The Quotable Newman

Dave Armstrong

The Quotable Newman

A Definitive Guide to His
Central Thoughts and Ideas

SOPHIA INSTITUTE PRESS

Manchester, New Hampshire

Sophia Institute Press
Box 5284, Manchester, NH 03108
1-800-888-9344
www.SophiaInstitute.com

Sophia Institute Press® is a registered trademark of Sophia Institute.

Library of Congress Cataloging-in-Publication Data
Newman, John Henry, 1801-1890.
    The quotable Newman : a definitive guide to his central
    thoughts and ideas / [edited by] Dave Armstrong.
      p. cm.
    Includes bibliographical references.
    ISBN 978-1-933184-84-5 (pbk. : alk. paper) 1. Newman, John
    Henry, 1801-1890—Quotations. I. Armstrong, Dave, 1958-
    II. Title.
BX4705.N5A25 2012
282—dc23

                                   2012010873

To the great man whose words were here compiled
with much pleasure by one whose entrance into the Catholic
Church was profoundly influenced by him. I feel very strongly
that Blessed Cardinal Newman will not only be proclaimed a
saint in due course, but also a Doctor of the Church.

Contents

Preface

by Joseph Pearce

In 2010, I was honored to be among the official press commentators for Pope Benedict XVI's visit to Britain. It was indeed a joy and a privilege to follow the Pope as he visited venues in London that resonated with Catholic significance. He visited Westminster Hall, in which St. Thomas More had stood trial, and visited Westminster Abbey to pray at the shrine of St. Edward the Confessor. He blessed the crowds in Hyde Park, only a stone's throw from the site of Tyburn Tree, the Machiavellian altar on which numerous Catholic martyrs were slain. It was as though the places selected for the Pope's visit had been carefully chosen to remind Englishmen of their Catholic heritage and to warn of the dangers inherent in secularist intolerance toward the Church. The purpose of the Pope's visit, however, was not primarily to celebrate England's Catholic heritage but to beatify John Henry Newman. In so doing, the Pope was not so much celebrating history as making it. Newman was the first Englishman, other than the martyrs, to be beatified since the Reformation; he was also the first Englishman born since the seventeenth century to be raised to the altar.

John Henry Newman was born in 1801, at the very dawn of the nineteenth century, and lived until 1890, as the sun began to set on this most catalytic and cataclysmic of epochs. During Newman's long and eventful life, new ideas would cause seismic shifts in the way modern man perceived himself. Karl Marx adapted the ideas of Hegel in the service of revolutionary politics, thereby unleashing an ideology that would claim the lives of tens of millions of people in the following century. Charles Darwin proposed the evolution of species from primitive beginnings, thereby initiating the notion of biological progressivism and the chronological snobbery that is its consequence. Friedrich Nietzsche declared brazenly that God was dead, thereby deifying man. Sigmund Freud supplanted the conscious will with subconscious complexes, thereby supplanting rational moral choices with irrational psychological urges. Revolutions swept across Europe as nationalism and socialism threatened the old order, sowing the seeds of National Socialism and its international communist Big Brother. The British Empire swept across the world, laying the foundations of globalism. It was a time of change and uncertainty and yet, at the same time and as the life of Newman testifies, it was also a time of religious revival and resurgent traditionalism.

Newman's own place within the Catholic Revival is paramount. He is indeed the very Father of the Revival itself.

At the time of Newman's birth, the Catholic Church in England had been largely rooted out of the national life and consciousness. Between the 1530s and the 1680s countless Catholics had been put to death for their faith. There are more than a hundred canonized and beatified English martyrs and many others whose final sacrifice for the Faith has not been officially recognized by the Church. In the wake of the so-called "Glorious" Revolution of 1688, which deposed the Catholic monarch, James II, two Jacobite uprisings sought the return of the true king's heirs to the throne. In the second of these uprisings the followers of Bonnie Prince Charlie were finally defeated at the Battle of Culloden in 1746, crushing any realistic hope of the return of a Catholic monarchy. At this point, after more than two hundred years of relentless persecution, all seemed lost for England's shrinking Catholic population. A small number of recusant families, who had clung to the Faith doggedly and dogmatically in defiance of the ongoing war of attrition against them, had resigned themselves to a place on the margins of English life, excluded from preferment in politics and society by the ingrained and institutionalized prejudice of their fellow countrymen. This was the world in which Newman was born and in which he was due to play a major role.

Newman's conversion in 1845, sixteen years after Catholic Emancipation and five years before the reestablishment of the Catholic hierarchy in England, heralded the birth of a revival that would see the resurrection of the Faith in the English-speaking world. Prior to Newman's conversion, Catholicism had been perceived by the British as a foreign religion, espoused by swarthy and superstitious Mediterranean types. As the power of Britain waxed into the fullness of an empire and as the power of Italy, Spain, and Portugal waned into relative impotence, it was easy for the British to feel superior and supercilious. Catholicism was a primitive and backward religion for primitive and backward people. Such snobbery was thrown into confusion by Newman's reception into the Catholic Church. It was difficult to dismiss the submission of such an intellectual giant to the historical and dogmatic claims of Rome.

Newman had made an intensive study of the early Church and had concluded that the Faith of the Church Fathers was the same holy, catholic, and apostolic Faith as that preached and taught by the Catholic Church of his own day. Newman's scholarship and his eloquence in expressing it shook the Anglican establishment, throwing into question the presumptions and prejudices on which the foundation of the Church of England was built.

A wave of converts from the higher echelons of society crossed the Tiber in Newman's wake as conversion became almost fashionable. At the same time, a huge influx of Irish immigrants, fleeing the potato famine, greatly increased the number of working-class Catholics. Almost overnight, Catholicism was becoming a significant force in British society, the presence of a growing number of erudite converts coinciding with the growing plebian presence of the Irish immigrants. The result would be a Catholic revival that would last for more than a century.

The first period of this revival could be called the Newman period, stretching from the great man's conversion in 1845 until his death in 1890. The second period, or what might be called the decadent interlude, spanned the final decade of the century in which the writers and artists of the fin de siècle flirted with Rome and ultimately succumbed to the charms of the Church. Among the converts from this decade were Oscar Wilde, Aubrey Beardsley, Ernest Dowson, and Lionel Johnson. The next major span of the revival could be called the Chesterbelloc period, in which the giant figures of G. K. Chesterton and Hilaire Belloc loomed large, which spanned from 1900, the year in which Chesterton was first published, until 1936, the year of his death. The final stage could be called the Inklings period, during which the figures of J.R.R. Tolkien and C. S. Lewis dominated, spanning from 1937, the year *The Hobbit* was published, until 1973, the year of Tolkien's death.

It is arguable that the enormity of the Catholic Revival, which placed Catholicism at the center and even at the pinnacle of the artistic and cultural life of Britain, would not have happened had it not been for Newman's conversion, the catalytic nature of which can hardly be overstated.

Having placed Newman's importance within its historical context, it is also necessary to look, albeit briefly, at his influence as a historian, theologian, philosopher, educationist, apologist, novelist, and poet.

Newman's importance as a historian is rooted in his pioneering work on the early Church, which convinced him, as it has convinced generations of those who have read his works, that a study of the Fathers and of the early heresies provides convincing evidence of the truth claims of Catholicism. Newman claimed and his work has shown that the more one is steeped in history, the more one becomes a Catholic.

As a theologian, Newman is rightly celebrated for his *Essay on the Development of Christian Doctrine* (1845), which has been hugely influential in the Church's understanding of how her doctrine develops without ever changing in its essentials. The most succinct encapsulation of this understanding of the development of Church doctrine was given by Tolkien in a letter to his son in which he likened the Church to a tree. It was wrong to see the full-grown tree, that is, the Church after two millennia of development, as being inferior to the seed from which it grew or the sapling that it had once been, that is, the early Church. The tree (the Church) is the same throughout all the ages, developing and growing organically without ever changing its essential "treeness" (that is, the truth that the Church teaches and the truth that she is).

In philosophy, Newman is best known for *An Essay in Aid of the Grammar of Assent* (1870), which shows the inadequacy of reductionist reasoning, such as logic, as a means of comprehending the fullness of truth. Faith is arrived at by the correlation of converging probabilities to which the will must assent. As an educationist, Newman championed the liberal arts in *The Idea of a University* (1852), uniting the classics of pagan antiquity to the inheritance of Christendom. As an apologist, his seminal *Apologia pro Vita Sua* (1864) remains one of the greatest spiritual autobiographies ever written, perhaps the greatest with the obvious exception of Augustine's *Confessions*. The role of the apologist is also manifested in his novels, *Loss and Gain* (1845) and *Callista* (1855), as well as in his sermons and his theological engagement with the errors of Anglicanism. Last but indubitably not least is Newman's position as a prose stylist of the highest order and a poet of the first rank.

Before concluding, passing reference must be made to later generations of famous converts on whom Newman had a major influence. These include Gerard Manley Hopkins, arguably the greatest poet in an age of great poets, who was received into the Church by Newman himself in 1866. Others who were helped significantly on their paths to Rome by Newman include Oscar Wilde, Maurice Baring, R. H. Benson, Christopher Dawson, Ronald Knox, Evelyn Waugh, Graham Greene, Muriel Spark, and Alec Guinness, to name but an illustrious few. Mention should also be made of Hilaire Belloc and J.R.R. Tolkien, two of the giants of the Catholic Revival, who were both educated at the Oratory School in Birmingham, which Newman had founded.

In so many multifarious ways, John Henry Newman has been a blessing to the Church. How appropriate, therefore, that the Church has now conferred a great blessing upon Newman by raising him to the altar. The beatified Newman is in the Presence of the Beatific Vision. He has achieved the only goal for which life is worth living. As such, praise should make way for prayers.

Blessed John Henry Newman, historian, theologian, philosopher, and poet, pray for us.

Introduction

The aim of this book is a simple, albeit very ambitious one: to compile notable quotations from Blessed John Henry Cardinal Newman (1801-1890) in the areas of theology and Church history, so that his thinking and wisdom might be more accessible to the reading public, and particularly to students of Christian theology and its history.

As with most works of this sort, the goal is to help make the quoted author more widely known: to spark interest and pique curiosity in more than a few readers. I envy those who will be embarking for the first time on a journey of serious reading of Cardinal Newman. It's pure joy for any thinker to do so.

I also seek to create a handy reference source that can be consulted when particular topics come up. Newman's thought is so full of insight that it seems to have no end. With the help of the Holy Spirit and whatever gifts granted to me by God's grace, I have done my best to compile the most substantive, pithy, and memorable quotations of Cardinal Newman that I can find.

The task of selection is necessarily subjective, and daunting, but this is a task I had to do, due to the huge debt I owe to John Henry Newman in relation to my own spiritual journey: one that brought me happily to the Catholic Church in 1990, exactly a hundred years after Newman's death.

This work is, therefore, the fruit of a proverbial "labor of love." Whether it was labor at all, however, is questionable, since the experience of perusing all of these wonderful books and letters, and the enjoyment obtained in so doing, made any "work" involved almost beside the point.

I do have some experience in putting together a book of quotations: I was the editor for *The Wisdom of Mr. Chesterton* (Charlotte, North Carolina: Saint Benedict Press, 2009). A major difference between that volume and this one, however, is the length of citations. I restricted myself in that instance to single sentences. But this would be impossible to do in Cardinal Newman's case, because of his flowing, elaborate, complex, Victorian prose. Nevertheless, I shall attempt to keep the excerpts as brief as I can, without giving up any essential meaning.

As in the Chesterton collection, I note sources with abbreviations and generally use chapter numbers rather than page numbers since the latter will vary with different editions. I have attempted to keep quotations chronological within categories. As indicated in the subtitles, I have narrowed the subject matter somewhat: primarily to theology and Church history. Newman also wrote widely on philosophy, education, spirituality, sociology, and current affairs and produced poetry and fiction, among other things. But in particularly notable instances or topics, I was quite willing to extend the parameters and make an exception to my own "rule"—out of love for Cardinal Newman's style, insight, and wisdom.

I chose to concentrate on theology and the history of theological doctrine and the Church, since those topics lend themselves to thematic unity and a coherent collection that can be referenced and used for the purpose of catechesis or apologetics. Given the vast amount of Newman's writing involved, I thought it best not to attempt to cover everything. But for the areas I *have* covered, I have sought to be quite comprehensive, in order to provide a reference work of lasting value and utility: something a little different from the hundreds of works on Newman, and various anthologies and collections of his writing thus far available.

I need to note two factors that were important in my selection process as an editor, so readers can be duly informed. As most who are reading this already are aware, Cardinal Newman was an Anglican for roughly the first half of his life, and a Catholic thereafter. Not infrequently in his earlier life, he not only explained, but vigorously advocated, positions that he later renounced. The question then arises as to the criteria for selection of quotations in the earlier period. Or, more specifically: are they to be conceptualized as presenting (all things considered), at least in part, the "polemical Anglican (at times, outright anti-Catholic), *Via Media* proponent Newman" or rather, "the proto-Catholic Newman who anticipates and looks forward to his later Catholic beliefs, and holds them in kernel form"? I have decided to follow the latter course. Generally, I have not included opinions that the later Newman would have disavowed, or literally did renounce as we see in his later corrective notes of his earlier writing. I am a Catholic, and I'm afraid that my natural bias in that direction considerably affected how the Anglican-period quotations were selected and edited.

Yet I don't think this is a *complete* "loss" for Anglican or otherwise non-Catholic readers, since the (ecumenical) result is an "Anglican Newman" who expresses ideas on which Catholics and more traditional or "high" Anglicans can readily agree. It is not unimportant to highlight agreement where it is present. Non-Catholic readers can also see how very much a Catholic can agree with the Anglican Newman's thinking, since I have deliberately set out to highlight the larger areas of agreement (in light of his later change of mind). The Anglican devotee of Cardinal Newman could, in this sense, particularly benefit from the earlier quotations insofar as they present a "Catholic Newman" who is not, in these compiled instances, expressing pointed disagreement with another "branch" of the universal Catholic Christian Church.

The second factor that ought to be highlighted is my determination to include, by and large, passages in Newman's writing that give *actual arguments* for positions, rather than being only beautifully expressed descriptions or sentiments and not necessarily defenses. Newman is such a good writer that virtually everything he writes is eloquent, in any event; but my goal is to emphasize the *apologist* Newman: the one who can provide a rationale for why we should *agree* with his positions.

Thus, it is apparent that my status as a Catholic, and as a Catholic *apologist* by occupation, has influenced how I edit. But I suppose this is to be expected, and I don't believe it detracts from the utility of the overall effort in the slightest, especially since I have stated my goals and "biases" up front, so as to avoid any misconception.

May the reader enjoy and be edified and educated by what I have compiled from Blessed John Henry Cardinal Newman's delightful writing.

The Quotable Newman

Absolution

'As My Father hath sent Me, even so send I you. And when He had said this, He breathed on them, and saith unto them, Receive ye the Holy Ghost. Whose soever sins ye remit, they are remitted unto them; and whose soever sins ye retain, they are retained.' [John xx. 21-23.] Here, then, the Apostles became Christ's representatives in the power of His Spirit, for the remission of sins, as before they were His representatives as regards miraculous cures, and preaching His Kingdom ... It might be thought that the power of remitting and retaining sins was too great to be given to sinful man over his fellows; but in matter of fact it was committed to the Apostles without restriction, though they were not infallible in what they did. (*PS* ii, Sermon 25: 'The Christian Ministry,' 14 December 1834)

Indeed, no one can be sufficiently aware, till he inquires into the subject, how very few texts can be produced from the Apostles' writings containing a promise of forgiveness when Christians sin ... There was nothing generous, nothing grateful, nothing of the high temper of faith, in sitting at home and merely praying for pardon ... If they wilfully transgressed, they *left* the road, they *abandoned* the work. Then they were like Demas, who went back, and they had to be restored; to be pardoned, not *in* the state of grace, but, if I may so say, *into* it. (*PS* v, Sermon 13: 'The State of Salvation,' 18 March 1838)

[T]hough your conscience witnesses against you, He can disburden it; whether you have sinned less or whether you have sinned more, He can make you as clean in His sight and as acceptable to Him as if you

3

had never gone from Him. Gradually will He destroy your sinful habits, and at once will He restore you to His favour. Such is the power of the Sacrament of Penance, that, be your load of guilt heavier or be it lighter, it removes it, whatever it is. (*Mix.*, Discourse 3: 'Men, Not Angels, the Priests of the Gospel')

[W]hen that Sacrament [of Penance] cannot be had, there is a high degree of contrition possible, such as (with the desire of that which cannot be had) avails in the mercy of God for forgiveness and restoration of grace. (*LD* xxxii, 308; Letter to Canon Charles Wellington Furse, 2 May 1870)

[N]or do pardons 'disparage His Sacraments,' for sacraments take away the guilt, and pardons the punishment, of sin. (*TT* #41, footnote 6 of 1883)

Adam

Though the Fathers, in accordance with Scripture, hold that Adam was created sinless, they also hold that he could not have persevered in his state of innocence and uprightness without a special grace, which he lost upon his fall, and which is regained for us, (and that in far greater measure,) by our Lord's sufferings and merits. The Catholic doctrine is, that Adam innocent was mortal, yet in fact would not have died; that he had no principle of eternal life within his body naturally, but was sustained continually by divine power till such time as immortality should have been given him. (*Ath.* ii, 'Adam')

Adam, from the time of his creation, was gifted, over and above his nature as man, with the grace of God, to unite him to God, and to make him holy. Grace is therefore called holy grace; and, as being holy, it is the connecting principle between God and man. Adam in Paradise might have had knowledge, and skill, and many virtues; but these gifts did not unite him to his Creator. It was holiness that united him, for it is said by St. Paul, 'Without holiness no man shall see God.' (*MD*, 'Meditations on the Litany of Loretto, for the Month of May: I. On the Immaculate Conception,' for May 9)

Angels

[C]oncerning them much more is told us than concerning the souls of
the faithful departed, because the latter 'rest from their labours;' but the
Angels are actively employed among us in the Church. They are said to
be 'ministering spirits, sent forth to minister for them who shall be heirs
of salvation' [Heb. i. 14]. No Christian is so humble but he has Angels to
attend on him, if he lives by faith and love. (*PS* iv, Sermon 13: 'The Invisible World,' 16 July 1837)

[T]he Ante-nicene Fathers ... speak of the Angelic visions in the Old
Testament as if they were appearances of the Son; but St. Augustine introduced the explicit doctrine, which has been received since his date,
that they were simply Angels, through whom the Omnipresent Son manifested Himself ... if anything was seen, that must have been some created
glory or other symbol, by which it pleased the Almighty to signify His
Presence. What was heard was a sound, as external to His Essence, and
as distinct from His Nature, as the thunder or the voice of the trumpet,
which pealed along Mount Sinai; what it was had not come under discussion ... St. Augustine ruled, and his ruling has been accepted in later
times, that it was not a mere atmospheric phenomenon, or an impression
on the senses, but the material form proper to an Angelic presence, or
the presence of an Angel in that material garb in which blessed Spirits do ordinarily appear to men. Henceforth the Angel in the bush, the
voice which spoke with Abraham, and the man who wrestled with Jacob,
were not regarded as the Son of God, but as Angelic ministers, whom He
employed, and through whom He signified His presence and His will ...
[A]s regards the instance of Angelic appearances itself, as St. Augustine
explained them, if those appearances were creatures, certainly creatures
were worshipped by the Patriarchs, not indeed in themselves, but as the
token of a Presence greater than themselves. When 'Moses hid his face,
for he was afraid to look upon God,' he hid his face before a creature;
when Jacob said, 'I have seen God face to face and my life is preserved,'
the Son of God was there, but what he saw, what he wrestled with, was
an Angel. When 'Joshua fell on his face to the earth and did worship

before the captain of the Lord's host, and said unto him, What saith my
Lord unto his servant?' what was seen and heard was a glorified creature, if St. Augustine is to be followed; and the Son of God was in him.
And there were plain precedents in the Old Testament for the lawfulness
of such adoration. When 'the people saw the cloudy pillar stand at the
tabernacle-door,' 'all the people rose up and worshipped, every man in his
tent-door.' When Daniel too saw 'a certain man clothed in linen' 'there
remained no strength in him,' for his 'comeliness was turned' in him 'into
corruption.' He fell down on his face, and next remained on his knees
and hands, and at length 'stood trembling,' and said 'O my Lord, by the
vision my sorrows are turned upon me, and I have retained no strength.
For how can the servant of this my Lord talk with this my Lord?' It might
be objected perhaps to this argument, that a worship which was allowable
in an elementary system might be unlawful when 'grace and truth' had
come 'through Jesus Christ;' but then it might be retorted surely, that that
elementary system had been emphatically opposed to all idolatry, and had
been minutely jealous of everything which might approach to favouring
it. (*Dev.*, Part I: ch. 4, sec. 2)

[H]ow *weary* the angels must get of the *history* of the world—every
generation beginning with sinners, and then some turning to repentance—looking at individual souls, seeing them plunge into sin fearlessly—yet they are afterwards to repent—they must feel indignation
that God should be trifled with. (*SN*, 'On the Gospel for Pentecost IX,'
29 July 1849)

Most perfect of creatures—the *image of God's attributes*. Their knowledge most comprehensive. They do not *learn*, they do not discover, but
at once from their nature they know intuitively all things of the world;
whereas the greatest philosophers with pains only knew a little. They
know God and His attributes by nature, even without grace. They understand His attributes, etc. They see God in all things ... Many wonderful
things in this world, but an angel more wonderful than all. If a creature so
wonderful, what the Creator? (*SN*, 'The Holy Angels — I,' 2 September
1860)

I had a bad accident there, with (thank God and my Guardian Angel) no harm whatever. (*Ward* i, 591; Letter to John Keble, 15 August 1863)

[T]he Angels have been considered by divines to have each of them a species to himself; and we may fancy each of them so absolutely *sui similis* as to be like nothing else, so that it would be as untrue to speak of a thousand Angels as of a thousand Hannibals or Ciceros. (GA, Part I, ch. 4, sec. 1)

[Y]our Guardian Angel will be faithful to the end. (*Ward* ii, 415; Letter to Sister Maria Pia, 22 January 1878)

[M]y good Guardian Angel, who never fails me, when the trial comes, has pulled me through. (*LD* xxix, 126; Letter to the Duke of Norfolk, 16 May 1879)

Angels were actually worshipped, in the proper sense of the word, by Gnostics and other heretics, who even ascribed to them a creative power; and certainly, to consider them the source of any good to man, and the acceptable channel intrinsically of approaching God, in derogation of our Lord's sole mediation, is idolatry. However, their presence in and about the Church, and with all of us individually, is an inestimable blessing, never to be slighted or forgotten; for, as by our prayers and our kind deeds we can serve each other, so Angels, but in a far higher way, serve us, and are channels of grace to us, as the Sacraments also are … As to the word 'worship,' as denoting the *cultus Angelorum*, worship is a very wide term, and has obviously more senses than one. Thus we read in one passage of Scripture that 'all the congregation … worshipped the Lord, and *the king*' [1 Chron 29:20]. (*Ath.* ii, 'Angels')

In the Old Testament, the angel sometimes appears by himself as a messenger from God and then receives homage as such; sometimes he is the manifestation of a Divine Presence and thus becomes relatively an object of worship. The angel in Judg. ii. 1, was a messenger, so was the angel in Dan. x. 5; but the angels in Exod. iii. 2, Acts vii. 30, Josh. v. 13, Judg. vi. 11 and xiii. 3, were the attendants upon God. In the last three passages the manifestation is first of the angel, then of the Lord of angels. First it was an angel that appeared to Gideon, then 'the Lord looked upon him,' on which, recognising the Divine Presence, he offered sacrifice. So Joshua first addressed the angel, but the words 'Loose thy shoes,' &c., told him who was there. (*TT* #71, footnote 10 of 1883)

Anglicanism

The Romanist gives to the existing *Church* the ultimate infallible decision in matters of saving faith; the Ultra-Protestant to the *individual*; and the Anglican to *antiquity*, giving authority to the Church, as being the witness and voice, or rather the very presence of Antiquity among us. (Review of *Lectures on the Principal Doctrines and Practices of the Catholic Church*, by Nicholas Wiseman, *British Critic*, vol. 19, Oct. 1836)

[W]e Anglo-Catholics do not profess a different religion from that of Rome, we profess their Faith *all but* their corruptions. (VM i, ch. 1)

The Anglican view, then, of the Church has ever been this, that its separate portions need not be united together, for their essential completeness, except by the tie of descent from one original. They are like a number of colonies sent out from a mother country, or as the tribes or nations which spring from a common parent. Jerusalem was the mother Church; they all come from her; they are Churches in that they come from her; but they are not bound to any union together in order to be Churches, any more than branches of an extended family, or colonies of a mother country, need have a common table or common purse, in order to have the blood and name of their ancestor. ('Catholicity of the Anglican Church,' *British Critic*, Jan. 1840; in *Ess.* ii, sec. X)

I am not here speaking for myself in one way or another; I am not examining the scripturalness, safety, propriety, or expedience of the points in question; but I desire that it may not be supposed as utterly unlawful for such private Christians as feel they can do it with a clear conscience, to allow a comprecation with the Saints as Bramball does, or to hold with

Andrewes that, taking away the doctrine of Transubstantiation from the Mass, we shall have no dispute about the Sacrifice; or with Hooker to treat even Transubstantiation as an opinion which by itself need not cause separation; or to hold with Hammond that no General Council, truly such, ever did, or shall err in any matter of faith; ... the Tract is grounded on the belief that the Articles need not be so closed as the received method of teaching closes them, and *ought* not to be for the sake of many persons. If we will close them, we run the risk of subjecting persons whom we should least like to lose or distress, to the temptation of joining the Church of Rome, or to the necessity of withdrawing from the Church as established, or to the misery of subscribing with doubt and hesitation. And, as to myself, I was led especially to exert myself with reference to this difficulty, from having had it earnestly set before me by parties I revere, to do all I could to keep members of our Church from straggling in the direction of Rome. (VM ii, IX. 'Letter to Rev. R. W. Jelf in Explanation of Tract 90,' 1841)

If it was promised to the Church that she should be 'the pillar and ground of the truth,' that her 'teachers should not be removed into a corner any more,' but that her 'ears should hear a voice behind her, saying, This is the way, walk ye in it;' and if, to us in this country, she is not such as this, surely we have forfeited something, surely are under a judgment; and if we are under a judgment, how inexpressibly it must offend Almighty God, that we do not 'humble ourselves under His mighty hand'! This being so, it is a very light thing indeed for one whose eyes are in his measure opened to see it, to find himself opposed for speaking plainly about it; and, even though opposed, it must be more difficult for him to keep silence *than* to speak. (SD, Sermon 22: 'Outward and Inward Notes of the Church,' 5 December 1841)

[T]here were persons who, if our Church committed herself to heresy, *sooner* than think that there was no Church any where, would believe the Roman to be the Church; and therefore would on faith accept what they could not otherwise acquiesce in. (Apo., ch. 4; Letter to R. W. Church, 24 December 1841)

[O]ur Church has through centuries ever been sinking lower and lower, till a good part of its pretensions and professions is a mere sham, though it be a duty to make the best of what we have received. (Moz. ii; Letter to R. W. Church, 25 December 1841)

It is not love of Rome that unsettles people, but fear of heresy at home … The Church of England has been ruined by people shutting their eyes and making the best of things … I distrust the Bishops altogether. (Moz. ii; Letter to John Keble, 26 December 1841)

I consider that, according to the great Anglican theory (by which I mean the theory of Laud, Bull, Butler, &c., upon which alone the English Church *can* stand, as being neither Roman nor Puritan), the present state of the Church is like that of an empire breaking or broken up. At least I know of no better illustration. (Moz. ii; Letter to W. R. Lyall, 16 July 1842)

How can that be practically a church, how can it teach, which speaks half a dozen things in the same breath? … No two clergymen, next door to each other, return the same answer to the question, 'What shall I do to be saved?' … It needs to be no theologian to be sure that 'a house divided against itself cannot stand.' (POL; Letter to S. L. Pope, 4 September 1842)

If I must specify what I mean by 'Anglican principles,' I should say, e.g., taking *Antiquity*, not the *existing Church*, as the oracle of truth; and holding that the *Apostolical Succession* is a sufficient guarantee of sacramental Grace, without *union with the Christian Church throughout the world*. I think them the firmest, strongest bulwark against Rome — that is, *if they can be held*. They *have* been held by many, and are far more difficult to refute than those of any other religious body. For myself, I found I *could not* hold them. I left them. From the time I began to suspect their unsoundness, I ceased to put them forward — when I was fairly sure of their unsoundness, I gave up my Living. When I was fully confident that the Church of Rome was the only true Church, I joined it. I have felt all along that Bishop Bull's theology was the only theology on which the English Church could stand — I have felt that opposition to the Church of Rome was *part* of that theology; and that he who could not protest against the Church of Rome was no true divine in the English Church. I have never said, nor attempted to say, that any one in office in the English Church, whether Bishop or incumbent, could be otherwise than in hostility to the Church of Rome. (*LD* xi, 27-28; Letter to Samuel Wilks, 8 November 1845)

Again in what sense are Rome and England one body in which the Church of England and Methodism may not be proved one body? ... I hold it impossible that you should remain in this half and half position, believing one thing on the same ground, on which you reject another ... When I admit that the English Church is in schism, I see a mass of facts confirmatory of it — its disorganised state of belief — its feebleness to resist heretics — its many changes — its freezing coldness. And on the other hand I have the portentous, the awful vitality of Rome. That is an overpowering confirmatory argument. (*LD* xi, 175; Letter to Henry Wilberforce, 8 June 1846)

[D]isunion in the Anglican Church is just what prejudices men of the world against it and makes it contemptible. They do not take hold of the possibility that one party in it may be contending for a truth against the other. The disunion is its condemnation. (*LD* xii, 159-160; Letter to Frederick Lucas, 20 January 1848)

The thought of Anglicanism with nothing fixed or settled, with Bishop contradicting Bishops within, and the whole world against it, without, is something so dreary and wretched, that I cannot speak of it without the chance of offence to those who still hold it. (*LD* xii, 168; Letter to A. J. Hanmer, 10 February 1848)

[T]he hollowness of High Churchism (or whatever it is called) is to me so very clear that it surprises me (not that persons should not see it at once), but that any should not see it at last, and, alas, I must add that I do not think it safe for any one who does see it, not to act on his conviction of it *at once* ... I do not disguise that Catholicism is a different religion from Anglicanism ... that religion which the Apostles introduced and which was in the world long before the Reformation was dreamed of. (*LD* xii, 223-225; Letter to Mrs. William Froude, 16 June 1848)

[T]he Anglican and the Catholic are two religions. I have professed both, and must know better than those who have professed one only ... This being so, it is a mere deceit, I fully think, to suppose that the difference between Catholics and Anglicans is that one believes a little more, and the other a little less; and therefore that they could unite. The religions never could unite; they never could be reconciled together ... because they proceed on different *ideas*; and, if they look in certain external aspects alike, or have doctrines in common, yet the way in which those doctrines are held, and the whole internal structure in the two religions is different; so that, even what a person has before he is a Catholic, being grafted on a new stock, becomes new, and he is like a Jew become Christian ... [T]he Anglo-catholic scarcely exists out of books, or in a hundred parsonages scattered through the land, and has had no continuous life or succession. Next, consider the vast difference between believing in a living authority, unerring because divine, in matters of doctrine, and believing none—between believing what an external authority defines, and believing what we ourselves happen to define as contained in Scripture and the Fathers, where no two individuals define quite the same set of doctrines ... In the one case, the living authority, deciding in controversies of faith, is the Church, in the other (whatever men pretend), it is we ourselves who are the ultimate authority. (*LD* xii, 234-235; Letter to E. J. Phipps, 3 July 1848)

I am much obliged to you for giving me the opportunity of setting right the misconception which is in circulation of the light in which I view the Anglican Church ... I respect and love the good men who belong to it; I have no wish to speak of it, but if I am forced to speak, by being misrepresented, I cannot help saying that I do not think the established Church is better off, as regards the Sacraments, than other non-Catholic bodies which have not renounced baptism. God's grace doubtless may be vouchsafed at his will both to Anglicans and to Protestants; and that I certainly may have said; but vouchsafed in order to bring them towards the Catholic Church; in this way it is doubtless given to one and the other; but in each case in order to draw them off from what they are; and if it does not do this to Anglicans as well as Protestants, it does not answer the purpose for which it is given. No wonder I say this, considering I have the greatest misgivings of the validity of Anglican orders ... If the Anglican Church has not orders, it has no Eucharist. (*LD* xii, 249; Second Letter to Robert Monteith, 21 July 1848)

Nothing is more day-clear than this, that unless there never was a Church and heretics round it, the Anglican Church is *a loco*, in the position of one of those early sects ... No one can maintain the Anglican Church from history (whatever they may try to do on the ground of doctrine). (*Ward* i, 238; Letter to Henry Wilberforce, 7 March 1849)

As a thing without a soul, it does not contemplate itself, define its intrinsic constitution, or ascertain its position. It has no traditions; it cannot be said to think; it does not know what it holds, and what it does not; it is not even conscious of its own existence ... Its fruits, as far as they are good, are to be made much of, as long as they last, for they are transient, and without succession; its former champions of orthodoxy are no earnest of orthodoxy now; they died, and there was no reason why they should be reproduced ... [I]ts Prayer-Book is an Act of Parliament of two centuries ago, and its cathedrals and its chapter-houses are the spoils of Catholicism. (*Dif.* i, Lecture 1)

[W]hat is sometimes called, or rather what calls itself, the Anglo-Catholic teaching, is not only a novelty in this age (for to prove a thing new to the age, is not enough in order to prove it uncongenial), but that, while it is a system adventitious and superadded to the national religion, it is, moreover, not supplemental, or complemental, or collateral, or correlative to it,—not implicitly involved in it, not developed from it,—nor combining with it,—nor capable of absorption into it; but, on the contrary, most uncongenial and heterogeneous, floating upon it, a foreign substance, like oil upon the water. (*Dif.* i, Lecture 2)

[H]e [himself] did not entertain the presumptuous thought of creating, at this time of day, a new theology himself; he considered that a theology true in itself, and necessary for the position of the Anglican Church, was to be found in the writings of Andrewes, Laud, Bramhall, Stillingfleet, Butler, and other of its divines, but had never been put together, — as he expressly declares. Nor, in spite of his misgivings, was he without a persuasion that the theological system contained in those writers, and derived, as he believed, from the primitive Fathers, not only ought to be, but might be, and, as he hoped, would be, acknowledged and acted upon by the Establishment. On the other hand, I allow, of course, and am not loth to allow, that, had he seen clearly that Antiquity and the Establishment were incompatible with each other, he would promptly have given up the Establishment, rather than have rejected Antiquity ... [T]hat movement of 1833 was from its very beginning engaged in propagating an unreality. (*Dif.* i, Lecture 2)

Protestantism is the dreariest of possible religions ... the thought of the Anglican service makes me shiver, and the thought of the Thirty-nine Articles makes me shudder. (*POL;* Letter to the Editor of the *Globe,* 28 June 1862)

[O]n my conversion, I was not conscious of any change in me of thought or feeling, as regards matters of doctrine; this, however, was not the case as regards some matters of fact, and, unwilling as I am to give offence to religious Anglicans, I am bound to confess that I felt a great change in my view of the Church of England. I cannot tell how soon there came on me, — but very soon, — an extreme astonishment that I had ever imagined it to be a portion of the Catholic Church. For the first time, I looked at it from without, and (as I should myself say) saw it as it was. Forthwith I could not get myself to see in it any thing else, than what I had so long fearfully suspected, from as far back as 1836, — a mere national institution. As if my eyes were suddenly opened, so I saw it — spontaneously, apart from any definite act of reason or any argument; and so I have seen it ever since. I suppose, the main cause of this lay in the contrast which was presented to me by the Catholic Church ... And so I recognise in the Anglican Church a time-honoured institution, of noble historical memories, a monument of ancient wisdom, a momentous arm of political strength, a great national organ, a source of vast popular advantage, and, to a certain point, a witness and teacher of religious truth. I do not think that if what I have written about it since I have been a Catholic, be equitably considered as a whole, I shall be found to have taken any other view than this; but that it is something sacred, that it is an oracle of revealed doctrine, that it can claim a share in St. Ignatius or St. Cyprian, that it can take the rank, contest the teaching, and stop the path of the Church of St. Peter, that it can call itself 'the Bride of the Lamb,' this is the view of it which simply disappeared from my mind on my conversion, and which it would be almost a miracle to reproduce ... Doubtless the National Church has hitherto been a serviceable breakwater against doctrinal errors, more fundamental than its own. How long this will last in the years now before us, it is impossible to say, for the Nation drags down its Church to its own level. (*Apo.*, Note E: 'The Anglican Church')

[I]t is no exaggeration to say that the Anglican ecclesiastical Establishment is an amalgamation of all these varieties of Protestantism, to which a considerable amount of Catholicism is superadded ... This remarkable Church has always been in the closest dependence on the civil power and has always gloried in this. It has ever regarded the Papal power with fear, with resentment, and with aversion, and it has never won the heart of the people. In this it has shown itself consistent throughout the course of its existence; in other concerns it has either had no opinions or has constantly changed them. In the sixteenth century it was Calvinist; in the first half of the seventeenth it was Arminian and quasi-Catholic; towards the close of that century and at the beginning of the next it was latitudinarian. In the middle of the eighteenth century it was described by Lord Chatham as having 'a papistical ritual and prayer-book, Calvinist articles of faith and an Arminian clergy.' ... In our days it contains three powerful parties in which are embodied the three principles of religion which appear constantly and from the beginning of its history in one form or another; the Catholic principle, the Protestant principle, and the sceptical principle. Each of these, it is hardly necessary to say, is violently opposed to the other two. (*Apo.* ii, Appendix to French translation of the *Apologia,* 1866)

[T]hose of its members who are what is called Evangelical, and those who are Liberals, cause a re-action in favour of Catholicism, and those who take the high line of Dr. Pusey are but educating souls for a communion holier and truer than their own. (*LD* xxxii, 277; Letter to C. C. Catcliffe, 6 January 1867)

As to the wonderful revival of religion in the Established Church, I certainly think it comes from God. If so, it must tend, as it visibly does tend, to the Church's benefit. One cannot conceive the generation which is brought up under it, when they come to maturity and to power, resting satisfied with the Anglican system. If their fathers, the present generation, yearn for unity, and for communion with St. Peter, much more will their children. There is nothing to prove that the present race of Catholicizing Anglicans is in bad faith; and there is much to show on the other hand that they are in good faith. It is possible indeed that the next generation may go off into Liberalism — as Hale and Chillingworth, the disciples of Laud. But I rather hope that Holy Church will arrest and win them over by her beauty and sanctity, her gentleness, serenity, and prudence. Anyhow we need not say that Anglicans at this time cast out devils through Beelzebub; rather they are like the man of whom Our Lord said: 'Forbid him not,' &c. (*Ward* ii, 553 [Appendix to Ch. 29]; Letter to Fr. John Walford, S.J., 19 May 1870)

Be sure there is as much chance of my turning an Anglican again as of my being ... the King of Clubs ... [T]he Anglican Church is ... a mere collection of men, a mere national body, a human society ... [I would be] the most asinine, as well as the most ungrateful of men, if I left that Gracious Lord who manifests Himself in the Catholic Church, for those wearisome Protestant shadows, out of which of His mercy he has delivered me. (*LD* xxv, 200; Letter to an Anglo-Catholic friend in August [?] 1870; cited in Ker, 656-657)

It is undeniable that the Anglican Church has retained large portions of the Catholic doctrine and ritual; so far forth as it has done so, of course, it will be called anti-Christian by those who call Rome pure Antichrist. (*Ess.* ii, sec. XI, footnote 2 from 1871)

As to the Anglican Orders, I certainly do think them doubtful and untrustworthy; and that, independent of any question arising out of Parker's consecration, into which I will not enter. Granting, for argument's sake, that that consecration was in all respects what its defenders say it was, still I feel a large difficulty in accepting the Anglican Succession and Commission of Ministry, arising out of the historical aspect of the Anglican Church and of its prelates, an aspect which suggests a grave suspicion of the validity of their acts from first to last ... That argument, which I maintain now as then, is as follows: — That the consecrations of 1559 were not only facts, they were acts; that those acts were not done and over once for all, but were only the first of a series of acts done in a long course of years; that these acts too, all of them, were done by men of certain positive opinions and intentions, and none of those opinions and views, from first to last, of a Catholic complexion, but on the contrary erroneous and heretical. And I questioned whether men of those opinions could by means of a mere rite or formulary, however correct in itself, start and continue in a religious communion, such as the Anglican, a ministerial succession which could be depended on as inviolate. I do not see what guarantee is producible for the faithful observance of a sacred rite, in form, matter, and intention, through so long a period in the hands of such administrators. And again, the existing state of the Anglican body, so ignorant of fundamental truth, so overrun with diversified error, would be but a sorry outcome of Apostolical ordinances and graces. 'By their fruits shall ye know them.' Revelation involves in its very idea a teaching and a hearing of Divine Truth. What clear and steady light of truth is there in the Church of England? What candlestick, upright and firm, on which it has been set? This seems to me what Leslie calls 'a short and easy method;' it is drawn out from one of the Notes of the Church. When we look at the Anglican communion, not in the books, in the imagination, or in the affections of its champions, but as it is in fact, its claims to speak in

Christ's Name are refuted by its very condition. An Apostolical ministry necessarily involves an Apostolical teaching ... As the matter stands, all we see is a hierarchical body, whose opinions through three hundred years compromise their acts, who do not themselves believe that they have the gifts which their zealous adherents ascribe to them, who in their hearts deny those sacramental formulas which their country's law obliges them to use, who conscientiously shudder at assuming real episcopal or sacerdotal power, who resolve 'Receive the Holy Ghost' into a prayer, 'Whose sins ye remit are remitted' into a licence to preach, and 'This is My Body, this is My Blood' into an allegory ... The difference of position between the two may be expressed in the following antithesis: — Catholics believe their Orders are valid, because they are members of the true Church; and Anglicans believe they belong to the true Church, because their Orders are valid ... That they can claim to have God's ministers among them, depends directly and solely upon the validity of their Orders; and to prove their validity, they are bound to trace their Succession through a hundred intermediate steps till at length they reach the Apostles; till they do this their claim is in abeyance. If it is improbable that the Succession has no flaws in it, they have to bear the brunt of the improbability; if it is presumable that a special Providence precludes such flaws, or compensates for them, they cannot take the benefit of that presumption to themselves; for to do so would be claiming to belong to the true Church, to which that high Providence is promised, and this they cannot do without arguing in a circle, first proving that they are of the true Church because they have valid Orders, and then that their Orders are valid because they are of the true Church ... Thus it would appear, that to Catholics the certainty of Apostolical Orders is not a point of prime necessity, yet they possess it; and for Anglicans it is absolutely indispensable, yet they have it not. On such grounds as these it is, that I consider the line of argument, which I have adopted against Anglican Orders, is neither open to the charge of scepticism, nor suicidal in the hands of a Catholic. (*Ess.* ii, Note on Essay X: 'Catholicity of the Anglican Church,' *British Critic*, Jan. 1840; from 1871)

Baptism marks *individuals* with an indelible character; but what spiritual promises have been made from heaven to the Anglican Church, as

such? ... The Almighty chose the *race* of Abraham to be His people, in
a sense in which He has not chosen the Anglo-Saxons. We cannot argue from Jerusalem to Canterbury and York ... [W]here is any promise of
divine Providence to the Anglican communion, when visibly separated
from the visible Catholic Church? (*VM* i, Lecture 14; footnotes 4, 7, and
12 from 1877)

   It is a body altogether cut off from the Church. It not only denounces
the Holy See, but it has allied itself with Protestantism. Its highest
Churchmen have looked favourably on the Nestorians and Monophysites. It allows its Clergy to preach all manner of false doctrines, to deny
the grace of baptism, to treat the Holy Eucharist as a mere outward rite,
and to make light of the necessity of ordination. It cannot interpret its
own formulas and definitions, and it cannot say what it holds and what it
does not hold. Therefore I cannot concern myself with the question of the
validity of its orders. (*LD* xxxii, 385; Letter to an Unknown Correspondent; undated, but thought [by the editors] to be from either December
1878 or January 1879)

   I left the Anglican Church because I could not believe it was a por-
tion of that Catholic Body which the Apostles founded and to which the
promises are made. I felt I could not be saved, if I remained where I was.
In my *Apologia* I think I have brought this out; that the bad reception by
Anglicans of Number 90 increased that conviction ... from first to last I
have had the clear conviction, independent of all such accidents, that the
Church of England is a Parliamentary Church. (*LD* xxx, 403; Letter to
Shirley Day, 27 September 1884)

   I never in arguing should think of entering upon your question whether
or not the Anglican Church was 'in schism' or whether or not it was in
possession of an 'Apostolical Succession.' These questions seem to me
beside the point in dispute. I never indeed, as I think, have said, that its
orders were certainly invalid; what I have said, if I have spoken against
them is that their validity was doubtful, and that doubtful orders were
unsafe ... But my direct and patent reason against the Catholicity of the

Anglican communion is quite clear of the question of orders. Anglicans consider the Church to be only a *family*; but it is more than that, it is a state, a polity, a *kingdom*, a visible kingdom … Our Lord announced that the kingdom of heaven was come, St. Paul speaks of the one body with many members (not branches, a body has not branches). If then the Church is a kingdom, and the one predicted Kingdom, the communion of Rome and the Anglican communion cannot *both* be that Kingdom, any more than King James and King William could each at the same time be King of England. (*LD* xxx, 407; Letter to an Unknown Correspondent, 7 October 1884)

A barrister, a dear friend of mine was converted to the Catholic Church, because, he said, the Church of England had taken the step of leaving the great Catholic body, and its first duty was to come back again. So I say now—the *move* towards union must first be taken by the party who committed the schism. When some Anglican ecclesiastic of name can be found to come to us and say he wishes, and is empowered, to lay before the Holy Father the repentant feelings existing and growing in the Church of England for the deeds of the 16th century, I shall receive the tidings with great joy and thankfulness. (*LD* xxxii, 468; Letter to an Unknown Correspondent, 18 September 1885)

Antiquity (the Early Church)

[T]he Primitive Church, which, in spite of the corruptions which disfigured it from the first, still in its collective holiness may be considered to make as near an approach to the pattern of Christ as fallen man ever will attain. (*US*, Sermon 5: 'Personal Influence, the Means of Propagating the Truth,' 22 January 1832)

[W]hatever doctrine the primitive ages unanimously attest, whether by consent of Fathers, or by Councils, or by the events of history, or by controversies, or in whatever way, whatever may fairly and reasonably be considered to be the universal belief of those ages, is to be received as coming from the Apostles. This Canon, as it may be called, rests upon the principle, which we act on daily, that what many independent and competent witnesses guarantee, is true. (*VM* i, ch. 2)

Neither individual, nor Bishop, nor Convocation, nor Council, may venture to decline the *Catholic interpretation* of its sacred mysteries. We have as little warrant for rejecting Ancient Consent as for rejecting Scripture itself. (*VM* i, ch. 11)

They who wish to dispense with Antiquity, should, in consistency, go further, and attempt to learn a language without a dictionary. (*Jfc.*, ch. 5)

[T]he mere name of Antiquity seems to produce a sudden collapse of the intellect in many quarters, certain shudders, and spasms, and indescribable inward sensations. ('Prospects of the Anglican Church,' *British Critic*, April 1839; in *Ess.* i, sec. VII)

And this utter incongruity between Protestantism and historical Christianity is a plain fact, whether the latter be regarded in its earlier or in its later centuries. Protestants can as little bear its Ante-nicene as its Post-tridentine period ... That Protestantism, then, is not the Christianity of history, it is easy to determine. (*Dev.*, Part I: Introduction)

It is indeed sometimes said that the stream is clearest near the spring. Whatever use may fairly be made of this image, it does not apply to the history of a philosophy or belief, which on the contrary is more equable, and purer, and stronger, when its bed has become deep, and broad, and full. It necessarily rises out of an existing state of things, and for a time savours of the soil. Its vital element needs disengaging from what is foreign and temporary, and is employed in efforts after freedom which become more vigorous and hopeful as its years increase. Its beginnings are no measure of its capabilities, nor of its scope. (*Dev.*, Part I: ch. 1)

Well, when I admit that the English Church is in schism, I see a mass of facts confirmatory of it — its disorganised state of belief — its feebleness to resist heretics — its many changes — its freezing coldness — and on the other hand, I have the portentous, the awful, vitality of Rome. This is an overpowering confirmatory argument. Another is this — that according to the lawyers' phrase, the doctrines of the Catholic Church (e.g. the Mass) go back to a time such that the memory of man 'knoweth not' anything different. It is the strongest ground in law. (*Ward* i, 619 [Appendix to Ch. 4]; Letter to Henry Wilberforce, 10 June 1846)

Antiquity, which was the basis of the doctrine of the *Via Media*, and by which was not to be understood a servile imitation of the past, but such a reproduction of it as is really new, while it is old. (*Apo.*, ch. 3)

The whole scene of pale, faint, distant Apostolic Christianity is seen in Rome, as through a telescope or magnifier. (*Apo.*, ch. 4)

Catholic controversialists only partially appeal to Antiquity. To interpret it they appeal to the principle of doctrinal development and to immemorial usage and belief and continuous tradition. (VM i, Lecture 4; footnote 16 from 1877)

The Anglican Church *should* thus act according to its *theory*, but does not in *fact*, because Antiquity *cannot* fulfil the office thus gratuitously put upon it. (VM i, Lecture 11; footnote 5 from 1877)

Apologetics and Evangelism

When St. Paul came to Athens, and found the altar dedicated to the Unknown God, he professed his purpose of declaring to the Heathen world Him 'whom they ignorantly worshipped.' He proceeded to condemn their polytheistic and anthropomorphic errors, to disengage the notion of a Deity from the base earthly attributes in which Heathen religion had enveloped it, and to appeal to their own literature in behalf of the true nature of Him in whom 'we live, and move, and have our being.' But, after thus acknowledging the abstract correctness of the philosophical system, as far as it went, he preaches unto them Jesus and the Resurrection; that is, he embodies the moral character of the Deity in those historical notices of it which have been made the medium of the Christian manifestation of His attributes. (*US*, Sermon 2: 'The Influence of Natural and Revealed Religion Respectively,' 13 April 1830)

Doubtless the degree in which we depend on argument in religious subjects varies with each individual, so that no strict line can be drawn: still, let it be inquired whether these Evidences are not rather to be viewed as splendid philosophical investigations than practical arguments; at best bulwarks intended for overawing the enemy by their strength and number, rather than for actual use in war. In matter of fact, *how* many men do we suppose, in a century, out of the whole body of Christians, have been primarily brought to belief, or retained in it, by an intimate and lively perception of the force of what are technically called the Evidences? And why are there so few? Because to the mind already familiar with the truths of Natural Religion, enough of evidence is at once afforded by the mere fact of the present existence of Christianity; which, viewed in its connexion with its principles and upholders and effects, bears on the face of it the signs of a divine ordinance in the very same way in which the visible world attests to us its own divine origin—a more accurate investigation, in which superior talents are brought into play, merely bringing to light an innumerable alternation of arguments, for and against it, which forms indeed an ever-increasing series in its behalf, but still does not get beyond the first suggestion of plain sense and religiously trained reason; and in fact, perhaps, never comes to a determination. Nay, so alert is the instinctive power of an educated conscience, that by some secret faculty, and without any intelligible reasoning process, it seems to detect moral truth wherever it lies hid, and feels a conviction of its own accuracy which bystanders cannot account for; and this especially in the case of Revealed Religion, which is one comprehensive moral fact,—according to the saying which is parallel to the text, 'I know My sheep, and am known of Mine.' [John x. 14] (*US*, Sermon 4: 'The Usurpations of Reason,' 11 December 1831)

Further, the warfare between Error and Truth is necessarily advantageous to the former, from its very nature, as being conducted by set speech or treatise; and this, not only for a reason already assigned, the deficiency of Truth in the power of eloquence, and even of words, but moreover from the very neatness and definiteness of method required in a written or spoken argument. Truth is vast and far-stretching, viewed as a system; and, viewed in its separate doctrines, it depends on the combination of a number of various, delicate, and scattered evidences; hence it can scarcely be exhibited in a given number of sentences. If this be attempted, its advocate, unable to exhibit more than a fragment of the whole, must round off its rugged extremities, and unite its straggling lines, by much the same process by which an historical narrative is converted into a tale. This, indeed, is the very *art* of composition, which, accordingly, is only with extreme trouble preserved clear of exaggeration and artifice; and who does not see that all this is favourable to the cause of error, — to that party which has not faith enough to be patient of doubt, and has just talent enough to consider perspicuity the chief excellence of a writer? (*US*, Sermon 5: 'Personal Influence, the Means of Propagating the Truth,' 22 January 1832)

[T]he Gospel Faith is a definite deposit, — a treasure, common to all, one and the same in every age, conceived in set words, and such as admits of being received, preserved, transmitted. We may safely leave the custody of it even in the hands of individuals; for in so doing, we are leaving nothing at all to private rashness and fancy, to pride, debate, and strife. We are but allowing men to 'contend earnestly for the Faith once delivered to the Saints;' the Faith which was put into their hands one by one at their baptism, in a form of words called the Creed, and which has come down to them in that very same form from the first ages. This Faith is what even the humblest member of the Church may and must contend for; and in proportion to his education, will the circle of his knowledge enlarge. The Creed delivered to him in Baptism will then unfold, first, into the Nicene Creed (as it is called), then into the Athanasian; and, according as his power of grasping the sense of its articles increases, so will it become his duty to contend for them in their fuller and more accurate form. (*PS* ii, Sermon 22: 'The Gospel, a Trust Committed to Us,' Dec. 1834)

[I]t must not be supposed from my expressing such sentiments, that I have any fear of argument for the cause of Christian truth, as if reason were dangerous to it, as if it could not stand before a scrutinizing inquiry. Nothing is more out of place, though it is too common, than such a charge against the defenders of Church doctrines. They may be right or they may be wrong in their arguments, but argue they do; they are ready to argue; they believe they have reason on their side; but they remind others, they remind themselves, that though argument on the whole will but advance the cause of truth, though so far from dreading it, they are conscious it is a great weapon in their hands; yet that, after all, if a man does nothing more than argue, if he has nothing deeper at bottom, if he does not seek God by some truer means, by obedience, by faith prior to demonstration, he will either not attain truth, or attain a shallow, unreal view of it, and have a weak grasp of it. Reason will prepare for the reception, will spread the news, and secure the outward recognition of the truth; but in all we do we ought to seek edification, not mere knowledge. (*TT* #85, Sep. 1838)

For it is our plain duty to preach and defend the truth in a straightforward way. Those who are to stumble must stumble, rather than the heirs of grace should not hear. While we offend and alienate one man, we secure another; if we drive one man further the wrong way, we drive another further the right way. The cause of truth, the heavenly company of saints, gains on the whole more in one way than in the other. A wavering or shallow mind does perhaps as much harm to others as a mind that is consistent in error, nay, is in no very much better state itself. (*TT* #85, Sep. 1838)

[T]he claims of truth must not be compromised for the sake of peace. No one has any cause to complain of those who, from a religious regard to purity of doctrine, denounce what others admire. But this I think may fairly be required of all persons, that they do not go so far as to denounce in another what they do not at the same time show to be inconsistent with the doctrine of our Church. (*VM* ii, VI. 'On Froude's Statements Concerning the Holy Eucharist,' 1838)

[R]eligious persons sometimes get perplexed and lose their way; are harassed by objections; see difficulties which they cannot surmount; are a prey to subtlety of mind or over-anxiety. Under these circumstances the varied proofs of Christianity will be a stay, a refuge, an encouragement, a rallying point for Faith, a gracious economy; and even in the case of the most established Christian they are a source of gratitude and reverent admiration, and a means of confirming faith and hope. Nothing need be detracted from the use of the Evidences on this score; much less can any sober mind run into the wild notion that actually no proof at all is implied in the maintenance, or may be exacted for the profession of Christianity. (US, Sermon 10: 'Faith and Reason, Contrasted as Habits of Mind,' Jan. 1839)

[T]o take the instance of St. Paul preaching at Athens: he told his hearers that he came as a messenger from that God whom they worshipped already, though ignorantly, and of whom their poets spoke. He appealed to the conviction that was lodged within them of the spiritual nature and the unity of God; and he exhorted them to turn to Him who had appointed One to judge the whole world hereafter. This was an appeal to the antecedent probability of a Revelation, which would be estimated variously according to the desire of it existing in each breast. Now, what was the evidence he gave, in order to concentrate those various antecedent presumptions, to which he referred, in behalf of the message which he brought? Very slight, yet something; not a miracle, but his own word that God had raised Christ from the dead; very like the evidence given to the mass of men now, or rather not so much. No one will say it was strong evidence; yet, aided by the novelty, and what may be called originality, of the claim, its strangeness and improbability considered as a mere invention, and the personal bearing of the Apostle, and supported by the full force of the antecedent probabilities which existed, and which he stirred within them, it was enough. It was enough, for some did believe, — enough, not indeed in itself, but enough for those who had love, and therefore were inclined to believe. To those who had no fears, wishes, longings, or expectations, of another world, he was but 'a babbler;' those who had such, or, in the Evangelist's words in another place, were 'ordained to eternal life,' 'clave unto him, and believed.' … St. Paul's arguments have been long ago abandoned even by men who professed to be defenders of Christianity. Nor can it be said surely that the line of thought (if I may dare so to speak), on which some of our Ever-blessed Saviour's discourses proceed, is more intelligible to our feeble minds. (US, Sermon 11: 'The Nature of Faith in Relation to Reason,' 13 January 1839)

'All that the Father giveth Me, shall come to Me. No man can come unto Me, except the Father which hath sent Me draw him. It is written in the Prophets, And they shall be all taught of God. Every man, therefore, that hath heard and hath learned of the Father, cometh unto Me.' It is the new life, and not the natural reason, which leads the soul to Christ. Does a child trust his parents because he has proved to himself that they are such, and that they are able and desirous to do him good, or from the instinct of affection? We *believe*, because we *love*. How plain a truth! What gain is it to be wise above that which is written? Why, O men, deface with your minute and arbitrary philosophy the simplicity, the reality, the glorious liberty of the inspired teaching? … [T]he second chapter of St. Paul's First Epistle to the Corinthians … distinctly teaches the nothingness of natural Reason, and the all-sufficiency of supernatural grace in the conversion of the soul … Again: — 'The anointing which ye have received of Him abideth in you, and ye need not that any man teach you, but as the same anointing teacheth you of all things, and is true and is no lie, and even as it hath taught you, ye shall abide in Him.' [1 Cor. ii. 1, 2, 4, 14-16. 1 John ii. 19, 20-27.] Surely the faculty by which we know the Truth is here represented to us, not as a power of investigation, but as a moral perception. (US, Sermon 12: 'Love the Safeguard of Faith Against Superstition,' 21 May 1839)

[E]ven as regards what are commonly called Evidences, that is, arguments *à posteriori*; conviction for the most part follows, not upon any one great and decisive proof or token of the point in debate, but upon a number of very minute circumstances together, which the mind is quite unable to count up and methodize in an argumentative form. (US, Sermon 13: 'Implicit and Explicit Reason,' Dec. 1840)

[O]f course I naturally think that I am right and they are wrong; but this persuasion is quite consistent both with my honouring their zeal for Christian truth and their anxiety for the welfare of our younger members, and with my very great consciousness that, even though I be right in my principle, I may have advocated truth in a wrong way. (VM ii, IX. 'Letter to Rev. R. W. Jelf in Explanation of Tract 90,' 1841)

I am not at all denying the use of either of those arguments for religion which are external to us, or of the practice of drawing out our reasons into form; but still so it is, we go by external reasons, before we have, or so far as we have not, inward ones; and we rest upon our logical proofs only when we get perplexed with objections, or are in doubt, or otherwise troubled in mind; or, again, we betake ourselves to the external evidence, or to argumentative processes, not as a matter of personal interest, but from a desire to gaze upon God's great work more intently, and to adore God's wisdom more worthily ... But still it holds good, that a man's real reason for attachment to his own religious communion, why he believes it to be true, why he is eager in its defence, why he feels indignant at being invited to abandon it, is not any series of historical or philosophical arguments, not any thing merely beautiful in its system, or supernatural, but what it has done for him and others; his confidence in it as a means by which men may be brought nearer to God, and may become better and happier ... it is very difficult to draw out our reasons for our religious convictions, and that on many accounts. It is very painful to a man of devout mind to do so; for it implies, or even involves a steadfast and almost curious gaze at God's wonder-working presence within and over him, from which he shrinks, as savouring of a high-minded and critical temper. And much more is it painful, not to say impossible, to put these reasons forth in explicit statements, because they are so very personal and private. Yet, as in order to the relief of his own perplexity, a religious man may at times try to ascertain them, so again for the service of others he will try, as best he may, to state them. (SD, Sermon 23: 'Grounds for Steadfastness in Our Religious Profession,' 19 December 1841)

I have spoken and have still to speak of the action of logic, implicit and explicit, as a safeguard, and thereby a note, of legitimate developments of doctrine: but I am regarding it here as that continuous tradition and habit in the Church of a scientific analysis of all revealed truth, which is an ecclesiastical principle rather than a note of any kind, as not merely bearing upon the process of development, but applying to all religious teaching equally, and which is almost unknown beyond the pale of Christendom. Reason, thus considered, is subservient to faith, as handling, examining, explaining, recording, cataloguing, defending the truths which faith, not reason, has gained for us, as providing an intellectual expression of supernatural facts, eliciting what is implicit, comparing, measuring, connecting each with each, and forming one and all into a theological system ... [T]here certainly is the opposite extreme of a readiness to receive any number of dogmas at a minute's warning, which, when it is witnessed, fairly creates a suspicion that they are merely professed with the tongue, not intelligently held. Our Lord gives no countenance to such lightness of mind; He calls on His disciples to use their reason, and to submit it. (*Dev.*, Part II: ch. 7, sec. 3)

We cannot beat and force people into belief ... I would say to a person, watch your season, avail yourself of opportunities, do not lose them — but still you cannot do more — you cannot make them. (*LD* xi, 224; Letter to the Marquise de Salvo, 18 August 1846)

There are, to be sure, many cogent arguments to lead one to join the Catholic Church, but they do not force the will. We may know them, and not be moved to act upon them. We may be convinced without being persuaded. The two things are quite distinct from each other, seeing you ought to believe, and believing; reason, if left to itself, will bring you to the conclusion that you have sufficient grounds for believing, but belief is the gift of grace. You are then what you are, not from any excellence or merit of your own, but by the grace of God who has chosen you to believe. (*Mix.*, Discourse 10: 'Faith and Private Judgment')

I know how very difficult it is to persuade others of a point which to one's self may be so clear as to require no argument at all ... It is not an easy thing to prove to men that their duty lies just in the reverse direction to that in which they have hitherto placed it. (*Dif.* i, Lecture 5)

As regards his Catholic readers, he would ask leave to express a hope that he may not be supposed in his concluding Lecture to recommend to the Laity the cultivation of a controversial temper, or a forwardness and rashness and unseasonableness in disputing upon religion. No one apprehends so clearly the difficulty of arguing on religious topics, consistently with their sacredness and delicacy, as he who has taken pains to do so well. No one shrinks so sensitively from its responsibility, when it is not a duty, as he who has learned by experience his own unavoidable inaccuracies in statement and in reasoning. It is no easy accomplishment in a Catholic to know his religion so perfectly, as to be able to volunteer a defence of it. (*PPC*, Preface)

Were my time my own, I should never shrink from any controversy, having the experience of twenty years, that the more Catholicism and its doctrines are sifted, the more distinct and luminous will its truth ever come out into view. (*PPC*, Lecture 8)

I want a laity, not arrogant, not rash in speech, not disputatious, but men who know their religion, who enter into it, who know just where they stand, who know what they hold, and what they do not, who know their creed so well, that they can give an account of it, who know so much of history that they can defend it. I want an intelligent, well-instructed laity; I am not denying you are such already: but I mean to be severe, and, as some would say, exorbitant in my demands, I wish you to enlarge your knowledge, to cultivate your reason, to get an insight into the relation of truth to truth, to learn to view things as they are, to understand how faith and reason stand to each other, what are the bases and principles of Catholicism, and where lie the main inconsistences and absurdities of the Protestant theory … You ought to be able to bring out what you feel and what you mean, as well as to feel and mean it; to expose to the comprehension of others the fictions and fallacies of your opponents; and to explain the charges brought against the Church, to the satisfaction, not, indeed, of bigots, but of men of sense, of whatever cast of opinion. (*PPC*, Lecture 9)

Nor will argument itself be out of place in the hands of laymen mixing with the world … Theologians inculcate the matter, and determine the details of that Revelation; they view it from within; philosophers view it from without, and this external view may be called the Philosophy of Religion, and the office of delineating it externally is most gracefully performed by laymen. In the first age laymen were most commonly the Apologists. Such were Justin, Tatian, Athenagoras, Aristides, Hermias, Minucius Felix, Arnobius, and Lactantius. In like manner in this age some of the most prominent defences of the Church are from laymen: as De Maistre, Chateaubriand, Nicolas, Montalembert, and others. (*IU*, Part II, ch. 4, sec. 4: 'General Religious Knowledge,' 1856)

I have said that minds in different states and circumstances cannot understand one another, and that in all cases they must be instructed according to their capacity, and, if not taught step by step, they learn only so much the less; that children do not apprehend the thoughts of grown people, nor savages the instincts of civilisation, nor blind men the perceptions of sight, nor pagans the doctrines of Christianity, nor men the experiences of Angels. (*Apo.* ii; 'Mr. Kingsley's Method of Disputation,' 21 April 1864)

I believed in a God on a ground of probability, that I believed in Christianity on a probability, and that I believed in Catholicism on a probability, and that these three grounds of probability, distinct from each other of course in subject matter, were still all of them one and the same in nature of proof, as being probabilities—probabilities of a special kind, a cumulative, a transcendent probability but still probability; inasmuch as He who made us has so willed, that in mathematics indeed we should arrive at certitude by rigid demonstration, but in religious inquiry we should arrive at certitude by accumulated probabilities. (*Apo.*, ch. 4)

I can never prophesy what will be useful to a given individual and what not ... [I]f there is a way of finding religious truth, it lies, not in exercises of the intellect, but close on the side of duty, of conscience, in the observance of the moral law ... to gain religious starting points, we must in a parallel way, interrogate our hearts, and (since it is a personal, individual matter,) our own hearts,—interrogate our own consciences, interrogate, I will say, the God who dwells there. (*POL*; Letter to Lady Louisa Simeon, 25 June 1869)

I prefer to rely on that of an *accumulation* of various probabilities ... from probabilities we may construct legitimate proof, sufficient for certitude ... since a Good Providence watches over us, He blesses such means of argument as it has pleased Him to give us, in the nature of man and of the world, if we use them duly for those ends for which He has given them; and that, as in mathematics we are justified by the dictate of nature in withholding our assent from a conclusion of which we have not yet a strict logical demonstration, so by a like dictate we are not justified, in the case of concrete reasoning and especially of religious inquiry, in waiting till such logical demonstration is ours, but on the contrary are bound in conscience to seek truth and to look for certainty by modes of proof, which, when reduced to the shape of formal propositions, fail to satisfy the severe requisitions of science. Here then at once is one momentous doctrine or principle, which enters into my own reasoning, and which another ignores, viz., the providence and intention of God; and of course there are other principles, explicit or implicit, which are in like circumstances. It is not wonderful then, that, while I can prove Christianity divine to my own satisfaction, I shall not be able to force it upon any one else. Multitudes indeed I ought to succeed in persuading of its truth without any force at all, because they and I start from the same principles, and what is a proof to me is a proof to them; but if any one starts from any other principles but ours, I have not the power to change his principles, or the conclusion which he draws from them, any more than I can make a crooked man straight. Whether his mind will ever grow straight, whether I can do anything towards its becoming straight, whether he is not responsible, responsible to his Maker, for being mentally crooked, is another matter; still the fact remains, that, in any inquiry about things in the concrete, men differ from each other, not so much in the soundness of their reasoning as in the principles which govern its exercise, that those principles are of a personal character, that where there is no common measure of minds, there is no common measure of arguments, and that the validity of proof is determined, not by any scientific test, but by the illative sense. (GA, Part II, ch. 10, sec. 2)

Christianity is addressed, both as regards its evidences and its contents, to minds which are in the normal condition of human nature, as believing in God and in a future judgment. Such minds it addresses both through the intellect and through the imagination; creating a certitude of its truth by arguments too various for direct enumeration, too personal and deep for words, too powerful and concurrent for refutation. Nor need reason come first and faith second (though this is the logical order), but one and the same teaching is in different aspects both object and proof, and elicits one complex act both of inference and of assent. It speaks to us one by one, and it is received by us one by one, as the counterpart, so to say, of ourselves, and is real as we are real. (GA, Part II, ch. 10, sec. 2)

I wish I could write a satisfactory answer to your question, but you will easily understand that the circumstance of my not knowing you personally makes it impossible to do so. I ever feel that religious questions are simply personal, and that the advice and arguments suitable to one inquirer are not suitable to another. (LD xxxii, 312; Letter to an Unknown Correspondent, 4 September 1870)

Of course every Catholic should have an intelligent appreciation of his religion, as St. Peter says, but still controversy is not the instrument by which the world is to be resisted and overcome. (FP, Sermon 9: 'The Infidelity of the Future,' 2 October 1873)

In controversy one has no right to complain of strong conclusions, but to assume them on starting is the act of a pleader or advocate, not of a theologian. I will not indeed say that this arm in polemical attack is altogether inadmissible, but at least it is not logical, and may without scruple be ignored and passed over by a respondent. (VM i, Preface to the Third Edition, 1877)

I hope it will not seem to your Holiness an intrusion upon your time if I address to you a few lines to thank you for the very seasonable and important encyclical which you bestowed upon us. All good Catholics must feel it a first necessity that the intellectual exercises, without which the Church cannot fulfil her supernatural mission duly, should be founded upon broad as well as true principles, that the mental creations of her theologians, and of her controversialists and pastors should be grafted on the Catholic tradition of philosophy, and should not start from a novel and simply original tradition, but should be substantially one with the teaching of St. Athanasius, St. Augustine, St. Anselm, and St. Thomas, as those great doctors in turn are one with each other. At a time when there is so much cultivation of mind, so much intellectual excitement, so many new views, true and false, and so much temptation to overstep the old truth, we need just what your Holiness has supplied us with in your recent pastoral. (*Ward* ii, 501-502; Letter to Pope Leo XIII, referring to his encyclical, *Aeterni Patris: On the Restoration of Christian Philosophy*, of 4 August 1879; presumably written shortly afterwards)

In trying to prove you *must have* assumptions, thus it is vain to attempt to *prove* your assumptions ... let us go back to the question of first principles. Of course there can from the nature of the case be no direct proof that one set of first principles is sound, another unsound. But there may be indirect proofs. You may show your young man that if there is a certain earnest and philosophical frame of mind which leads to truth in various subject matters, it is probable that under normal circumstances such a frame of mind will also lead to the adoption of sound first principles. So far as the sceptical habit of mind goes with want of depth and earnestness, you have a strong argument against the probability of sceptical first principles. (*Ward* ii, 491, 493; personal conversations recorded by the author, Wilfrid Ward, 30 and 31 January 1885)

Apostles

An Apostle, as inspired, had his mind absolutely enlightened on revealed matters. Ask him any question on the subject of revelation and he could answer it, unless for some special reason it was withheld from him. Also, of course his inspiration might grow in fulness. Still it was a state of mind, and made him different from all other men. (*LD* xxxii, 292; Letter to an Unknown Correspondent, 12 February 1869)

Apostolic Deposit of Faith

The notion of doctrinal knowledge absolutely novel, and of simple addition from without, is intolerable to Catholic ears, and never was entertained by any one who was even approaching to an understanding of our creed. Revelation is all in all in doctrine; the Apostles its sole depository, the inferential method its sole instrument, and ecclesiastical authority its sole sanction. The Divine Voice has spoken once for all, and the only question is about its meaning ... Christian Truth is purely of revelation; that revelation we can but explain, we cannot increase, except relatively to our own apprehensions; without it we should have known nothing of its contents, with it we know just as much as its contents, and nothing more. And, as it was given by a divine act independent of man, so will it remain in spite of man. (*IU*, Part I, Discourse 9: 'Duties of the Church Towards Knowledge,' 1852)

What is known in Christianity is just that which is revealed, and nothing more; certain truths, communicated directly from above, are committed to the keeping of the faithful, and to the very last nothing can really be added to those truths. From the time of the Apostles to the end of the world no strictly new truth can be added to the theological information which the Apostles were inspired to deliver. It is possible of course to make numberless deductions from the original doctrines; but, as the conclusion is ever in its premisses, such deductions are not, strictly speaking, an addition. (*IU*, Part II, ch. 7: 'Christianity and Physical Science,' November 1855)

[N]either Pope nor Council are on a level with the Apostles. To the Apostles the whole revelation was given, by the Church it is transmitted; no simply new truth has been given to us since St. John's death; the one office of the Church is to guard 'that noble deposit' of truth, as St. Paul speaks to Timothy, which the Apostles bequeathed to her, in its fulness and integrity. Hence the infallibility of the Apostles was of a far more positive and wide character than that needed by and granted to the Church. (*Dif.* ii, Letter to the Duke of Norfolk, ch. 9, 1875)

Catholics will not instance one doctrine merely, but, as has been noted above, there are many doctrines, which, though not in the Apostolic Creed (as the developed doctrine of the Holy Trinity, original sin, the necessity of grace, eternal punishment), still the high Anglican considers to have a place in the Apostolic *depositum* of faith ... [C]ommonly truths of the Apostolic *depositum* are not made dogmas or articles of faith, till they have been publicly denied. (VM i, Lecture 10; footnotes 1 and 2 from 1877)

Revealed truth, to be what it professes, must have an uninterrupted descent from the Apostles; its teachers must be unanimous, and persistent in their unanimity; and it must bear no human master's name as its designation ... [W]hat is over and above nature must come from divine revelation; and, if so, it must descend from the very date when it was revealed, else it is but matter of opinion; and opinions vary, and have no warrant of permanence, but depend upon the relative ability and success of individual teachers, one with another, from whom they take their names. (*Ath.* ii, 'Heretics')

Apostolic Succession

Christ promised He should be with His Apostles always, as ministers of His religion, even unto the end of the world. In one sense the Apostles were to be alive till He came again; but they all died at the natural time. Does it not follow, that there are those now alive who represent them? Now who were the most probable representatives of them in the generation next their death? They surely, whom they had ordained to succeed them in the ministerial work. (*TT* #7, 1833)

Further, take that remarkable passage in Matt. xxiv. 45-51. Luke xii. 42-46, 'Who then is that faithful and wise Steward, whom his Lord shall make ruler over His household, to give them their portion of meat in due season? Blessed is that servant, whom his Lord, *when He cometh*, shall find so doing!' &c ... I do not ask who are the stewards, but surely the words, *when He cometh*, imply that they are to continue till the end of the world ... there must be those with whom Christ is present, who are His 'Stewards,' and whom it is our duty to obey. (*TT* #11, 1833)

[A]ll sects think it necessary that their Ministers should be ordained by other Ministers. Now, if this be the case, then the validity of ordination, even with *them*, rests on a *succession*; and is it not plain that they ought to trace that succession to the Apostles? Else, why are they ordained at all? And, any how, if *their* Ministers have a commission, who derive it from private men, much more do the Ministers of our Church, who actually do derive it from the Apostles. Surely those who dissent from the Church have *invented* an ordinance, as they themselves must allow; whereas Churchmen, whether rightly or wrongly, still maintain *their* succession not to be an invention, but to be God's ordinance ... [T]heir succession, not professing to come from God, has no power to restrain any fanatic from setting up to preach of his own will, and a people with itching ears choosing for themselves a teacher. (*TT* #15, 1833)

The doctrine in dispute is this; that Christ founded a visible Church as an ordinance for ever, and endowed it once for all with spiritual privileges, and set His Apostles over it, as the first in a line of ministers and rulers, like themselves except in their miraculous gifts, and to be continued from them by successive ordination; in consequence, that to adhere to this Church thus distinguished, is among the ordinary duties of a Christian, and is the means of his appropriating the Gospel blessings with an evidence of his doing so not attainable elsewhere. (*TT* #74, 1836)

A body of doctrine had been delivered by the Apostles to their first successors, and by them in turn to the next generation, and then to the next, as we have said above. 'The things that thou hast heard from me through many witnesses,' says St. Paul to Timothy, 'the same commit thou to faithful men, who shall be able to teach others also.' This body of truth was in consequence called the 'depositum,' as being a substantive teaching, not a mere accidental deduction from Scripture. Thus St. Paul says to his disciple and successor Timothy, 'Keep the deposit,' 'hold fast the form of sound words,' 'guard the noble deposit.' This important principle is forcibly insisted on by Irenaeus and Tertullian before the Nicene era, and by Vincent after it. ('Apostolical Tradition,' *British Critic*, Vol. 19, July 1836; in *Ess.* i, sec. III)

[A] person who denies the Apostolical Succession of the Ministry, because it is not clearly taught in Scripture, ought, I conceive, if consistent, to deny the divinity of the Holy Ghost, which is nowhere literally stated in Scripture. (*TT* #85, Sep. 1838)

I will but add, by way of specimen, how such interpretations as our Lord's of 'I am the God of Abraham,' etc., would, were we not accustomed to them, startle and offend reasoning men. Is it not much further from the literal force of the words, than the doctrine of the Apostolical Succession is from the words, 'I am with you alway, even unto the end of the world'? In the one case we argue, 'Therefore, the Apostles are in one sense *now* on earth, because Christ says 'with *you* alway;' in the other, Christ Himself argues, 'therefore in one sense the bodies of the patriarchs are still alive; for God calls Himself '*their* God.' We say, 'therefore the Apostles live in their successors.' Christ implies, 'therefore the body never died, and therefore it will rise again.' His own divine mouth hereby shows us that doctrines may be in Scripture, though they require a multitude of links to draw them thence. (*TT* #85, Sep. 1838)

The principle indeed of Dogmatism developes into Councils in the course of time; but it was active, nay sovereign from the first, in every part of Christendom. A conviction that truth was one; that it was a gift from without, a sacred trust, an inestimable blessing; that it was to be reverenced, guarded, defended, transmitted; that its absence was a grievous want, and its loss an unutterable calamity ... Councils and Popes are the guardians and instruments of the dogmatic principle: they are not that principle themselves; they presuppose the principle; they are summoned into action at the call of the principle. (*Dev.*, Part II: ch. 8, sec. 1)

Our starting-point is not the fact of a faithful transmission of Orders, but the standing fact of the Church, the Visible and One Church, the reproduction and succession of herself age after age. It is the Church herself that vouches for our Orders, while she authenticates herself to be the

Church not by our Orders, but by her Notes. It is the great Note of an ever-enduring *cœtus fidelium*, with a fixed organisation, a unity of jurisdiction, a political greatness, a continuity of existence in all places and times, a suitableness to all classes, ranks, and callings, an ever-energizing life, an untiring, ever-evolving history, which is her evidence that she is the creation of God, and the representative and home of Christianity. She is not based upon her Orders; she is not the subject of her instruments; they are not necessary for her idea ... If Providence had so willed, she might have had her ministers without any lineal descent from the Apostles at all. Her mere nomination might have superseded any rite of Ordination; there might have been no indelible character in her ministers; she might have commissioned them, used them, and recalled them at her pleasure. She might have been like a civil state, in which there is a continuation of office, but not a propagation of official life. The occupant of the See of St. Peter, himself made such by mere election, might have made bishops and unmade them. Her Divine Founder has chosen a better way, better because He has chosen it. A transmission of ministerial power ever has been, and ever shall be; and He who has so ordained, will carry out His ordinance, preserve it from infraction or make good any damage to it, because it is His ordinance, but still that ordinance is not simply of the essence of the Church; it is not more than an inseparable accident and a necessary instrument. Nor is the Apostolic descent of her priests the direct warrant of their power in the eyes of the faithful; their warrant is her immediate, present, living authority; it is the word of the Church which marks them out as the ministers of God, not any historical or antiquarian research, or genealogical table; and while she is most cautious and jealous that they should be ordained aright, yet it is sufficient in proof of their ordination that they belong to her. (*Ess.* ii, Note on Essay X: 'Catholicity of the Anglican Church,' *British Critic*, Jan. 1840; from 1871)

Atonement

The Jewish sacrifices indeed are done away, but still there remains One Great Sacrifice for sin, infinitely higher and more sacred than all other conceivable sacrifices. According to the Gospel message, Christ has voluntarily suffered, 'the just for the unjust, to bring us to God.' Here is the mystery continued. Why was this suffering necessary to procure for us the blessings which we were in ourselves unworthy of? We do not know. We should not be better men or knowing why God did not pardon us without Christ's death; so He has not told us ... We are saved by the death of Christ; but who is Christ? Christ is the Very Son of God, Begotten of God and One with God from everlasting, God incarnate. This is our inexpressible comfort, and a most sanctifying truth if we receive it rightly; but how stupendous a mystery *is* the incarnation and sufferings of the Son of God! (*PS* i, Sermon 16: 'The Christian Mysteries,' 14 June 1829)

And so it has ever been in very deed; to approach Him has been, from the first, to be partaker, more or less, in His sufferings; I do not say in the case of every individual who believes in Him, but as regards the more conspicuous, the more favoured, His choice instruments, and His most active servants; that is, it has been the lot of the Church, on the whole, and of those, on the whole, who had been most like Him, as Rulers, Intercessors, and Teachers of the Church. (*PS* iii, Sermon 11: 'Bodily Suffering,' 3 May 1835)

Thus the Atonement:—*why* it was necessary, *how* it operates, is a Mystery; that is, the heavenly truth which is revealed, extends on each side of it into an unknown world. We see but the skirts of God's glory in it. (*TT* #73, 1836)

When He spoke, it was literally God speaking; when He suffered, it was God suffering. Not that the Divine Nature itself could suffer, any more than our soul can see or hear; but, as the soul sees and hears through the organs of the body, so God the Son suffered *in* that human nature which He had taken to Himself and made His own. And in that nature He did truly suffer ... We believe, then, that when Christ suffered on the cross, our nature suffered in Him. Human nature, fallen and corrupt, was under the wrath of God, and it was impossible that it should be restored to His favour till it had expiated its sin by suffering ... thus, as the Apostle says, 'If one died for all, then did *all* die;' 'our old man is crucified *in Him*, that the *body* of sin might be destroyed;' and 'together' with Christ 'when we were dead in sins, hath He quickened us, and raised us up together, and made us sit together in heavenly places in Christ Jesus.' Thus 'we are members of His body, from His flesh, and from His bones: for whosoever eateth His flesh and drinketh His blood, hath eternal life,' for His flesh is meat indeed, and His blood is drink indeed; and 'he that eateth His flesh and drinketh His blood dwelleth in Him, and He in him' [2 Cor. v. 14. Rom. vi. 6. Eph. ii. 5, 6; v. 30. John vi. 54]. (*PS* vi, Sermon 6: 'The Incarnate Son, a Sufferer and Sacrifice,' 1 April 1836)

It is called *the state of grace*, and it is the state to die in, and since we may die any moment, the state to live in, if we would be safe. And though few are in this state, it is the state in which God wills all to be in, for Christ died for *all*. As He sends out *preachers* all over the earth, and as still more, guardian angels, so *graces*. To all He gives grace, even to those who are not yet in His favour, or *in* grace. He gives them this grace in order that they may *come* into a state of grace—heathens, idolaters, Jews, heretics, all who are not Catholics. All have grace without knowing it. (*SN*, 'No One Can Come to Me Except the Father,' Etc.,' 6 August 1854)

I conceive that the atonement is a 'mystery,' a glorious 'mystery,' to be gloried in *because* it is a mystery, to be received by a pure act of faith, inasmuch as reason does not *see how* the death of God Incarnate can stand instead of, can be a Vicarious Satisfaction for, the eternal death of his sinful brethren. (*LD* xxx, 204; Letter to George T. Edwards, 15 April 1883)

[W]e are saved solely by the vicarious suffering of our Lord for us. (*LD* xxx, 211; Letter to George T. Edwards, 2 May 1883)

Atonement: Universal

No one is punished except for his own fault. No one is punished except for rejecting light. God gives light all over the earth—enough to make men advance forward. (*SN*, 'Faith,' 31 January 1858)

Baptism

St. Paul says of himself, that he was not sent to baptize, but to preach the Gospel. *He* did not baptize, because so great a gift was baptism, that the Apostles wished to avoid the chance of seeming to baptize in their own name, and of seeming to be setting up *themselves* for the meritorious means through which men are saved. St. Paul says, then, 'I thank my God that I baptized *none* of you,' except one or two whom he mentions, 'lest any should say that I had baptized in mine own name.' [1 Cor. i. 14, 15.] As water is a feeble element, so the minister chosen was the feeblest vessel in the Church, to show that all was of God. Accordingly, the Apostle generally had with him some friend, who, while a companion and comfort to him, administered those offices which he did not take upon himself. (*PS* vi, Sermon 12: 'Faith the Title for Justification,' 24 January 1841)

Baptism and Regeneration

The ordinary and intelligible reason for the Baptism of infants, is the securing to them remission of sins, and the gift of the Holy Ghost — Regeneration; but if this sacred privilege is not given to them in Baptism, why, it may be asked, should Baptism be administered to them at all? Why not wait till they can understand the meaning of the rite, and can have faith and repentance themselves? ... It does seem as if those who deny the regeneration of infants ought, if they were consistent (which happily they are not), to refrain from baptizing them. Surely, if we go by Scripture, the question is decided at once; for no one can deny that there is much more said in Scripture in behalf of the connexion between Baptism and Divine grace, than about the duty of Infant Baptism. The passage can scarcely be named, in the New Testament, where Baptism is referred to, without the mention, direct or indirect, of spiritual influences. What right have we to put asunder what God has united? ... [O]n the day of Pentecost, St. Peter said to the multitude, who asked what they must do, 'Repent, and be baptized every one of you in the name of Jesus Christ for the remission of sins, and ye shall receive the gift of the Holy Ghost.' Accordingly, 'they that gladly received His word were baptized,' in order to obtain these privileges; and, forthwith, we hear of their continuing 'in gladness and singleness of heart, praising God.' Again, when the Ethiopian Eunuch had been baptized by Philip, he 'went on his way rejoicing.' After St. Paul had been struck down by the Saviour whom he was persecuting, and sent to Damascus, he began to pray; but though in one sense a changed man already, he had not yet received the gift of regeneration, nor did he receive it except by the ministry of Ananias, who was sent to Him from Christ, expressly that he 'might be filled with the Holy Ghost.' Accordingly, Ananias said to him, 'And now why tarriest thou? Arise and be baptized, and wash away thy sins, calling on the name of the Lord.' So again Cornelius, religious man as he was, and that doubtless by God's secret aid, yet was not received into Christ's family except by Baptism. Even the descent of the Holy Ghost upon him and his friends miraculously, while St. Peter was preaching to them, did not supersede the necessity of the Sacrament. And lastly, when the jailer at Philippi had been baptized, he 'rejoiced, believing in God with all his house.' [Acts ii. 38-47; viii. 39; ix. 17; xxii. 16; x. 44-48; xvi. 34.] ... Is it possible, then, now that the Spirit is come, we can be under dead rites and ordinances? It is plainly impossible. If Baptism then has no spiritual virtue in it, can it be intended for us Christians? If it has no regenerating power, surely they only are consistent who reject it altogether. (*PS* iii, Sermon 19: 'Regenerating Baptism,' 15 November 1835)

[T]he Sacrament of Baptism is not a mere *sign* or *promise*, but actually a *means* of grace, an *instrument*, by which, when rightly received, the soul is admitted to the benefits of Christ's Atonement, such as the forgiveness of sin, original and actual, reconciliation to God, a new nature, adoption, citizenship in Christ's kingdom, and the inheritance of heaven,—in a word, Regeneration. And next, Baptism is considered to be rightly received, when there is no positive obstacle or hindrance to the reception in the recipient, such as impenitence or unbelief would be in the case of an adult; so that infants are necessarily right recipients of it, as not being yet capable of actual sin. (*TT* #76, 1836)

Let us consider a doctrine much debated and much resisted at this day,—the doctrine of Baptismal Regeneration. Scripture tells us expressly that, 'except a man be born of water and of the Spirit, he cannot enter the kingdom of God;' and that God has saved us 'by the washing of regeneration;' and that 'Baptism saves us;' and that we 'wash away our sins' by Baptism. No other means have been pointed out to us for attaining regeneration, or the new birth; so that, while Baptism is said to take us out of a state of nature into a state of grace, if a man is not born again in Baptism, it does not appear how he is to be born again. Such is the true doctrine, which has ever been received in the whole Church. (*SD*, Sermon 6: 'Faith and Experience,' 25 November 1838)

No other appointed, means but [B]aptism is revealed in Scripture for regeneration. (*Keb.*, 207; Letter of 4 March 1843)

[W]hen man fell and lost this holy grace, he had various gifts still adhering to him; he might be, in a certain measure, true, merciful, loving, and just; but these virtues did not unite him to God. What he needed was holiness; and therefore the first act of God's goodness to us in the Gospel is to take us out of our *unholy* state by means of the sacrament of Baptism, and by the grace then given us to re-open the communications, so long closed, between the soul and heaven. (*MD*, 'Meditations on the Litany of Loretto, for the Month of May: I. On the Immaculate Conception,' for May 9)

Baptism, Infant

For instance, if the cases of Lydia, of the jailer, of Stephanas, were brought to show our Lord's *wish* as to the baptism of households, the actions of his apostles to *interpret* his own commands, it was answered; 'This is no satisfactory *proof*; it is not *certain* that every one of those households was not himself a believer; it is not *certain* there were any children among them:' — though surely, in as many as *three* households, the probability is on the side which the Church has taken, especially viewing the texts in connexion with our Saviour's words, 'Suffer the little children,' &c. (*TT* #45, 1834)

[O]ur gracious Lord has done much more than tell us that some souls are elected to the mercies of redemption and others not. He has not left

Christians thus uncertain about their children. He has expressly assured us that children are in the number of his chosen; and, if you ask, whether all children, I reply, all children you can bring to Baptism, all children who are within reach of it … He has disclosed His secret election in a visible Sacrament, and thus enables Christians to bear to be, what otherwise they would necessarily shrink from being—parents. He relieves, my brethren, your anxious minds, anxious (as they must ever be) for your children's welfare, even after all the good promises of the Gospel, but unspeakably anxious before you understand *how* you are to be rid of the extreme responsibility of bestowing an eternal being upon sinful creatures whom you cannot change … Now that Christ receives us in our infancy, no one has any ground for complaining of his fallen nature. He receives by birth a curse, but by Baptism a blessing, and the blessing is the greater. (*PS* iii, Sermon 20: 'Infant Baptism,' 24 May 1835)

[I]nfants are by and at baptism unconditionally translated from a state of wrath into a state of grace and acceptance for Christ's sake. (*TT* #76, 1836)

Baptism placed you in this blessed state. God did not wait till you should do some good thing before He blessed you. No! He knew you could do no good thing of yourselves. So He came to you first; He loved you before you loved Him; He gave you a work which He first made you able to do. He placed you in a new and heavenly state, in which, while you remain, you are safe. He said not to you, 'Obey Me, and I will give you a kingdom;' but 'Lo I give you a kingdom freely and first of all; now obey Me henceforth, for you can, and you shall remain in it;' not 'Obey Me, and I will then give you the Holy Spirit as a reward;' but 'I give you that great gift in order that you may obey Me.' (*PS* viii, Sermon 4: 'The Call of David,' 25 June 1837)

[I]n defending such doctrines and practices of the Church as Infant Baptism or the Episcopal Succession, the Tracts have argued that they rested on substantially the same basis as the Canon of Scripture, viz., the testimony of ancient Christendom. (*VM* ii, X. 'Letter to Richard, Lord Bishop of Oxford, in Explanation of Tract 90,' 1841)

[C]ircumcision ... is altogether done away with in the Gospel; yet not so done away with, but it leaves behind it a representative. It is abolished as a type fulfilled, a type of Christian renewal; yet still there is such a rite as Christian circumcision, and it is called Baptism. This is what St. Paul expressly says in the chapter before us. 'Ye are complete in Christ,' he says, 'which is the Head of all principality and power. In whom all ye are circumcised with the circumcision made without hands, in putting off the body of the sins of the flesh by the circumcision of Christ: buried with Him in baptism.' Here he says, first, that the Colossians *had* received a circumcision, though not the Jewish; and then names what it is, 'buried with Him in Baptism.' Thus, though circumcision is abolished, Scripture has not left us without its substitute, lest the great and fundamental rule which circumcision implied, of entering God's service by a formal act of dedication, should be slighted. And on account of this correspondence between the two rites, we infer the duty of baptizing infants, because infants were circumcised, though there is no command to that effect in Scripture. Nor need there be, if, as I am here showing, the Law contains in it the ecclesiastical and ritual rules of the Gospel, only under a veil. (*SD*, Sermon 15: 'The Principle of Continuity Between the Jewish and Christian Churches,' 20 November 1842)

One of the passages of St. Chrysostom to which I might refer is this, 'We baptize infants, though they are not defiled with sin, that they may receive sanctity, righteousness, adoption, heirship, brotherhood with Christ, and may become His members.' (*Aug. contr. Jul.* i. 21.) This at least shows that he had a clear view of the importance and duty of infant baptism, but such was not the case even with saints in the generation immediately before him ... [I]nfant baptism, which is a fundamental rule of Christian duty with us, was less earnestly insisted on in early times. Even in the fourth century St. Gregory Nazianzen, St. Basil, and St. Augustine, having Christian mothers, still were not baptized till they were adults. (*Dev.*, Part I: ch. 4, sec. 1)

Certainly no Catholic controversialist will say that his real ground for considering (e.g.) infant baptism obligatory, is the testimony of the first three centuries. *Of course* he must appeal to the voice of the infallible Church. On what do Anglicans rest its obligation? (*VM* i, Lecture 2; footnote 29 from 1877)

Baptism of Desire

So again, contrition of a certain kind is sufficient as a disposition or condition, or what is called matter, for receiving absolution in Penance *ex opere operato* or by virtue of the sacrament; but it may be heightened and purified into so intense an act of divine love, of hatred and sorrow for sin, and of renunciation of it, as to cleanse and justify the soul, without the sacrament at all, or *ex opere operantis*. (*Dif.* i, Lecture 3)

Church (Ecclesiology)

Too many persons at this day … do not obey Him in that way in which it is His will that He should be obeyed. They do not obey Him in His Kingdom; they think to be His people, without being His subjects. They determine to serve Him in their own way; and though He has formed His chosen into one body, they think to separate from that body, yet to remain in the number of the chosen. Far different is the doctrine suggested to us by the text. In St. Peter, who is there made the rock on which the Church is founded, we see, as in a type, its unity, stability, and permanence. It is set up in one name, not in many, to show that it is one; and that name is Peter, to show that it will last, or, as the Divine Speaker proceeds, that 'the gates of hell shall not prevail against it.' In like manner, St. Paul calls it 'the pillar and ground of the truth.' [1 Tim. iii. 15.] (*PS* vii, Sermon 17: 'The Unity of the Church,' 22 November 1829)

To the millions for whom Redemption has been wrought, creeds and catechisms, liturgies and a theological system, the multitudinous eversounding voice, the categorical, peremptory incisiveness, the (so to say) full chime, of ecclesiastical authority, is a first necessity, if they are to realize the world unseen. ('Apostolical Tradition,' *British Critic*, Vol. 19, July 1836; in *Ess.* i, sec. III)

There have ever been from the first these two kinds of Christians — those who belonged to the Church, and those who did not. There never was a time since the Apostles' day, when the Church was not; and there never was a time but men were to be found who preferred some other way of worship to the Church's way. (*PS* viii, Sermon 1: 'Reverence in Worship,' 30 October 1836)

Roman Catholics having ever insisted upon it, and Protestants having neglected it, to speak of the Church at all. (*VM* i, Introduction)

He who could make St. Peter walk the waves, could make even a corrupt or defective creed a mode and way of leading us into truth, even were ours such; much more can He teach us by the witness of the Church Catholic. It is far more probable that her witness should be true, whether about the Canon or the Creed, than that God should have left us without any witness at all. (*TT* #85, Sep. 1838)

'The *Church* of the living God,' says St. Paul, '*the pillar and ground of the truth.*' The simple question then for Private Judgment to exercise itself upon is, what and where is the Church? ('Private Judgment,' *British Critic*, July 1841; in *Ess.* ii, sec. XIV)

We hear much of Bible Christians, Bible Religion, Bible preaching; it would be well if we heard a little of the Bible Church also; we venture to say, that Dissenting Churches would vanish thereupon at once, for, since it is their fundamental principle that they are not a pillar or ground of truth, but voluntary societies, without authority and without gifts, the Bible Church they cannot be. ('Private Judgment,' *British Critic*, July 1841; in *Ess.* ii, sec. XIV)

Has there not, in fact, been a great corporation, or continuous body politic, all over the world, from the Apostles' days to our own, bearing the name of Church — one, and one only? Has it not spread in spite of all opposition, and maintained itself marvellously against the power of the world? Has it not ever taken the cause of the poor and friendless against the great and proud? Has it not succeeded by the use of weapons, not earthly and carnal, but by righteousness and mercy, as was foretold? Has it not broken in pieces numberless kingdoms and conquerors which opposed it, and risen again, and flourished more than before, after the most hopeless reverses? Has it not ever been at war with the spirit of the world, with pride, and luxury, and cruelty, and tyranny, and profaneness? (*SD*, Sermon 16: 'The Christian Church an Imperial Power,' 27 November 1842)

There is a religious communion claiming a divine commission, and holding all other religious bodies around it heretical or infidel; it is a well-organised, well-disciplined body; it is a sort of secret society, binding together its members by influences and by engagements which it is difficult for strangers to ascertain. It is spread over the known world; it may be weak or insignificant locally, but it is strong on the whole from its continuity; it may be smaller than all other religious bodies together, but is larger than each separately. It is a natural enemy to governments external to itself; it is intolerant and engrossing, and tends to a new modelling of society; it breaks laws, it divides families. It is a gross superstition; it is charged with the foulest crimes; it is despised by the intellect of the day; it is frightful to the imagination of the many. And there is but one communion such. Place this description before Pliny or Julian; place it before Frederick the Second or Guizot. '*Apparent diræ facies.*' Each knows at once, without asking a question, who is meant by it. One object, and only one, absorbs each item of the detail of the delineation. (*Dev.*, Part II: ch. 6)

[T]he whole world, heresies inclusive, were irresistibly constrained to call God's second election by its prophetical title of the 'Catholic' Church. St. Paul tells us that the heretic is 'condemned by himself;' and no clearer witness against the sects of the earlier centuries was needed by the Church, than their own testimony to this contrast between her actual position and their own. Sects, say the Fathers, are called after the name of their founders, or from their locality or from their doctrine. So was it from the beginning: 'I am of Paul, and I of Apollos, and I of Cephas;' but it was promised to the Church that she should have no master upon earth, and that she should 'gather together in one the children of God that were scattered abroad.' Her every-day name, which was understood in the market place and used in the palace, which every chance comer knew, and which state-edicts recognised, was the 'Catholic' Church. This was that very description of Christianity in those times which we are all along engaged in determining. And it had been recognised as such from the first ... On the whole, then, we have reason to say, that if there be a form of Christianity at this day distinguished for its careful organisation, and its consequent power; if it is spread over the world; if it is conspicuous for zealous maintenance of its own creed; if it is intolerant towards what it considers error; if it is engaged in ceaseless war with all other bodies called Christian; if it, and it alone, is called 'Catholic' by the world, nay, by those very bodies, and if it makes much of the title; if it names them heretics, and warns them of coming woe, and calls on them one by one, to come over to itself, overlooking every other tie; and if they, on the other hand, call it seducer, harlot, apostate, Antichrist, devil; if, however much they differ one with another, they consider it their common enemy; if they strive to unite together against it, and cannot; if they are but local; if they continually subdivide, and it remains one; if they fall one after another, and make way for new sects, and it remains the same; such a re-ligious communion is not unlike historical Christianity, as it comes before us at the Nicene Era. (*Dev.*, Part II: ch. 6, sec. 2)

When we consider the succession of ages during which the Catholic system has endured, the severity of the trials it has undergone, the sudden and wonderful changes without and within which have befallen it, the incessant mental activity and the intellectual gifts of its maintainers, the enthusiasm which it has kindled, the fury of the controversies which have been carried on among its professors, the impetuosity of the assaults made upon it, the ever-increasing responsibilities to which it has been commit-ted by the continuous development of its dogmas, it is quite inconceivable that it should not have been broken up and lost, were it a corruption of Christianity. Yet it is still living, if there be a living religion or philoso-phy in the world; vigorous, energetic, persuasive, progressive; *vires acquirit eundo*; it grows and is not overgrown; it spreads out, yet is not enfeebled; it is ever germinating, yet ever consistent with itself. Corruptions indeed are to be found which sleep and are suspended; and these, as I have said, are usually called 'decays:' such is not the case with Catholicity; it does not sleep, it is not stationary even now; and that its long series of developments should be corruptions would be an instance of sustained error, so novel, so unaccountable, so preternatural, as to be little short of a miracle, and to rival those manifestations of Divine Power which constitute the evidence of Christianity ... It is true, there have been seasons when, from the operation of external or internal causes, the Church has been thrown into what was almost a state of *deliquium*; but her wonderful revivals, while the world was triumphing over her, is a further evidence of the absence of corruption in the system of doctrine and worship into which she has developed. If corruption be an incipient disorganisation, surely an abrupt and absolute recurrence to the former state of vigour, after an interval, is even less conceivable than a corruption that is permanent. Now this is the case with the revivals I speak of. After violent exertion men are exhausted and fall asleep; they awake the same as before, refreshed by the temporary cessation of their activity; and such has been the slumber and such the restoration of the Church. She pauses in her course, and almost suspends her functions; she rises again, and she is herself once more; all things are in their place and ready for action. Doctrine is where it was, and usage, and precedence, and principle, and policy; there may be changes, but they are consolidations or adaptations; all is unequivocal and determinate, with an identity which there is no disputing. Indeed it is one of the most popular charges against the Catholic Church at this very time, that she is 'incorrigible;' change she cannot, if we listen to St. Athanasius or St. Leo; change she never will, if we believe the controversialist or alarmist of the present day. (*Dev.*, Part II: ch. 12)

The system of the Church of Rome is not corruption because it has *lasted so long*—not decay because it is so *energetic and vigorous* ... [T]he sustained, steady, unwearied action of the Church of Rome I think is quite incompatible with decay. (*LD* xi, 111; Letter to Miss M. R. Giberne, 11 February 1846)

And, as the Jews then passed over passages in Scripture, which ought to have set them right, so do Christians now pass over passages, which would, if dwelt on, extricate them from their error. For example, the Jews passed over the texts: 'They pierced my hands and my feet,' 'My God, My God, why hast Thou forsaken Me?' 'He was rejected of men, a man of sorrows and acquainted with grief,'—which speak of Christ. And men nowadays pass over such passages as the following which speak of the Church: 'Whosoever sins ye remit, they are remitted to them'; 'Thou art Peter and upon this rock I will build my Church'; 'Anointing them with oil in the Name of the Lord'; 'The Church the pillar and foundation of the truth'; and the like. They are so certain that the doctrine of the one Holy Catholic Church is not true, that they will not give their mind to these passages, they pass them over. They cannot tell you what they mean, but they are quite sure they do not mean what Catholics say they mean, because Catholicism is not true. In fact a deep prejudice is on their minds, or what Scripture calls blindness. They cannot tell what these passages and many others mean, but they do not care. They say that after all they are not important—which is just begging the question—and when they are urged and forced to give them a meaning, they say any thing that comes uppermost, merely to satisfy or to perplex the questioner, wishing nothing more than to get rid of what they think a troublesome, but idle, question. (*FP*, Sermon 4: 'Prejudice and Faith,' 5 March 1848)

[T]hat religion, to which alone a beginning short of the Apostles cannot be assigned. (*LD* xii, 236; Letter to E. J. Phipps, 3 July 1848)

Protestants ... laugh at the notion itself of men pinning their faith (as they express themselves) upon Pope or Council; they think it simply superstitious and narrow-minded, to profess to believe just what the Church believes, and to assent to whatever she will say in time to come on matters of doctrine. That is, they laugh at the bare notion of doing what Christians undeniably did in the time of the Apostles ... they quarrel with the very state of mind which all Christians had in the age of the Apostles (*Mix.*, Discourse 10: 'Faith and Private Judgment')

None but the Catholic has *been able* to be everywhere ... even earthly empires do not spread over the world so *widely as* this and so diversely—now from east to west, now from north to south. Mahomet by the sword ... even empires of this world gained by the *sword* do not *last*. Not only is this a single religious empire, but it has lasted out earthly empires, and now shows as little decay as ever. (*SN*, 'On the Catholic Church,' 6 January 1850)

She is the good Samaritan to Protestants. (*SN*, 'On Christ the Good Samaritan,' 31 August 1851)

I recognised at once a reality which was quite a new thing with me. Then I was sensible that I was not making for myself a Church by an effort of thought; I needed not to make an act of faith in her; I had not painfully to force myself into a position, but my mind fell back upon itself in relaxation and in peace, and I gazed at her almost passively as a great objective fact. I looked at her;—at her rites, her ceremonial, and her precepts; and I said, 'This *is* a religion;' and then, when I looked back upon the poor Anglican Church, for which I had laboured so hard, and upon all that appertained to it, and thought of our various attempts to dress it up doctrinally and esthetically, it seemed to me to be the veriest of nonentities. (*Apo.*, Note E: 'The Anglican Church')

It is the Catholic Church, *not* because of its orders, but because it is the one visible body from which the Apostles set off once for all, and from which the Anglican Church split off, just as the present English nation is the representative of the past English nation, and not the United States, though they came out of it. The Catholic Church does not depend on its orders, but its orders depend on it. (*LD* xxxii, 317; Letter to an Unknown Correspondent, 30 May 1871)

[I]t is *one*: true though it be that St. Paul, St. Luke, and St. John, when engaged on historical fact speak of many 'churches,' the style of Scripture changes when it speaks of the great Christian gifts doctrinally. In presence of these gospel prerogatives there is but one body with many members. Our Lord builds, upon the rock of Peter and of Peter's faith, not churches, but 'My Church;' St. Paul speaks of the 'House of God, the Church of the Living God' in which St. Timothy is called to be a ruler, and not of 'churches;' of the Church 'being the pillar and ground of the truth.' Again he speaks, as of 'One God and Father of all, one Lord, one Spirit, one faith, one hope, one baptism,' so also of but 'one body;' and again our Lord as 'the Head of the body, the Church,' not of the churches. This one Church, as it necessarily follows, is *Catholic*, because it embraces all Christians at once in one extended whole, its catholicity being coincident with its unity. This is a subject on which St. Paul delights to expatiate. Where has he a word of dioceses or bishoprics, each a complete whole, each independent of the rest, each with the power of the keys, each a facsimile of each? On the contrary, he declares 'we are *all* baptized by one Spirit into *one* body,' the Spirit who is one, being the pledge of the body's unity, and the one body being the condition of the Spirit's presence. Both Jews and Gentiles 'are fellow-heirs, and of the same body;' are 'framed together and grow into a holy temple,' 'a habitation of God through the Spirit.' 'There is neither Jew nor Greek, ye are *all one* in Christ Jesus.' 'To the peace of God ye are called in *one* body.' We, *being many*, are *one body* in Christ.' 'The body is one and hath many members; ye are the body of Christ and members in particular.' Is it not clear then that according to St. Paul, the whole Church comes first, and its portions or individual members come second, that its portions are not wholes, that they are accidents, but the one whole body is no accident, no conglomerate, but the object of Apostolic zeal, and the direct and primary recipient of divine grace? Once more, this visible, one, and whole or Catholic body, is, as indeed the word 'body' implies, an *organisation*, with many members converging and concurring into one ecclesiastical corporation or power. I mean, this the Church was, in matter of fact, in the days of the Apostles. Even Apostles, though each of them had a universal jurisdiction, had not the power to break up the one Church into fragments, and each of them to make a communion of his own in it. 'Who is Paul, who is Apollos,' says the Apostle, 'but ministers?' 'Ye are *God's* husbandry, ye are *God's* building, ye are the temple of God.' In like manner St. Luke tells us that those who were baptized 'continued steadfastly in the Apostles' doctrine and *fellowship;*' and St. Paul that the many members of the body have not the same office, nor are all equally honourable, — implying in all he writes a formed ecclesiastical polity ... If then the New Testament is to be our guide in matters ecclesiastical, one thing at least is certain ... of one thing we cannot doubt, that all Christians were in that first age bound together in one body, with an actual intercommunion and mutual relations between them, with ranks and offices, and with a central authority; and that this organised association was 'the body of Christ,' and that in it, considered as One, dwelt the 'One Spirit.' This external unity is a duty prior in order and idea to Episcopacy; in it, and not in Episcopacy, lies the transmission and warrant of Divine privilege. (*Ess.* ii, Note on Essay X: 'Catholicity of the Anglican Church,' *British Critic*, Jan. 1840; from 1871)

Church, Indefectibility of

The grant of permanency was made in the beginning, not to the mere doctrine of the Gospel, but to the Association itself built upon the doctrine; in prediction, not only of the indestructibility of Christianity, but of the medium also through which it was to be manifested to the world. Thus the Ecclesiastical Body is a divinely-appointed means, towards realizing the great evangelical blessings. (*Ari.*, ch. 3, sec. 2)

[W]hat can be better news to the bulk of mankind than to be told that Christ when He ascended, did not leave us orphans, but appointed representatives of Himself to the end of time? ... One Church on earth from Christ's coming to the end of all things. (*TT #2*, 1833)

In truth, do what he will, Satan cannot quench or darken the light of the Church. He may incrust it with his own evil creations, but even opaque bodies transmit rays, and Truth shines with its own heavenly lustre, though 'under a bushel.' The Holy Spirit has vouchsafed to take up His abode in the Church, and the Church will ever bear, on its front, the visible signs of its hidden privilege. (*PS* iii, Sermon 17: 'The Visible Church an Encouragement to Faith,' 14 September 1834)

Another gift bestowed upon Elisha, and on the Christian Church which he prefigured, that is on her saints, and at times on her rulers, is the gift of discerning of spirits. Of our Saviour it is said, 'He knew what was in man;' He knew the thoughts of His disciples; He knew what was happening in other places. Of His fulness His disciples received. St. Peter detected Ananias; St. Paul speaks as if he could have been in spirit at Corinth, while in the flesh he was absent. And in all ages the Catholic Church is promised an instinctive perception of Christian truth, detecting the grosser or the more insidious forms of heresy, though at a distance, as if by some subtle sense; and thus transmitting the faith of the Gospel pure and inviolate to the latest times. (*SD*, Sermon 13: 'Elisha a Type of Christ and His Followers,' 14 August 1836)

[T]he Church Catholic is indefectible in matters of necessary and saving truth … [T]he whole Church, all over the world, will never agree together in teaching and enforcing what is not true. (Review of *Lectures on the Principal Doctrines and Practices of the Catholic Church*, by Nicholas Wiseman, *British Critic*, vol. 19, Oct. 1836)

Not that the Church has not this peculiar prerogative with it, which no other religious body has, that as it began with Christ's first coming, so it will never fail till He comes again; but that for a time, in the course of single generations, nay, I may say in every age and at all times, it seems to be failing, and its enemies to be prevailing. It is the peculiarity of the warfare between the Church and the world, that the world seems ever gaining on the Church, yet the Church is really ever gaining on the world. Its enemies are ever triumphing over it as vanquished, and its members ever despairing; yet it abides. It abides, and it sees the ruin of its oppressors and enemies. 'O how suddenly do they consume, perish, and come to a fearful end!' Kingdoms rise and fall; nations expand and contract; dynasties begin and end; princes are born and die; confederacies are made and unmade, and parties, and companies, and crafts, and guilds, and establishments, and philosophies, and sects, and heresies. They have their day, but the Church is eternal; yet *in* their day they seem of much account. (*SD*, Sermon 6: 'Faith and Experience,' 25 November 1838)

Christianity has been too often in what seemed deadly peril, that we should fear for it any new trial now. So far is certain; on the other hand, what is uncertain, and in these great contests commonly is uncertain, and what is commonly a great surprise, when it is witnessed, is the particular mode by which, in the event, Providence rescues and saves His elect inheritance. Sometimes our enemy is turned into a friend; sometimes he is despoiled of that special virulence of evil which was so threatening; sometimes he falls to pieces of himself; sometimes he does just so much as is beneficial, and then is removed. Commonly the Church has nothing more to do than to go on in her own proper duties, in confidence and peace; to stand still and to see the salvation of God. (*Ward* ii, 462; 'Biglietto Speech' upon becoming a Cardinal, 12 May 1879)

Church, Infallibility of

And if the very claim to infallible arbitration in religious disputes is of so weighty importance and interest in all ages of the world, much more is it welcome at a time like the present, when the human intellect is so busy, and thought so fertile, and opinion so manifold. The absolute need of a spiritual supremacy is at present the strongest of arguments in favour of the fact of its supply ... if these ideas have various aspects, and make distinct impressions on different minds, and issue in consequence in a multiplicity of developments, true, or false, or mixed, as has been shown, what power will suffice to meet and to do justice to these conflicting conditions, but a supreme authority ruling and reconciling individual judgments by a divine right and a recognised wisdom? In barbarous times the will is reached through the senses; but in an age in which reason, as it is called, is the standard of truth and right, it is abundantly evident to any one, who mixes ever so little with the world, that, if things are left to themselves, every individual will have his own view of them, and take his own course; that two or three will agree today to part company tomorrow; that Scripture will be read in contrary ways, and history, according to the apologue, will have to different comers its silver shield and its golden; that philosophy, taste, prejudice, passion, party, caprice, will find no common measure, unless there be some supreme power to control the mind and to compel agreement ... If Christianity is both social and dogmatic, and intended for all ages, it must humanly speaking have an infallible expounder. Else you will secure unity of form at the loss of unity of doctrine, or unity of doctrine at the loss of unity of form; you will have to choose between a comprehension of opinions and a resolution into parties, between latitudinarian and sectarian error. You may be tolerant or intolerant of contrarieties of thought, but contrarieties you will have. By the Church of England a hollow uniformity is preferred to an infallible chair; and by the sects of England, an interminable division. Germany and Geneva began with persecution, and have ended in scepticism. The doctrine of infallibility is a less violent hypothesis than this sacrifice either of faith or of charity. It secures the object, while it gives definiteness and force to the matter, of the Revelation. I have called the doctrine of infallibility an hypothesis: let it be so considered for the sake of argument, that is, let it be considered to be a mere position, supported by no direct evidence, but required by the facts of the case, and reconciling them with each other. That hypothesis is indeed, in matter of fact, maintained and acted on in the largest portion of Christendom, and from time immemorial; but let this coincidence be accounted for by the need. (*Dev.*, Part I: ch. 2, sec. 2)

You ask lastly for 'the *foundation* of the doctrine, the right to teach it at all and believe it at all etc etc' I answer, as above, the infallible Church is the warrant. (*LD* xii, 335; Letter to Catherine Ward, 18 November 1848)

[T]he infallibility of the Holy See, or of the Church ... For myself, I firmly believe that in Scripture the Catholic doctrine on the subject *is* contained. (*PPC*, Lecture 8)

[T]he Church has a sovereign authority, and, when she speaks *ex cathedrâ*, must be obeyed. (*IU*, Part II, ch. 8: 'Christianity and Scientific Investigation,' 1855)

Supposing then it to be the Will of the Creator to interfere in human affairs, and to make provisions for retaining in the world a knowledge of Himself, so definite and distinct as to be proof against the energy of human scepticism, in such a case, — I am far from saying that there was no

other way, — but there is nothing to surprise the mind, if He should think
fit to introduce a power into the world, invested with the prerogative of
infallibility in religious matters. Such a provision would be a direct, immediate, active, and prompt means of withstanding the difficulty; it would
be an instrument suited to the need; and, when I find that this is the very
claim of the Catholic Church, not only do I feel no difficulty in admitting
the idea, but there is a fitness in it, which recommends it to my mind. And
thus I am brought to speak of the Church's infallibility, as a provision,
adapted by the mercy of the Creator, to preserve religion in the world,
and to restrain that freedom of thought, which of course in itself is one
of the greatest of our natural gifts, and to rescue it from its own suicidal
excesses ... a power, possessed of infallibility in religious teaching, is happily adapted to be a working instrument, in the course of human affairs,
for smiting hard and throwing back the immense energy of the aggressive,
capricious, untrustworthy intellect. (*Apo.*, ch. 5)

Every exercise of Infallibility is brought out into act by an intense and
varied operation of the Reason, both as its ally and as its opponent, and
provokes again, when it has done its work, a re-action of Reason against
it; and, as in a civil polity the State exists and endures by means of the
rivalry and collision, the encroachments and defeats of its constituent
parts, so in like manner Catholic Christendom is no simple exhibition of
religious absolutism, but presents a continuous picture of Authority and
Private Judgment alternately advancing and retreating as the ebb and flow
of the tide; — it is a vast assemblage of human beings with wilful intellects
and wild passions, brought together into one by the beauty and the Majesty of a Superhuman Power ... St. Paul says in one place that his Apostolical power is given him to edification, and not to destruction. There
can be no better account of the Infallibility of the Church. It is a supply
for a need, and it does not go beyond that need. Its object is, and its effect
also, not to enfeeble the freedom or vigour of human thought in religious
speculation, but to resist and control its extravagance ... Nor does it at all
follow, because there is a gift of infallibility in the Catholic Church, that
therefore the parties who are in possession of it are in all their proceedings
infallible. (*Apo.*, ch. 5)

[N]or is it the fact, that the Church imposes dogmatic statements on the interior assent of those who cannot apprehend them. The difficulty is removed by the dogma of the Church's infallibility, and of the consequent duty of 'implicit faith' in her word. The 'One Holy Catholic and Apostolic Church' is an article of the Creed, and an article, which, inclusive of her infallibility, all men, high and low, can easily master and accept with a real and operative assent. It stands in the place of all abstruse propositions in a Catholic's mind, for to believe in her word is virtually to believe in them all. Even what he cannot understand, at least he can believe to be true; and he believes it to be true because he believes in the Church. The *rationale* of this provision for unlearned devotion is as follows: — It stands to reason that all of us, learned and unlearned, are bound to believe the whole revealed doctrine in all its parts and in all that it implies according as portion after portion is brought home to our consciousness as belonging to it; and it also stands to reason, that a doctrine, so deep and so various, as the revealed *depositum* of faith, cannot be brought home to us and made our own all at once. No mind, however large, however penetrating, can directly and fully by one act understand any one truth, however simple. (GA, Part I, ch. 5, sec. 3)

St. Paul ... calls the Church 'the pillar and ground of the Truth;' and he bids his convert Timothy, when he had become a ruler in that Church, to 'take heed unto his doctrine,' to 'keep the deposit' of the faith, and to 'commit' the things which he had heard from himself 'to faithful men who should be fit to teach others.'... if the Church, initiated in the Apostles and continued in their successors, has been set up for the direct object of protecting, preserving, and declaring the Revelation, and that, by means of the Guardianship and Providence of its Divine Author, we are led on to perceive that, in asserting this, we are in other words asserting, that, so far as the message entrusted to it is concerned, the Church is infallible; for what is meant by infallibility in teaching but that the teacher in his teaching is secured from error? and how can fallible man be thus secured except by a supernatural infallible guidance? And what can have been the object of the words, 'I am with you all along to the end,' but to give thereby an answer by anticipation to the spontaneous, silent alarm of the feeble company of fishermen and labourers, to whom they were addressed, on their finding themselves laden with superhuman duties and responsibilities? (*Dif.* ii, Letter to the Duke of Norfolk, ch. 9, 1875)

All this was foreseen certainly by the Divine Mind, when He committed to his Church so complex a mission; and, by promising her infallibility in her formal teaching, He indirectly protected her from serious error in worship and political action also. This aid, however, great as it is, does not secure her from all dangers as regards the problem which she has to solve; nothing but the gift of impeccability granted to her authorities would secure them from all liability to mistake in their conduct, policy, words and decisions, in her legislative and her executive, in ecclesiastical and disciplinarian details; and such a gift they have not received. (VM i, Preface to the Third Edition, 1877)

St. Paul was infallible; first he gave proofs of it, viz., by miracles, &c., then he acted upon it. He did not appeal to James, Cephas, and John for his doctrine, though they were 'pillars.' Was he then 'inconsistent'? Supposing the Church is infallible, that very thing must happen which does happen, viz., she must assert her infallibility, and then act upon it as decisive in every controversy of faith ... As I have said, the infallible Church supersedes the ancient Fathers, just as much as St. Paul's infallibility put aside the procedure of Peter in Gal. ii., and St. Peter and St. James St. Paul, in James ii., 2 Pet. iii ... [I]f infallibility exists in the Church, it *must* supersede, as far us the gift is exercised, all argument and all authority of doctors. (VM i, Lecture 2; footnotes 2, 3, and 26 from 1877)

The Church does not profess to 'know the whole dispensation;'... Nor is it axiomatic, just the contrary, that to be infallible in what is revealed, implies a profession of knowing what to the Apostles was not revealed ... Her infallible voice is seldom exercised, and comparatively few dogmas have been promulgated to be accepted *de fide* ... Of these various points of doctrine, those which have been made *de fide* in Catholic teaching, as being determined by the Church's infallibility, are also to be met with and are taught as revealed truths in those writings of the Fathers, which Anglicans call 'Antiquity.' So they do not serve as specimens of the 'bold speculativeness of Romanism.' (VM i, Lecture 3; footnotes 15, 20, and 25 from 1877)

We are *certain* of the Church's infallibility by means not of *a* probability, but of an accumulation of probabilities. I am certain that I am in England by physical sense and common sense, not because I am infallible. Else, we must all be exercising a supernatural gift every hour of our lives. (VM i, Lecture 4; footnote 10 from 1877)

New questions, new opinions are ever rising in the Church, and she has the power of answering those questions, and judging those opinions with infallible exactness, when they relate to faith and morals. If she cannot say Yes or No, how can she teach the Truth? (VM i, Lecture 9; footnote 7 from 1877)

No promise of inspiration is given to the Church, but of infallibility, which is not a habit or permanent faculty, but consists in an external divine protection, when the Church speaks *ex cathedrâ*, against her falling into error. (VM i, Lecture 13; footnote 1 from 1877)

As to 'points of faith' they accept them all on the *ground* that the infallible Church proposes them. If we doubt of some, why believe any? They all come on the same authority. It is a fundamental doctrine of the Catholic Church that as to matters of Christian Faith she cannot err in her teaching. It follows at once that whoever denies anything she teaches, as her power to grant Indulgences, denies an article of faith, and necessarily falls under an anathema. Of course then no one can belong to the Church who rejects what the Church, the 'pillar and ground of the Truth,' professes to have received from heaven. (*TT* #71, footnotes 4 and 5 of 1883)

Confession

How many are the souls, in distress, anxiety or loneliness, whose one need is to find a being to whom they can pour out their feelings unheard by the world? Tell them out they must; they cannot tell them out to those whom they see every hour. They want to tell them and not to tell them; and they want to tell them out, yet be as if they be not told; they wish to tell them to one who is strong enough to bear them, yet not too strong to despise them; they wish to tell them to one who can at once advise and can sympathise with them; they wish to relieve themselves of a load, to gain a solace, to receive the assurance that there is one who thinks of them, and one to whom in thought they can recur, to whom they can betake themselves, if necessary, from time to time, while they are in the world. How many a Protestant's heart would leap at the news of such a benefit, putting aside all distinct ideas of a sacramental ordinance, or of a grant of pardon and the conveyance of grace! If there is a heavenly idea in the Catholic Church, looking at it simply as an idea, surely, next after the Blessed Sacrament, Confession is such. And such is it ever found in fact, — the very act of kneeling, the low and contrite voice, the sign of the cross hanging, so to say, over the head bowed low, and the words of peace and blessing. Oh what a soothing charm is there, which the world can neither give nor take away! Oh what piercing, heart-subduing tranquillity, provoking tears of joy, is poured, almost substantially and physically upon the soul, the oil of gladness, as Scripture calls it, when the penitent at length rises, his God reconciled to him, his sins rolled away for ever! This is confession as it is in fact; as those bear witness to it who know it by experience. (*PPC*, Lecture 8)

Your ideas about confession are most unreal and romantic. The Priest is nothing—God is everything. They are the greatest friends who know each other most intimately. The Confessor's sympathy so flows out upon a penitent that it is as if he were making, not hearing a Confession. (*POL*; Letter to William Froude, 11 August 1851)

Neither did I say that 'Sacramental confession' was 'a note of the Church.' Nor is it. Nor could I with any cogency have brought this as an argument against the Church of England, for the Church of England has retained Confession, nay, Sacramental Confession. No fair man can read the form of Absolution in the Anglican Prayer in the Visitation of the Sick, without seeing that that Church *does* sanction and provide for

Confession and Absolution. If that form does not contain the profession of a grave Sacramental act, words have no meaning. (*Apo.* ii, Appendix One, section 2: 'My Sermon on 'Wisdom and Innocence')

Conscience

Our great internal teacher of religion is, as I have said in an earlier part of this Essay, our Conscience. Conscience is a personal guide, and I use it because I must use myself; I am as little able to think by any mind but my own as to breathe with another's lungs. Conscience is nearer to me than any other means of knowledge. And as it is given to me, so also is it given to others; and being carried about by every individual in his own breast, and requiring nothing besides itself, it is thus adapted for the communication to each separately of that knowledge which is most momentous to him individually, — adapted for the use of all classes and conditions of men, for high and low, young and old, men and women, independently of books, of educated reasoning, of physical knowledge, or of philosophy. Conscience, too, teaches us, not only that God is, but what He is; it provides for the mind a real image of Him, as a medium of worship; it gives us a rule of right and wrong, as being His rule, and a code of moral duties. Moreover, it is so constituted that, if obeyed, it becomes clearer in its injunctions, and wider in their range, and corrects and completes the accidental feebleness of its initial teachings. Conscience, then, considered as our guide, is fully furnished for its office ... Now Conscience suggests to us many things about that Master, whom by means of it we perceive, but its most prominent teaching, and its cardinal and distinguishing truth, is that he is our Judge. (GA, Part II, ch. 10, sec. 1)

I say, then, that the Supreme Being is of a certain character, which, expressed in human language, we call ethical. He has the attributes of justice, truth, wisdom, sanctity, benevolence and mercy, as eternal characteristics in His nature, the very Law of His being, identical with Himself; and next, when He became Creator, He implanted this Law, which is Himself, in the intelligence of all His rational creatures. The Divine Law, then, is the rule of ethical truth, the standard of right and wrong, a sovereign, irreversible, absolute authority in the presence of men and Angels ... This law, as apprehended in the minds of individual men, is called 'conscience;' and though it may suffer refraction in passing into the intellectual medium of each, it is not therefore so affected as to lose its character of being the Divine Law, but still has, as such, the prerogative of commanding obedience ... This view of conscience, I know, is very different from that ordinarily taken of it, both by the science and literature, and by the public opinion, of this day. It is founded on the doctrine that conscience is the voice of God, whereas it is fashionable on all hands now to consider it in one way or another a creation of man ... Conscience is not a long-sighted selfishness, nor a desire to be consistent with oneself; but it is a messenger from Him, who, both in nature and in grace, speaks to us behind a veil, and teaches and rules us by His representatives ... When men advocate the rights of conscience, they in no sense mean the rights of the Creator, nor the duty to Him, in thought and deed, of the creature; but the right of thinking, speaking, writing, and acting, according to their judgment or their humour, without any thought of God at all ... It becomes a licence to take up any or no religion, to take up this or that and let it go again, to go to church, to go to chapel, to boast of being above all religions and to be an impartial critic of each of them. Conscience is a stern monitor, but in this century it has been superseded by a counterfeit, which the eighteen centuries prior to it never heard of, and could not have mistaken for it, if they had. It is the right of self-will ... [C]onscience is not a judgment upon any speculative truth, any abstract doctrine, but bears immediately on conduct, on something to be done or not done ... Hence conscience cannot come into direct collision with the Church's or the Pope's infallibility; which is engaged in general propositions, and in the condemnation of particular and given errors ... Since then infallibility alone could block the exercise of conscience, and the Pope is not infallible in that subject-matter in which conscience is of supreme authority, no deadlock, such as is implied in the objection which I am answering, can take place between conscience and the Pope. (*Dif.* ii, Letter to the Duke of Norfolk, ch. 5, 1875)

Conversion and Converts

When men change their religious opinions really and truly, it is not merely their opinions that they change, but their hearts; and this evidently is not done in a moment — it is a slow work; nevertheless, though gradual, the change is often not uniform, but proceeds, so to say, by fits and starts, being influenced by external events, and other circumstances. This we see in the growth of plants, for instance; it is slow, gradual, continual; yet one day by chance they grow more than another, they make a shoot, or at least we are attracted to their growth on that day by some accidental circumstance, and it remains on our memory. So with our souls: we all, by nature, are far from God; nay, and we have all characters to form, which is a work of time … Others, again, continue forming a religious character and religious opinions as the result of it, though holding at the same time some outward profession of faith inconsistent with them; as, for instance, suppose it has been their unhappy condition to be brought up as heathens, Jews, infidels, or heretics. They hold the notions they have been taught for a long while, not perceiving that the character forming within them is at variance with these, till at length the inward growth forces itself forward, forces on the opinions accompanying it, and the dead outward surface of error, which has no root in their minds, from some accidental occurrence, suddenly falls off; suddenly, — just as a building might suddenly fall, which had been going many years, and which falls at this moment rather than that, in consequence of some chance cause, as it is called, which we cannot detect. (*PS* viii, Sermon 15: 'Sudden Conversions,' 25 January 1832)

I fully sympathise in what you say about the temper of some younger men. I suppose the case is simply this, that we have raised desires, of which our Church does not supply the objects, and that they have not the patience, or humility, or discretion to keep from seeking those objects where they are supplied. I have from the first thought that nothing but a quasi miracle would carry us through the trial with no proselytes whatever to Rome and, though I shall fairly have to bear my share in them, shall not feel surprise, nor I trust self-reproach at what is not my doing. (*Keb.*, 41-42; Letter to Rev. W. Dodsworth, 19 November 1839)

I am not surprised at any one being drawn to the Roman Church under your feelings, wrong as I think it. And I lament as much as any one can our present state in the English, in which high aspirations have so little means of exercise. If you will allow me to add it, I think you were *hasty* in your resolve. So great a matter as a change of religion ought not to be thought of without years (I may say) of prayer and preparation. (*Moz.* ii; Letter to a Lady of 'excitable temperament,' April 1841)

And if the voice of men in general is to weigh at all in a matter of this kind, it does but corroborate these instinctive feelings. A convert is undeniably in favour with no party; he is looked at with distrust, contempt, and aversion by all. His former friends think him a good riddance, and his new friends are cold and strange; and as to the impartial public, their very first impulse is to impute the change to some eccentricity of character, or fickleness of mind, or tender attachment, or private interest ... Why should we go out of our way, one and all of us, to impute personal motives in explanation of the conversion of every individual convert, as he comes before us, if there were in us, the public, an adhesion to that absolute, and universal, and unalienable principle, as its titles are set forth in heraldic style, high and broad, sacred and awful, the right, and the duty, and the possibility of Private Judgment? Why should we confess it in the general, yet promptly and pointedly deny it in every particular, if our hearts retained more than the 'magni nominis umbra,' when we preached up the Protestant principle?... If a staunch Protestant's daughter turns Roman, and betakes herself to a convent, why does he not exult in the occurrence? Why does he not give a public breakfast, or hold a meeting, or erect a memorial, or write a pamphlet in honour of her, and of the great undying principle she has so gloriously vindicated? ('Private Judgment,' *British Critic*, July 1841; in *Ess.* ii, sec. XIV)

Do not believe any absurd reports. They talk in the papers of secessions among us to Rome. Do not believe it. Not one will go. At the same time I cannot answer for *years hence*, if the present state of things is persevered in. (*Moz.* ii; Letter to Jemima Mozley, 16 November 1841)

[I]f men who believed the articles of the Creed were taught from authority that the English Church was not the Church Catholic, they would seek it elsewhere. (*Moz.* ii; Letter to J. R. Hope, 19 November 1841)

[W]ho can be startled, not I, if a person here or there, painfully sensitive of this fearful eclipse of the Sun of Truth, and hoping, if that be possible, to find something better elsewhere; and either not having cherished, or neglecting to look for those truer tokens of Christ's presence in the Church, which are personal to himself, leaves us for some other communion? Alas! and we, instead of being led to reflect on our own share in his act, instead of dwelling on our own sin, are eloquent about his; instead of confessing our own most unchristian divisions, can but cry out against his dividing from us; instead of repenting of our own profaneness which has shocked him, protest against his superstition; instead of calling to mind the lying and slandering, the false witness, the rejoicing in evil, the ungenerousness and unfairness which abound among us, our low standard of duty and scanty measures of holiness, our love of the world and our dislike of the Cross; instead of acknowledging that our brother has left us because we have left God, that we have lost him because we have lost our claim to keep him; we, forsooth, think we 'do well to be angry,' and can but enlarge on his impatience, or obstinacy, or wilfulness, or infatuation. (*SD*, Sermon 22: 'Outward and Inward Notes of the Church,' 5 December 1841)

Almighty God, it may be said, often seems to be fighting against a man, and to be driving him away from the religion he at present professes, as the Angel resisted Balaam. Providences befall him which he is justified in interpreting as a suggestion to seek God elsewhere; and thus the search after religious truth is made a matter of mere feeling, or imagination. I reply, that I have said nothing to sanction such a proceeding. I have said nothing to lead men to consult the fluctuations of their minds in the passing hour, for information concerning God's will. We all are depressed at one time, and encouraged and revived at another; we have our times of gloom, of disquiet, of doubt, of impatience, of disgust ... All this we certainly may do, but without any sanction from the doctrine which I have been laying down. The simple question is, whether such temporary frames of mind can be proved to come from God ... there seem to be two reasons which may lead a man to leave the communion in which he was born: first, some clear indisputable command of God to leave it,

and secondly, some plain experience that God does not acknowledge it
… Nothing that is here said about uncovenanted mercies must be taken
to imply that individuals ought to be satisfied in remaining external to
the Catholic Church, when they are once *convinced* of the fact; but mere
impressions, impulses, fancies, frames of mind, logical deductions, or the
blindness which follows on religious carelessness, may easily be mistaken
for convictions. (*SD*, Sermon 23: 'Grounds for Steadfastness in Our Religious Profession,' 19 December 1841)

[T]his is a great triumph to the Roman Catholics … it inclines people
to them. Many persons say to themselves, 'We are more certain that the
discord and variety of opinions which surround us is from beneath, than
that the Creed of Pope Pius is not from above.' (*POL*; Letter to S. L. Pope,
4 September 1842)

I *do* wish people to agree with me in turning Romeward; but, as I do
not wish them so to feel because *I* am so feeling, so do I deprecate their
so feeling from mere disgust with what is happening among ourselves.
Disgust makes no good converts; change of opinion is, commonly speaking, the work of a long time. People who are disgusted one way, may be
disgusted the other. (*Ble.*, 445; Letter to Jemima Mozley, 11 February
1845)

[O]rdinarily, the test of our being called is, not any great vividness of
impression, but its continuance. I have generally said to persons, Fix a
time, and observe whether your conviction lasts through it, and how it
stands at the end of it … Persons then, in waiting to be certain, may be
waiting for that which from the nature of the case cannot be theirs …
[Doubt is the condition of our nature … the merit of faith consists in
making ventures. (*LD* xi, 60-61; Letter to A. J. Hanmer, 11 December
1845)

You say you have to pain relations by your step—alas, that is the trial
which *all* have to go through. (*LD* xi, 71; Letter to the Marquise de Salvo,
18 December 1845)

Divine Wisdom uses most distinct and opposite ways of leading us to the Catholic Church. (*LD* xi, 73; Letter to Mrs. Elizabeth Anstice, 20 December 1845)

I suppose nothing is more common among educated converts than partial, incomplete knowledge — inconsistencies in knowledge — some things known thoroughly, and the simplest things unknown — the fault of being ill grounded. (*LD* xi, 108; Letter to Miss M. R. Giberne, 2 February 1846)

[A] number of persons are making great sacrifices in credit and circumstances; their brethren, who feel called to remain as they were, pass this over altogether, and in the face of it have the heart to scrutinize the details of their manner in conversation, in order to find a charge against them. They do not see what tells for them, they do see what tells against them. Surely such critics are in want either of arguments for their own cause, or of charity. May none of us hereafter be judged by so severe a judgment as is now exercised towards the converts generally! And after all, that severity perhaps has no other foundation than the newness of their position, which their censors have not entered into. (*LD* xi, 124; Letter to E. B. Pusey, 21 February 1846)

What *does* distress me is, when a person is setting himself to oppose the movement, as is Pusey. It is one thing not to see one's way to move, another to stop and turn back those who are moving ... Pusey says, 'Trust in me that you are safe' and 'to move would be a mortal sin.' (*LD* xi, 135; Letter to Henry Wilberforce, 10 March 1846)

[D]id you make up your mind to the step of which I have been speaking, you might have great temptations at the last minute, to make you change it. This occurs to many persons, and in various ways. (*LD* xi, 141; Letter to Mrs. J. W. Bowden, 22 March 1846)

Indeed I have thought a good deal of you and your troubles; and was about to write daily, but for a reason I will state presently. I have thought more of your wife, and still more of Mrs. Sargent, whose repeated trials I have talked over and mused upon with St. John. It is all very mysterious. So too is the distress of mind at this moment of other friends of mine, of a different kind—I mean, their struggling to know whether or not they should join the Church of Rome, and not seeing their way—a most consuming, exhausting trial. Yet it will, doubtless, all turn to good. Perhaps, if we knew all, we should know it is impossible for the elect of God to emerge from darkness to light in any other way. Such travail is necessary for the new birth. Perhaps if we saw our way too soon, there might be a re-action and old habits and associations might come over one again. I know too well of the state of those in doubt not to believe that the long trial of some is no sin of theirs, but God's way with them, imparting light slowly that He may impart it more effectually. My only dread is, and it is in some cases very great, when they are not, to all appearance, using the light given them, but shutting their eyes. And as doubt, long continued, may be the fiery process by which one person is brought into the Church, so the loss or alienation of friends by their conversion may be the divinely sent trial of others. It may be the gradual operation by which He prepares their own soul for the trial. (*Ward* i, 619 [Appendix to Ch. 4]; Letter to Henry Wilberforce, 29 May 1846)

The sight of a convert is the most cogent and withal the most silent and subduing of arguments. If persons are not persuaded, or at least moved by it, words will not do. It may lead the way to words, words may suitably follow, but if it does not do something, words will do still less. (*LD* xi, 224; Letter to the Marquise de Salvo, 18 August 1846)

I have met with nothing which has been any difficulty to me—nor do I personally know any one of the converts who has—but this is plain, and must never be forgotten, that every one who joins the Church, must come in the spirit of a child to a Mother—not to criticize any thing, but to accept ... Earnestly as I desire all persons I know to become Catholics, I wish them first to pray for faith—for a mere outward conformity to the Church, or rebellion of the reason after joining it, would be miserable. (*LD* xii, 168; Letter to A. J. Hanmer, 10 February 1848)

I *have myself* found all I seek — 'I have all and abound' — my every want has been supplied — and so it has in all persons, whom I know at all well, who have become Catholics. (*LD* xii, 223; Letter to Mrs. William Froude, 16 June 1848)

The truth is, that the world, knowing nothing of the blessings of the Catholic faith, and prophesying nothing but ill concerning it, fancies that a convert, after the first fervour is over, feels nothing but disappointment, weariness, and offence in his new religion, and is secretly desirous of retracing his steps. This is at the root of the alarm and irritation which it manifests at hearing that doubts are incompatible with a Catholic's profession, because it is sure that doubts will come upon him, and then how pitiable will be his state! That there can be peace, and joy, and knowledge, and freedom, and spiritual strength in the Church, is a thought far beyond the world's imagination; for it regards her simply as a frightful conspiracy against the happiness of man, seducing her victims by specious professions, and, when they are once hers, caring nothing for the misery which breaks upon them, so that by any means she may detain them in bondage. Accordingly, it conceives we are in perpetual warfare with our own reason, fierce objections ever rising within us, and we forcibly repressing them. It believes that, after the likeness of a vessel which has met with some accident at sea, we are ever bailing out the water which rushes in upon us, and have hard work to keep afloat; we just manage to linger on, either by an unnatural strain on our minds, or by turning them away from the subject of religion. The world disbelieves our doctrines itself, and cannot understand our own believing them. It considers them so strange, that it is quite sure, though we will not confess it, that we are haunted day and night with doubts, and tormented with the apprehension of yielding to them. (*Mix.*, Discourse 11: 'Faith and Doubt')

Be convinced in your reason that the Catholic Church is a teacher sent to you from God, and it is enough. I do not wish you to join her, till you are. If you are half convinced, pray for a full conviction, and wait till you have it. It is better indeed to come quickly, but better slowly than carelessly; and sometimes, as the proverb goes, the more haste, the worse speed. Only make yourselves sure that the delay is not from any fault of yours, which you can remedy. God deals with us very differently; conviction comes slowly to some men, quickly to others; in some it is the result of much thought and many reasonings, in others of a sudden illumination. One man is convinced at once, as in the instance described by St. Paul: 'If all prophesy,' he says, speaking of exposition of doctrine, 'and there come in one that believeth not, or one unlearned, he is convinced of all, he is judged of all. The secrets of his heart are made manifest; and so, falling down on his face, he will worship God, and say that God is among you of a truth.' The case is the same now; some men are converted merely by entering a Catholic Church; others are converted by reading one book; others by one doctrine. They feel the weight of their sins, and they see that that religion must come from God which alone has the means of forgiving them. Or they are touched and overcome by the evident sanctity, beauty, and (as I may say) fragrance of the Catholic Religion. Or they long for a guide amid the strife of tongues; and the very doctrine of the Church about faith, which is so hard to many, is conviction to them. Others, again, hear many objections to the Church, and follow out the whole subject far and wide; conviction can scarcely come to them except as at the end of a long inquiry. (*Mix.*, Discourse 11: 'Faith and Doubt')

One after another, moving not as a party, but one by one, unwittingly, because they could not help it, men of mature age, from 40 to past 50, in all professions and states, numbers have done what I have done ... It is surely much easier to account for Keble and Pusey not moving, Catholicism being true, than for all these persons moving, Catholicism being not true. And, whereas it was the fashion at first to use this argument, as W[illiam]. F[roude]. does in 1847, against us, I think it ought to have its weight now for us. It was the fashion then to say 'O, Newman is by himself. We don't deny his weight — but no one else of any name has gone — and are we to go by one man?' Times are altered now ... When then a certain portion of our race are certain they have found religious truth, should we not feel as we might do, if, while ignorant of mathematics, we found a number of educated persons simply confident of Newton's conclusions? I mean, admit that truth was attainable in religion, though we had not attained it. Nor do I think it matters that many men are 'certain' of what is opposite to Catholic truth—or 'certain' that Catholicism is false—for men have been 'certain' that Newton was false—yet that would not move us against Newton, because, though we are no judge of Newton's reasonings, we may be judges of the persons who use and embrace them—and all the Dominicans in the world might not move us in favour of any theory but Newton's—though we understood the argument on neither side. In like manner there are men rationally certain in religion—and irrationally certain—and we may be judges of this, though not as yet judges of their reasons. And here, recurring to what I said before, I do really think the character and variety of the converts to Catholicism of late in England form a most powerful argument, that there is such a thing as ascertainable truth in religion—and I am willing that a man should set against them, Luther, Cranmer, and Co., if he wishes. Next, it must be considered that, though there is a profession of certainty among Protestants, and pious earnest people among them, yet their certainty commonly relates to, and their religious life is seated in, doctrines which are included in Catholicism—so that their certainty cannot be considered to contradict and invalidate the certainty of Catholics ... Keble is not certain of anything—and if I put him on one side, and men like R. Wilberforce, Hope Scott, or Allies on the other, he does not pretend to collide with them; he only has not what they have. Again, as to Pusey, he indeed is most 'certain'—but the greater part of things, far, of which he is certain, are those of which Catholics are certain—and as to other points, in which he differs from Catholics, how he can be said to be certain of them I cannot tell, for, if his words are fairly quoted, he contradicts himself continually, or affirms to one person what he denies to another. (*Ward* i, 622-624 [Appendix to Ch. 8]; Letter of 1850)

Those surely who are advancing towards the Church would not have advanced so far as they have, had they not had sufficient arguments to bring them still further. What retards their progress is not any weakness in those arguments, but the force of opposite considerations, speculative or practical, which are urged, sometimes against the Church, sometimes against their own submitting to her authority. They would have no doubt

about their duty, but for the charges brought against her, or the remon-
strances addressed to themselves; ... Such persons, then, have a claim
on us to be fortified in their right perceptions and their good resolutions,
against the calumnies, prejudices, mistakes, and ignorance of their friends
and of the world, against the undue influence exerted on their minds by
the real difficulties which unavoidably surround a religion so deep and
manifold in philosophy, and occupying so vast a place in the history of
nations ... Here is the plain reason why so many are brought near to the
Church, and then go back, or are so slow in submitting to her ... Every
one is obliged, by the law of his nature, to act by reason; yet no one likes
to make a great sacrifice unnecessarily; such difficulties, then, just avail to
turn the scale, and to detain men in Protestantism, who are open to the
influence of tenderness towards friends, reliance on superiors, regard for
their position, dread of present inconvenience, indolence, love of independence, fear of the future, regard to reputation, desire of consistency,
attachment to cherished notions, pride of reason, or reluctance to go to
school again. No one likes to take an awful step, all by himself, without
feeling sure he is right; no one likes to remain long in doubt whether he
should take it or not; he wishes to be settled ... [I]n what he has been saying in explanation, he must not be supposed to forget that faith depends
upon the will, not really on any process of reasoning, and that conversion
is a simple work of divine grace ... [T]o clear away from the path of an
inquirer objections to Catholic truth, is to subserve his conversion by
giving room for the due and efficacious operation of divine grace. (*Dif.* i,
Preface)

I think many a Protestant has principles in him which ought to make
him a Catholic, if he followed them out. (*POL;* Letter to Francis William
Newman, 18 January 1860)

Catholics did not make us Catholics; Oxford made us Catholics. (*Ward*
ii, 57; Letter to Canon Estcourt, 2 June 1860)

Rogers the other day asked Ward why it was that Catholics understood
me so little? i.e., I suppose, why they thought so little of me. And the

Saturday Review, writing apropos of my letter to the *Globe* of last summer, said that I had disappointed friends and enemies, since I had been a Catholic, by doing nothing. The reason is conveyed in the remark, of Marshall of Brighton to Fr. Ambrose last week; 'Why, he has made no converts, as Manning and Faber have.' Here is the real secret of my 'doing nothing.' The only thing of course which it is worth producing, is *fruit*, — but with the Cardinal, immediate show is fruit, and conversions the sole fruit. At Propaganda, conversions, and nothing else, are the proof of doing anything. Everywhere with Catholics, to make converts, is doing something; and not to make them is 'doing nothing.' And further still, in the estimate of Propaganda, of the Cardinal, and of Catholics generally, they must be splendid conversions of great men, noble men, learned men, not simply of the poor. It must be recollected that at Rome they have had visions of the whole of England coming over to the Church, and that their notion of instrumentality of this conversion *en masse* is the conversion of persons of rank ... But I am altogether different, — my objects, my theory of acting, my powers, go in a different direction, and one not understood or contemplated at Rome or elsewhere ... To me conversions were not the first thing, but the edification [building up] of Catholics. So much have I fixed upon the latter as my object, that up to this time the world persists in saying that I recommend Protestants not to become Catholics. And, when I have given as my true opinion, that I am afraid to make hasty converts of educated men, lest they should not have counted the cost, and should have difficulties after they have entered the Church, I do but imply the same thing, that the Church must be prepared for converts, as well as converts prepared for the Church. How can this be understood at Rome? What do they know there of the state of English Catholics? of the minds of English Protestants? What do they know of the antagonism of Protestantism and Catholicism in England? ... Now from first to last, education, in this large sense of the word, has been my line, and, over and above the disappointment it has caused as putting conversions comparatively in the background, and the offence it has given by insisting that there was room for improvement among Catholics, it has seriously annoyed the governing body here and at Rome: — at Rome on the side of the philosophy of polemic. (*Ward* i, 583-585; *Journal*, 21 January 1863)

For who can know himself, and the multitude of subtle influences which act upon him? And who can recollect, at the distance of twenty-five years, all that he once knew about his thoughts and his deeds, and that, during a portion of his life, when, even at the time his observation, whether of himself or of the external world, was less than before or after, by very reason of the perplexity and dismay which weighed upon him, — when, in spite of the light given to him according to his need amid his darkness, yet a darkness it emphatically was? (*Apo.*, ch. 3)

I recognised in the sentiment what is one of the delusions of *many* who are not converts but old Catholics, (perhaps of some converts too) that Catholics are on an intellectual and social equality with Protestants. This idea I have ever combated, and been impatient at; and, till we allow that there are greater natural gifts and human works in the Protestant world of England than in the little Catholic flock, we only make ourselves ridiculous and hurt that just influence by which alone we can hope to convert men. (*Ward* ii, 45; Letter to Henry Wilberforce, 24 August 1864)

[A] convert comes to learn, and not to pick and choose. He comes in simplicity and confidence, and it does not occur to him to weigh and measure every proceeding, every practice which he meets with among those whom he has joined. He comes to Catholicism as to a living system, with a living teaching, and not to a mere collection of decrees and canons, which by themselves are of course but the framework, not the body and substance of the Church. And this is a truth which concerns, which binds, those also who never knew any other religion, not only the convert ... The convert comes, not only to believe the Church, but also to trust and obey her priests, and to conform himself in charity to her people. (*Dif.* ii, Letter to Pusey, ch. 2, 1865)

It is grievous that people are so hard. In converts it is inexcusable; it is a miserable spirit in them. (*POL*; Letter to Emily Bowles, 16 April 1866)

One of the greatest trials is, to have it cast upon one to make up one's mind, — on some grave question, with great consequences spreading into the future—and to be in doubt what one ought to do. (*POL*; Letter to Marianne Frances Bowden, 5 June 1866)

A mere liking for Catholic devotions or opinions is no sure ground for conversion. You have no call on you to leave your present position, unless you believe that such a step is necessary in order to save your soul ... if you have a clear view that the Catholic Church is the true and only Fold of Christ you are *bound* at all hazard and suffering to join it, and God will give you strength. (*LD* xxxii, 312; Letter to an Unknown Correspondent, 4 September 1870)

I am not surprised at your pausing at the last moment before you take a very momentous and solemn step ... while the clouds last, you have to wait ... You must earnestly and perseveringly ask for light. It is better to doubt before you join the Church than after joining. (*LD* xxix, 193; Letter to Mrs. Lydia Rose Christie, 5 November 1879)

Conversion (His Own)

[N]ow in my rooms in Oriel College, slowly advancing, &c. and led on by God's hand blindly, not knowing whither He is taking me. (*Apo.*, ch. 3; citing a memorandum of 7 September 1829)

I had no opinion about the Catholic Question till 1829. No one can truly say I was ever *for* the Catholics; but I was not against them. In fact I did not enter into the state of the question at all. (*Apo.*, 'Additional Notes'; Letter to Archbishop Richard Whately, 11 November 1834)

I would say, 'I would be a Romanist, if I could. I wish I could be a Romanist.' But I cannot—there is that mixture of error in it, which (though unseen of course by many many pious Christians who have been brought up in it) effectually cuts off the chance of my acquiescing in it ... The more I examine into the R. C. system, the less sound it appears to me to be; and the less safely could I in conscience profess to receive it. (*POL*; Letter to Mrs. William Wilberforce, 17 November 1834)

My stronghold was Antiquity; now here, in the middle of the fifth century, I found, as it seemed to me, Christendom of the sixteenth and the nineteenth centuries reflected. I saw my face in that mirror, and I was a Monophysite. The Church of the *Via Media* was in the position of the Oriental communion, Rome was where she now is; and the Protestants were the Eutychians ... It was difficult to make out how the Eutychians or Monophysites were heretics, unless Protestants and Anglicans were heretics also; difficult to find arguments against the Tridentine Fathers, which did not tell against the Fathers of Chalcedon; difficult to condemn the Popes of the sixteenth century, without condemning the Popes of the fifth. The drama of religion, and the combat of truth and error, were ever one and the same. The principles and proceedings of the Church now, were those of the Church then; the principles and proceedings of heretics then, were those of Protestants now. I found it so, — almost fearfully; there was an awful similitude, more awful, because so silent and unimpassioned, between the dead records of the past and the feverish chronicle of the present. The shadow of the fifth century was on the sixteenth. It was like a spirit rising from the troubled waters of the old world, with the shape and lineaments of the new. The Church then, as now, might be called peremptory and stern, resolute, overbearing, and relentless; and heretics were shifting, changeable, reserved, and deceitful, ever courting civil power, and never agreeing together, except by its aid; and the civil power was ever aiming at comprehensions, trying to put the invisible out of view, and substituting expediency for faith. What was the use of continuing the controversy, or defending my position, if, after all, I was forging arguments for Arius or Eutyches, and turning devil's advocate against the much-enduring Athanasius and the majestic Leo? Be my soul with the Saints! and shall I lift up my hand against them? ... my friend, an anxiously religious man, now, as then, very dear to me, a Protestant still, pointed out the palmary words of St. Augustine, ... '*Securus judicat orbis terrarum*' ['the secure judgment of the whole world'] ... they were words which went beyond the occasion of the Donatists: they applied to that of the Monophysites. They gave a cogency to the Article, which had escaped me at first. They decided ecclesiastical questions on a simpler rule than that of Antiquity; nay, St. Augustine was one of the prime oracles of

Antiquity; here then Antiquity was deciding against itself. What a light was hereby thrown upon every controversy in the Church! ... the deliberate judgment, in which the whole Church at length rests and acquiesces, is an infallible prescription and a final sentence against such portions of it as protest and secede ... For a mere sentence, the words of St. Augustine, struck me with a power which I never had felt from any words before ... By those great words of the ancient Father, interpreting and summing up the long and varied course of ecclesiastical history, the theory of the *Via Media* was absolutely pulverized ... He who has seen a ghost, cannot be as if he had never seen it. The heavens had opened and closed again. The thought for the moment had been, 'The Church of Rome will be found right after all;' and then it had vanished. My old convictions remained as before ... Down had come the *Via Media* as a definite theory or scheme, under the blows of St. Leo ... I had no longer a distinctive plea for Anglicanism, unless I would be a Monophysite ... I had no positive Anglican theory. I was very nearly a pure Protestant. Lutherans had a sort of theology, so had Calvinists; I had none. (*Apo.*, ch. 3; referring [in 1865] to the time-period of August 1839; second section cited from his writing in 1850, recalling his thoughts in 1839)

I have had the first real hit from Romanism which has happened to me ... You see the whole history of the Monophysites has been a sort of alternative. And now comes this dose at the end of it. It does certainly come upon one that we are not at the bottom of things. At this moment we have sprung a leak; ... there is an uncomfortable vista opened which was closed before. I am writing upon my first feelings. (*Moz.* ii; Letter to Frederick Rogers, 22 September 1839)

Indeed his [Nicholas Wiseman's] last article comparing us to the Donatists has taken in quarters where I should not have expected it would excite an interest. Indeed he has fixed on our weak point ... It is plainly necessary to stop up the leak in our boat which he has made, if we are to proceed. (*Keb.*, 49; Letter to J. W. Bowden, 5 January 1840)

As to Dr. Wiseman's article I do not think you have hit the point of it. It made a very great impression here, and to say, what of course I would only say to such as yourself, it made me for a while very uncomfortable in my own mind. He maintains first that the present look of Christendom is such, that St. Austin or St. Basil coming among us would say at once 'That is the Catholic Church and those are the heretics' meaning Rome and us respectively ... I frankly confess I cannot deny either of his positions that the Fathers would at first sight so judge of us or that they did so teach. (*Keb.*, 54; Letter to J. W. Bowden, 21 February 1840)

I begin to have serious apprehensions lest any religious body is strong enough to withstand the league of evil but the Roman Church. At the end of the first millenary it withstood the fury of Satan, and now the end of the second is drawing on. Certainly the way that good principles have shot up is wonderful; but I am not clear that they are not tending to Rome—not from any necessity in the principles themselves, but from the much greater proximity between Rome and us than between infidelity and us, and that in a time of trouble we naturally look about for allies. (*Moz.* ii; Letter to Jemima Mozley [sister], 25 February 1840)

[W]e don't know yet what the English Church will bear of infused Catholic truth. We are, as it were, proving cannon. I know that there is a danger of bursting; but still, one has no right to assume that our Church will not stand the test. (2) If I fear the tendency of what I teach towards Rome, it is no more than I see in Hooker or Taylor ... We all create a sympathy towards Rome so far as our system does not realise what is realised in Rome ... It is quite consistent to say that I think Rome the centre of unity, and yet not to say that she is infallible, when she is by herself. (*Moz.* ii; Letter to Frederick Rogers, 25 November 1840)

I think I never shall believe that so much piety and earnestness would be found among Protestants, if there were not some very grave errors on the side of Rome. To suppose the contrary is most unreal, and violates all one's notions of moral probabilities ... That I am an advocate for Protestantism, you cannot suppose;—but I am forced into a *Via Media*, short of Rome, as it is at present. (*Apo.*, ch. 4; Letter to a Catholic, 26 April 1841)

[W]ere I ever so much to change my mind on this point, this would not tend to bring me from my present position, providentially appointed in the English Church. That your communion was unassailable, would not prove that mine was indefensible ... We have (I trust) the principle and temper of obedience too intimately wrought into us to allow of our separating ourselves from our ecclesiastical superiors because in many points we may sympathise with others. We have too great a horror of the principle of private judgment to trust it in so immense a matter as that of changing from one communion to another ... That my *sympathies* have grown towards the religion of Rome I do not deny; that my *reasons* for *shunning* her communion have lessened or altered it would be difficult perhaps to prove. And I wish to go by reason, not by feeling. (*Apo.*, ch. 4; Letter to a Catholic, 5 May 1841)

In the *Arian History* I found the very same phenomenon, in a far bolder shape, which I had found in the Monophysite ... I had not sought it out; I was reading and writing in my own line of study, far from the controversies of the day, on what is called a 'metaphysical' subject; but I saw clearly, that in the history of Arianism, the pure Arians were the Protestants, the semi-Arians were the Anglicans, and that Rome now was what it was then. The truth lay, not with the *Via Media*, but with what was called 'the extreme party.' (*Apo.*, ch. 3; referring to his state of mind between July and November 1841)

I fear I must say that I am beginning to think that the only way to keep in the English Church is steadily to contemplate and act upon the possibility of leaving it ... At all events, I am sure that, to leave the English Church, unless something very flagrant happens, must be the work of years. (*Moz.* ii; Letter to J. R. Hope, 17 October 1841)

For myself, I am too anxious for others, nay for myself, to say anything light about going to Rome. Our Church seems fast Protestantising itself. (*Moz.* ii; Letter to John Keble, 24 October 1841)

I have been for a long while assuring persons that the English Church was a branch of the Catholic Church. If, then a measure is in progress [the

Jerusalem bishopric] which in my judgment tends to cut from under me the very ground on which I have been writing and talking, and to prove all I hold a mere theory and illusion a paper theology which facts contradict, who will not excuse it if I am deeply pained at such proceedings? When friends who rely on my word come to me and say, 'You told us the English Church was Catholic,' what am I to say to this reproach? (*Keb.*, 157; Letter to J. R. Hope, 24 November 1841)

For two years and more I have been in a state of great uneasiness as to my position here, owing to the consciousness I felt, that my opinions went far beyond what had been customary in the English Church ... the contest is no longer one of what would be represented as a quasi-Romanism against Anglicanism but of Catholicism against heresy. (*Moz.* ii; Letter to Mr. Rickards, 1 December 1841)

I fully think that if this particular measure comes off, it will all but unchurch us ... if it takes place, I think it clear that, though one might remain where one was, oneself yet we should have no arguments to prevent others going to Rome. (*Keb.*, 164; Letter to J. R. Hope, 2 December 1841)

We are in so bad a way, that there seems no medium between taking very strong measures in time to come or acknowledging we are not a Church. I wish there were some possible way of interfering in this Jerusalem matter. Is there no shape in which it could be thrown at present, or prospectively, in which the Presbytery could interfere? (*Keb.*, 160; Letter to S. F. Wood, 6 December 1841)

R. Wilberforce, ... thinks I am turning R.C ... What have you said to him to make him think so? ... R. W. makes me think that your mind is also getting unsettled on the subject of Rome. I think you will give me credit, Carissime, of not undervaluing the strength of the feelings which draw one that way and yet I am (I trust) quite clear about my duty to remain where I am. Indeed much clearer than I was some time since. (*Keb.*, 160-161; Letter to S. F. Wood, 13 December 1841)

[T]here is indefinitely more in the Fathers against our own state of alienation from Christendom than against the Tridentine Decrees. (*Apo.*, ch. 4; Letter to R. W. Church, 24 December 1841)

I believe a very general misgiving is beginning to show itself about our Church's Catholicity and that on the ground of those most painful things which some of the Bishops are saying and doing. Of course preaching the doctrine of the Holy Catholic Church will lead men to Rome, supposing our Bishops declare we are not part of the Catholic Church, or that we do not hold the Catholic doctrines … I am sure that they are the worst friends of the Church who refuse to look dangers in the face. Her best friends are those who, instead of shutting their eyes, tell us when she is in danger. For centuries she has been wasting away, because persons have made the best of things and palliated serious faults. Of course directly one speaks out, one is accused of intending to Romanise but I would speak out to prevent what silence would not tend a whit to prevent, but to excuse. As it is, I fear irremediable evil is done by the acts I allude to. Confidence is shaken and when once a doubt of our Catholicity gets into the mind, it is like a seed: it lies for years to appearance dead but alas, it has its hour of germinating or is ever threatening. It should ever be borne in mind that no serious movement towards Rome took place, in fact, till the year 1841, when the authorities of the Church had more or less declared themselves against Catholic truth. (*Keb.*, 162-163; Letter to Rev. W. Dodsworth, 27 December 1841)

[C]ertainly hardly anything is said to me or comes to me, even from friends, of a sympathetic character. The truth is, I suppose it is difficult for them to put themselves into my place. (*Keb.*, 184; Letter to Edward Bellasis, 16 February 1842)

[O]f course Church principles will lead to Rome, if our Bishops repudiate them. Did our whole communion solemnly and formally enact that there was no Church, or that itself was not part of it, in so unequal a contest between the Creed and a human decree it is quite clear which would be worsted … And what would be awfully fulfilled by a formal act, is fulfilled in its measure by the act of individual bishops, or local parties of our Church. They are taking part against Christ when they speak against the Church, and will lose her children. I make no excuse then, I do but grieve while I say that many secessions will to a certainty take place, should our authorities infringe that Apostolic Creed which is the necessary condition of their power, and warrant of their claim upon a Christian's allegiance. It is my confident trust that so deplorable an event will not take place, but I say now, as I have always said, that, while I will pay unlimited obedience to the Bishop set over me while he comes in Christ's name, yet to one who comes in the name of man, in his own name, in the name of mere expedience, reason, national convenience and the like, to the neglect of that Creed which speaks of the Catholic Church, I should not be bound to pay him any at all ... [T]he general cry that the Church of Rome is spreading, makes young people curious, and incites them to take up with its doctrines and practices, though none of us had written a word ... If all the world agrees in telling a man he has no business in our Church, he will at length begin to think he has none. (*Keb.*, 185-187; Letter of 6 March 1842)

Of course the fact that the Roman Church *has* so developed and maintained, adds great weight to the antecedent plausibility. I cannot assert that it is not true; but I cannot, with that keen perception which some people have, appropriate it. It is a nuisance to me to be *forced* beyond what I can fairly accept. (*Apo.*, ch. 4; Letter to Edward B. Pusey, 16 October 1842)

Your feelings are in favour of Rome, so are mine. Yet I would not trust myself among R Catholics without recollecting how apt feeling is to get the better of judgment. (*Ble.*, 321; Letter to Miss Holmes, 8 February 1843)

[W]hat influence I exert is simply and exactly, be it more or less, in the direction of the Church of Rome and that whether I will or no. What men learn from me, who learn anything, is to lean towards doctrines and practices which our Church does not sanction. There was a time when I tried to balance this by strong statements against Rome, which I suppose to a certain extent effected my object. But now, when I feel I can do this no more, how greatly is the embarrassment of my position increased! I am in danger of acting as a traitor to that system, to which I must profess attachment or I should not have the opportunity of acting at all. But what increases my difficulty most heavily is the gradual advance, which is making, to a unanimous condemnation of No. 90 on the part of the Bishops. Here I stand on a different footing from all who agree to that Tract on the whole, even from you. No one but myself can be answerable for every word of it. The Bishops condemn it, without specifying what they condemn in it. This gives an opening to every reader who agrees with it on the whole, to escape the force of their censure. I alone cannot escape it. Two years have passed, and one Bishop after another has pronounced an unmitigated sentence against it ... I declare I wonder at myself that I have remained so long without moving ... I am conscious too, as I have said above, that I am not advocating, that I am not promoting, the Anglican system of doctrine, but one very much more resembling in matter of fact, the doctrine of the Roman Church. (*Keb.*, 210-212; Letter to John Keble, 14 March 1843)

Is not the RC system the nearest far to the primitive? ... I said that we ought to wait for a union with Rome, till Rome was holier. What has affected my feelings very much lately is to find the holiness of the Roman saints since our separation—which seems a sufficient answer to my demand; especially the Jesuits, whose Exercises I have been lately studying. (*Ble.*, 332; *Diary*, 12 April 1843)

At present I fear, as far as I can analyze my own convictions, I consider the Roman Catholic Communion to be the Church of the Apostles, and that what grace is among us (which, through God's mercy, is not little) is extraordinary, and from the over-flowings of His dispensation. I am very far more sure that England is in schism, than that the Roman additions to the Primitive Creed may not be developments, arising out of a keen and vivid realizing of the Divine Depositum of Faith. (*Apo.*, ch. 4; Letter to John Keble, 4 May 1843)

I have spoken very confidently about our being in no danger from Rome; and I doubt not with much presumption and recklessness. But I had a full conviction, (and have still) of the independence of the Anglican view compared with the Roman, and the formidableness of the former to the latter, and I had great faith in our Divines, so as to take (I suppose) for granted, what I had not duly examined, the irrelevancy of the charge of schism as urged against us. If I have been very bold in nearing the Roman system, this has risen mainly from over-secure reliance on our position, and from a keen impression of our great need of what the Roman system contains. I have spoken strongly against that system itself, that I might use it without peril ... my present feelings have arisen naturally and gradually, and have been resisted ... I have, to the utmost of my power and with some success, tried to keep persons from Rome. (*Keb.*, 226-227; Letter to John Keble, 18 May 1843)

These are reasons enough to make me give up St. Mary's, but, were there no other, this feeling would be sufficient, that I am not so zealous a defender of the established and existing system of religion as I ought to be for such a post. (*Moz.* ii; Letter to Jemima Mozley, 28 August 1843)

The truth then is, I am not a good son enough of the Church of England to feel I can in conscience hold preferment under her. I love the Church of Rome too well. (*Moz.* ii; Letter to J. B. Mozley, 1 September 1843)

I suppose the Catholic theory is, that creeds, sacraments, succession etc. are nothing without unity vid. St. Cyprian of the Novatians, and St. Austin of the Donatists. The only way I have ever attempted to answer this, is by arguing that we really were, or in one sense were, in unity with the rest of the Church but, as you know; I never have been thoroughly satisfied with my arguments, and grew more and more to suspect them. (*Keb.*, 259-260; Letter to John Keble, 6 September 1843)

You cannot estimate what so many (alas!) feel at present, the strange effect produced on the mind when the conviction flashes, or rather pours, in upon it that Rome is the true Church. Of course it is a most revolutionary, and therefore a most exciting, tumultuous conviction. For this reason persons should not act under it, for it is impossible in such a state of emotion that they can tell whether their conviction is well founded or not. They cannot judge calmly. (*Moz.* ii; Letter to Jemima Mozley, 22 September 1843)

May He not 'do what He will with His own?' [Matt. xx. 15.] May not His sun set as it has risen? and must it not set, if it is to rise again? and must not darkness come first, if there is ever to be morning? and must not the sky be blacker, before it can be brighter? And cannot He, who can do all things, cause a light to arise even in the darkness? ... And, O my brethren, O kind and affectionate hearts, O loving friends, should you know any one whose lot it has been, by writing or by word of mouth, in some degree to help you thus to act; if he has ever told you what you knew about yourselves, or what you did not know; has read to you your wants or feelings, and comforted you by the very reading; has made you feel that there was a higher life than this daily one, and a brighter world than that you see; or encouraged you, or sobered you, or opened a way to the inquiring, or soothed the perplexed; if what he has said or done has ever made you take interest in him, and feel well inclined towards him; remember such a one in time to come, though you hear him not, and pray for him, that in all things he may know God's will, and at all times he may be ready to fulfil it. (*SD*, Sermon 26: 'The Parting of Friends,' 25 September 1843)

I do so despair of the Church of England, and am so evidently cast off by her, and, on the other hand, I am so drawn to the Church of Rome, that I think it *safer*, as a matter of honesty, *not* to keep my living. This is a very different thing from having any *intention* of joining the Church of Rome. However, to avow generally as much as I have said would be wrong for ten thousand reasons. People cannot understand a man being in a state of *doubt*, of *misgiving*, of being unequal to *responsibilities*, &c.; but they will conclude that he has clear views either one way or the other. All I know is, that I could not without hypocrisy profess myself any longer a *teacher* and a *champion* for our Church. Very few persons know this—hardly one person, only one (I think) in Oxford, viz., James Mozley. I think it would be most cruel, most unkind, most unsettling to tell them. (*Moz.* ii; Letter to Harriett Mozley, 29 September 1843)

I fear that I must confess, that, in proportion as I think the English Church is showing herself intrinsically and radically alien from Catholic principles, so do I feel the difficulties of defending her claims to be a branch of the Catholic Church. It seems a dream to call a communion Catholic, when one can neither appeal to any clear statement of Catholic doctrine in its formularies, nor interpret ambiguous formularies by the received and living Catholic sense, whether past or present. Men of Catholic views are too truly but a party in our Church. I cannot deny that many other independent circumstances, which it is not worth while entering into, have led me to the same conclusion. (*Apo.*, ch. 4; Letter to Henry Edward Manning, 14 October 1843)

[I]t is not from disappointment, irritation, or impatience, that I have, whether rightly or wrongly, resigned St. Mary's; but because I think the Church of Rome the Catholic Church, and ours not part of the Catholic Church, because not in communion with Rome; and because I feel that I could not honestly be a teacher in it any longer. (*Apo.*, ch. 4; Letter to Henry Edward Manning, 25 October 1843)

Last summer four years (1839) it came strongly upon me, from reading first the Monophysite controversy, and then turning to the Donatist, that we were external to the Catholic Church. I have never got over this. I did not, however, yield to it at all, but wrote an article in the 'British Critic' on the Catholicity of the English Church, which had the effect of quieting me for two years. Since this time two years the feeling has revived and gradually strengthened. (*Moz.* ii; Letter to J. B. Mozley, 24 November 1843)

I have honestly trusted our Church and wished to defend her as she wishes to be defended. I wasn't surely wrong in defending her on that basis which our divines have ever built and on which alone they can pretend to build. And how could I foresee that when I examined that basis I should feel it to require a system different from hers and that the Fathers to which she led me would lead me from her? I do not see then that I have been to blame; yet it would be strange if I had heart to blame others who are honest in maintaining what I am abandoning. It is no pleasure to me to differ from friends, no comfort to be estranged from them, no satisfaction or boast to have said things which I must unsay. Surely I will remain where I am as long as ever I can. I think it right to do so. If my misgivings are from above, I shall be carried on in spite of my resistance. I cannot regret in time to come having struggled to remain where I found myself placed. And believe me the circumstance of such men as yourself being contented to remain is the strongest argument in favour of my own remaining. It is my constant prayer, that if others are right I may be drawn back — that nothing may part us. (*Keb.*, 292-293; Letter to Henry Edward Manning, 24 December 1843)

I fear I must say I have a steadily growing conviction about the English Church ... The early Church has all along been my line of study and I am still occupied upon it ... It is this line of reading, and no other, which has led me Romeward. Not that I read it with that view. I wish to resist, as I always have and think it a duty. I am sure, if it be right to go forward, I shall be forced on in spite of myself. Somehow I cannot feel the question of dutifulness so strongly as it is sometimes put. Was it undutifulness to the Mosaic Law, to be led on to the Gospel? was not the Law from God? How could a Jew, formerly or now, ever, become a Christian, if he must at all hazards resist convictions and for ever? How could a Nestorian or Monophysite join the Catholic Church but by a similar undutifulness? What I wish is, not to go by my own judgment, but by something external, like the pillar of the cloud in the desert ... letters, which I receive continually from persons whom I know and whom I know not, show me that a movement is going on in cases which are little suspected and in minds which are struggling against it ... If my thoughts had been led through the early Church to Rome, why should not others? ... I have lately been praying that 'if I am right, Pusey, Manning etc. may be brought forward; but if Pusey, Manning etc. are right, I may be brought back that nothing, if it be possible, may separate us. One thing I will add I sometimes have uncomfortable feelings as if I should not like to die in the English Church. It seems to me that, while Providence gives one time, it is even a call upon one to make use of it in deliberateness and waiting but that, did He cut short one's hours of grace, this would be a call to make up one's mind on what seemed most probable. (*Keb.*, 300-301; Letter to John Keble, 23 January 1844)

I fear that I must say that for four years and a half I have had a conviction, weaker or stronger, but on the whole constantly growing, and at present very strong, that we are not part of the Catholic Church. I am too much accustomed to this idea to feel pain at it. I could only feel pain, if I found it led me to action. At present I do not feel any such call. Such feelings are not hastily to be called convictions, though this seems to me to be such. Did I ever arrive at a full persuasion that it was such, then I should be anxious and much perplexed. (*Ble.*, 364; Letter to Edward B. Pusey, 19 February 1844)

With my opinions, to the full of which I dare not confess, I feel like a guilty person with others, though I trust I am not so. People kindly think that I have much to bear externally—disappointment, slander, &c. No, I have nothing to bear but the anxiety which I feel for my friends' anxiety for me, and perplexity. (*Moz.* ii; Letter to J. W. Bowden, 21 February 1844)

To remain in the English Church from a motive of expediency seems to me altogether unjustifiable both in a theological and a religious point of view. (*Ble.*, 365; Letter to Rev. C. J. Myers, 25 February 1844)

[I]f I judge of the future by the past, and when I recollect the long time, now nearly five years, that certain views and feelings have been more or less familiar to me, and sometimes pressing on me, it would seem as if anything might happen. And I must confess that they are very much clearer and stronger than they were even a year ago. I can no more calculate how soon they may affect my will and become practical, than a person who has long had a bodily ailment on him (though I hope and trust it is not an ailment) can tell when it may assume some critical shape, though it may do so any day … Unless any thing happened which I considered a divine call, and beyond all calculation, I never should take any one by surprise. (*Moz.* ii and *Ble.*, 368; Letter to Jemima Mozley, 21 May 1844)

Am I in a delusion, given over to believe a lie? Am I deceiving myself and thinking myself convinced when I am not? Does any subtle feeling or temptation, which I cannot detect, govern me, and bias my judgment? But is it possible that Divine Mercy should not wish me, if so, to discover and escape it? Has He led me thus far to destroy me in the wilderness? … month by month my convictions grow in one direction … what is my own state? Why, that for the last five years (almost) of it, I have had a strong feeling, often rising to an habitual conviction, though in the early portion of it after a while dormant, but very active now for two years and a half, and growing more urgent and imperative continually, that the Roman Communion is the only true Church — and this conviction came upon me while I was reading the Fathers and from the Fathers — and when I was reading them theologically, not ecclesiastically, in that particular line of study, that of the ancient heresies … as far as I see, all inducements and temptations are for remaining quiet, and against moving … It is no proud thing to unsay what I have said, to pull down what I have attempted to build up … The time for argument is past. I have been in one settled conviction for so long a time, which every new thought seems to strengthen. (*Ble.*, 369, and *POL*; Letter to John Keble, 8 June 1844)

The second point was my conviction that certain definite doctrines of Rome were not to be found in Antiquity — and this objection has been removed from my mind by a consideration of the principle of *development*, which I implied … in what I said in my last about the growth of the Papal power. (*Ble.*, 370; Letter to Mrs. William Froude, 9 June 1844)

I cannot tell how soon my feelings may change, or external circumstances interpose. And it comes upon me that when persons are on the brink of serious actions and afraid to plunge into the stream, Providence in mercy takes them by surprise. (*Keb.*, 322; Letter to John Keble, 13 June 1844)

No acts at this time of the day surely can unchurch us, if we have not been unchurched by the events of the Reformation but they may bring out, they may force on the mind, the fact we are, that we long have been unchurched. The Jerusalem Bishoprick three years ago disturbed me in a way very few people know, inflicting on my imagination what my reason had been unable to withstand some years before that. And now comes this formidable transaction whispering the same thing into my ear, or rather to my heart. Every form of heresy is tolerated, but there is an instinctive irritation, or shudder, at anything too Catholic. Six hundred clergymen can condense a legion of heresies into a manifesto, and the Bishops (one exception, if so, is not much) can be quite silent ... A clergyman of popular celebrity can in print deny a theological phrase which a General Council imposed, and not a word is said ... What do such facts, (true in substance though perhaps I have not expressed myself accurately in detail,) what do they show, but that we are not 'built upon the foundation of the Apostles and Prophets'? These are very fearful thoughts, which have long, very long, crowded upon my mind, and oppressed it, and which really do seem likely one day to come to something, I feel I should [be] almost a hypocrite, if I went on much longer without giving utterance to them. (*Keb.*, 327-328; Letter to E. L. Badely, 23 August 1844)

I have a great dread of going merely by my own feelings, lest they should mislead me. By one's sense of duty one must go, but external facts support one in doing so. (*Ble.*, 380; Letter to Miss Giberne, 7 November 1844)

The pain I feel at the distress I am causing others, at the great unsettlement of mind I am causing, and the ties I am rending, is keener than I can say. On Saturday for some time my heart literally ached, and is still uneasy. And I have the griefs, not of one, but of so many upon me. And all this in addition to the original and principal trial itself, which has been a secret anxiety upon me for years. Everyone must see at a glance how many and strong natural feelings and motives I have against committing myself to such acts, as nevertheless seem likely to be urged on me as imperative to my salvation but none can know the dismal thing it is to me to trouble and unsettle and wound so many quiet, kind, and happy minds. (*Keb.*, 343; Letter to Rev. Edward Coleridge, 12 November 1844)

I am going through what must be gone through; and my trust only is that every day of pain is so much taken from the necessary draught which must be exhausted. There is no fear (humanly speaking) of my moving for a long time yet. This has got out without my intending it; but it is all well. As far as I know myself, my one great distress is the perplexity, unsettlement, alarm, scepticism, which I am causing to so many; and the loss of kind feeling and good opinion on the part of so many, known and unknown, who have wished well to me. And of these two sources of pain it is the former that is the constant, urgent, unmitigated one. I had for days a literal ache all about my heart; and from time to time all the complaints of the Psalmist seemed to belong to me. And as far as I know myself, my one paramount reason for contemplating a change is my deep, unvarying conviction that our Church is in schism, and that my salvation depends on my joining the Church of Rome ... I have no existing sympathies with Roman Catholics; I hardly ever, even abroad, was at one of their services; I know none of them, I do not like what I hear of them. And then, how much I am giving up in so many ways! and to me sacrifices irreparable, not only from my age, when people hate changing, but from my especial love of old associations and the pleasures of memory. Nor am I conscious of any feeling, enthusiastic or heroic, of pleasure in the sacrifice; I have nothing to support me here. (*Apo.*, ch. 4; Letter of 16 November 1844)

Nothing but the feeling that I should forfeit God's favour by not acting can be a warrant for my acting. Nothing but the feeling that I am not safe in remaining where I am, can warrant my not remaining. (*Ble.*, 382; Letter to Robert Wilberforce, 16 November 1844)

[A]s far as I know myself the one single over-powering feeling is that our Church is in schism and that there is no salvation in it for one who is convinced of this. It is now more than five years since a consideration of the Monophysite and Donatist controversies wrought in me a clear conviction that we were now, what those heretics were then ... I dwelt upon the Roman corruptions, as we consider them, and balanced them against our difficulties. But this time three years the conviction came on me again, and now for that long time it has been clear and unbroken under all change of circumstance, place, and spirits. Through this time my own question has been 'Is it a delusion?' and I have waited, not because my conviction was not clear, but because I doubted whether it was a duty to trust it. I am still waiting on that consideration ... If I once am absolutely convinced that our Church is in schism, there is, according to the doctrine (I believe) of every age, no safety for me in it. (*Keb.*, 345-346; Letter to Rev. Edward Coleridge, 16 November 1844)

The only feeling I am at all suspicious of, is one which for an instant I have felt once or twice, but which has not remained to my consciousness on my mind, a feeling of intellectual contempt for the paralogisms of our ecclesiastical and theological theory. That I do think it full of paralogisms is quite certain that I could, if I chose, indulge myself in extreme contempt of it, I know; and that nothing passes in my mind of this consciously, I know also and I trust I have no latent feeling of this kind, i.e. anything to bias, to influence me. What I have asked myself is, 'Are you not perhaps ashamed to hold a system which is so inconsistent, so untenable?' I cannot deny I should be ashamed of having to profess it yet I think the feeling, whatever be its strength, is not at all able to do so great a thing as to make me tear myself from my friends, from their good opinion, from my reputation for consistency, from my habitual associations, from all that is naturally dear to me ... My sole ascertainable reason for moving is a feeling of indefinite risk to my soul in staying. This, I seem to ascertain in the following manner. I don't think I could die in our Communion ... I am kept first from deference to my friends next by the fear of some dreadful delusion being over me. (*Keb.*, 352-353; Letter to John Keble, 21 November 1844)

I have gone through a great deal of pain, and have been very much cut up. The one predominant distress upon me has been this unsettlement of mind I am causing. This is a thing that has haunted me day by day ... I cannot make out that I have any motive but a sense of indefinite risk to my soul in remaining where I am. A clear conviction of the substantial identity of Christianity and the Roman system has now been on my mind for a full three years. It is more than five years since the conviction first came on me, though I struggled against it and overcame it. I believe all my feelings and wishes are against change. I have nothing to draw me elsewhere. I hardly ever was at a Roman service; even abroad I knew no Roman Catholics. I have no sympathies with them as a party. I am giving up everything. I am not conscious of any resentment, disgust, or the like to repel me from my present position; and I have no dreams whatever — far from it indeed. I seem to be throwing myself away. Unless something occurs which I cannot anticipate I have no intention of any early step even now. But I cannot but think — though I can no more realise it than being made Dean of Ch. Ch. or Bishop of Durham — that some day it will be, and at a definite distance of time. As far as I can make out I am in the state of mind which divines call *indifferentia*, inculcating it as a duty to be set on nothing, but to be willing to take whatever Providence wills. How *can* I at my age and with my past trials be set upon anything? I really don't think I am. What keeps me here is the desire of giving every chance for finding out if I am under the power of a delusion. Various persons have sent me very kind letters, and I really trust that many are bearing me in mind in their prayers. (*Moz.* ii; Letter to Jemima Mozley, 24 November 1844)

I do think the unsettlement of quiet people quite a reason for not moving without a clear and settled conviction that to move is a duty. It throws the *onus probandi* on the side of moving, were it not so before. And this is what has kept me quiet hitherto. Still there is a point beyond which this impediment will not act. (*Moz.* ii; Letter to Jemima Mozley, December 1844)

I do not wonder at anyone's first impression being, when he hears of the change of religion of another, that he is influenced by some wrong motive. It is the necessary consequence of his thinking himself right; and I fully allow that, the *onus probandi* that he is not so influenced lies with the person influenced. While, then, I think you are rather hard on the various persons who have joined the Church of Rome, I think you are justified in being so, for they have to prove that they do not deserve a hard opinion. I say the same of myself. A person's feeling naturally is, that there must be something wrong at bottom; that I must be disappointed, or restless, or set on a theory, or carried on by a party, or coaxed into it by admirers, or influenced by any of the ten thousand persuasions which are as foreign from my mind as from my heart, but which it is easy for others to assign as an hypothesis. I do not quarrel with persons so thinking. But still I think that as time goes on, and persons have the opportunity of knowing me better, they will see that all these suppositions do not hold; and they will be led to see that my motive simply is that I believe the Roman Church to be true, and that I have come to this belief without any assignable fault on my part. Far indeed am I from saying 'without fault' absolutely, but I say without fault that can be detected and assigned. Were I sure that it was without fault absolutely, I should not hesitate to move tomorrow. It is the fear that there is some secret undetected fault which is the cause of my belief which keeps me where I am, waiting. But I really can say that nothing occurs to me indicative of any such fault, and the longer the time without such discovery the more hope I have that there is none such. I cannot detect such. Some time ago I wrote down for Keble everything of every sort I could detect as passing in my mind in any respect wrong, or leading to wrong, day by day, for a certain period, and he could detect nothing bearing on this particular belief of mine. I have been as open with him as possible. Now I am far from saying I can find in myself good motives—I have not any confidence whatever that I am acting from faith and love; but what I say is that I cannot detect bad motives, ... If God gives me certain light, supposing it to be such, this is a reason for *me* to act—yet in so doing I am not condemning those who do not so act. There *is* one truth, yet it may not please Almighty God to show every one in the same degree or way what and where it is. (*Moz*. ii and *Ble*., 381; Letter to Jemima Mozley, 22 December 1844)

Any thing I say must be abrupt—nothing can I say which will not leave a bewildering feeling, as needing so much to explain it, and being isolated and, as it were, unlocated, and not having any thing to show its bearing upon other subjects … This I am sure of, that nothing but a simple, direct call of duty is a warrant for any one leaving our Church; no preference of another Church, no delight in its services, no hope of greater religious advancement in it, no indignation, no disgust, at the persons and things, among which we may find ourselves in the Church of England. The simple question is, Can *I* (it is personal, not whether another, but can *I*) be saved in the English Church? am *I* in safety, were I to die tonight? Is it a mortal sin in *me*, not joining another communion? (*Ble.*, 385 and *Apo.*, ch. 4; Letter to Miss Giberne, 8 January 1845)

[A]s far as such outward matters go, I am as much gone over as if I *were already gone*. It is a matter of time only. I'm waiting, if so be, that if I am under a delusion, it may be revealed to me though I am quite unworthy of it — but outward events have never been the *causes* of my actions, or in themselves touched *feelings*. They have had a *confirmatory*, *aggravating* effect often. (*Ble.*, 387; Letter to Edward B. Pusey, 25 February 1845)

Is it not like a death-bed repentance to put off what one feels one ought to do? As to my convictions, I can but say what I have told you already, that I cannot at all make out *why* I should determine on moving, except as thinking I should offend God by not doing so. I cannot make out what I am at except on this supposition. At my time of life men love ease. I love ease myself. I am giving up a maintenance involving no duties, and adequate to all my wants. What in the world am I doing this for (I ask *myself* this), except that I think I am called to do so? I am making a large income by my sermons, I am, to say the very least, risking this; the chance is that my sermons will have no further sale at all. I have a good name with many; I am deliberately sacrificing it. I have a bad name with more. I am fulfilling all their worst wishes, and giving them their most coveted triumph. I am distressing all I love, unsettling all I have instructed or aided. I am going to those whom I do not know, and of whom I expect very little. I am making myself an outcast, and that at my age. Oh, what can it be but a stern necessity which causes this? Pity me, my dear Jemima. What have I done thus to be deserted, thus to be left to take a wrong course, if it is wrong? I began by defending my own Church with all my might when others would not defend her. I went through obloquy in defending her. I in a fair measure succeed. At the very time of this success, before any reverse, in the course of my reading it breaks upon me that I am in a schismatical Church. I oppose myself to the notion; I write against it—year after year I write against it, and I do my utmost to keep others in the Church … Continually do I pray that He would discover to me if I am under a delusion … Have the multitude who will judge me any right to judge me? Who of my equals, who of the many who will talk flippantly about me, has a right? Who has a right to judge me but my Judge? (*Moz.* ii; Letter to Jemima Mozley, 15 March 1845)

So if I had my will I should like to wait till the summer of 1846, which would be a full seven years from the time that my convictions first began to fall on me. But I don't think I shall last so long. (*Ble.*, 387; Letter to Miss Giberne, 30 March 1845)

I say to myself, if I am under a delusion, what have I done, what grave sin have I committed, to bring such a judgment on me? O that it may be revealed to me, and the delusion broken! But I go on month after month, year after year, without change of feeling except in one direction; not floating up and down, but driving one way. (*Moz.* ii; Letter to J. B. Mozley, 2 April 1845)

How dreadful it is to have to act on great matters so much in the dark—yet I, who have preached so much on the duty of following in the night wherever God may call, am the last person who have [sic] a right to complain. (*Ble.*, 385; Letter to Henry Wilberforce, 27 April 1845)

You are quite right in saying I do not take Ward and Oakeley's grounds that all Roman doctrine may be held in our Church and that as Roman. I have always and everywhere resisted it. (*Keb.*, 380; Letter to J. R. Hope, 14 May 1845)

I am very much more made up both in steady conviction and preparation of my feelings, to change my place but am suffering from fatigue of mind, partly from former distress, partly from other causes. (*Keb.*, 380; Letter to J. R. Hope, 10 June 1845)

[H]ow should it be but right in acting on so very long a conviction as that which obliges me to acknowledge that Christ's home is elsewhere and that I must seek him there? (*Ble.*, 394; Letter to Rev. Edward Coleridge, 3 July 1845)

[I]t is morally certain I shall join the R.C. Church … It has been the conviction of six years—from which I have never receded … My conviction has nothing whatever to do with the events of the day. It is founded on my study of early Church history. I think the Church of Rome in every respect the continuation of the early Church. I think she is the early Church *in* these times, … They differ in doctrine and discipline as child and grown man differ, not otherwise. I do not see any medium between disowning Christianity, and taking the Church of Rome … I cannot believe only just as much as our Reformers out of their own heads have chosen we should believe—I must believe less or more. If Christianity is one and the same at all times, then I must believe, not what the Reformers have carved out of it, but what the Catholic Church holds. (*POL;* Letter to Richard Westmacott, 11 July 1845)

And now, dear Reader, time is short, eternity is long. Put not from you what you have here found; regard it not as mere matter of present controversy; set not out resolved to refute it, and looking about for the best way of doing so; seduce not yourself with the imagination that it comes of disappointment, or disgust, or restlessness, or wounded feeling, or undue sensibility, or other weakness. Wrap not yourself round in the associations of years past, nor determine that to be truth which you wish to be so, nor make an idol of cherished anticipations. Time is short, eternity is long. (*Dev.*, Part II: ch. 12; Conclusion [the very end of the work])

If I thought any other body but that which I recognise to be the Catholic to be recognised by the Saviour of the world, I would not have left that body. (*LD* xi, 14; Letter to Jemima Mozley, 9 October 1845)

The pain indeed, which I knew I was giving individuals, has affected me much ... With what conscience could I have remained? How could I have answered it at the last day, if, having opportunities of knowing the Truth which others have not, I had not availed myself of them? What a doom would have been mine, if I had kept the Truth a secret in my own bosom, and when I knew which the One Church was, and which was not part of the One Church, I had suffered friends and strangers to die in an ignorance from which I might have relieved them! Impossible. One may not act hastily and unsettle others when one has not a clear view — but when one has, it is impossible not to act upon it. (*LD* xi, 16; Letter to Jemima Mozley, 14 October 1845)

I have taken a long time about my own change. My book on 'the Prophetical Office etc.' was written 9 years ago — Six years ago the Catholicity of the Church of Rome broke on my mind suddenly and clearly. I have never shaken off the impression, though for a long while I dreaded to allow it, lest it should be a delusion. Nay the dread of delusion has kept me where I was till the last month. I do not mean to say that every one who comes to the same views with myself must be as long about it. Mine was a peculiar case. But I can easily understand that in many minds a conviction will be the work of time. (*LD* xi, 18; Letter to Edward Badeley, 19 October 1845)

Since the above was written, the Author has joined the Catholic Church. It was his intention and wish to have carried his Volume through the Press before deciding finally on this step. But when he had got some way in the printing, he recognised in himself a conviction of the truth of the conclusion to which the discussion leads, so clear as to supersede further deliberation. Shortly afterwards circumstances gave him the opportunity of acting upon it, and he felt that he had no warrant for refusing to do so. (*Dev.*, Advertisement to the First Edition: Postcript, October 1845)

Pray be quite assured that I would not have left the English Church, had I thought it possible for me to remain in God's favour and remain a member of it. To my own mind it is as clear as light that it is a Church which the Fathers would not have acknowledged. I had no alternative but to leave it, unless I gave up the Fathers, nay all revealed religion. It would have been a gross hypocrisy in me, to profess to rule myself by the early Church, and yet to remain in a communion which resembled the Donatists, or Nestorians, or Monophysites, and not the ancient Catholic Church. It was impossible for me to know this, yet keep it as a secret in my own breast, and be the cause of others perishing who were satisfied with the English Church because they thought I was. (*LD* xi, 26-27; Letter to Harmood W. Banner, 8 November 1845)

I never could think it right to change my religion on any ground short of the *absolute necessity* of the act, as a condition of *everlasting salvation*. (*LD* xi, 63; Letter to the Marquise de Salvo, 14 December 1845)

As time went on and I read the Fathers more attentively, I found the Via Media less and less satisfactory. It broke down with me in 1839. So much on the *theory* of the Anglican Church—but as to the Church itself I implicitly believed in her divinity till a late date ... When I was driven back from the theory of the Via Media, I retreated upon the Church her-self—I did not at once give her up. There cannot be a more cogent proof of my confidence in the Church, in some way or other, any how; whatever might turn out to be her real evidence, evidence there was I was sure. (*LD* xi, 100-101; Letter to Henry Wilberforce, 27 January 1846)

[C]an you point to any one who has lost more in the way of friendship, whether by death or alienation, than I have? ... So many dead, so many separated ... dear friends who *are* preserved in life *not* moving with me; Pusey strongly bent on an opposite course, Williams protesting against my conduct as rationalistic, and dying—Rogers and J. Mozley viewing it with utter repugnance. Of my friends a dozen years ago whom have I now? (*LD* xi, 102; Letter to Miss M. R. Giberne, 28 January 1846)

I do not know how to do justice to my reasons for becoming a Catholic in ever so many words—but if I attempted to do so in few, and that in print, I should wantonly expose myself and my cause to the hasty and prejudiced criticisms of opponents. This I will not do. People shall not say, 'We have now got his reasons, and know their worth.' No, you have not got them, you cannot get them, except at the cost of some portion of the trouble I have been at myself. You cannot buy them for a crown piece — You cannot take them in your hand at your will, and toss them about, You must consent to *think* — and you must exercise such resignation to the Divine Hand which leads you, as to follow it any whither. I am not assuming that my reasons are sufficient or unanswerable, when I say this — but describing the way in which alone our intellect can be successfully exercised on the great subject in question, if the intellect is to be the instrument of conversion. Moral proofs are grown into, not learnt by heart. (*LD* xi, 110; Letter to J. Spencer Northcote, 8 February 1846)

It has been sometimes objected that some of us have gone over for the privileges we hoped to gain in the Catholic Church. That has not been our case here. We went over not realizing those privileges which we have found *by* going. (*LD* xi, 131; Letter to Mrs. J. W. Bowden, 1 March 1846)

[N]ot for one moment have I felt otherwise than most grateful to God that I did what I did last October ... [D]ay by day I seem to gain a nearer approach to Him who condescends to dwell with man upon earth under sensible forms — but what would I have given for a clearer view at the time of acting, and for a year before! ... God's ways are not as ours. I was left to myself, that is, to the ordinary guidance of His grace ... and He has given me after acting that confidence which He denied me before. (*LD* xi, 140-141; Letter to Mrs. J. W. Bowden, 22 March 1846)

I am sometimes tempted now to reproach myself that I did not move faster, when it was of such importance to others that I should have done so. (*LD* xi, 151; Letter to Mrs. J. W. Bowden, 18 April 1846)

[T]he deep and awful [awesome] joy which membership with the Catholic Church imparts is something different in kind from any peace I had in the Anglican. (*LD* xi, 185; Letter to Mrs. Lockhart, 26 June 1846)

This day I have been a year in the Catholic Church — and every day I bless Him who led me into it more and more. I have come from clouds and darkness into light, and cannot look back on my former state without the dreary feeling which one has on looking back upon a wearisome miserable journey. (*LD* xi, 257; Letter to Miss Parker, 9 October 1846)

[F]rom the time I became a Catholic, the shadow of a misgiving has not crossed my mind that I was not doing God's will in becoming one — not a shadow of regret ... were the loss a hundred fold, it would indeed have been a cheap bargain. It is coming out of shadows into truth — into that which is beyond mistake a real religion — not a mere opinion ... but an external objective substantive creed and worship ... I have had no exercise whatever for my faith (i.e. in the sense of combating with *doubt*). (*LD* xii, 168; Letter to A. J. Hanmer, 10 February 1848)

I for one was converted to the Church, not by the medieval age, but by the primitive centuries. (*LD* xxxii, 43; Letter to Lady Shrewsbury, 29 April 1848)

I have not had any feeling whatever but one of joy and gratitude that God called me out of an insecure state into one which is sure and safe, out of the war of tongues into a realm of peace and assurance. (*LD* xii, 218; Letter to Henry Bourne, 13 June 1848)

I joined the Catholic Church to save my soul; I said so at the time. No inferior motive would have drawn me from the Anglican. And I came to it to learn, to receive what I should find, whatever it was. Never for an instant have I had since any misgiving I was right in doing so — never any misgiving that the Catholic religion was not the religion of the Apostles. (*LD* xii, 236; Letter to E. J. Phipps, 3 July 1848)

Having been one of a party who were led on to the Catholic Church by her stronger doctrines, and who despised half measures and uncertain statements. (*LD* xii, 319; Letter to Bishop William B. Ullathorne, 2 November 1848)

[T]hey [the Church Fathers] had been the beginning of my doubts ... [H]ere is truth, and all else is shadow, and I have had ... not even the *temptation* to doubt. Yes, I believe that God's grace so accompanies that great act, whereby we unite ourselves to His visible dwelling place, that the devil does not touch us. (*LD* xii, 357; Letter to Henry Wilberforce, 30 November 1848)

Having experienced for many months, nay I would say for a year or two before I became a Catholic, while my convictions were growing, that very distressing feeling which you describe, 'How do I know, confident as I may be, that it may not be a false confidence, that I am not in a dream, and the act of conversion will break it? I am sure, but how can I be sure that I ought to be sure?'—I can both sympathise with you, and perhaps have some right to advise you. (*LD* xii, 377; Letter to Catherine Ward, 19 December 1848)

I cannot forget, that when, in the year 1839, a doubt first crossed my mind of the tenableness of the theological theory on which Anglicanism is based, it was caused in no slight degree by the perusal of a controversial paper, attributed to your Lordship, on the schism of the Donatists. (*LD* xxxii, 45; Letter to Nicholas Cardinal Wiseman [then a bishop], 4 October 1849; also part of *Mix.*, Dedication)

Nor was it solely the conspicuous parallel which I have been describing in outline, which, viewed in its details, was so fatal a note of error against the Anglican position. I soon found it to follow, that the grounds on which alone Anglicanism was defensible formed an impregnable stronghold for the primitive heresies, and that the justification of the Primitive Councils was as cogent an apology for the Council of Trent. It was difficult to make out how the Eutychians or Monophysites were heretics, unless Protestants and Anglicans were heretics also; difficult to find arguments against the Tridentine Fathers which did not tell against the Fathers of Chalcedon; difficult to condemn the Popes of the sixteenth century, without condemning the Popes of the fifth. The drama of religion and the combat of truth and error were ever one and the same. The principles

and proceedings of the Church now were those of the Church then; the
principles and proceedings of heretics then were those of Protestants now.
I found it so — almost fearfully; there was an awful similitude, more awful,
because so silent and unimpassioned, between the dead records of the past
and the feverish chronicle of the present. The shadow of the fifth century
was on the sixteenth. It was like a spirit rising from the troubled waters
of the Old World with the shape and lineaments of the new. The Church
then, as now, might be called peremptory and stern, resolute, overbearing, and relentless; and heretics were shifting, changeable, reserved, and
deceitful, ever courting the civil power, and never agreeing together, except by its aid; and the civil power was ever aiming at comprehensions,
trying to put the invisible out of view, and to substitute expediency for
faith. What was the use of continuing the controversy, or defending my
position, if, after all, I was but forging arguments for Arius or Eutyches,
and turning devil's advocate against the much-enduring Athanasius and
the majestic Leo? Be my soul with the Saints! and shall I lift up my hand
against them? (*Dif.* i, Lecture 12)

[W]hen I became a Catholic, grave persons, Protestant clergymen, at-
tested (what they said was well known to others besides themselves) that
either I was mad, or was in the most imminent danger of madness. They
put it into the newspapers, and people were sometimes quite afraid to
come and see me ... it has lately been put into the papers, under the sanction of respectable names, that I am not a believer in the Catholic doctrines; and broader still in private letters, that I have given up Revealed
Religion altogether. I mention these instances, not for their own sake,
but to illustrate the power of prejudice. Men are determined they will *not*
believe that an educated Protestant can find peace and satisfaction in the
Catholic Church; and they invent catastrophes for the occasion, which
they think too certain to need testimony or proof. In the reports I have
been setting down, there was not even a rag or a shred of evidence to give
plausibility to them. (*PPC*, Lecture 6)

I have not had one moment's wavering of trust in the Catholic
Church ever since I was received into her fold, and ever have held, that

her Sovereign Pontiff is the centre of unity and the Vicar of Christ. And I ever have had, and have still, an unclouded faith in her creed in all its articles; a supreme satisfaction in her worship, discipline and teaching; and an eager longing and a hope against hope that the many dear friends whom I have left in Protestantism may be partakers of my happiness. This being my state of mind, to add, as I hereby go on to do, that I have no intention, and never had any intention, of leaving the Catholic Church and becoming a Protestant again, would be superfluous, except that Protestants are always on the look-out for some loophole or evasion in a Catholic's statement of fact ... Return to the Church of England! No; 'the net is broken, and we are delivered.' I should be a consummate fool (to use a mild term) if in my old age I left 'the land flowing with milk and honey' for the city of confusion and the house of bondage. (*POL*; Letter to the Editor of the *Globe*, 28 June 1862)

I have said that 'I owe nothing to Protestantism.' I say so deliberately ... By Protestantism I meant that system of theology which came into the world in the 16th century — its characteristics are such as these — the doctrine of justification by faith only — the Bible the sole rule of faith — the denial of sacramental influence — assurance of personal salvation — and, as regards Calvinism, the doctrine of reprobation. Some of them I professed ... when I was young — some I never could stomach — but, at least afterwards, I unlearned them all ... I hold none of the distinguishing doctrines of Protestantism nor have I for these (almost) forty years ... But I *do* owe much to Anglicanism. It was in the divines of the Anglican Church, Laud, Hooker, Bull, Beveridge, Stillingfleet and others, that I found those doctrines, which either are Catholic or directly tended in my own case to Catholic doctrine. (*LD* xxxii, 261-262; Letter to an Unknown Correspondent, 1 November 1864)

It is not my present accuser alone who entertains, and has entertained, so dishonourable an opinion of me and of my writings. It is the impression of large classes of men; the impression twenty years ago and the impression now. There has been a general feeling that I was for years where I had no right to be; that I was a 'Romanist' in Protestant livery and service;

that I was doing the work of a hostile Church in the bosom of the English Establishment, and knew it, or ought to have known it. There was no need of arguing about particular passages in my writings, when the fact was so patent, as men thought it to be ... But I do not like to be called to my face a liar and a knave; nor should I be doing my duty to my faith or to my name, if I were to suffer it. I know I have done nothing to deserve such an insult, and if I prove this, as I hope to do, I must not care for such incidental annoyances as are involved in the process. (*Apo.*, Preface)

Alas! it was my portion for whole years to remain without any satisfactory basis for my religious profession, in a state of moral sickness, neither able to acquiesce in Anglicanism, nor able to go to Rome. But I bore it, till in course of time my way was made clear to me. If here it be objected to me, that as time went on, I often in my writings hinted at things which I did not fully bring out, I submit for consideration whether this occurred except when I was in great difficulties, how to speak, or how to be silent, with due regard for the position of mind or the feelings of others. (*Apo.*, ch. 2)

Since I have been a Catholic, people have sometimes accused me of backwardness in making converts; and Protestants have argued from it that I have no great eagerness to do so. It would be against my nature to act otherwise than I do; but besides, it would be to forget the lessons which I gained in the experience of my own history in the past. (*Apo.*, ch. 3)

There are no friends like old friends; but of those old friends, few could help me, few could understand me, many were annoyed with me, some were angry, because I was breaking up a compact party, and some, as a matter of conscience, could not listen to me. (*Apo.*, ch. 4)

I had a great dislike of paper logic. For myself, it was not logic that carried me on; as well might one say that the quicksilver in the barometer changes the weather. It is the concrete being that reasons; pass a number of years, and I find my mind in a new place; how? the whole man moves; paper logic is but the record of it. All the logic in the world would not have made me move faster towards Rome than I did … Great acts take time. At least this is what I felt in my own case; and therefore to come to me with methods of logic had in it the nature of a provocation. (*Apo.*, ch. 4)

I could not continue in this state, either in the light of duty or of reason. My difficulty was this: I had been deceived greatly once; how could I be sure that I was not deceived a second time? I thought myself right then; how was I to be certain that I was right now? How many years had I thought myself sure of what I now rejected? how could I ever again have confidence in myself? As in 1840 I listened to the rising doubt in favour of Rome, now I listened to the waning doubt in favour of the Anglican Church. To be certain is to know that one knows; what inward test had I, that I should not change again, after that I had become a Catholic? I had still apprehension of this, though I thought a time would come, when it would depart. (*Apo.*, ch. 4)

From the time that I became a Catholic, of course I have no further history of my religious opinions to narrate. In saying this, I do not mean to say that my mind has been idle, or that I have given up thinking on theological subjects; but that I have had no variations to record, and have had no anxiety of heart whatever. I have been in perfect peace and contentment; I never have had one doubt. I was not conscious to myself, on my conversion, of any change, intellectual or moral, wrought in my mind. I was not conscious of firmer faith in the fundamental truths of Revelation, or of more self-command; I had not more fervour; but it was like coming into port after a rough sea; and my happiness on that score remains to this day without interruption. Nor had I any trouble about receiving those additional articles, which are not found in the Anglican Creed. Some of them I believed already, but not any one of them was a trial to me. I made a profession of them upon my reception with the greatest ease, and I have the same ease in believing them now. (*Apo.*, ch. 5)

If the arguments used in the foregoing Essay did not retain me in the Anglican Church, I do not see what could keep me in it; yet the time came, when I wrote to Mr. Keble [in October 1840], 'I seem to myself almost to have shot my last arrow [against Rome], in the article on English Catholicity.' The truth is, I believe, I was always asking myself what would the Fathers have done, what would those whose works were around my room, whose names were ever meeting my eyes, whose authority was ever influencing my judgment, what would these men have said, how would they have acted in my position? I had made a good case on paper, but what judgment would be passed on it by Athanasius, Basil, Gregory, Hilary, and Ambrose? The more I considered the matter, the more I thought that these Fathers, if they examined the antagonist pleas, would give it against me. (*Ess.* ii, Note on Essay X: 'Catholicity of the Anglican Church,' *British Critic*, Jan. 1840; from 1871)

If it be asked of me how, with my present views of the inherent impracticability of the Anglican theory of Church polity, I could ever have held it myself, I answer that, though swayed by great names, I never was without misgivings about the difficulties which it involved; and that as early as 1837, in my Volume in defence of Anglicanism as contrasted with 'Romanism and popular Protestantism,' I expressed my sense of these difficulties. (*Ess.* ii, Note on Essay X: 'Catholicity of the Anglican Church,' *British Critic*, Jan. 1840; from 1871)

[A]m I a contented Roman Catholic? I will but say that I have been a Catholic for nearly 30 years, and I never have had through that time one misgiving as to the Catholic Roman Church being the One Ark of salvation and oracle of Truth given to man by the mercy of God. Moreover, I bless Him that of His great grace He has brought me into it, and I wish and pray that all men were partakers of His wonderful gift. Also I challenge any one to say that by writing or by word of mouth I had said any thing to any one inconsistent with this statement. (*LD* xxxii, 334; Letter to Mrs. Albon Woodroffe, 16 August 1873)

For seventeen years, I do not say by whose fault, if by any one's, my own or that of others, I was simply cut off from my former friends. Many of them died in that estrangement; some of that old generation still remains unforgiving. But since 1862 there has been a wide expression of feeling towards me on the part of those who recollect me when they were young, and on the part of some of my contemporaries. You must not, and will not, for an instant suppose, that I have ever, since I left my early religious home, had one single misgiving or doubt that I have transferred myself to a better place, ... but this confidence is surely not [in]consistent with a loving remembrance of old time and old labours. (*LD* xxxii, 335; Letter to Canon Charles Wellington Furse, 29 August 1873)

In the years which followed the publication of this Volume, in proportion as he read the Fathers more carefully, and used his own eyes in determining the faith and worship of their times, his confidence in the Anglican divines was more and more shaken, and at last it went altogether. And, according as this change of mind came over him, he felt of course disturbance at that strong language he had used against the Roman teaching, ... which, though he had used it with a full belief that it was merited and was necessary for the Anglican argument, had never been quite according to his taste. At length he published a Retractation of the chief passages which were coloured with it. (*VM* i, Preface to the Third Edition, 1877)

I should not myself allow that I was driven out of the Anglican Church, instead of leaving it because the Truth was elsewhere. (*LD* xxix, 93; Letter to Alfred Reginald Perring, 29 March 1879)

Sir William Palmer, in his republication of his 'Narrative,' &c., in spite of using words of me, of which I feel the kindness, ventures to say that 'Newman and Froude had consulted [Dr. Wiseman] at Rome upon the feasibility of being received *as English Churchmen* into the Papal communion, retaining their doctrines.' If this means that Hurrell Froude and I thought of being received into the Catholic Church while we still remained outwardly professing the doctrine and the communion of the Church of England, I utterly deny and protest against so calumnious a statement. Such an idea never entered into our heads. I can speak for myself, and, as far as one man can speak for another, I can answer for my dear friend also. (*VM* ii, XI, 'Retractation of Anti-Catholic Statements,' footnote of 11 October 1883)

Councils, Ecumenical

If a Council is attended by many Bishops from various parts of Christendom, and if they speak one and all the same doctrine, without constraint, and bear witness to their having received it from their Fathers, having never heard of any other doctrine, and verily believing it to be Apostolic, — great consideration is due to its decisions. (*VM* i, ch. 2)

While Councils are a thing of earth, their infallibility of course is not guaranteed; when they are a thing of heaven, their deliberations are overruled, and their decrees authoritative. In such cases they are *Catholic* councils; and it would seem, from passages which will be quoted in Section 11, that the Homilies recognise four, or even six, as bearing this character. (*TT* #90, Jan. 1841)

Heretical questionings have been transmuted by the living power of the Church into salutary truths. The case is the same as regards the Ecumenical Councils. Authority in its most imposing exhibition, grave Bishops, laden with the traditions and rivalries of particular nations or places, have been guided in their decisions by the commanding genius of individuals, sometimes young and of inferior rank. Not that uninspired intellect overruled the super-human gift which was committed to the Council, which would be a self-contradictory assertion, but that in that process of inquiry and deliberation, which ended in an infallible enunciation, individual reason was paramount. Thus Malchion, a mere presbyter, was the instrument of the great Council of Antioch in the third century in meeting and refuting, for the assembled Fathers, the heretical Patriarch of that see. Parallel to this instance is the influence, so well known, of a young deacon, St. Athanasius, with the 318 Fathers at Nicaea. (*Apo.*, ch. 5)

Of course what the General Council speaks is the word of God — but still we may well feel indignant at the intrigue, trickery, and imperiousness which is the human side of its history—and it seems a dereliction of duty not to do one's part to meet them. (*Ward* ii, 240; Letter to Canon William Walker, 10 November 1867)

The same is the idea of the Infallibility of the *Church* in Council. The Bishops are fallible one by one—their reasoning may be bad—and their facts—their evidence—their motives—their purpose—but their ultimate definition is overruled, and is the Word of God, as Balaam was overruled ... Thus Perrone says that 'infallibilitas is not given to the Church *ad modum inspirationis* ['in the way of inspiration'], but *ad modum peculiaris subsidii, sive, ut aiunt, adsistentiae* ['in the way of a particular aid, or, as they say, assistance']. *Nunquam Catholici docuerunt donum infallibilitatis a deo Ecclesiae tribui ad modum inspirationis*' ['Furthermore, Catholics have never taught that God has given the Church the gift of infallibility in the manner of inspiration']. (*LD* xxxii, 293; Letter to an Unknown Correspondent, 12 February 1869)

[A] Council's proper office is, when some great heresy or other evil impends, to inspire the faithful with hope and confidence. (*POL*; Letter to Bishop William B. Ullathorne, 28 January 1870)

Now we have lately had an ecumenical Council. Councils have generally acted as a lever, displacing and disordering portions of the existing theological system. Not seldom have they been followed by bitter quarrels in the Catholic body. Time is necessary to put things to rights. (*POL*; Letter to Lord Howard of Glossop, 27 April 1872)

Of course there is a sense of the word 'inspiration' in which it is common to all members of the Church, and therefore especially to its Bishops, and still more directly to those rulers, when solemnly called together in Council, after much prayer throughout Christendom, and in a frame of mind especially serious and earnest by reason of the work they have in hand. The Paraclete certainly is ever with them, and more effectively in a Council, as being 'in Spiritu Sancto congregata;' but I speak of the special and promised aid necessary for their fidelity to Apostolic teaching; and, in order to secure this fidelity, no inward gift of infallibility is needed, such as the Apostles had, no direct suggestion of divine truth, but simply an external guardianship, keeping them off from error (as a man's good Angel, without at all enabling him to walk, might, on a night journey, keep him from pitfalls in his way), a guardianship, saving them, as far as their ultimate decisions are concerned, from the effects of their inherent infirmities, from any chance of extravagance, of confusion of thought, of collision with former decisions or with Scripture, which in seasons of excitement might reasonably be feared. (*Dif.* ii, Letter to the Duke of Norfolk, ch. 9, 1875)

Creation; Nature

There is motion and activity in Nature, but it is *without effort*; all creation is as it were hung upon wheels, and moves noiselessly and gracefully — the sun, the stream, the breeze, life. (*SN*, 'On Labour and Rest,' 27 January 1850)

Nothing lives without Him; nothing is. Animated nature, vegetables, nay, the very material substances, have their life, if it may be so called, their motion and activity in Him — the elements. What is called Nature, a principle of life, is from Him. (*SN*, 'On Grace, the Principle of Eternal Life,' 24 February 1850)

His are the substance, and the operation, and the results of that system of physical nature into which we are born ... The laws of the universe, the principles of truth, the relation of one thing to another, their qualities and virtues, the order and harmony of the whole, all that exists, is from Him; ... All we see, hear, and touch, the remote sidereal firmament, as well as our own sea and land, and the elements which compose them, and the ordinances they obey, are His. The primary atoms of matter, their properties, their mutual action, their disposition and collocation, electricity, magnetism, gravitation, light, and whatever other subtle principles or operations the wit of man is detecting or shall detect, are the work of His hands. (*IU*, Part I, Discourse 3: 'Bearing of Theology on Other Branches of Knowledge,' 1852)

It is true, then, that Revelation has in one or two instances advanced beyond its chosen territory, which is the invisible world, in order to throw light upon the history of the material universe. Holy Scripture, it is perfectly true, does declare a few momentous facts, so few that they may be counted, of a physical character. It speaks of a process of formation out of chaos which occupied six days; it speaks of the firmament; of the sun and moon being created for the sake of the earth; of the earth being immovable; of a great deluge; and of several other similar facts and events. It is true; nor is there any reason why we should anticipate any difficulty in accepting these statements as they stand, whenever their meaning and drift are authoritatively determined; for, it must be recollected, their meaning has not yet engaged the formal attention of the Church, or received any interpretation which, as Catholics, we are bound to accept, and in the absence of such definite interpretation, there is perhaps some presumption in saying that it means this, and does not mean that. And this being the case, it is not at all probable that any discoveries ever should be made by physical inquiries incompatible at the same time with one and all of those senses which the letter admits, and which are still open. (*IU*, Part II, ch. 7: 'Christianity and Physical Science,' November 1855)

The whole universe comes from the good God. It is His creation; *it* is good; it is all good, as being the work of the Good, though good only in its degree, and not after His Infinite Perfection. The physical nature of man is good; nor can there be any thing sinful in itself in acting according to that nature. Every natural appetite or function is lawful, speaking abstractedly. No natural feeling or act is in itself sinful. (*IU*, Part II, ch. 10: 'Christianity and Medical Science,' November 1858)

I do not see anything in the text of Scripture which obliges us, or even leads us, to consider the six days of Genesis i to be literal days. (*LD* xxx, 101; Letter printed in the *Illustrated Century Magazine*, June 1882)

Demons (Fallen Angels)

[T]he present war with evil spirits would seem to be very different from what it was in former ages. They attack a civilised age in a more subtle way than they attack a rude age. We read in lives of saints and others of the evil spirit showing himself and fighting with them face to face, but now those subtle and experienced spirits find it is more to their purpose not to show themselves, or at least not so much. They find it their interest to let the idea of them die away from the minds of men, that being unrecognised, they may do the more mischief. And they assault men in a more subtle way—not grossly, in some broad temptation, which everyone can understand, but in some refined way they address themselves to our pride or self-importance, or love of money, or love of ease, or love of show, or our depraved reason, and thus have really the dominion over persons who seem at first sight to be quite superior to temptation. (*FP*, Sermon 5: 'Surrender to God,' 12 March 1848)

[S]ome have been cut off and sent to hell for their first sin. This was the case, as divines teach, as regards the rebel Angels. For their first sin, and that a sin of thought, a single perfected act of pride, they lost their first estate, and became devils. (*Mix.*, Discourse 2: 'Neglect of Divine Calls and Warnings')

The sin of the angels, one and the same in all, from imitation. Lucifer led them. *What* [was] the sin? All [sins] in one doubtless, but especially pride. What *kind* of pride? Obstinacy, ambition, disobedience, arrogance?—all doubtless, but especially and initially reliance [on] and contentment in *natural* gifts, with despising *supernatural*. Additions to this pride (1) a sort of *sensual* love of self; (2) presumption, ambition, hatred of God; (3) jealousy of man who was to be created. (*SN*, 'The Holy Angels—III,' 16 September 1860)

Deuterocanon ('Apocrypha')

For though I believe the Old and New Testament alone to be *plenarily* inspired, yet I do believe, according to the Homily, what you do not believe, that the Holy Ghost did speak by the mouth of Tobit. (*TT* #82, 3 March 1837)

Development (of Doctrine)

No prophet ends his subject: his brethren after him renew, enlarge, transfigure, or reconstruct it. (*Ari.*, ch. 1, sec. 3)

[T]he secondary and distinct meaning of prophecy, is commonly hidden from view by the veil of the literal text, lest its immediate scope should be overlooked; when that is once fulfilled, the recesses of the sacred language seem to open, and give up the further truths deposited in them. (*Ari.*, ch. 1, sec. 3)

Surely everything our Saviour did and said is characterized by mingled simplicity and mystery. His emblematical actions, His typical miracles, His parables, His replies, His censures, all are evidences of a legislature in germ, afterwards to be developed, a code of divine truth which was ever to be before men's eyes, to be the subject of investigation and interpretation, and the guide in controversy. (*VM* i, ch. 12)

The testimony given at the latter date is the limit to which all that has been before given converges … Viewing the matter as one of moral evidence, we seem to see in the testimony of the fifth the very testimony which every preceding century gave, accidents excepted, … The fifth century acts as a comment on the obscure text of the centuries before it, and brings out a meaning which, with the help of that comment, any candid person sees really to belong to them. And in the same way as regards the Catholic Creed, though there is not so much to explain and account for. Not so much, for no one, I suppose, will deny that in the Fathers of the fourth century it is as fully developed, and as unanimously adopted, as it is in the fifth century; and, again, there had been no considerable doubts about any of its doctrines previously, as there were about the Epistle to the Hebrews or the Apocalypse: … And as the unanimity of the fifth century as regards the Canon, clears up and overcomes all previous differences, so the abundance of the fourth as to the Creed interprets, develops, and combines all that is recondite or partial, in previous centuries, as to doctrine, acting in a parallel way as a comment, not, indeed, as in the case of the Canon, upon a perplexed and disordered, but upon a concise text. In both cases, the after centuries contain but the termination and summing up of the testimony of the foregoing. (*TT* #85, Sep. 1838)

Christianity lay *beneath* the letter; that the letter slew those who for whatever cause went by it; that when Christ came, He shed a light on the sacred text and brought out its secret meaning. Now, is not this just the case I have been stating, as regards Catholic doctrines, or rather a more difficult case? The doctrines of the Church are not hidden so deep in the New Testament, as the Gospel doctrines are hidden in the Old; but they are hidden. (*TT* #85, Sep. 1838)

All systems, then, which live and are substantive, depend on some or other inward principle or doctrine, of which they are the development. They are not a fortuitous assemblage of atoms from without, but the expansion of a moral element from within. They cannot die a natural death till this moral element dies, though, of course, they, as all things below, may be overcome by violence. But they are indestructible, considered internally, while their informing principle continues; for it is their life. Within they have nothing of a self-destructive nature; everything is evolved from one and the same formula; part cannot quarrel with part, both being results or transformations of that one. Their parts cohere, not from any immediate junction or direct association, but because they all spring from a principle, and into that principle resolve. While their inward life remains, they repair their losses; if existing portions are cut off, they put out fresh branches. But when that life goes, they are no more; they have no being, they dissolve. However fair they may look for a time, whether state, nation, society, church, university, moral agent, they are dead; and if they in appearance continue, still are they but phantoms, kept together by extraneous influences acting for extraneous purposes. ('The Anglo-American Church,' *British Critic*, Oct. 1839; in *Ess.* i, sec. VIII)

Allowing the Church Catholic ever so much power over the faith, allowing that it may add what it will, provided it does not contradict what has been determined in former times, yet let us come to the plain question, Does the Church, according to Romanists, know more now than the Apostles knew? Their theory seems to be that the whole faith was present in the minds of the Apostles, nay, of all saints at all times, but in great measure as a matter of mere temper, feeling, and unconscious opinion, that is, implicitly, not in the way of exact statements and in an intellectual form. All men certainly hold a number of truths, and act on them, without knowing it; when a question is asked about them, then they are obliged to reflect what their opinion has ever been, and they bring before themselves and assent to doctrines which before were but latent within them … [T]he Roman Catholics, we suppose, would maintain that the Apostles were implicit Tridentines; that the Church held in the first age what she holds now; only that heresy, by raising questions, has led to her throwing her faith into dogmatic shape, and has served to precipitate truths which before were held in solution. ('Catholicity of the Anglican Church,' *British Critic*, Jan. 1840; in *Ess*. ii, sec. X)

[O]ur doctrines also, as those of the Trinity and Incarnation, are developments; so that it may in turn be asked of us, did the Apostles hold the Athanasian doctrine, or, on the other hand, do we know more than they? But we avow they *did* hold the Athanasian doctrine; they did hold those developments which afterwards were incorporated in the Church system. There is no paradox in maintaining of any individual in the Apostles' lifetime that he held them; for heresies arose while they were on earth, quite sufficient to lead to their holding and transmitting to the Church views as explicit and formal as those which were afterwards recognised and adopted in Councils and fixed in creeds; not to say that a mystery naturally leads the mind of itself, without external stimulus, to trace it to its ultimate points. ('Catholicity of the Anglican Church,' *British Critic*, Jan. 1840; in *Ess*. ii, sec. X)

I have said enough to explain St. Paul's statement in the text, that 'old things are passed away,' and 'all things new' under the Gospel. By all things being '*new*' is meant that they are *renewed*; by 'old things *passing away*' is meant that they are *changed*. The substance remains; the form, mode, quality, and circumstances are different and more excellent. Religion has still forms, ordinances, precepts, mysteries, duties, assemblies, festivals, and temples as of old time; but, whereas all these were dead and carnal before, now, since Christ came, they have a life in them. He has brought life to the world; He has given life to religion; He has made everything spiritual and true by His touch, full of virtue, full of grace, full of power: so that ordinances, works, forms, which before were unprofitable, now, by the inward meritorious influence of His blood imparted to them, avail for our salvation. (*PS* v, Sermon 12: 'The New Works of the Gospel,' 26 January 1840)

But every existing establishment, whatever be its nature, is a *fact*, a thing *sui simile*, which cannot be resolved into any one principle, nor can be defended and built up upon one idea. Its position is the result of a long history, which has moulded it and stationed it in the form and place which characterize it. It has grown into what it is by the influence of a number of concurrent causes in time past. (*VM* ii, X. 'Letter to Richard, Lord Bishop of Oxford, in Explanation of Tract 90,' 1841)

The history of the Old Dispensation affords us a remarkable confirmation of what I have been arguing from these words; for in the time of the Law there was an increase of religious knowledge by fresh revelations. From the time of Samuel especially to the time of Malachi, the Church was bid look forward for a growing illumination, which, though not necessary for religious obedience, subserved the establishment of religious comfort. Now, I wish you to observe how careful the inspired prophets of Israel are to prevent any kind of disrespect being shown to the memory of former times, on account of that increase of religious knowledge with which the later ages were favoured; and if such reverence for the past were a duty among the Jews when the Saviour was still to come, much more is it the duty of Christians, who expect no new revelation, and who, though they look forward in hope, yet see the future only in the mirror of times and persons past, who (in the Angel's words) 'wait for that same Jesus: ... so to come in like manner as they saw Him go into heaven.' (*PS* vii, Sermon 18: 'Steadfastness in Old Paths,' 1842)

Consider again the state of Israel in Babylon; or its state when Christ came, partly settled in a part of Canaan, partly in Alexandria, with a rival temple, and partly scattered all over the face of the earth, like a mist, or like the drops of rain. And let it be observed, as this last instance suggests, its change when Christ came, from a local into a Catholic form, was not abrupt but gradual. What was first a dispersion, became a diffusion; during the last centuries of Judaism, the Church was in great measure Catholic already. Besides Jerusalem and Alexandria, it had a number of centres or metropolitan posts scattered over the Roman empire, as we read in the book of Acts; and about these were collected a number of proselytes from the heathen, waiting for the promised Paraclete to make the dead bones live. And, in matter of fact, these centres did become the first channels of the Gospel, and starting-points of its propagation, as we learn from the same inspired history. Such changes, however, whether gradual or not, do not interfere with the Church's being considered one and the same under them. How different is a human being in different stages of his existence! how different all his states here below from that body which shall be! yet the same body shall rise which dies, though it be made a spiritual body. It is no objection, then, rather it gives countenance, to the notion of the identity of the Jewish Church with the Christian, that it is so different from it; for the Jewish Church was at various eras very different from itself; and worms of the earth at length gain wings, yet are the same, and man dies in corruption, and rises incorrupt, yet without losing his original body ... [I]f the Gospel may be considered as a new state or condition of the Law, surely it is not stranger or harsher to consider the Church of the Gospel as a continuation of the Church of the Law. (*SD*, Sermon 14: 'The Christian Church a Continuation of the Jewish,' 13 November 1842)

The Gospel has not put aside, it has incorporated into itself, the revelations which went before it. It avails itself of the Old Testament, as a great gift to Christian as well as to Jew. It does not dispense with it, but it dispenses it. Persons sometimes urge that there is no code of duty in the New Testament, no ceremonial, no rules for Church polity. Certainly not; they are unnecessary; they are already given in the Old. Why should the Old Testament be retained in the Christian Church, but to be used?

There are we to look for our forms, our rites, our polity; only illustrated, tempered, spiritualized, by the Gospel. The precepts remain; the observance of them is changed. This, I say, is what many persons are slow to understand. They think the Old Testament must be supposed to be our rule directly and literally, or not at all; and since we cannot put ourselves under it absolutely and without explanation, they conclude that in no sense it is binding on us; but surely there is such a thing as the *application* of Scripture; this is no very difficult or strange idea. (*SD*, Sermon 15: 'The Principle of Continuity Between the Jewish and Christian Churches,' 20 November 1842)

Mary's faith did not end in a mere acquiescence in Divine providences and revelations: as the text informs us, she 'pondered' them. When the shepherds came, and told of the vision of Angels which they had seen at the time of the Nativity, and how one of them announced that the Infant in her arms was 'the Saviour, which is Christ the Lord,' while others did but wonder, 'Mary kept all these things, and pondered them in her heart' [Lk 2:19]. Again, when her Son and Saviour had come to the age of twelve years, and had left her for awhile for His Father's service, and had been found, to her surprise, in the Temple, amid the doctors, both hearing them and asking them questions, and had, on her addressing Him, vouchsafed to justify His conduct, we are told, 'His mother kept all these sayings in her heart.' ... Thus St. Mary is our pattern of Faith, both in the reception and in the study of Divine Truth. She does not think it enough to accept, she dwells upon it; not enough to possess, she uses it; not enough to assent, she develops it; not enough to submit the Reason, she reasons upon it; not indeed reasoning first, and believing afterwards, with Zacharias, yet first believing without reasoning, next from love and reverence, reasoning after believing. And thus she symbolizes to us, not only the faith of the unlearned, but of the doctors of the Church also, who have to investigate, and weigh, and define, as well as to profess the Gospel; to draw the line between truth and heresy; to anticipate or remedy the various aberrations of wrong reason; to combat pride and recklessness with their own arms; and thus to triumph over the sophist and the innovator. (*US*, Sermon 15: 'The Theory of Developments in Religious Doctrine,' Feb. 1843)

Let us ... descend to the history of the formation of any Catholic dogma. What a remarkable sight it is, as almost all unprejudiced persons will admit, to trace the course of the controversy, from its first disorders to its exact and determinate issue. Full of deep interest, to see how the great idea takes hold of a thousand minds by its living force, and will not be ruled or stinted, but is 'like a burning fire,' as the Prophet speaks, 'shut up' within them, till they are 'weary of forbearing, and cannot stay,' and grows in them, and at length is born through them, perhaps in a long course of years, and even successive generations; so that the doctrine may rather be said to use the minds of Christians, than to be used by them. Wonderful it is, to see with what effort, hesitation, suspense, interruption, — with how many swayings to the right and to the left — with how many reverses, yet with what certainty of advance, with what precision in its march, and with what ultimate completeness, it has been evolved; till the whole truth 'self-balanced on its centre hung,' part answering to part, one, absolute, integral, indissoluble, while the world lasts! Wonderful, to see how heresy has but thrown that idea into fresh forms, and drawn out from it farther developments. (*US*, Sermon 15: 'The Theory of Developments in Religious Doctrine,' Feb. 1843)

1. I am far more certain (according to the Fathers) that we *are* in a state of culpable separation, *than* that developments do *not* exist under the Gospel, and that the Roman developments are not the true ones. 2. I am far more certain, that *our* (modern) doctrines are wrong, *than* that the *Roman* (modern) doctrines are wrong. 3. Granting that the Roman (special) doctrines are not found drawn out in the early Church, yet I think there is sufficient trace of them in it, to recommend and prove them, *on the hypothesis* of the Church having a divine guidance, though not sufficient to prove them by itself. So that the question simply turns on the nature of the promise of the Spirit, made to the Church. 4. The proof of the Roman (modern) doctrine is as strong (or stronger) in Antiquity, as that of certain doctrines which both we and Romans hold: e.g. there is more of evidence in Antiquity for the necessity of Unity, than for the Apostolical Succession; for the Supremacy of the See of Rome, than for the Presence in the Eucharist; for the practice of Invocation, than for certain books in

the present Canon of Scripture, &c. &c. 5. The analogy of the Old Testament, and also of the New, leads to the acknowledgment of doctrinal developments. (*Apo.*, ch. 4; Letter of 14 July 1844)

The following Essay is directed towards a solution of the difficulty which has been stated, — the difficulty, as far as it exists, which lies in the way of our using in controversy the testimony of our most natural informant concerning the doctrine and worship of Christianity, viz., the history of eighteen hundred years. The view on which it is written has at all times, perhaps, been implicitly adopted by theologians, and, I believe, has recently been illustrated by several distinguished writers of the continent, such as De Maistre and Möhler: viz., that the increase and expansion of the Christian Creed and Ritual, and the variations which have attended the process in the case of individual writers and Churches, are the necessary attendants on any philosophy or polity which takes possession of the intellect and heart, and has had any wide or extended dominion; that, from the nature of the human mind, time is necessary for the full comprehension and perfection of great ideas; and that the highest and most wonderful truths, though communicated to the world once for all by inspired teachers, could not be comprehended all at once by the recipients, but, as being received and transmitted by minds not inspired and through media which were human, have required only the longer time and deeper thought for their full elucidation. This may be called the *Theory of Development of Doctrine;* and, before proceeding to treat of it, one remark may be in place. It is undoubtedly an hypothesis to account for a difficulty; but such too are the various explanations given by astronomers from Ptolemy to Newton of the apparent motions of the heavenly bodies, and it is as unphilosophical on that account to object to the one as to object to the other. Nor is it more reasonable to express surprise, that at this time of day a theory is necessary, granting for argument's sake that the theory is novel, than to have directed a similar wonder in disparagement of the theory of gravitation, or the Plutonian theory in geology. Doubtless, the theory of the Secret and the theory of doctrinal Developments are expedients, and so is the dictum of Vincentius; so is the art of grammar or the use of the quadrant; it is an expedient to enable us to solve what has now become a necessary and an anxious problem … An argument is needed, unless Christianity is to abandon the province of argument; and those who find fault with the explanation here offered of its historical phenomena will find it their duty to provide one for themselves. (*Dev.*, Part I: Introduction)

As to Christianity, supposing the truths of which it consists to admit of development, that development will be one or other of the last five kinds. Taking the Incarnation as its central doctrine, the Episcopate, as taught by St. Ignatius, will be an instance of political development, the *Theotokos* of logical, the determination of the date of our Lord's birth of historical, the Holy Eucharist of moral, and the Athanasian Creed of metaphysical. (*Dev.*, Part I: ch. 1)

No one doctrine can be named which starts complete at first, and gains nothing afterwards from the investigations of faith and the attacks of heresy. (*Dev.*, Part I: ch. 2, sec. 1)

In one of our Lord's parables 'the Kingdom of Heaven' is even compared to 'a grain of mustard-seed, which a man took and hid in his field; which indeed is the least of all seeds, but when it is grown it is the greatest among herbs, and becometh a tree,' and, as St. Mark words it, 'shooteth out great branches, so that the birds of the air come and lodge in the branches thereof.' And again, in the same chapter of St. Mark, 'So is the kingdom of God, as if a man should cast seed into the ground, and should sleep, and rise night and day, and the seed should spring and grow up, he knoweth not how; for the earth bringeth forth fruit of herself.' Here an internal element of life, whether principle or doctrine, is spoken of rather than any mere external manifestation; and it is observable that the spontaneous, as well as the gradual, character of the growth is intimated. This description of the process corresponds to what has been above observed respecting development, viz., that it is not an effect of wishing and resolving, or of forced enthusiasm, or of any mechanism of reasoning, or of any mere subtlety of intellect; but comes of its own innate power of expansion within the mind in its season, though with the use of reflection and argument and original thought, more or less as it may happen, with a dependence on the ethical growth of the mind itself, and with a reflex influence upon it. Again, the Parable of the Leaven describes the development of doctrine in another respect, in its active, engrossing, and interpenetrating power. From the necessity, then, of the case, from the history of all sects and parties in religion, and from the analogy and example of Scripture, we may fairly conclude that Christian doctrine admits of formal, legitimate, and true developments, that is, of developments contemplated by its Divine Author. (*Dev.*, Part I: ch. 2, sec. 1)

[I]n like manner, Christians were not likely to entertain the question of the abstract allowableness of images in the Catholic ritual, with the actual superstitions and immoralities of paganism before their eyes. Nor were they likely to determine the place of the Blessed Mary in our reverence, before they had duly secured, in the affections of the faithful, the supreme glory and worship of God Incarnate, her Eternal Lord and Son … Nor could ecclesiastical liberty be asserted, till it had been assailed. Nor would a Pope arise, but in proportion as the Church was consolidated. Nor would monachism be needed, while martyrdoms were in progress … nor St. Irenaenus denounce the Protestant view of Justification, nor St. Cyprian draw up a theory of toleration. There is 'a time for every purpose under the heaven;' 'a time to keep silence and a time to speak.' (*Dev.*, Part I: ch. 3, sec. 2)

I venture to set down seven Notes of varying cogency, independence and applicability, to discriminate healthy developments of an idea from its state of corruption and decay, as follows: — There is no corruption if it retains one and the same type, the same principles, the same organisation; if its beginnings anticipate its subsequent phases, and its later phenomena protect and subserve its earlier; if it has a power of assimilation and revival, and a vigorous action from first to last. (*Dev.*, Part II: ch. 5)

Preservation of type. This is readily suggested by the analogy of physical growth, which is such that the parts and proportions of the developed form, however altered, correspond to those which belong to its rudiments. The adult animal has the same make, as it had on its birth; young birds do not grow into fishes, nor does the child degenerate into the brute, wild or domestic, of which he is by inheritance lord. Vincentius of Lerins adopts this illustration in distinct reference to Christian doctrine. 'Let the soul's religion,' he says, 'imitate the law of the body, which, as years go on, developes indeed and opens out its due proportions, and yet remains identically what it was. Small are a baby's limbs, a youth's are larger, yet they are the same.' ... this unity of type, characteristic as it is of faithful developments, must not be pressed to the extent of denying all variation, nay, considerable alteration of proportion and relation, as time goes on, in the parts or aspects of an idea. Great changes in outward appearance and internal harmony occur in the instance of the animal creation itself. The fledged bird differs much from its rudimental form in the egg. The butterfly is the development, but not in any sense the image, of the grub. (*Dev.*, Part II: ch. 5, sec. 1)

Continuity of principles. Pagans may have, heretics cannot have, the same principles as Catholics; if the latter have the same, they are not real heretics, but in ignorance. Principle is a better test of heresy than doctrine. Heretics are true to their principles, but change to and fro, backwards and forwards, in opinion; for very opposite doctrines may be exemplifications of the same principle. Thus the Antiochenes and other heretics sometimes were Arians, sometimes Sabellians, sometimes Nestorians, sometimes Monophysites, as if at random, from fidelity to their common principle, that there is no mystery in theology. Thus Calvinists become Unitarians from the principle of private judgment. The doctrines of heresy are accidents and soon run to an end; its principles are everlasting ... Protestantism, viewed in its more Catholic aspect, is doctrine without active principle; viewed in its heretical, it is active principle without doctrine. Many of its speakers, for instance, use eloquent and glowing language about the Church and its characteristics: some of them do not realize what they say, but use high words and general statements about 'the faith,' and 'primitive truth,' and 'schism,' and 'heresy,' to which they attach no definite meaning; while others speak of 'unity,' 'universality,' and 'Catholicity,' and use the words in their own sense and for their own ideas. (*Dev.*, Part II: ch. 5, sec. 2)

Power of assimilation. In the physical world, whatever has life is characterized by growth, so that in no respect to grow is to cease to live. It grows by taking into its own substance external materials; and this absorption or assimilation is completed when the materials appropriated come to belong to it or enter into its unity. Two things cannot become one, except there be a power of assimilation in one or the other ... Thus, a power of development is a proof of life, not only in its essay, but especially in its success; for a mere formula either does not expand or is shattered in expanding. A living idea becomes many, yet remains one ... The idea never was that throve and lasted, yet, like mathematical truth, incorporated nothing from external sources. So far from the fact of such incorporation implying corruption, as is sometimes supposed, development is a process of incorporation. (*Dev.*, Part II: ch. 5, sec. 3)

Logical sequence. An idea under one or other of its aspects grows in the mind by remaining there; it becomes familiar and distinct, and is viewed in its relations; it leads to other aspects, and these again to others, subtle, recondite, original, according to the character, intellectual and moral, of the recipient; and thus a body of thought is gradually formed without his recognising what is going on within him. And all this while, or at least from time to time, external circumstances elicit into formal statement the thoughts which are coming into being in the depths of his mind; and soon he has to begin to defend them; and then again a further process must take place, of analyzing his statements and ascertaining their dependence one on another. And thus he is led to regard as consequences, and to trace to principles, what hitherto he has discerned by a moral perception and adopted on sympathy; and logic is brought in to arrange and inculcate what no science was employed in gaining ... Thus, the holy Apostles would without words know all the truths concerning the high doctrines of theology, which controversialists after them have piously and charitably reduced to formulæ, and developed through argument. Thus, St. Justin or St. Irenaeus might be without any digested ideas of Purgatory or Original Sin, yet have an intense feeling, which they had not defined or located, both of the fault of our first nature and the responsibilities of our nature regenerate ... A doctrine, then, professed in its mature years by a philosophy or religion, is likely to be a true development, not a corruption, in proportion as it seems to be the *logical issue* of its original teaching. (*Dev.*, Part II: ch. 5, sec. 4)

Anticipation of its future. Since, when an idea is living, that is, influential and effective, it is sure to develope according to its own nature, and the tendencies, which are carried out on the long run, may under favourable circumstances show themselves early as well as late, and logic is the same in all ages, instances of a development which is to come, though vague and isolated, may occur from the very first, though a lapse of time be necessary to bring them to perfection. And since developments are in great measure only aspects of the idea from which they proceed, and all of them are natural consequences of it, it is often a matter of accident in what order they are carried out in individual minds; and it is in no wise strange that here and there definite specimens of advanced teaching should very early occur, which in the historical course are not found till a late day. The fact, then, of such early or recurring intimations of tendencies which afterwards are fully realized, is a sort of evidence that those later and more systematic fulfilments are only in accordance with the original idea ... Another evidence, then, of the faithfulness of an ultimate development is its definite anticipation at an early period in the history of the idea to which it belongs. (*Dev.*, Part II: ch. 5, sec. 5)

Conservative action upon its past. As developments which are preceded by definite indications have a fair presumption in their favour, so those which do but contradict and reverse the course of doctrine which has been developed before them, and out of which they spring, are certainly corrupt; for a corruption is a development in that very stage in which it ceases to illustrate, and begins to disturb, the acquisitions gained in its previous history ... A true development, then, may be described as one which is conservative of the course of antecedent developments being really those antecedents and something besides them: it is an addition which illustrates, not obscures, corroborates, not corrects, the body of thought from which it proceeds; and this is its characteristic as contrasted with a corruption ... as regards the Jewish Law, our Lord said that He came 'not to destroy, but to fulfil.' (*Dev.*, Part II: ch. 5, sec. 6)

Chronic vigour. Since the corruption of an idea, as far as the appearance goes, is a sort of accident or affection of its development, being the end of a course, and a transition-state leading to a crisis, it is, as has been observed above, a brief and rapid process. While ideas live in men's minds, they are ever enlarging into fuller development: they will not be stationary in their corruption any more than before it; and dissolution is that further state to which corruption tends. Corruption cannot, therefore, be of long standing; and thus *duration* is another test of a faithful development … The course of heresies is always short; it is an intermediate state between life and death, or what is like death; or, if it does not result in death, it is resolved into some new, perhaps opposite, course of error, which lays no claim to be connected with it. And in this way indeed, but in this way only, an heretical principle will continue in life many years, first running one way, then another … while a corruption is distinguished from decay by its energetic action, it is distinguished from a development by its *transitory character*. (*Dev.*, Part II: ch. 5, sec. 7)

[I]f it be true that the principles of the later Church are the same as those of the earlier, then, whatever are the variations of belief between the two periods, the later in reality agrees more than it differs with the earlier, for principles are responsible for doctrines. Hence they who assert that the modern Roman system is the corruption of primitive theology are forced to discover some difference of principle between the one and the other; for instance, that the right of private judgment was secured to the early Church and has been lost to the later, or, again, that the later Church rationalizes and the earlier went by faith. (*Dev.*, Part II: ch. 7, sec. 6)

Supposing then the so-called Catholic doctrines and practices are true and legitimate developments, and not corruptions, we may expect from the force of logic to find instances of them in the first centuries. And this I conceive to be the case: the records indeed of those times are scanty, and we have little means of determining what daily Christian life then was: we know little of the thoughts, and the prayers, and the meditations, and the discourses of the early disciples of Christ, at a time when these professed developments were not recognised and duly located in the theological system; yet it appears, even from what remains, that the atmosphere of the Church was, as it were, charged with them from the first, and delivered itself of them from time to time, in this way or that, in various places and persons, as occasion elicited them, testifying the presence of a vast body of thought within it, which one day would take shape and position. (*Dev.*, Part II: ch. 10)

[I]n all fair reasoning, when no great existing objections or suspicions are in the way, we should take the later state of the Church as the interpretation of the words and deeds of the earlier. Thus the fulfilment of a prophecy interprets the wording in which it is conveyed—the event is made the legitimate comment upon the text. As when we take the decision of Nicaea as the true measure of the words of the Ante-Nicene Fathers, so we ought to take other decisions on the question of the Papacy as the rule and standard of the variable acts and words (if so) which preceded them. (*LD* xi, 238-239; Letter to Lord Adare, 31 August 1846)

I have no reason to be displeased with the theory, as far as any thing I have learned here is concerned—and I still hold it, under submission to the Church of course. I may have used words in my book which are inadvisable, made extreme statements, or in matters of detail scraped against definitions of the Church, but this is a very different thing from an error of theory. (*LD* xii, 128; Letter to John Walker, 2 November 1847)

[T]here are many truths which have remained implicit, (or in less theological language, undeveloped) for ages. (*LD* xii, 333; Letter to Catherine Ward, 18 November 1848)

It is well known that, though the creed of the Church has been one and the same from the beginning, yet it has been so deeply lodged in her bosom as to be held by individuals more or less implicitly, instead of being delivered from the first in those special statements, or what are called definitions, under which it is now presented to us, and which preclude mistake or ignorance. These definitions, which are but the expression of portions of the one dogma which has ever been received by the Church, are the work of time; they have grown to their present shape and number in the course of eighteen centuries, under the exigency of successive events, such as heresies and the like, and they may of course receive still further additions as time goes on. Now this process of doctrinal development, as you might suppose, is not of an accidental or random character; it is conducted upon laws, as everything else which comes from God; and the study of its laws and of its exhibition, or, in other words, the science and history of the formation of theology, was a subject which had interested me more than anything else from the time I first began to read the Fathers, and which had engaged my attention in a special way. Now it was gradually brought home to me, in the course of my reading, so gradually, that I cannot trace the steps of my conviction, that the decrees of later Councils, or what Anglicans call the Roman corruptions, were but instances of that very same doctrinal law which was to be found in the history of the early Church; and that in the sense in which the dogmatic truth of the prerogatives of the Blessed Virgin may be said, in the lapse of centuries, to have grown upon the consciousness of the faithful, in that same sense did, in the first age, the mystery of the Blessed Trinity also gradually shine out and manifest itself more and more completely before their minds. Here was at once an answer to the objections urged by Anglicans against the present teaching of Rome; and not only an answer to objections, but a positive argument in its favour; for the immutability and uninterrupted action of the laws in question throughout the course of Church history is a plain note of identity between the Catholic Church of the first ages and that which now goes by that name. (*Dif.* i, Lecture 12)

Language then requires to be refashioned even for sciences which are based on the senses and the reason; but much more will this be the case, when we are concerned with subject-matters, of which, in our present state, we cannot possibly form any complete or consistent conception, such as the Catholic doctrines of the Trinity and Incarnation. Since they are from the nature of the case above our intellectual reach, and were unknown till the preaching of Christianity, they required on their first promulgation new words, or words used in new senses, for their due enunciation; and, since these were not definitely supplied by Scripture or by tradition, nor, for centuries, by ecclesiastical authority, variety in the use, and confusion in the apprehension of them, were unavoidable in the interval ... The very confidence which would be felt by Christians in general that Apostolic truth would never fail, ... would indispose them to define it, till definition became an imperative duty. (*Atlantis*, July 1858; *Ari.*, App., Note 4)

As to development of doctrine and action in the Church I should hold to Vincentius's account of it, who compares it to bodily growth. (*Ward* i, 639 [Appendix to Ch. 18]; Letter to Lord Acton, 19 July 1862)

[T]he principle of development of doctrine in the Christian Church ... is certainly recognised in the *Treatise of Vincent of Lerins*, which has so often been taken as the basis of Anglicanism ... I saw that the principle of development not only accounted for certain facts, but was in itself a remarkable philosophical phenomenon, giving a character to the whole course of Christian thought. It was discernible from the first years of the Catholic teaching up to the present day, and gave to that teaching a unity and individuality. It served as a sort of test, which the Anglican could not exhibit, that modern Rome was in truth ancient Antioch, Alexandria, and Constantinople, just as a mathematical curve has its own law and expression. (*Apo.*, ch. 4)

[A]s to my hypothesis of Doctrinal Development, I am sorry to find you do not look upon it with friendly eyes; though how, without its aid, you can maintain the doctrines of the Holy Trinity and Incarnation, and others which you hold, I cannot understand. You consider my principle may be the means, in time to come, of introducing into our Creed, as portions of the necessary Catholic faith, the Infallibility of the Pope, and various opinions, pious or profane, as it may be, about our Blessed Lady. I hope to remove your anxiety as to the character of these consequences. (*Dif.* ii, Letter to Pusey, ch. 2, 1865)

Certainly we all hold the '*Quod semper, quod ubique*' &c., as much as we ever did, as much as Anglicans do. It is a great and general principle, involving of course a certain range of variation in the fulness in which it has been, here and there, now and then, received and exemplified. For instance, the eternal pre-existence of the Divine Son was taught far more consistently after the Council of Nicaea in A.D. 325, than before it, and in some cases, as, for instance, the validity of baptisms by heretics, and the like, there have been remarkable differences of opinion; but the Rule is a great and useful one on the whole. There is no rule, against which exceptions cannot be brought. As to the question of development in the doctrines of the *depositum*, that is provided for in the Rule expressly. You know the Rule comes from Vincentius Lerinensis, who wrote at the end (I think) of the 4th century, and who illustrates and enforces it with great eloquence. He says (I use Charles Marriott's, as I think it is, translation), 'Let the religion of our souls imitate the nature of our bodies, which, although with process of time they develop and unfold their proportions, yet remain the same that they were. The limits of infants be small, of young men great, yet not divers, but the same. No new thing doth come forth in old men, which before had not *lain hid* in them, being children. The Christian doctrine must follow these laws of increasing.' (*Ward* ii, 377; Letter to Mrs. William Froude, March 1871)

The hypothesis about the *depositum fidei* in which I gradually acquiesced was that of doctrinal development, or the evolution of doctrines out of certain original and fixed *dogmatic truths*, which were held inviolate from first to last, and the more firmly established and illustrated by the very process of enlargement. (*Ess.* i, sec. VII, footnote 5 from 1871)

The Jewish history is the beginning of Christianity and of its evidences. The mustard seed. Abraham the mustard seed, the father of the faithful. God has founded one church, and that from the beginning. Slow, *as geological formations.* As we cherish a plant—in *the hothouse*, etc. (*SN*, 'Divine Judgments Continued,' 17 September 1871)

The Jews, then, God's people, and their Church God's Church. It was the Ark. The world lay in wickedness, and in the wrath of God, except that holy Church which God founded by Moses. The Pharisees its rulers … Indefectible, never to end. You will say it ended. No, it changed into the Christian Church. (*SN*, 'The Jewish and the Christian Church,' 28 June 1874)

It is not in the course of Providence that new wine should be poured into old bottles. What a change it was in Judaism to become Christianity; it took centuries—and witness what anxious longing holy men felt from age to age that the great change should be accomplished in the birth of the Redeemer. (*LD* xxxii, 351; Letter to Augustus Craven, 13 April 1875)

What has been said applies also to those other truths, with which Ratiocination has more to do than History, which are sometimes called developments of Christian doctrine, truths which are not upon the surface of the Apostolic *depositum*—that is, the legacy of Revelation,—but which from time to time are brought into form by theologians, and sometimes have been proposed to the faithful by the Church, as direct objects of faith. No Catholic would hold that they ought to be logically deduced in their fulness and exactness from the belief of the first centuries, but only this,—that, on the assumption of the Infallibility of the Church (which will overcome every objection except a contradiction in thought), there is nothing greatly to try the reason in such difficulties as occur in reconciling those evolved doctrines with the teaching of the ancient Fathers; such development being evidently the new form, explanation, transformation, or carrying out of what in substance was held from the first, what the Apostles said, but have not recorded in writing, or would necessarily have said under our circumstances, or if they had been asked, or in view of certain uprisings of error, and in that sense being really portions of the legacy of truth, of which the Church, in all her members, but especially in her hierarchy, is the divinely appointed trustee ... As to the ecclesiastical Acts of 1854 and 1870, I think with Mr. Gladstone that the principle of doctrinal development, and that of authority, have never in the proceedings of the Church been so freely and largely used as in the Definitions then promulgated to the faithful; but I deny that at either time the testimony of history was repudiated or perverted. (*Dif.* ii, Letter to the Duke of Norfolk, ch. 8, 1875)

The answer to this is an exposition of the doctrine of the growth and development in the Catholic mind, as time goes on, of the Apostolic *depositum*. It is difficult for any one to deny that there are points of doctrine on which the Church is clearer now than in the first age. We are not the only parties who maintain this; our opponents maintain it also, in their own creed. Will any Anglican deny that (say) Dr. Pusey has a more exact, a truer view of the '*Filioque*' than Theodoret or St. John Damascene? Will any Protestant deny that Luther ... saw Gospel truth with a luminousness and assurance which, they consider, was not enjoyed by St. Basil, St. Ambrose, and St. Chrysostom? (VM i, Lecture 2; footnote 21 from 1877)

The following pages were not in the first instance written to prove the divinity of the Catholic Religion, though ultimately they furnish a positive argument in its behalf, but to explain certain difficulties in its history, felt before now by the author himself, and commonly insisted on by Protestants in controversy, as serving to blunt the force of its *primâ facie* and general claims on our recognition. However beautiful and promising that Religion is in theory, its history, we are told, is its best refutation; the inconsistencies, found age after age in its teaching, being as patent as the simultaneous contrarieties of religious opinion manifest in the High, Low, and Broad branches of the Church of England. In reply to this specious objection, it is maintained in this Essay that, granting that some large variations of teaching in its long course of 1800 years exist, nevertheless, these, on examination, will be found to arise from the nature of the case, and to proceed on a law, and with a harmony and a definite drift, and with an analogy to Scripture revelations, which, instead of telling to their disadvantage, actually constitute an argument in their favour, as witnessing to a Superintending Providence and a great Design in the mode and in the circumstances of their occurrence. (*Dev.*, Preface to 2nd Edition, 2 February 1878)

As Newton's theory is the development of the laws of motion and of the first principles of geometry, so the corpus of Catholic doctrine is the outcome of Apostolic preaching. That corpus is the slow working out of conclusions by means of meditation, prayer, analytical thought, argument, controversy, through a thousand minds, through eighteen centuries and the whole of Europe. There has been a continual process in operation of correction, refinement, adjustment, revision, enucleation, etc, and this from the earliest times, as recognised by Vincent of Lerins … Our teaching, as well as yours, requires the preparation and exercise of long thought and of a thorough imbuing in religious ideas. (*LD* xxix, 117; Letter to William Froude, 29 April 1879)

Divorce

As to divorce, our Lord expressly says to the Pharisees, that 'Moses, by reason of the hardness of their hearts, permitted them to put away their wives;' yet this was a breach of a natural and primeval law, which was in force at the beginning as directly and unequivocally as the law against fratricide. (VM i, Preface to the Third Edition, 1877)

Doctrine; Dogma

The proof of reality in a doctrine is its holding together when actually attempted. (VM i, Introduction)

Religion cannot but be dogmatic; it ever has been. All religions have had doctrines; all have professed to carry with them benefits which could be enjoyed only on condition of believing the word of a supernatural informant, that is, of embracing some doctrines or other. And it is a mere idle sophistical theory, to suppose it can be otherwise. Destroy religion, make men give it up, if you can; but while it exists, it will profess an insight into the next world, it will profess important information about the next world, it will have points of faith, it will have dogmatism, it will have anathemas. Christianity, therefore, ever will be looked on, by the multitude, what it really is, as a rule of faith as well as of conduct. (*TT* #85, Sep. 1838)

[N]o one person, not even a Bishop *ex cathedrâ*, may at his mere word determine what doctrine shall be received and what not. He is bound to appeal to the established faith. He is bound conscientiously to try opinions by the established faith, and in doing so appeals to an Unseen Power. (VM ii, VI. 'On Froude's Statements Concerning the Holy Eucharist,' 1838)

The doctrines of original and actual sin, of Christ's Divinity and Atonement, and of Holy Baptism, are so vast, that no one can realize them without very complicated and profound feelings. Natural reason tells a man this, and that if he simply and genuinely believes the doctrines, he must have these feelings; and he professes to believe the doctrines absolutely, and therefore he professes the correspondent feelings. But in truth he perhaps does *not* really believe them absolutely, because such absolute belief is the work of long time, and therefore his profession of feeling outruns the real inward existence of feeling, or he becomes unreal … we all say the Creed, but who comprehends it fully? All we can hope is, that we are in the way to understand it; that we partly understand it; that we desire, pray, and strive to understand it more and more. Our Creed becomes a sort of prayer. (PS v, Sermon 3: 'Unreal Words,' 2 June 1839)

The absence, or partial absence, or incompleteness of dogmatic statements is no proof of the absence of impressions or implicit judgments, in the mind of the Church. Even centuries might pass without the formal expression of a truth, which had been all along the secret life of millions of faithful souls. (US, Sermon 15: 'The Theory of Developments in Religious Doctrine,' Feb. 1843)

The principle of *dogma,* that is, supernatural truths irrevocably committed to human language, imperfect because it is human, but definitive and necessary because given from above. (*Dev.*, Part II: ch. 7, sec. 1)

That there is a truth then; that there is one truth; that religious error is in itself of an immoral nature; that its maintainers, unless involuntarily such, are guilty in maintaining it; that it is to be dreaded; that the search for truth is not the gratification of curiosity; that its attainment has nothing of the excitement of a discovery; that the mind is below truth, not above it, and is bound, not to descant upon it, but to venerate it; that truth and falsehood are set before us for the trial of our hearts; that our choice is an awful giving forth of lots on which salvation or rejection is inscribed; that 'before all things it is necessary to hold the Catholic faith;' that 'he that would be saved must thus think,' and not otherwise; that, 'if thou criest after knowledge, and liftest up thy voice for understanding, if thou seekest her as silver, and searchest for her as for hid treasure, then shalt thou understand the fear of the Lord, and find the knowledge of God,'—this is the dogmatical principle, which has strength … What Conscience is in the history of an individual mind, such was the dogmatic principle in the history of Christianity. Both in the one case and the other, there is the gradual formation of a directing power out of a principle. (*Dev.*, Part II: ch. 8, sec. 1)

The de fide doctrine keeps us in the Church, but we are saved by something more than what is just necessary, as by works, so by thoughts, so by devotions. I conceive it is not *safe* to take the least possible sufficient in *itself* for salvation. We should *wish* at least to hold all that is received, though not *de fide*. (*LD* xii, 333; Letter to Catherine Ward, 18 November 1848)

I ended yesterday by saying that such writers as Veron and Chrissman and Denzinger, in laying down what was '*de fide*,' never pretended to exclude the principle that it was '*de fide*' because the Church taught it as such, and that she could teach other things as '*de fide*' by the same right as she taught what she now teaches as such. This is our broad principle, held by all of whatever shade of theological opinion. While it would be illogical not to give an inward assent to what she has already declared to be revealed, so it is pious and religious to believe, or at least not to doubt, what, though in fact not defined, still it is *probable* she might define as revealed, or that she *will* define, or seems to *consider* to be revealed … Doctrine is the *voice* of a religious body; its principles are of its *substance*. The principles may turn into doctrines by being defined; but they live as necessities before definition, and are the less likely to be defined, *because* they are so essential to life. (*Ward* ii, 220, 223; Letter to Edward B. Pusey, 23 March 1867)

A dogma is a proposition; it stands for a notion or for a thing; and to believe it is to give the assent of the mind to it, as it stands for the one or for the other. To give a real assent to it is an act of religion; to give a notional, is a theological act. It is discerned, rested in, and appropriated as a reality, by the religious imagination; it is held as a truth, by the theological intellect. (GA, Part I, ch. 5)

Every consideration, the fullest time should be given to those who have to make up their minds to hold an article of faith which is new to them. To take up at once such an article may be the act of a vigorous faith; but it may also be the act of a man who will believe anything because he believes nothing, and is ready to profess whatever his ecclesiastical, that is, his political party requires of him. There are too many high ecclesiastics in Italy and England, who think that to believe is as easy to obey. (LD xxv, 430; letter of late 1871; cited in Ker, 665)

[D]e fide, that is, a truth necessary to be believed, as being included in the original divine revelation, for those terms, revelation, depositum, dogma, and de fide, are correlatives ... so difficult a virtue is faith, even with the special grace of God, in proportion as the reason is exercised, so difficult is it to assent inwardly to propositions, verified to us neither by reason nor experience, but depending for their reception on the word of the Church as God's oracle, that she has ever shown the utmost care to contract, as far as possible, the range of truths and the sense of propositions, of which she demands this absolute reception ... She only speaks when it is necessary to speak; but hardly has she spoken out magisterially some great general principle, when she sets her theologians to work to explain her meaning in the concrete, by strict interpretation of its wording, by the illustration of its circumstances, and by the recognition of exceptions, in order to make it as tolerable as possible, and the least of a temptation, to self-willed, independent, or wrongly educated minds. (Dif. ii, Letter to the Duke of Norfolk, ch. 9, 1875)

[T]he Church, as divinely guided, has not formulated her doctrines all at once, but has taken in hand, first one, and then another. (Ath. ii, 'Angels')

From the first the Church had the power, by its divinely appointed representatives, to declare the truth upon such matters in the revealed message or gospel-tidings as from time to time came into controversy ... and these representatives, of course, were the Rulers of the Christian people who received, as a legacy, the depositum of doctrine from the Apostles, and by means of it, as need arose, exercised their office of teaching. Each Bishop was in his own place the Doctor Ecclesiæ for his people; there was an appeal, of course, from his decision to higher courts; to the Bishops of a province, of a nation, of a partriarchate, to the Roman Church, to the Holy See, as the case might be; and thus at length a final determination was arrived at, which in consequence was the formal teaching of the Church, and as far as it was direct and categorical, was, from the reason of the case, the Word of God. And being such, was certain, irreversible, obligatory on the inward belief and reception of all subjects of the Church, or what is called *de fide*. All this could not be otherwise if Christianity was to teach divine truth in contrast to the vague opinions and unstable conjectures of human philosophers and moralists, and if, as a plain consequence, it must have authoritative organs of teaching, and if true doctrines never can be false, but what is once true is always true. What the Church proclaims as true never can be put aside or altered, ... Decrees or definitions of Councils come to us as formal notices or memoranda, setting forth in writing what has ever been held orally or implicitly in the Church. (*Ath.* ii, 'Definitions')

I allow, then, that the Church, certainly, does 'insist,' when she speaks dogmatically, nay or rather she more than insists, she obliges; she obliges us to an internal assent to that which she proposes to us. So far I admit, or rather maintain. And I admit that she obliges us in a most forcible and effective manner, that is, by the penalty of forfeiting communion with her, if we refuse our internal assent to her word. We cannot be real Catholics, if we do not from our heart accept the matters which she puts forward as divine and true. This is plain. Next, to what does the Church oblige us? and what is her warrant for doing so? I answer, The matters which she can oblige us to accept with an internal assent are the matters contained in that Revelation of Truth, written or unwritten, which came to the world from our Lord and His Apostles; and this claim on our faith in her decisions as to the matter of that Revelation rests on her being the divinely appointed representative of the Apostles and the expounder of their words; so that whatever she categorically delivers about their formal acts or their writings or their teaching, is an Apostolic deliverance. I repeat, the only sense in which the Church 'insists' on any statement, Biblical or other, the only reason of her so insisting, is that that statement is part of the original Revelation, and therefore must be unconditionally accepted,—else, that Revelation is not, as a revelation, accepted at all. (*OIS*, sections 3- 4)

Doctrines and History

For myself, I would simply confess that no doctrine of the Church can be rigorously proved by historical evidence: but at the same time that no doctrine can be simply disproved by it. Historical evidence reaches a certain way, more or less, towards a proof of the Catholic doctrines; often nearly the whole way; sometimes it goes only as far as to point in their direction; sometimes there is only an absence of evidence for a conclusion contrary to them; nay, sometimes there is an apparent leaning of the evidence to a contrary conclusion, which has to be explained;—in all cases there is a margin left for the exercise of faith in the word of the Church. He who believes the dogmas of the Church only because he has reasoned them out of History, is scarcely a Catholic. It is the Church's dogmatic use of History in which the Catholic believes; and she uses other informants also, Scripture, tradition, the ecclesiastical sense ... and a subtle ratiocinative power, which in its origin is a divine gift. There is nothing of bondage or 'renunciation of mental freedom' in this view, any more than in the converts of the Apostles believing what the Apostles might preach to them or teach them out of Scripture ... it has ever been our teaching and our protest that, as there are doctrines which lie beyond the direct evidence of history, so there are doctrines which transcend the discoveries of reason; and, after all, whether they are more or less recommended to us by the one informant or the other, in all cases the immediate motive in the mind of a Catholic for his reception of them is, not that they are proved to him by

Reason or by History, but because Revelation has declared them by means of that high ecclesiastical *Magisterium* which is their legitimate exponent. (*Dif.* ii, Letter to the Duke of Norfolk, ch. 8, 1875)

Doctrines: 'Primary vs. Secondary'

Let us join issue then on this plain ground, whether or not the doctrine of 'the Church,' and the duty of obeying it, be laid down *in Scripture*. If so, it is no matter as regards our practice, whether the doctrine is primary or secondary, whether the duty is much or little insisted on. A Christian mind will aim at obeying the *whole* counsel and will of God; on the other hand, to those who are tempted arbitrarily to classify and select their duties, it is written, 'Whosoever shall break one of these least commandments, and shall teach men so, he shall be called the least in the kingdom of heaven.' (*TT* #11, 1833)

Many men, … would fain discern one or two doctrines in Scripture clearly, and no more; or some generalized form, yet not so much as a *body* of doctrine of any character. They consider that a certain message, consisting of one or two great and simple statements, makes up the whole of the Gospel, and that these *are* plainly in Scripture; accordingly, that he who holds and acts upon these is a Christian, and ought to be acknowledged by all to be such, for in holding these he holds all that is necessary. These statements they sometimes call the essentials, the peculiar doctrines, the vital doctrines, the leading idea, the great truths of the Gospel, — and all this sounds very well; but when we come to realize what is abstractedly so plausible, we are met by this insurmountable difficulty, that no great number of persons agree together what *are* these great truths, simple views, leading ideas, or peculiar doctrines of the Gospel. (*TT* #85, Sep. 1838)

Eden, Garden of

Adam's state in Eden seems to have been like the state of children now — in being simple, inartificial, inexperienced in evil, unreasoning, uncalculating, ignorant of the future, or (as men now speak) unintellectual. The tree of the knowledge of good and evil was kept from him. (*PS* v, Sermon 8: 'The State of Innocence,' 11 February 1838)

Election

[I]t is not (as I have many times urged) as if God did not give enough to all, but He gives more to one than another. Why, we know not ... In your own nature you are indefinitely removed from Him; it is only by super-abundant grace that you come near Him. He is not bound to give grace, but He does give it to all. And as He is not bound to give at all, He is not bound in measure. He has full right to give so much as He pleases, more to one than to another ... You do not know but this may be the last grace given you, if you resist it. (*SN*, 'On the Necessity of Securing Our Election,' 6 October 1850)

Eucharist

[I]t seems so very irreverent and profane a thing to say that our Saviour's own body is carnally present on the Altar. That He is in some mysterious incomprehensible way present I fully believe; but I do not know what way—and since that way is not told us in Scripture or the ancient fathers I dare pronounce nothing. (*POL*; Letter to Mrs. William Wilberforce, 17 November 1834)

The Roman Church, we know, considers that the elements of Bread and Wine depart or are taken away on Consecration, and that the Body and Blood of Christ take their place. This is the doctrine of Transubstantiation ... what neither our Church, nor any of the late maintainers of her doctrine on the subject, even dreams of holding. (*VM* ii, VI. 'On Froude's Statements Concerning the Holy Eucharist,' 1838)

[C]onsider our Lord's allusion to the Manna. Persons there are who explain our eating Christ's flesh and blood, as merely meaning our receiving a *pledge* of the *effects* of the *passion* of His Body and Blood; that is, in other words, of the *favour* of Almighty God: but how can Christ's giving us His Body and Blood mean merely His giving us a pledge of His favour? Surely these awful words are far too clear and precise to be thus carelessly treated. Christ, as I have said, surely would not use such definite terms, did He intend to convey an idea so far removed from their meaning and so easy of expression in simple language. Now it increases the force of this consideration to observe that the manna, to which He compares His gift, was not a figure of speech, but a something definite and particular, really given, really received. The manna was not simply health, or life, or God's favour, but a certain something which caused health, continued life, and betokened God's favour. The manna was a gift external to the Israelites, and external also to God's own judgment of them and resolve concerning them, a gift created by Him and partaken by His people. And Christ, in like manner, says, that He Himself is to us the *true* Manna, the *true* Bread that came down from heaven; not like that manna which could not save its partakers from death, but a life-imparting manna. What therefore the manna was in the wilderness, that surely is the spiritual manna in the Christian Church; the manna in the wilderness was a real gift, taken and eaten; so is the manna in the Church. It is not God's mercy, or favour, or imputation; it is not a state of grace, or the promise of eternal life, or the privileges of the Gospel, or the new covenant; it is not, much less, the doctrine of the Gospel, or faith in that doctrine; but it is what our Lord says it is, the gift of His own precious Body and Blood, really given, taken, and eaten as the manna might be. (*PS* vi, Sermon 11: 'The Eucharistic Presence,' 13 May 1838)

If obscurity of texts, for instance, about the grace of the Eucharist, be taken as a proof that no great benefit is therein given, it is an argument against there being any benefit. On the other hand, when certain passages are once interpreted to refer to it, the emphatic language used in those passages shows that the benefit is not small. We cannot say that the subject is unimportant, without saying that it is not mentioned at all. Either no gift is given in the Eucharist, or a great gift. If only the sixth chapter of St. John, for instance, does allude to it, it shows it is not merely an edifying rite, but an awful communication beyond words. Again, if the phrase, 'the communication of the Body of Christ,' used by St. Paul, means any gift, it means a great one. You may say, if you will, that it does not mean any gift at all, but means only a representation or figure of the communication; this I call explaining away, but still it is intelligible; but I do not see how, if it is to be taken literally as a real *communication* of something, it can be other than a communication of *His Body*. Again, though the Lord's Table be but twice called an Altar in Scripture, yet, granting that it *is* meant in those passages, it is there spoken of so solemnly, that it matters not though it be nowhere else spoken of. (*TT* #85, Sep. 1838)

Especially should we turn our thoughts to the consideration of Holy Communion, which in ancient times was used in many or most places to be celebrated daily, but now is celebrated commonly but three or four times a year. If that holy ordinance be the continual life of the Church, if the Jews 'did eat manna in the wilderness, and are dead,' but if any man 'eat of this bread he shall live for ever,' [John vi. 51.] is it wonderful that those of us who relinquish this Gospel gift, and rest in our faith for salvation, should fall back into a state like the Jews? Is it wonderful that we who are the children of promise should not enjoy the promise, seeing we will not accept it; seeing we think it enough to believe that we already have it, or though God offers it, will not put out our hand to take it? (*PS* vi, Sermon 13: 'Judaism of the Present Day,' 28 February 1841)

Without going so far as to speak of miracles, which I do not mean to do, yet really things have happened to me in connexion with the Most Holy Sacrament which quite prove to me it is a reality and not an empty show. (*LD* viii, 367; Letter to Miss Holmes, 6 December 1841)

If it is not presumptuous to say, I trust I have been favoured with a much more definite view of the (promised) inward evidence of the Presence of Christ with us in the Sacraments, now that the outward notes of it are being removed. And I am content to be with Moses in the desert or with Elijah excommunicated from the Temple. I say this, putting things at the strongest. (*Keb.*, 161; Letter to Samuel F. Wood, 13 December 1841)

People say that the Holy Communion obscures the doctrine of Gospel grace; that in obeying Christ's command we are forgetting His atonement; that in coming for His benefits, we tend to deny His all-sufficient merits. Can any imputation be more preposterous and wild, however estimable the persons may be who cast it? Certainly none. (*SD*, Sermon 9: 'Indulgence in Religious Privileges,' 1 May 1842)

[H]ow far the Anglican doctrine of the Eucharist depends on the times before the Nicene Council, how far on the times after it, may be gathered from the circumstance that, when a memorable Sermon [1878 footnote: Dr. Pusey's University Sermon of 1843] was published on the subject, out of about one hundred and forty passages from the Fathers appended in the notes, not in formal proof, but in general illustration, only fifteen were taken from Ante-nicene writers. (*Dev.*, Part I: Introduction)

[A]fter tasting the awful [i.e., awesome] delight of worshipping God in His Temple, how unspeakably cold is the idea of a Temple without that Divine Presence! One is tempted to say what is the meaning, what is the use of it? (*LD* xi, 131; Letter to Mrs. J. W. Bowden, 1 March 1846)

He [does] not [merely] present Himself before us as the object of worship, but God actually gives Himself to us to be received into our breasts … It is the life of our religion. (*SN*, 'Devotion to the Holy Eucharist,' 25 May 1856)

Next, there is the actual entrance of Himself, soul and body, and divinity, into the soul and body of every worshipper who comes to Him for the gift, a privilege more intimate than if we lived with Him during His long-past sojourn upon earth. (GA, Part II, ch. 10, sec. 2)

Eucharist: Communion in One Species

Now the question is, whether the doctrine here laid down, and carried into effect in the usage here sanctioned, was entertained by the early Church, and may be considered a just development of its principles and practices.

I answer that, starting with the presumption that the Council has ecclesiastical authority, which is the point here to be assumed, we shall find quite enough for its defence, and shall be satisfied to decide in the affirmative; we shall readily come to the conclusion that Communion under either kind is lawful, each kind conveying the full gift of the Sacrament. For instance, Scripture affords us two instances of what may reasonably be considered the administration of the form of Bread without that of Wine; viz., our Lord's own example towards the two disciples at Emmaus, and St. Paul's action at sea during the tempest. Moreover, St. Luke speaks of the first Christians as continuing in the '*breaking of bread,* and in prayer,' and of the first day of the week 'when they came together to *break bread.*' And again, in the sixth chapter of St. John, our Lord says absolutely, 'He that eateth Me, even he shall live by Me.' And, though He distinctly promises that we shall have it granted to us to drink His blood, as well as to eat His flesh; nevertheless, not a word does He say to signify that, as He is the Bread from heaven and the living Bread, so He is the heavenly, living Wine also. Again, St. Paul says that 'whosoever shall eat this Bread *or* drink this Cup of the Lord unworthily, shall be guilty of the Body and Blood of the Lord.' Many of the types of the Holy Eucharist, as far as they go, tend to the same conclusion; as the Manna, to which our Lord referred, the Paschal Lamb, the Shewbread, the sacrifices from which the blood was poured out, and the miracle of the loaves, which are figures of the bread alone; while the water from the rock, and the Blood from our Lord's side correspond to the wine without the bread. Others are representations of both kinds; as Melchizedek's feast, and Elijah's miracle of the meal and oil. And, further, it certainly was the custom in the early Church, under circumstances, to communicate in one kind, as we learn from St. Cyprian, St. Dionysius, St. Basil, St. Jerome, and others. For instance, St. Cyprian speaks of the communion of an infant under Wine, and of a woman under Bread; and St. Ambrose speaks of his brother in shipwreck folding the consecrated Bread in a handkerchief, and placing it round his neck; and the monks and hermits in the desert can hardly be supposed to have been ordinarily in possession of consecrated Wine as well as Bread. From the following letter of St. Basil, it appears that, not only the monks, but the whole laity of Egypt ordinarily communicated in Bread only ... Moreover, children, not to say infants, were at one time admitted to the Eucharist, at least to the Cup; on what authority are they now excluded from Cup and Bread also? St. Augustine considered the usage to be of Apostolical origin; and it continued in the West down to the twelfth century; it continues in the East among Greeks, Russo-Greeks, … and that on the ground of its almost universality in the primitive Church. Is it a greater innovation to suspend the Cup, than to cut off children from Communion altogether? Yet we acquiesce in the latter deprivation without a scruple. It is safer to acquiesce with, than without, an authority; safer with the belief that the Church is the pillar and ground of the truth, than with the belief that in so great a matter she is likely to err. (*Dev.*, Part I: ch. 4, sec. 1)

Catholics believe that 'totus Christus,' our Lord in body and blood, in soul, in divinity, in all that is included in His Personality, is present at once whether in the consecrated Host or in the Chalice. Indeed, how else can His Presence be spiritual? He who partakes of either species receives Him in His whole human nature as well as in His Divine; but His whole humanity is not present, if His blood be absent. And in fact communion was received from the first in one species only; in Scripture, Acts ii. 42, xx. 7; it is recognised as a custom by St. Cyprian and St. Dionysius in the ante-Nicene era, as well as by St. Basil, St. Jerome, and others later. It is known to have been in use in Pontus, Egypt, Africa, and Lombardy during the same period; perhaps also in Spain and Syria afterwards. Again: communion of children was almost universal in primitive times; it is still the custom in the Greek, Russian, and Monophysite Churches: is it then a less innovation to deny infant communion, as Anglicans do, than to deny communion in both species? (*TT* #71, footnote 1 of 1883)

Eucharistic Adoration and Benediction

You will have the blessedness of finding, when you enter a Church, a Treasure Unutterable—the Presence of the Eternal Word Incarnate—the Wisdom of the Father who, even when He had done His work, would not leave us, but rejoices still to humble Himself by abiding in mean places on earth for our sakes, while He reigns not the less on the right hand of God. (*LD* xii, 224; Letter to Mrs. William Froude, 16 June 1848)

[T]he Benediction of the Blessed Sacrament is one of the simplest rites of the Church. The priests enter and kneel down; one of them unlocks the Tabernacle, takes out the Blessed Sacrament, inserts it upright in a Monstrance of precious metal, and sets it in a conspicuous place above the altar, in the midst of lights, for all to see. The people then begin to sing; meanwhile the Priest twice offers incense to the King of heaven, before whom he is kneeling. Then he takes the Monstrance in his hands, and turning to the people, blesses them with the Most Holy, in the form of a cross, while the bell is sounded by one of the attendants to call attention to the ceremony. It is our Lord's solemn benediction of His people, as when He lifted up His hands over the children, or when He blessed His chosen ones when He ascended up from Mount Olivet. As sons might come before a parent before going to bed at night, so, once or twice a week the great Catholic family comes before the Eternal Father, after the bustle or toil of the day, and He smiles upon them, and sheds upon them the light of His countenance. It is a full accomplishment of what the Priest invoked upon the Israelites, 'The Lord bless thee and keep thee; the Lord show His face to thee and have mercy on thee; the Lord turn His countenance to thee and give thee peace.' Can there be a more touching rite, even in the judgment of those who do not believe in it? How many a man, not a Catholic, is moved, on seeing it, to say 'Oh, that I did but believe it!' when he sees the Priest take up the Fount of Mercy, and the people bent low in adoration! It is one of the most beautiful, natural, and soothing actions of the Church. (*PPC*, Lecture 6)

He is not past, He is present now. And though He is not seen, He is here. The same God who walked the water, who did miracles, etc., is in the Tabernacle. We come before Him, we speak to Him just as He was spoken to 1800 years ago, etc. (*SN*, 'Devotion to the Holy Eucharist,' 25 May 1856)

Wherefore, on the contrary, those spontaneous postures of devotion? why those unstudied gestures? why those abstracted countenances? why that heedlessness of the presence of others? why that absence of the shame-facedness which is so sovereign among professors of other creeds?

The spectator sees the effect; he cannot understand the cause of it. *Why is this simple earnestness of worship? we* have no difficulty in answering. It is because the Incarnate Saviour is present in the tabernacle; and then, when suddenly the hitherto silent church is, as it were, illuminated with the full piercing burst of voices from the whole congregation, it is because He now has gone up upon His throne over the altar, there to be adored. It is the visible Sign of the Son of Man, which thrills through the congregation, and makes them overflow with jubilation. (*SVO*, Sermon 3: 'Waiting for Christ,' preached on the 27th Sunday after Pentecost, 1856)

[A]ll the images that a Catholic church ever contained, all the Crucifixes at its Altars brought together, do not so affect its frequenters, as the lamp which betokens the presence or absence there of the Blessed Sacrament. (*Dif.* ii, Letter to Pusey, ch. 5, 1865)

We have a more wonderful, soothing time of silence than the Quakers. It is the silent half hour, spent, solus cum solo, before the Tabernacle. (*LD* xxx, 146-147; Letter to George T. Edwards, 8 November 1882)

Evil

When we hear speak of the wicked, we are apt to think that men of abandoned lives and unprincipled conduct, cruel, crafty, or profligate men, can alone be meant. This obtains almost universally; we think that evil, in any sufficient sense of the word, is something external to us, and at a distance. Thus in the case of children, when they hear of bad men and wicked men, they have no conception that evil can really be near them. They fancy, with a fearful curiosity, something which they have not seen, something foreign and monstrous, as if brought over the seas, or the production of another sphere; though, in truth, evil, and in its worst and most concentrated shape, is born with them, lives within them, is not subdued except by a supernatural gift from God, and is still in them, even when God's grace has brought it under. (*SD*, Sermon 7: 'Faith and the World,' 18 November 1838)

[I]f evil is not from Him, as assuredly it is not, this is because evil has no substance of its own, but is only the defect, excess, perversion, or corruption of that which has substance. (*IU*, Part I, Discourse 3: 'Bearing of Theology on Other Branches of Knowledge,' 1852)

Faith Alone (Protestant Notion of *Sola Fide*)

Still dwelling on the sin and misery of our unrenewed nature! still anxiously turning to the corruption and odiousness of the flesh, and refusing to contemplate the work of *the Spirit, lest* grace should fail of being exalted, *lest* glory should be given to man, *lest* Christ's work should be eclipsed! What a strange and capricious taste, to linger in the tomb, to sit down with Job among the ashes, by way of knowing him who has called us to light, to liberty, to perfection! How eccentric and how inconsequent, — how like, (unless sometimes seen in serious and well-judging men,) how like an aberration, to argue that to extol the work of the Spirit, must be to obscure the grace of Christ? Yet this is firmly held, — held as if in the spirit of confessors and martyrs, — held, *mordicus*, as a vital, sovereign, glorious, transporting truth, by the dominant ultra-Protestantism. Regenerate man must, to the day of his death, have in him nothing better than man unregenerate. In spite of the influences of grace, there must be nothing in him to admire, nothing to kindle the beholder, nothing to gaze upon, dwell on, or love, lest we glory in man. Grace must do nothing in him, or it is not duly upheld. The triumph of grace is to act entirely externally to him, not in him. To save and sanctify is not so great a work as to save and leave sinful. There must be nothing saintly, nothing super-human, nothing angelic in man regenerate, because man unregenerate is the child and slave of evil. Sin must be his sole characteristic, his sole theme, his sole experience ... Faith is to be made everything, as being the symbol and expression of this negative or degraded state; and charity, which is the fulfilling of the law, the end of the commandment, and the greatest of Christian graces, must not be directly contemplated or enforced at all, lest it be thereby implied that the Christian can be better with grace than he is without it. Such is supposed to be, ... spiritual religion, the religion in which the Spirit is supposed to do little or nothing for us. (Review of *The Life of Augustus Hermann Franké*, by H.E.F. Guerike, *British Critic*, vol. 21, July 1837)

But in truth, after all, men do not make up their mind from Scripture, though they profess to do so; they go by what they consider their inward experience. They fancy they have reasons in their own spiritual history for concluding that God has taught them the doctrine of justification without good works; and by these they go. They cannot get themselves to throw their minds upon Scripture; they argue from Scripture only to convince others, but you may defeat them again and again, without moving or distressing them; they are above you, for they do not depend on Scripture for their faith at all, but on what has taken place within them. (*Jfc.*, ch. 12)

[A] system of doctrine has risen up during the last three centuries, in which faith or spiritual-mindedness is contemplated and rested on as the end of religion instead of Christ. I do not mean to say that Christ is not mentioned as the Author of all good, but that stress is laid rather on the believing than on the Object of belief, on the comfort and persuasiveness of the doctrine rather than on the doctrine itself. And in this way religion is made to consist in contemplating ourselves instead of Christ; not simply in looking to Christ, but in ascertaining that we look to Christ, not in His Divinity and Atonement, but in our conversion and our faith in those truths ... The fault here spoken of is the giving to our 'experiences' a more prominent place in our thoughts than to the nature, attributes, and work of Him from whom they profess to come, — the insisting on them as a special point for the consideration of all who desire to be recognised as converted and elect. (*Jfc.*, ch. 13)

[T]he Church considers the doctrine of justification by faith only to be a *principle*, and the religion of the day takes it as *a rule of conduct*. (*Jfc.*, ch. 13)

Now justification by faith only is a principle, not a rule of conduct; and the popular mistake is to view it as a rule. This is where men go wrong. They think that the long and the short of religion is to have faith; that is the whole, faith independent of every other duty; a something which can exist in the mind by itself, and from which all other holy exercises follow (*Jfc.*, ch. 13)

True faith is what may be called colourless, like air or water; it is but the medium through which the soul sees Christ; and the soul as little really rests upon it and contemplates it, as the eye can see the air. When, then, men are bent on holding it (as it were) in their hands, curiously inspecting, analyzing, and so aiming at it, they are obliged to colour and thicken it, that it may be seen and touched. That is, they substitute for it something or other, a feeling notion, sentiment, conviction, or act of reason, which they may hang over, and doat upon. They rather aim at experiences (as they are called) within them, than at Him that is without them. They are led to enlarge upon the signs of conversion, the variations of their feelings, their aspirations and longings, and to tell all this to others; — to tell others how they fear, and hope, and sin, and rejoice, and renounce themselves, and rest in Christ only; how conscious they are that their best deeds are but 'filthy rags,' and all is of grace, till in fact they have little time left them to guard against what they are condemning, and to exercise what they think they are so full of. (*Jfc.*, ch. 13)

To look to Christ is to be justified by faith; to think of being justified by faith is to look from Christ and to fall from grace. (*Jfc.*, ch. 13)

[I]t is not an uncommon notion at this time, that a man may be an habitual sinner, and yet be in a state of salvation, and in the kingdom of grace. And this doctrine many more persons hold than think they do; not in words, but in heart. They think that faith is all in all; that faith, if they have it, blots out their sins as fast as they commit them. They sin in distinct acts in the morning, — their faith wipes all out; at noon, — their faith still avails; and in the evening, — still the same. Or they remain contentedly in sinful habits or practices, under the dominion of sin, not warring against it, in ignorance what is sin and what is not; and they think that the only business of a Christian is, not to be holy, but to have faith, and to think and speak of Christ; and thus, perhaps, they are really living, whether by habit or by act, in extortion, avarice, envy, rebellious pride, self-indulgence, or worldliness, and neither know nor care to know it. If they sin in habits, they are not aware of these at all; if by acts, instead of viewing them one and all together, they take them one by one, and set their faith against each separate act. (*PS* v, Sermon 13: 'The State of Salvation,' 18 March 1838)

Faith is the tenure upon which this divine life is continued to us: by faith the Christian lives, but if he draws back he dies; his faith profits him nothing; or rather, his drawing back to sin is a reversing of his faith; after which, God has no pleasure in him. And yet, clearly as this is stated in Scripture, men in all ages have fancied that they might sin grievously, yet maintain their Christian hope. They have comforted themselves with thoughts of the infinite mercy of God, as if He could not punish the sinner; or they have laid the blame of their sins on their circumstances; or they have hoped that zeal for the truth, or that almsgiving, would make up for a bad life; or they have relied upon repenting in time to come. And not the least subtle of such excuses is that which results from a doctrine popularly received at this day, that faith in Christ is compatible with a very imperfect state of holiness, or with unrighteousness, and avails for the pardon of an unrighteous life. So that a man may, if so be, go on pretty much like other men, with this only difference, that he has what he considers faith, — a certain spiritual insight into the Gospel scheme, a renunciation of his own merit, and a power of effectually pleading and applying to his soul Christ's atoning sacrifice, such as others have not; — that he sins indeed much as others, but then is deeply grieved that he sins; that he *would* be under the wrath of God as others are, had he not faith to remove it withal. And thus the necessity of a holy life is in fact put out of sight quite as fully as if he said in so many words, that it was not required; and a man may, if it so happen, be low-minded, sordid, worldly, arrogant, imperious, self-confident, impure, self-indulgent, ambitious or covetous, nay, may allow himself from time to time in wilful acts of sin which he himself condemns, and yet, by a great abuse of words, may be called spiritual … Instead of faith blotting out transgressions, transgressions blot out faith. (*PS* v, Sermon 14: 'Transgressions and Infirmities,' 25 March 1838)

'Whosoever shall call upon the Name of the Lord shall be saved;' a promise is given, but the how, the when, the where, the by what, these particulars are by the very form of the proposition left uncertain. Time is not mentioned, nor mode; — but a *promise* given, that it *shall* be ... 'Ask, and it shall be given you; seek, and ye shall find; knock, and it shall be opened unto you.' Here salvation is, as it were, put in our own power; to *hear* the invitation is our sufficient title for coming; to *pray* for the gift is the sure and certain means of receiving it. Most true; but does the word *seek* imply one act, and one only? does it imply that we gain at once what we ask for? The contrary: we are elsewhere told to '*strive* to enter in at the strait gate, for many will *seek* to enter in,' that is, seek *without* striving, 'and shall not be able.' [Luke xiii. 24.] ... Sometimes, doubtless, God mercifully answers upon one prayer, and sometimes He justifies on one act of faith; but I am speaking of what we have a right to gather from such passages; and I say, that all they can prove is this, that he who has faith has a *promise* from God that he *shall*, shall in God's own way, in God's own time, shall certainly and surely in the event, be justified; that, as he who begins to pray will sooner or later obtain, so he who believes shall, unless he 'draw back,' be justified ... Take again the instance of St. Paul himself. By faith he obeyed the heavenly vision, and went into Damascus, and waited. But he *had* to wait, he was not justified. He waited three days — he prayed; then Ananias was sent; and *he* said, 'Arise, and be baptized, and *wash away thy sins*, calling on the Name of the Lord.' [Acts xxii. 16.] To believe, to confess, to pray, to call, were the sufficient *title* for the gift; but baptism was the instrument of receiving it. (*PS* vi, Sermon 12: 'Faith the Title for Justification' 24 January 1841)

Catholics hold that, not faith only, but faith, hope, and charity, are the 'sustaining cause' of justification. — Concil. Trid. Sess. vi. 7. (*Jfc.*, ch. 10, footnote 2 from 1874)

Faith and Reason

The grace promised us is given, not that we may know more, but that we may do better. It is given to influence, guide, and strengthen us in performing our duty towards God and man; it is given to us as creatures, as sinners, as men, as immortal beings, not as mere reasoners, disputers, or philosophical inquirers. It teaches what we are, whither we are going, what we must do, how we must do it; it enables us to change our fallen nature from evil to good, 'to make ourselves a new heart and a new spirit.' ... As knowledge about earth, sky, and sea, and the wonders they contain, is in itself valuable, and in its place desirable, so doubtless there is nothing sinful in gazing wistfully at the marvellous providences of God's moral governance, and wishing to understand them. But still God has not given us such knowledge in the Bible, ... [T]hey have argued, that no doctrine which was *mysterious*, i.e. too deep for human reason, or inconsistent with their self-devised notions, could be contained in Scripture; as if it were honouring Christ to maintain that when He said a thing, He could not have meant what He said, because *they* would not have said it. (*PS* i, Sermon 16: 'The Christian Mysteries,' 14 June 1829)

Now it should not surprise us when men of acute and powerful understandings more or less reject the Gospel, for this reason, that the Christian revelation addresses itself to our hearts, to our love of truth and goodness, our fear of sinning, and our desire to gain God's favour; and quickness, sagacity, depth of thought, strength of mind, power of comprehension, perception of the beautiful, power of language, and the like, though they are excellent gifts, are clearly quite of a different kind from these spiritual excellences—a man may have the one without having the other. *This*, then, is the plain reason why able, or again why learned men are so often defective Christians, because there is no necessary connexion between faith and ability; because faith is one thing and ability is another; because ability of mind is a *gift*, and faith is a *grace* ... These gifts are different in kind. In like manner, powers of mind and religious principles and feelings are distinct gifts; and as all the highest spiritual excellence, humility, firmness, patience, would never enable a man to read an unknown tongue, or to enter into the depths of science, so all the most brilliant mental endowments, wit, or imagination, or penetration, or depth, will never of themselves make us wise in religion. And as we should fairly and justly deride the savage who wished to decide questions of science or literature by the sword, so may we justly look with amazement on the error of those who think that they can master the high mysteries of spiritual truth, and find their way to God, by what is commonly called reason, i.e. by the random and blind efforts of mere mental acuteness, and mere experience of the world. (*PS* viii, Sermon 13: 'Truth Hidden When Not Sought After,' 17 October 1830)

This opposition between Faith and Reason takes place in two ways, when either of the two encroaches upon the province of the other. It would be an absurdity to attempt to find out mathematical truths by the purity and acuteness of the moral sense. It is a form of this mistake which has led men to apply such Scripture communications as are intended for religious purposes to the determination of physical questions. This error is perfectly understood in these days by all thinking men. This was the usurpation of the schools of theology in former ages, to issue their decrees to the subjects of the Senses and the Intellect. No wonder Reason and Faith were at variance. The other cause of disagreement takes place when Reason is the aggressor, and encroaches on the province of Religion, attempting to judge of those truths which are subjected to another part of our nature, the moral sense. (*US*, Sermon 4: 'The Usurpations of Reason,' 11 December 1831)

Right reason, then, and faith combine to lead us, instead of measuring a divine revelation by human standards, or systematizing, except so far as it does so itself, to take what is given as we find it, to use it and be content. For instance, Scripture says that Christ died for sinners; that He rose for our justification, that He went that the Spirit might come; *so far* we may systematize. Such and such-like portions of a scheme are revealed, and we may use them, but no farther. (*TT* #73, 1836)

Reason may be the judge, without being the origin, of Faith; and that Faith may be justified by Reason, without making use of it ... Faith, then, as I have said, does not demand evidence so strong as is necessary for what is commonly considered a rational conviction, or belief on the ground of Reason; and why? For this reason, because it is mainly swayed by antecedent considerations. In this way it is, that the two principles are opposed to one another: Faith is influenced by previous notices, prepossessions, and (in a good sense of the word) prejudices; but Reason, by direct and definite proof. The mind that believes is acted upon by its own hopes, fears, and existing opinions; whereas it is supposed to reason severely, when it rejects antecedent proof of a fact, — rejects every thing but the actual evidence producible in its favour ... It is the reckoning that to be, which it hopes or wishes to be; not 'the realizing of things proved by evidence.' Its desire is its main evidence; or, as the Apostle expressly goes on to say, it makes its own evidence, 'being the *evidence* of things not seen.' And this is the cause, as is natural, why Faith seems to the world so irrational, as St. Paul says in other Epistles. Not that it has no grounds in Reason, that is, in evidence; but because it is satisfied with so much less than would be necessary, were it not for the bias of the mind, that to the world its evidence seems like nothing. (*US*, Sermon 10: 'Faith and Reason, Contrasted as Habits of Mind,' Jan. 1839)

It is usual at this day to speak as if Faith were simply of a moral nature, and depended and followed upon a distinct act of Reason beforehand, — Reason warranting, on the ground of evidence, both ample and carefully examined, that the Gospel comes from God, and *then* Faith embracing it. On the other hand, the more Scriptural representation seems to be this, which is obviously more agreeable to facts also, that, instead of there being really any such united process of reasoning first, and then believing, the act of Faith is sole and elementary, and complete in itself, and depends on no process of mind previous to it: ... the imputation brought against Faith, [is] that it is the reasoning of a weak mind, whereas it is in truth the reasoning of a divinely enlightened one. (*US*, Sermon 11: 'The Nature of Faith in Relation to Reason,' 13 January 1839)

Faith, then, and Reason, are popularly contrasted with one another; Faith consisting of certain exercises of Reason which proceed mainly on presumption, and Reason of certain exercises which proceed mainly upon proof. Reason makes the particular fact which is to be ascertained the point of primary importance, contemplates it, inquires into its evidence, not of course excluding antecedent considerations, but not beginning with them. Faith, on the other hand, begins with its own previous knowledge and opinions, advances and decides upon antecedent probabilities, that is, on grounds which do not reach so far as to touch precisely the desired conclusion, though they tend towards it, and may come very near it. It acts, before actual certainty or knowledge. (*US*, Sermon 12: 'Love the Safeguard of Faith Against Superstition,' 21 May 1839)

Faith cannot exist without grounds or without an object; but it does not follow that all who have faith should recognise, and be able to state what they believe, and why … True Faith, then, admits, but does not require, the exercise of what is commonly understood by Reason. (*US*, Sermon 13: 'Implicit and Explicit Reason,' Dec. 1840)

Surely, as the only true religion is that which is seated within us, a matter, not of words, but of things, so the only satisfactory test of religion is something within us. If religion be a personal matter, its reasons also should be personal. Wherever it is present, in the world or in the heart, it produces an effect, and that effect is its evidence. When we view it as set up in the world, it has its external proofs, when as set up in our hearts, it has its internal; and that, whether we are able to elicit them ourselves, and put them into shape, or not. Nay, with some little limitation and explanation, it might be said, that the very fact of a religion taking root within us, is a proof, so far, that it is true. If it were not true, it would not take root. (*SD*, Sermon 23: 'Grounds for Steadfastness in Our Religious Profession,' 19 December 1841)

I do not mean of course that the Fathers were opposed to inquiries into the intellectual basis of Christianity, but that they held that men were not obliged to wait for logical proof before believing; on the contrary, that the majority were to believe first on presumptions and let the intellectual proof come as their reward. (*Dev.*, Part II: ch. 7, sec. 2)

The old Catholic notion, which still lingers in the Established Church, was, that Faith was an intellectual act, its object truth, and its result knowledge … in proportion as the Lutheran leaven spread, it became fashionable to say that Faith was, not an acceptance of revealed doctrine, not an act of the intellect, but a feeling, an emotion, an affection,

an appetency; and, as this view of Faith obtained, so was the connexion
of Faith with Truth and Knowledge more and more either forgotten or
denied. At length the identity of this (so-called) spirituality of heart and
the virtue of Faith was acknowledged on all hands. Some men indeed disapproved the pietism in question, others admired it; but whether they admired or disapproved, both the one party and the other found themselves
in agreement on the main point, viz. — in considering that this really was
in substance Religion, and nothing else; that Religion was based, not on
argument, but on taste and sentiment, that nothing was objective, every
thing subjective, in doctrine. I say, even those who saw through the af-
fectation in which the religious school of which I am speaking clad itself,
still came to think that Religion, as such, consisted in something short of
intellectual exercises, viz., in the affections, in the imagination, in inward
persuasions and consolations, in pleasurable sensations, sudden changes,
and sublime fancies ... Religion was based on custom, on prejudice, on
law, on education, on habit, on loyalty, on feudalism, on enlightened expedience, on many, many things, but not at all on reason; reason was neither its warrant, nor its instrument, and science had as little connexion
with it as with the fashions of the season, or the state of the weather. (*IU*,
Part I, Discourse 2: 'Theology a Branch of Knowledge,' 1852)

Not that they are opposed, but faith has the power of anticipating, and
arrives at first at what reason scarcely guesses at at last. (*SN*, 'Faith,' 12
April 1863)

My argument is in outline as follows: that that absolute certitude
which we were able to possess, whether as to the truths of natural theology, or as to the fact of a revelation, was the result of an *assemblage* of
concurring and converging probabilities, and that, both according to the
constitution of the human mind and the will of its Maker; that certitude
was a habit of mind, that certainty was a quality of propositions; that
probabilities which did not reach to logical certainty, might suffice for
a mental certitude; that the certitude thus brought about might equal
in measure and strength the certitude which was created by the strictest
scientific demonstration; and that to possess such certitude might in given

cases and to given individuals be a plain duty, though not to others in other circumstances. (*Apo.*, ch. 1)

I am far of course from denying that every article of the Christian Creed, whether as held by Catholics or by Protestants, is beset with intellectual difficulties; and it is simple fact, that, for myself, I cannot answer those difficulties. Many persons are very sensitive of the difficulties of Religion; I am as sensitive of them as any one; but I have never been able to see a connexion between apprehending those difficulties, however keenly, and multiplying them to any extent, and on the other hand doubting the doctrines to which they are attached. Ten thousand difficulties do not make one doubt, as I understand the subject; difficulty and doubt are incommensurate. There of course may be difficulties in the evidence; but I am speaking of difficulties intrinsic to the doctrines themselves, or to their relations with each other. A man may be annoyed that he cannot work out a mathematical problem, of which the answer is or is not given to him, without doubting that it admits of an answer, or that a certain particular answer is the true one. Of all points of faith, the being of a God is, to my own apprehension, encompassed with most difficulty, and yet borne in upon our minds with most power. (*Apo.*, ch. 5)

Let us have a little faith; which ought to be no great hardship to those, who starting with the profession that there *is* a God, ought not to be surprised that we cannot always understand him, who is infinite. (*LD* xxx, 400; Letter to Edward Hayes Plumptre, 14 September 1884)

Faith and Works

The whole history of redemption, the covenant of mercy in all its parts and provisions, attests the necessity of holiness in order to salvation; as indeed even our natural conscience bears witness also. (*PS* i, Sermon 1: 'Holiness is Necessary for Future Blessedness,' 1834)

I conceive that we are in danger, in this day, of insisting on neither of these as we ought; regarding all true and careful consideration of the

Object of faith, as barren orthodoxy, technical subtlety, and the like, and all due earnestness about good works as a mere cold and formal morality; and, instead, making religion, or rather (for this is the point) making the test of our being religious, to consist in our having what is called a spiritual state of heart, to the comparative neglect of the Object from which it must arise, and the works in which it should issue ... how is a man to know that his motives and affections are right except by their fruits? Can they possibly be their own evidence? ... deeds of obedience are an intelligible evidence, nay, the sole evidence possible, and, on the whole, a satisfactory evidence of the reality of our faith. I do not say that this or that good work tells anything; but a course of obedience says much. (*PS* ii, Sermon 14: 'Saving Knowledge,' Feb. 1835)

[T]he two states of mind are altogether one and the same: it is quite indifferent whether we say a man seeks God in faith, or say he seeks Him by obedience; and whereas Almighty God has graciously declared He will receive and bless all that seek Him, it is quite indifferent whether we say, He accepts those who *believe*, or those who *obey*. To believe is to look beyond this world to God, and to obey is to look beyond this world to God; to believe is of the heart, and to obey is of the heart; to believe is not a solitary act, but a consistent habit of trust; and to obey is not a solitary act, but a consistent habit of doing our duty in all things. I do not say that faith and obedience do not stand for separate ideas in our minds, but they stand for nothing more; they are not divided one from the other in fact. They are but one thing viewed differently ... viewed as sitting at Jesus' feet, it is called *faith*; viewed as running to do His will, it is called *obedience* ... in proportion as a man obeys, is he driven to faith, in order to learn the remedy of the imperfections of his obedience ... from the beginning to the end of Scripture, the one voice of inspiration consistently maintains, not an uniform contrast between faith and obedience, but this *one* doctrine, that the only way of salvation open to us is the *surrender* of ourselves to our Maker in all things—supreme devotion, resignation of our will, the turning with all our heart to God; and this state of mind is ascribed in Scripture sometimes to the believing, sometimes to the obedient, according to the particular passage; and it is no matter to which it is ascribed … Abraham found favour in God's sight, *because he gave himself up to Him*: this is faith or obedience, whichever we please to call it. No matter whether we say, Abraham was favoured because his faith embraced God's *promises*, or because his obedience cherished God's *commands*, for God's commands are promises, and His promises commands to a heart devoted to Him; so that, as there is no substantial difference between command and promise, so there is likewise none between obedience and faith. (*PS* iii, Sermon 6: 'Faith and Obedience,' 21 February 1830)

[T]he Gospel leaves us just where it found us, as regards the necessity of our obedience to God; that Christ has not obeyed instead of us, but that obedience is quite as imperative as if Christ had never come; nay, is pressed upon us with additional sanctions; the difference being, not that He relaxes the strict rule of keeping His commandments, but that He gives us spiritual aids, which we have not except through Him, to enable us to keep them. Accordingly Christ's service is represented in Scripture, not as different from that religious obedience which conscience teaches us naturally, but as the perfection of it. (*PS* viii, Sermon 14: 'Obedience to God the Way to Faith in Christ,' 31 October 1830)

Why be so bent upon forcing two inspired teachers into a real and formal discordance of doctrine? If you could prove ever so cogently that when St. Paul said, 'deeds of the Law,' he meant to include Christian works, you would not have advanced one step towards interpreting St. James, or impairing his authority; you would have only plunged into a more serious perplexity. Difficult if it be to account for St. Paul insisting on faith, and St. James at a later date insisting on works, surely it is a greater difficulty when it is insisted on that St. Paul excludes the very works which St. James includes. Is our Gospel like the pretended revelation of the Arabian impostor, a variable rule, the latter portion contradicting the former? (*Jfc.*, ch. 12)

[F]aith only may justify in one sense, good works in another, — and this is all that I here maintain … in the sense in which faith justifies, it only justifies. (*Jfc.*, ch. 12)

It does not follow that works done in faith do not justify, because works done without faith do not justify; that works done in the Holy Ghost, and ordinances which are His instruments, do not justify, because carnal works and dead rites do not justify. (*Jfc.*, ch. 12)

Nothing surely is more suitable than to explain justifying faith to be a principle of action, a characteristic of obedience, a sanctifying power, if by doing so we reconcile St. Paul with St. James, and moreover observe the while the very same rule of interpretation which we apply to Scripture generally. (*Jfc.*, ch. 12)

Sacrifices and purifications, circumcision and the sabbath, could not take away sins, could not justify. Visible things are but means of grace at best; and they were not so much, before grace was purchased ... Such was human nature in its best estate before Christ came; its worst was when it mistook the tatters of its poverty for the garments of righteousness, and, as in our Lord's age, prided itself on what it was and what it did, because its own, — its sacrifices, ceremonies, birth-place, and ancestry, — as if these could stand instead of that justification which it needed. This was that reliance on the works of the Law, which St. Paul denounces, a reliance utterly incompatible of course with the doctrine of free grace, and, in consequence, of faith. (*Jfc.*, ch. 12)

St. Paul says, we are justified without works; what works? 'works of,' or done under, 'the Law,' the Law of Moses, through which the Law of Nature spoke in the ears of the Jews. But St. James speaks of works done under what he calls 'the royal Law,' 'the Law of liberty,' which we learn from St. Paul is 'the Law of the Spirit of Life,' for 'where the Spirit of the Lord is, there is liberty;' in other words, the Law of God, as written on the heart by the Holy Ghost. St. Paul speaks of works done under the letter, St. James of works done under the Spirit. This is surely an important difference in the works respectively mentioned. Or, to state the same thing differently: St. James speaks, not of mere works, but of works of faith, of good and acceptable works. I do not suppose that any one will dispute this, and therefore shall take it for granted. St. James then says, we are justified, not by faith only, but by *good* works. Now St. Paul is not speaking at all of good works, but of works done *in the flesh* and of themselves 'deserving God's wrath and damnation.' He says, 'without *works;*' he does not say without *good* works; whereas St. James is speaking of good works solely. St. Paul speaks of 'works done before the grace of Christ and the inspiration of His Spirit;' St. James of 'good works which are the fruits of faith and follow after justification.' (*Jfc.*, ch. 12)

St. Paul never calls those works which he says do not justify 'good works,' but simply 'works,'—'works of the Law,'—'deeds of the Law,'—'works not in righteousness,'—'dead works;' what have these to do with works or fruits of the Spirit? Of these latter also St. Paul elsewhere speaks, and by a remarkable contrast he calls them again and again 'good works.' For instance, 'By grace are ye saved through faith, … not of *works*, lest any man should boast; for we are His workmanship, created in Christ Jesus unto *good* works.' This surely is a most pointed intimation that the works which do not justify are not good, or, in other words, are works *before* justification. As to works after, which *are* good, whether they justify or not, he does not decide so expressly as St. James, the error which he had to resist leading him another way. He only says, against the Judaizing teachers, that our works must begin, continue, and end in faith. But to proceed; he speaks elsewhere of 'abounding in every *good* work,' of being 'fruitful in every *good* work,' of being 'adorned with *good* works,' of being 'well reported of for *good* works,' 'diligently following every *good* work,' of 'the *good* works of some being open beforehand,' of being 'rich in *good* works,' of being 'prepared unto every *good* work,' of being 'throughly furnished unto all *good* works,' of being 'unto every *good* work reprobate,' of being 'a pattern of *good* works,' of being 'zealous of *good* works,' of being 'ready to every *good* work,' of being 'careful to maintain *good* works,' of 'provoking unto love and to *good* works,' and of being 'made perfect in every *good* work.' [2 Cor. ix. 8. Eph. ii. 10. Col. i. 10. 2 Thess. ii. 17. 1 Tim. ii. 10; v. 10, 25; vi. 18. 2 Tim. ii. 21; iii. 17. Tit. i. 16; ii. 7, 14; iii. 8, 14. Heb. x. 24; xiii. 21.] Now surely this is very remarkable. St. James, though he means good works, drops the epithet, and only says works. Why does not St. Paul the same? why is he always careful to add the word *good*, except that he had also to do with a sort of works with which St. James had not to do,—that the word *works* was already appropriated by him to those of the Law, and therefore that the epithet *good* was necessary, lest deeds done in the Spirit should be confused with them? St. Paul, then, by speaking of faith as justifying without works, means without corrupt and counterfeit works, not without good works. (*Jfc.*, ch. 12)

'By works,' says St. James, 'a man is justified, and not by faith only.' Now, let me ask, what texts do their opponents shrink from as they from this? do they even attempt to explain it? or if so, is it not by some harsh and unnatural interpretation? Next, do they not proceed, as if distrusting their own interpretation, to pronounce the text difficult, and so to dispose of it? yet who can honestly say that it is in itself difficult? rather, can words be plainer, were it not that they are forced into connexion with a theory of the sixteenth century. (*Jfc.*, ch. 12)

We know that faith justifies us; but what is the test of true faith? Works are its evidence; but they are so on the whole, after a sufficient period of time, to others, and at the judgment of the last day. (*PS* v, Sermon 17: 'The Testimony of Conscience,' 9 December 1838)

They might do as many works and services as they would in their present state, but these would not advance them at all, and why?—not that works were not necessary, God forbid! but that such works were not good works; that no works were good works but those done in the Spirit, and that nothing could gain them the gift of the Spirit but faith in Christ. (*PS* v, Sermon 11: 'The Law of the Spirit,' 12 January 1840)

Our best obedience in our own strength is worth nothing; it is altogether unsound, it is ever failing, it never grows firmer, it never can be reckoned on, it does nothing well, it has nothing in it pleasing or acceptable to God:—and not only so, it is the obedience of souls born and living under God's wrath, for a state of nature is a state of wrath. On the other hand, obedience which is done in faith is done with the aid of the Holy Spirit; it is holy and acceptable in God's sight; it grows habitual and consistent; it tends to possess the soul wholly; and it leads straight onward to heaven. This was the very promise of the Gospel as the prophet Isaiah announces it. 'An highway shall be there and a way, and it shall be called the *way of holiness:* the unclean shall not pass over it ... the wayfaring men, though fools, shall not err therein.' [Isa. xxxv. 8.] This being understood, we shall have no difficulty in understanding St. Paul's language. The way of salvation is by works, as under the Law, but it is by 'works which spring out of faith,' and which come of 'the inspiration of the Spirit.' It is because works are living and spiritual, from the heart, and by faith, that the Gospel is a new covenant. Hence in the passages above quoted we are told again and again of 'the law *in our inward parts;*' 'a new *heart;*' 'a new *spirit;*' the Holy '*Spirit within us;*' 'newness of *life;*' and 'circumcision of the *heart* in the Spirit.' And hence St. Paul says, that though we have not been 'saved by works,' yet we are '*created* unto *good* works;' and that 'the blood of Christ purges the conscience from *dead* works to *serve* the *living* God.' Salvation then is not by dead works, but by living works ... And thus there is no opposition between St. Paul and St. James. St. James says, that justification is by works, and St. Paul that it is by faith: but, observe, St. James does not say that it is by dead or Jewish works; he mentions expressly *both* faith *and* works; he only says, 'not faith *only* but works also:'—and St. Paul is far from denying it is by works, he only says that it is by faith and denies that it is by *dead* works. And what proves this, among other circumstances, is, that he never calls those works, which he condemns and puts aside, *good* works, but simply works: whenever he speaks of good works in his Epistles, he speaks of Christian works; not of Jewish. On the whole, then, salvation is both by faith and by works. St. James says, not *dead* faith, and St. Paul, not *dead* works. St. James, 'not by faith *only,*' for that *would* be dead faith: St. Paul, 'not by works only,' for such *would* be dead works. Faith alone can make works living; works alone can make faith living. Take away either, and you take away both;—he alone has faith who has works,—he alone has works who has faith. (*PS* v, Sermon 12: 'The New Works of the Gospel,' 26 January 1840)

Are you sure that you do not take 'obedience,' ... *instead* of faith, when you should only take it *as the way* to faith? (*LD* xii, 227; Letter to Mrs. William Froude, 27 June 1848)

Catholics hold that our good works, as proceeding from the grace of the Holy Ghost, cannot be worthless, but have a real and proper value; on the other hand, that the great reward of eternal life is due to them only in consequence of the promise of God. Good works have on this ground a claim on God's faithfulness to His promises, and thereby a claim on His justice, for it would be unjust to promise and not fulfil. (*Jfc*., ch. 1, footnote 1 from 1874)

Fathers of the Church

But it should be remembered, that it is we in after times who systematize the statements of the Fathers, which, as they occur in their works, are for the most part as natural and unpremeditated as those of the inspired volume itself. (*Ari*., ch. 2, sec. 4)

The Rule of Vincent is not of a mathematical or demonstrative character, but moral, and requires practical judgment and good sense to apply it. For instance: what is meant by being 'taught *always*'? does it mean in every century, or every year, or every month? Does '*everywhere*' mean in every country, or in every diocese? And does 'the *Consent of Fathers*' require us to produce the direct testimony of every one of them? How many Fathers, how many places, how many instances constitute a fulfilment of the test proposed? It is, then, from the nature of the case, a condition which never can be satisfied as fully as it might have been; it admits of various and unequal application in various instances. (VM i, ch. 2)

To maintain that the Fathers cannot be trusted, does not prove that one's own private judgment can. (VM i, ch. 6)

When they speak of doctrines, they speak of them as being universally held. They are witnesses to the fact of those doctrines having been received, not here or there, but everywhere. We receive those doctrines which they thus teach, not merely because they teach them, but because they bear witness that all Christians everywhere then held them ... They do not speak of their *own private* opinion; they do not say, 'This is true, *because* we see it in Scripture' — about which there might be differences of judgment — but, 'this is true, because in matter of fact it is held, and has ever been held, by all the Churches, down to our times, without interruption, ever since the Apostles.' (*TT* #83, 1838)

Accordingly, the controversy between those who appeal to them for and against the Catholic system of doctrine, or any portions of it, turns upon this issue — whether the Catholic and later statements are due developments, or but ingenious perversions of those passages from St. Clement or St. Ignatius, which are brought forward as proofs of them. ('The Theology of St. Ignatius,' *British Critic*, Jan. 1839; in *Ess.* i, sec. VI)

Whatever then be the true way of interpreting the Fathers, and in particular the Apostolical Fathers, if a man begins by summoning them before him, instead of betaking himself to them, — by seeking to make them evidence for modem dogmas, instead of throwing his mind upon their text, and drawing from them their own doctrines, — he will to a certainty miss their sense ... Nothing then is more common than a supercilious way of dealing with the writings of the Fathers, as if it were enough to measure the nature and value of their contents by antecedent reasoning, without having the trouble of a personal inspection of them. ('The Theology of St. Ignatius,' *British Critic,* Jan. 1839; in *Ess.* i, sec. VI)

To read then a particular Father to advantage, we must, as a preliminary, do these two things — divest ourselves of modern ideas and prejudices, and study theology. ('The Theology of St. Ignatius,' *British Critic*, Jan. 1839; in *Ess.* i, sec. VI)

For some years the argument in favour of our Church drawn from Antiquity has been met by the assertion, that that same Antiquity held also other opinions which no one now would think of maintaining; that if it were mistaken in one set of opinions, it might be in the other; that its mistakes were of a nature which argued feebleness of intellect, or unsoundness of judgment, or want of logical acumen in those who held them, which would avail against its authority in the instances in which it was used, as well as in those in which it had been passed over. Moreover it was said that those who used it in defence of the Church knew this well, but were not honest enough to confess it. They were challenged to confess or deny the charges thus brought against the Fathers; and, since to deny the fact was supposed impossible, they were bid to draw out a case, such, as either would admit of a defence of the fact on grounds of reason, or of its surrender without surrendering the authority of the Fathers altogether. Such challenges, and they have not been unfrequent, afford, I conceive, a sufficient reason for any one who considers that the Church of England derives essential assistance from Christian Antiquity in her interpretation of Scripture, to enter upon the examination of the particular objections by which certain authors have assailed its authority. (VM ii, X. 'Letter to Richard, Lord Bishop of Oxford, in Explanation of Tract 90,' 1841)

When I began to read the 'Fathers' many years ago, I began at the Apostolical, and took a great deal of pains with them and Justin Martyr all which I count now almost wasted and that for this reason, that I did not understand what was in them, what I was to look for, what were the strong and important points, etc. I measured and systematized them by the Protestant doctrines and views, and by this sort of cross division I managed to spend a good deal of time on them and got nothing from them ... This has ever since made me averse to persons reading the 'Fathers' without first getting some acquaintance with divinity; or at least letting the study of the two proceed together ; or again some acquaintance with Ecclesiastical History ... Bishop Kaye, to judge from his publications, has proceeded in the same orderly way accordingly, since a man must have some system, he has naturally taken his own with him, and transforms Tertullian into the Thirty-nine Articles one after another. I think Tertullian would be surprised to see himself in the Bishop's pages. (*Keb.*, 196-197; Letter to Rev. T. W. Allies, 30 September 1842)

It is true indeed that the subsequent profession of the doctrine in the Universal Church creates a presumption that it was held even before it was professed; and it is fair to interpret the early Fathers by the later ... To give a deeper meaning to their letter, we must interpret them by the times which came after. (*Dev.*, Part I: Introduction)

On the whole, all parties will agree that, of all existing systems, the present communion of Rome is the nearest approximation in fact to the Church of the Fathers, possible though some may think it, to be nearer still to that Church on paper. Did St. Athanasius or St. Ambrose come suddenly to life, it cannot be doubted what communion he would take to be his own. All surely will agree that these Fathers, with whatever opinions of their own, whatever protests, if we will, would find themselves more at home with such men as St. Bernard or St. Ignatius Loyola, or with the lonely priest in his lodging, or the holy sisterhood of mercy, or the unlettered crowd before the altar, than with the teachers or with the members of any other creed. (*Dev.*, Part I: ch. 2, sec. 3)

[T]here could not be a more thorough refutation of its foundation and superstructure than was to be found in the volumes of the Fathers. There was no mistaking that the principles professed, and doctrines taught by those holy men, were utterly anti-Protestant ... it was a patent fact, open to all, written on the face of their works, that they were anti-Protestant ... the time at length came, when first of all turning their minds (some of them, at least) more carefully to the doctrinal controversies of the early Church, they saw distinctly that in the reasonings of the Fathers, elicited by means of them, and in the decisions of authority, in which they issued, were contained at least the rudiments, the anticipation, the justification of what they had been accustomed to consider the corruptions of Rome ... The Fathers *would* protect 'Romanists' as well as extinguish Dissenters. The Anglican divines *would* misquote the Fathers, and shrink from the very doctors to whom they appealed. The Bishops of the seventeenth century were shy of the Bishops of the fourth; and the Bishops of the nineteenth were shy of the Bishops of the seventeenth ... it was at length plain that primitive Christianity ignored the National Church, and that the National Church cared little for primitive Christianity, or for those who appealed to it as her foundation. (*Dif.* i, Lecture 5)

[I]t is the fashion of the mass of Protestants, whenever they think on the subject, to accuse the Church of the Fathers of what they call Popish superstition and intolerance; and some have even gone so far as to say, that in these respects that early Church was more Popish than the Papists themselves ... [N]o candid person who has fairly examined the state of the case can doubt, that, if we differ from the Fathers in some things, Protestants differ from them in all, and if we vary from them in accidentals, Protestants contradict them in essentials ... I say, then, that the writings of the Fathers, so far from prejudicing at least one man against the modern Catholic Church, have been simply and solely the one intellectual cause of his having renounced the religion in which he was born and submitted himself to her. What other causes there may be, not intellectual, unknown, unsuspected by himself, though freely imputed on mere conjecture by those who would invalidate his testimony, it would be unbecoming and impertinent to discuss; for himself, if he is asked why he became a Catholic, he can only give that answer which experience and consciousness bring home to him as the true one, viz., that he joined the Catholic Church simply because he believed it, and it only, to be the Church of the Fathers; because he believed that there was a Church upon earth till the end of time, and one only. (*Dif.* i, Lecture 12)

[W]e need not by an officious piety arbitrarily force the language of separate Fathers into a sense which it cannot bear; nor by an unjust and narrow criticism accuse them of error; nor impose upon an early age a distinction of terms belonging to a later. (*Atlantis*, July 1858; *Ari.*, App., Note 4)

We are bound to interpret all Scripture by the unanimous consent of the Fathers. (*Ward* i, 543; Letter to Thomas Arnold, 12 October 1862)

I had not read the Fathers cautiously enough; that in such nice points, as those which determine the angle of divergence between the two Churches, I had made considerable miscalculations. (*Apo.*, ch. 4)

I recollect well what an outcast I seemed to myself, when I took down from the shelves of my library the volumes of St. Athanasius or St. Basil, and set myself to study them; and how, on the contrary, when at length I was brought into Catholic communion, I kissed them with delight, with a feeling that in them I had more than all that I had lost; and, as though I were directly addressing the glorious saints, who bequeathed them to the Church, how I said to the inanimate pages, 'You are now mine, and I am now yours, beyond any mistake.' (*Dif.* ii, Letter to Pusey, ch. 1, 1865)

I am not ashamed still to take my stand upon the Fathers, and do not mean to budge. The history of their times is not yet an old almanac to me ... The Fathers made me a Catholic, and I am not going to kick down the ladder by which I ascended into the Church. It is a ladder quite as service-able for that purpose now, as it was twenty years ago. Though I hold, as you know, a process of development in Apostolic truth as time goes on, such development does not supersede the Fathers, but explains and com-pletes them. (*Dif.* ii, Letter to Pusey, ch. 2, 1865)

[T]hey who loved the Fathers, could have no place in the Church of England. (*LD* xxv, 352-353; Letter of July 1871; cited in Ker, 663)

Justice has not been done here to the ground of tradition, on which the Fathers specially took their stand. For example, 'Whoever heard such doctrine?' says Athanasius; 'whence, from whom did they gain it? Who thus expounded to them when they were at school?' Orat. i. § 8. (*Ari.*, ch. 3, sec. 1; footnote 14 from 1871)

[H]istory and the patristical writings do not absolutely decide the truth or falsehood of all important theological propositions, any more than Scripture decides it. As to such propositions, all that one can safely say is, that history and the Fathers look in one determinate direction. They make a doctrine more or less probable, but rarely contain a statement, or suggest a conclusion, which cannot be plausibly evaded. The definition of the Church is commonly needed to supply the defects of logic. (*VM* i, Lecture 1; footnote 1 from 1877)

[W]e do not hold even the greatest of them to be infallible, whereas the Church *is* infallible. (*VM* i, Lecture 2; footnote 10 from 1877)

Antiquity, in these respects, is as bold and minute as Catholicity can be said to be. St. Augustine and other Fathers recognise the distinction between mortal and venial sins; determine that mortal sins merit an eternal punishment; that souls are kept in prison till their lesser sins are purged away; that prayers, e.g. the Lord's Prayer, satisfy for light and daily, that is, venial sins; that post-baptismal falls are remitted through Penance, as a raft may save after shipwreck; that after such remission punishment remains due; that this punishment is averted by good works and bodily mortifications, and by the Eucharistic Sacrifice, which, by Apostolic tradition, is profitably offered for the dead. (VM i, Lecture 3; footnote 26 from 1877)

But in order to determine what the Fathers say, and in what they agree, the Church's witness involves a judgment. Judges in our Courts of law are primarily witnesses to the law, written and unwritten, but still they are called judges of the law, and are truly such. And who can deny that a Jury judges of facts? The facts of Antiquity are not too clear to dispense with the exercise of a judgment upon them. (VM i, Lecture 11; footnote 4 from 1877)

At the time of the translation, in 1841-1844, to be literal in the English used in the work was a foremost duty. Those who at that date took part in Dr. Pusey's great undertaking were regarded with much suspicion, both by Catholics and Protestants, as if they were introducing the Fathers to the English public with a covert view of recommending thereby certain religious theories of their own. It was alleged that in truth the only high-church doctrine to be found in the Fathers was Baptismal Regeneration; translators, it was said, who went beyond this were to be watched, and any departure from grammatical and literal accuracy in their renderings was sure to be scored against them as a controversial artifice ... I yield to no one still in special devotion to those centuries of the Catholic Church which the Holy Fathers represent. (*Select Treatises of St. Athanasius*, Vol. 1, Advertisement to the Third Edition, 2 February 1881)

God

If, then, the infinite benevolence of God wins our love, certainly His justice commands it; and were we able, as the Saints made perfect are able, to combine the notion of both in their separate perfections, as displayed in the same acts, doubtless our awe and admiration of the glorious vision would be immeasurably increased. (*US*, Sermon 6: 'On Justice, as a Principle of Divine Governance,' 8 April 1832)

In Him there are no parts or passions, nothing inchoate or incomplete, nothing by communication, nothing of quality, nothing which admits of increase, nothing common to others. He is separate from all things, and whole, and perfect, and simple, and like Himself and none else; and one, not in name, or by figure, or by accommodation, or by abstraction, but one in Himself, or, as the Creed speaks, one in substance or essence. All that He is, is Himself, and nothing short of Himself; His attributes are He. Has He wisdom? this does but mean that He is wisdom. Has He love? that is, 'God is love,' as St. John speaks. Has He omnipresence? that is, He is omnipresent. Has He omniscience? He is all-knowing. Has He power? He is almighty. He is holy, and just, and true, and good, not in the way of qualities of His essence, but holiness, justice, truth, and goodness, are all one and the self-same He, according as He is contemplated by His creatures in various aspects and relations. We men are incapable of conceiving of Him as He is; we cannot attain to more than glimpses, accidental or partial views, of His Infinite Majesty, and these we call by different names, as if He had attributes, and were of a compound nature; and thus He deigns in mercy to us to speak of Himself, using even human, sensible, and material terms; as if He could be angry, who is not touched by evil; or could repent, in whom is no variableness; or had eyes, or arms, or breath, who is a Spirit; whereas He is at once and absolutely all perfection, and whatever is He, is all He is, and He is Himself always and altogether. (*PS* vi, Sermon 24: 'The Mystery of the Holy Trinity,' 1842)

[A]ccording to the teaching of Monotheism, God is an Individual, Self-dependent, All-perfect, Unchangeable Being; intelligent, living, personal, and present; almighty, all-seeing, all-remembering; between whom and His creatures there is an infinite gulf; who has no origin, who is all-sufficient for Himself; who created and upholds the universe; who will judge every one of us, sooner or later, according to that Law of right and wrong which He has written on our hearts. He is One who is sovereign over, operative amidst, independent of, the appointments which He has made; One in whose hands are all things, who has a purpose in every event, and a standard for every deed, and thus has relations of His own towards the subject-matter of each particular science which the book of knowledge unfolds; who has with an adorable, never-ceasing energy implicated Himself in all the history of creation, the constitution of nature, the course of the world, the origin of society, the fortunes of nations, the action of the human mind. (*IU*, Part I, Discourse 2: 'Theology a Branch of Knowledge,' 1852)

[A]s in the human frame there is a living principle, acting upon it and through it by means of volition, so, behind the veil of the visible universe, there is an invisible, intelligent Being, acting on and through it, as and when He will. Further, I mean that this invisible Agent is in no sense a soul of the world, after the analogy of human nature, but, on the contrary, is absolutely distinct from the world, as being its Creator, Upholder, Governor, and Sovereign Lord. Here we are at once brought into the circle of doctrines which the idea of God embodies. I mean then by the Supreme Being, one who is simply self-dependent, and the only Being who is such; moreover, that He is without beginning or Eternal, and the only Eternal; that in consequence He has lived a whole eternity by Himself; and hence that He is all-sufficient, sufficient for His own blessedness, and all-blessed, and ever-blessed. Further, I mean a Being, who, having these prerogatives, has the Supreme Good, or rather is the Supreme Good, or has all the attributes of Good in infinite intenseness; all wisdom, all truth, all justice, all love, all holiness, all beautifulness; who is omnipotent, omniscient, omnipresent; ineffably one, absolutely perfect; and such, that what we do not know and cannot even imagine of Him, is far more wonderful than what we do and can. I mean One who is sovereign over His own will and actions, though always according to the eternal Rule of right and wrong, which is Himself. I mean, moreover, that He created all things out of nothing, and preserves them every moment, and could destroy them as easily as He made them; and that, in consequence, He is separated from them by an abyss, and is incommunicable in all His attributes. And further, He has stamped upon all things, in the hour of their creation, their respective natures, and has given them their work and mission and their length of days, greater or less, in their appointed place. I mean, too, that He is ever present with His works, one by one, and confronts every thing He has made by His particular and most loving Providence, and manifests Himself to each according to its needs: and has on rational beings imprinted the moral law, and given them power to obey it, imposing on them the duty of worship and service, searching and scanning them through and through with His omniscient eye, and putting before them a present trial and a judgment to come. Such is what Theology teaches about God. (*IU*, Part I, Discourse 3: 'Bearing of Theology on Other Branches of Knowledge,' 1852)

[W]hat we know of Him is infinitely less than what we do not know. (*SN*, 'First Article of the Creed,' 28 February 1858)

And I hold this still: I am a Catholic by virtue of my believing in a God; and if I am asked why I believe in a God, I answer that it is because I believe in myself, for I feel it impossible to believe in my own existence (and of that fact I am quite sure) without believing also in the existence of Him, who lives as a Personal, All-seeing, All-judging Being in my conscience. Now, I dare say, I have not expressed myself with philosophical correctness, because I have not given myself to the study of what metaphysicians have said on the subject; but I think I have a strong true meaning in what I say which will stand examination. (*Apo.*, ch. 4)

I speak then of the God of the Theist and of the Christian: a God who is numerically One, who is Personal; the Author, Sustainer, and Finisher of all things, the life of Law and Order, the Moral Governor; One who is Supreme and Sole; like Himself, unlike all things besides Himself which all are but His creatures; distinct from, independent of them all; One who is self-existing, absolutely infinite, who has ever been and ever will be, to whom nothing is past or future; who is all perfection, and the fulness and archetype of every possible excellence, the Truth Itself, Wisdom, Love, Justice, Holiness; One who is All-powerful, All-knowing, Omnipresent,

Incomprehensible. These are some of the distinctive prerogatives which I ascribe unconditionally and unreservedly to the great Being whom I call God. (GA, Part I, ch. 5, sec. 1)

God, Omnipotence of

God is almighty, but still this does not mean that He can do everything whatever, for if so He could do contradictions. There are some things, of course, which are impossible to Him because the very thought of them is an absurdity, *e.g.* He can never cease to be holy; He can never wish to cease to be holy, etc., etc. (SN, 'The Omnipotence of God and Man's Free-Will,' 7 August 1870)

Gospel; Good News

Again, if by speaking of the Gospel as clear and intelligible, a man means to imply that this is the whole of it, then I answer, No; for it is also deep, and therefore necessarily mysterious. This is too often forgotten. (TT #73, 1836)

[T]he Gospel is not a mere scheme or doctrine, but a reality and a life; not a subject for books only, for private use, for individuals, but for public profession, for combined action, for outward manifestation. (SD, Sermon 9: 'Indulgence in Religious Privileges,' 1 May 1842)

The Gospel is but a development of the Law; and creeds and systems may at first sight be very far removed from certain known originals, and yet, after all, be but developments of them. (SD, Sermon 15: 'The Principle of Continuity Between the Jewish and Christian Churches,' 20 November 1842)

I do not object to bringing forward the Atonement explicitly and prominently in itself ... I think it should be taught all baptized children that it is the life of all true Christians but that it is not the means of conversion (ordinarily speaking or in the divine appointment) of those who are not religious. I think it ought not to be preached to infidels, immoral men, backsliders, at first, but be reserved till they begin to feel the need of it. Consequently I object to the use of it so often made in our pulpits as the one doctrine to be addressed to all. It is but one out of others, and not adapted to all. There are various instruments of persuasion given in Scripture; the most familiar distinction is that of the Law and the Gospel. I consider that at this time the mass of our congregations who have lapsed after baptism require the Law rather than the Gospel. They require to be brought to a sense of sin, and I do not think the preaching of the doctrine of the Atonement is intended to bring them to a sense of sin. Dr. Chalmers ... would cast pearls before swine; he would excite the feelings rather than mend the heart; that is, this is the result of his mode of preaching, for, of course, he would wish to renew the heart, though I think he takes the wrong way. I will add, first that in preaching the Law, I do not mean, of course, to exclude the preaching of Divine Love and Mercy but the insisting specially on the Atonement. Secondly the Atonement is not the only doctrine which under circumstances; I would withhold the Incarnation is another. The Apostles in the Acts are almost silent both about the Divinity of Christ and the Atonement. I only wish to follow their example. St. Paul is said to preach the faith of Christ to Festus, where he but insists on righteousness, temperance, and judgment to come. Our Saviour Himself is said to preach the Gospel, yet even His death, and much more His Atonement, was a secret during His Ministry. (*Keb.*, 205-206; Letter of 4 March 1843)

[T]he imagination that the Atonement is the necessary instrument of conversion, results in what seems to me a superstition, viz the fancied obligation of introducing the whole gospel into every Sermon. Thus all Sermons are repetitions of each other. Robert Wilberforce used to call them '180-degrees Sermons'. You heard the same thing, the 'Scheme,' 'Plan' etc, every Sunday, and nothing else. (*LD* xxx, 225; Letter to George T. Edwards, 2 June 1883)

Grace

Christ has not only died for sinners, but also vouchsafes from above the influences of grace, to enable them to love what by nature they cannot love, and to do what they cannot do—to believe and obey ... though God mercifully gives His grace to enable men to believe in His Son, yet it is as certain as the truth of Scripture itself, that He does not give His grace to *all*, but to those to whom He will. If any word of Scripture be true, it is this—that there is an election, that 'it is not of him that willeth, nor of him that runneth, but of God that showeth mercy,' that some men are brought near unto God, and gifted with his regenerating grace, and others not. (*PS* iii, Sermon 20: 'Infant Baptism,' 24 May 1835)

There are different degrees in which we may stand in God's favour; we may be rising or sinking in His favour; we may not have forfeited it, yet we may not be securing it; we may be safe for the present, but have a dangerous prospect before us. We may be more or less 'hypocrites,' 'slothful,' 'unprofitable,' and yet our day of grace not be passed. We may still have the remains of our new nature lingering on us, the influences of grace present with us, and the power of amendment and conversion within us. We may still have talents which we may put to account, and gifts which we may stir up. We may not be cast out of our state of justification, and yet may be destitute of that love of God, love of God's truth, love of holiness, love of active and generous obedience, that honest surrender of self, which alone will secure to us hereafter the blessed words, 'Well done, good and faithful servant; enter thou into the joy of thy Lord.' [Matt. xxv. 21.] (*PS* v, Sermon 24: 'The Power of the Will,' 1 March 1840)

Once more, it may so happen that we find ourselves, how or why we cannot tell, much more able to obey God in certain respects than heretofore. Our minds are so strangely constituted, it is impossible to say whether it is from the growth of habit suddenly showing itself, or from an unusual gift of Divine grace poured into our hearts, but so it is; let our temptation be to sloth, or irresolution, or worldly anxiety, or pride, or to other more base and miserable sins, we may suddenly find ourselves possessed of a power of self-command which we had not before. Or again, we may have a resolution grow on us to serve God more strictly in His house and in private than heretofore. This is a call to higher things; let us beware lest we receive the grace of God in vain. (*PS* viii, Sermon 2: 'Divine Calls,' 1843)

It is our Lord's intention in His Incarnation to make us what He is Himself; this is the principle of *grace*, which is not only holy but sanctifying. (*Dev.*, Part II: ch. 7, sec. 1)

And if you are conscious that your hearts are hard, and are desirous that they should be softened, do not despair. All things are possible to you, through God's grace. Come to Him for the will and the power to do that to which He calls you. He never forsakes anyone who calls upon him. He never puts any trial on a man but He gives Him grace to overcome it. Do not despair then; nay do not despond, even though you do come to Him, yet are not at once exalted to overcome yourselves. He gives grace by little and little. It is by coming daily into His presence, that by degrees we find ourselves awed by that presence and able to believe and obey Him. (*FP*, Sermon 3: 'The Calls of Grace,' 27 February 1848)

Why we know not, but God, who shows mercy and gives grace to all, shows greater mercy and gives more abundant grace to one man than another. To all He gives grace sufficient for their salvation; to all He gives far more than they have any right to expect, and they can claim nothing; but to some He gives far more than to others. He tells us Himself, that, if the inhabitants of Tyre and Sidon had seen the miracles done in Chorazin, they would have done penance and turned to Him. That is, there was that which would have converted them, and it was not granted to them. (*Mix.*, Discourse 2: 'Neglect of Divine Calls and Warnings')

Grace is given for the merits of Christ all over the earth; there is no corner, even of Paganism, where it is not present, present in each heart of man in real sufficiency for his ultimate salvation. Not that the grace presented to each is such as at once to bring him to heaven; but it is sufficient for a beginning. It is sufficient to enable him to plead for other grace; and that second grace is such as to impetrate a third grace; and thus the soul may be led from grace to grace, and from strength to strength, till at length it is, so to say, in very sight of heaven, if the gift of perseverance does but complete the work ... It is the teaching of the Catholic Church from time immemorial, and independently of the present controversy, that grace is given in a sacred ordinance in two ways, viz.—to use the scholastic distinction, *ex opere operantis*, and *ex opere operato*. Grace is given *ex opere operato*, when, the proper dispositions being supposed in the recipient, it is given through the ordinance itself; it is given *ex opere operantis*, when, whether there be outward sign or no, the inward energetic act of the recipient is the instrument of it. (*Dif.* i, Lecture 3)

[W]hen men get old, as I do, then they see how little grace is in them, and how much what seemed grace was but nature. Then the soul is left to lassitude, torpor, dejection, and coldness which is its real state ... Then it understands at length its own nothingness, and that it has less grace than it had but it has nothing but grace to aid it. It is the sign of a saint to *grow*; common minds, even though they are in the grace of God, dwindle, (i.e. seem to do so) as time goes on. The energy of grace alone can make a soul strong in age. (*POL*; Letter to Miss Mary Holmes, 31 July 1850)

No one can come up to the strength of God's grace—stronger than the elements; stronger than miracles. It bears up against anything; it overcomes everything. (*SN*, 'On the Strong Man of Sin and Unbelief,' 23 March 1851)

Grace ever works by few; it is the keen vision, the intense conviction, the indomitable resolve of the few, it is the blood of the martyr, it is the prayer of the saint, it is the heroic deed, it is the momentary crisis, it is the concentrated energy of a word or a look, which is the instrument of heaven. Fear not, little flock, for He is mighty who is in the midst of you, and will do for you great things. (*PPC*, Lecture 9)

Nature not simply evil. We do not say that Nature cannot do good actions without God's grace. Far from it. Instances of great heathens. What we say is that no one can get to *heaven* without God's grace. (*SN*, 'Nature and Grace,' 23 July 1854)

I know perfectly well, and thankfully confess to Thee, O my God, that Thy wonderful grace turned me right round when I was more like a devil than a wicked boy, at the age of fifteen, and gave me what by Thy con-tinual aids I never lost. Thou didst change my heart, and in part my whole mental complexion at that time (*Ward* i, 575; *Journal*, 15 December 1859)

Great things are done through grace, and one attribute of the great things which grace enables the soul to do is their *lastingness*, their con-tinuance, their permanent life and strength, as years roll past. I say, the works of grace are *permanent*. (*LD* xxx, 357; Letter to P. Sprague Oram, 6 May 1884)

History

[T]he study of history is said to enlarge and enlighten the mind, and why? because, as I conceive, it gives it a power of judging of passing events, and of all events, and a conscious superiority over them, which before it did not possess. (*IU*, Part I, Discourse 6: 'Knowledge Viewed in Relation to Learning,' 1852)

History and Christianity

History is not a creed or a catechism, it gives lessons rather than rules; still no one can mistake its general teaching in this matter, whether he accept it or stumble at it. Bold outlines and broad masses of colour rise out of the records of the past. They may be dim, they may be incomplete; but they are definite. And this one thing at least is certain; whatever his-tory teaches, whatever it omits, whatever it exaggerates or extenuates, whatever it says and unsays, at least the Christianity of history is not Prot-estantism. If ever there were a safe truth, it is this. And Protestantism has ever felt it so. I do not mean that every writer on the Protestant side has felt it; for it was the fashion at first, at least as a rhetorical argument against Rome, to appeal to past ages, or to some of them; but Protestant-ism, as a whole, feels it, and has felt it. This is shown in the determination already referred to of dispensing with historical Christianity altogether, and of forming a Christianity from the Bible alone: men never would have put it aside, unless they had despaired of it ... To be deep in history is to cease to be a Protestant. (*Dev.*, Part I: Introduction)

Holy Spirit

I consider the gifts and operations of the Blessed Spirit to be manifold; some are outward, some inward, some sanctify, some are grants of power, some of knowledge, some of moral goodness ... what He is in the Church, in the individual, in the Evangelist, in the Apostle, in the Prophet, in the Apocryphal writer, in the Doctor and Teacher, — is all holy, but admits of differences of kind and of degree ... the spiritual gift in like manner may be the same, yet diverge; it may be applied to the heart or to the head, as an inward habit or an external impression; for one purpose, not for another; for a time, or for ever. Thus inspiration may be partial or plenary. (*TT* #82, 3 March 1837)

He is 'the Spirit of God;' He 'proceedeth from the Father;' He is in God as 'the spirit of a man that is in him;' He 'searcheth all things, even the deep things of God;' He is 'the Spirit of Truth;' the 'Holy Spirit;' at the creation, He 'moved upon the face of the waters;' 'Whither shall I go,' says the Psalmist, 'from Thy Spirit?' He is the Giver of all gifts, 'dividing to every man severally as He will;' we are born again 'of the Spirit.' To resist Divine grace is to grieve, to tempt, to resist, to quench, to do despite to the Spirit. He is the Comforter, Ruler, and Guide of the Church; He reveals things to come; and blasphemy against Him has never forgiveness. In all such passages, it is surely implied both that the Holy Ghost has a Personality of His own, and that He is God. (*PS* vi, Sermon 24: 'The Mystery of the Holy Trinity,' 1842)

Holy Spirit: Indwelling of

Who can be personally present at once with every Christian, but God Himself? ... It is plain that such an inhabitation brings the Christian into a state altogether new and marvellous, far above the possession of mere gifts, exalts him inconceivably in the scale of beings, and gives him a place and an office which he had not before. In St. Peter's forcible language, he becomes 'partaker of the Divine Nature,' and has 'power' or authority, as St. John says, 'to become the son of God.' Or, to use the words of St.

Paul, 'he is a new creation; old things are passed away, behold all things are become new.' His rank is new; his parentage and service new. He is 'of God,' and 'is not his own,' 'a vessel unto honour, sanctified and meet for the Master's use, and prepared unto every good work.' [2 Pet. i. 4. John i. 12. 2 Cor. v. 17. 1 John iv. 4. 1 Cor. vi. 19, 20. 2 Tim. ii. 21.] (*PS* ii, Sermon 19: 'The Indwelling Spirit,' Dec. 1834)

[S]ensible and sober-minded men, ... acquiesce in the notion, that the gift of the Holy Ghost was almost peculiar to the Apostles' day, that now, at least, it does nothing more than make us decent and orderly members of society; the privileges bestowed upon us in Scripture being, as they conceive, but of an external nature, education and the like, or, at the most, a pardon of our sins and admission to God's favour, unaccompanied by any actual and inherent powers bestowed upon us. (*PS* iii, Sermon 18: 'The Gift of the Spirit,' 8 November 1835)

But now, by the coming of our Saviour Christ, we have received *more abundantly* the Spirit of God in our hearts, ... Whatever might be the spiritual aid that was vouchsafed before, afterwards it was a Divine Presence in the soul, abiding, abundant, and efficacious. In a word, it was the Holy Ghost Himself: He influenced indeed the heart before, but is not revealed as residing in it. (*TT* #82, 11 January 1837)

The prophets had announced the *promise*. Ezek. xxxvi. 25-27: 'I will sprinkle clean water upon you, and ye shall be clean ... a *new heart* also will I give you, and *a new spirit* will I put *within* you ... and I will put My *spirit within you*.' Again, xxxvii. 27: 'My *tabernacle* also shall be with them.' Vid. also Heb. viii. 10. In Isa. xliv. 3, the gift is expressly connected with the person of the Messiah: 'I will pour water upon him that is thirsty, and floods upon the dry ground: I will pour My *Spirit* upon Thy seed, and My blessing upon Thine offspring.' Our Saviour refers to this gift as the *promise* of His Father, Luke xxiv. 49; Acts i. 4. He enlarges much upon it, John xiv.-xvi. It flows to us from Him: 'Of His fulness have all we received.' (John i. 16.) St. John expressly tells us it was *not* given *before* Christ was glorified. (John vii. 39.) In like manner St. Paul says, that though the old fathers lived by faith, yet they received not the *promise*. (Heb. xi. 39.) And St. Peter, that even the prophets, though they *had* the prophetic Spirit—'the Spirit of Christ which was in them'—yet, after all, had not 'the glory which should follow;' which was 'the Gospel *with the Holy Ghost sent down from heaven;*' that is, the Spirit, in the special Christian sense. Consider also St. Paul's use of the term 'spirit,' e.g. Rom. viii, as being the characteristic of the Gospel. It is described in the New Testament under the same images as it is promised in the Old,—a tabernacle in us, and a fount of living water (1 Cor. iii. 17; vi. 19; 2 Cor. vi. 16-18; John iv. 14; vii. 38). (*TT* #82, 11 January 1837)

A brute differs less from a man, than does man, left to himself with his natural corruption allowed to run its course, differ from man fully formed and perfected by the habitual indwelling of the Holy Spirit. (*PS* v, Sermon 13: 'The State of Salvation,' 1840)

Honorius (Pope)

I will not pass from this question of History without a word about Pope Honorius, whose condemnation by anathema in the Sixth Ecumenical Council, is certainly a strong *primâ facie* argument against the Pope's doctrinal infallibility. His case is this:—Sergius, Patriarch of Constantinople, favoured, or rather did not condemn, a doctrine concerning our Lord's Person which afterwards the Sixth Council pronounced to be heresy. He consulted Pope Honorius upon the subject, who in two formal letters declared his entire concurrence with Sergius's opinion. Honorius died in peace, but, more than forty years after him, the Sixth Ecumenical Council was held, which condemned him as a heretic on the score of those two letters. The simple question is, whether the heretical documents proceeded from him as an infallible authority or as a private Bishop. Now I observe that, whereas the Vatican Council has determined that the Pope is infallible only when he speaks *ex cathedrâ*, and that, in order to speak *ex cathedrâ*, he must at least speak 'as exercising the office of Pastor and Doctor of all Christians, defining, by virtue of his Apostolical authority, a doctrine whether of faith or of morals for the acceptance of the universal

Church' ... from this Pontifical and dogmatic explanation of the phrase it follows, that, whatever Honorius said in answer to Sergius, and whatever he held, his words were not *ex cathedrâ,* and therefore did not proceed from his infallibility. I say so first, because he could not fulfil the above conditions of an *ex cathedrâ* utterance, if he did not actually *mean* to fulfil them ... The Pope cannot address his people East and West, North and South, without meaning it, as if his very voice, the sounds from his lips, could literally be heard from pole to pole; nor can he exert his 'Apostolical authority' without knowing he is doing so; nor can he draw up a form of words and use care and make an effort in doing so accurately, without intention to do so; and, therefore, no words of Honorius proceeded from his prerogative of infallible teaching, which were not accompanied with the intention of exercising that prerogative; and who will dream of saying, be he Anglican, Protestant, unbeliever, or on the other hand Catholic, that Honorius on the occasion in question did actually intend to exert that infallible teaching voice which is heard so distinctly in the *Quantâ curâ* and the *Pastor Æternus?* ... Secondly, it is no part of our doctrine, as I shall say in my next section, that the discussions previous to a Council's definition, or to an *ex cathedrâ* utterance of a Pope, are infallible, and these letters of Honorius on their very face are nothing more than portions of a discussion with a view to some final decision. For these two reasons the condemnation of Honorius by the Council in no sense compromises the doctrine of Papal Infallibility. At the utmost it only decides that Honorius in his own person was a heretic, which is inconsistent with no Catholic doctrine; but we may rather hope and believe that the anathema fell, not upon him, but upon his letters in their objective sense, he not intending personally what his letters legitimately expressed. (*Dif.* ii, Letter to the Duke of Norfolk, ch. 8, 1875)

Ignatius of Antioch, St.

We do not assume for Ignatius more than this, that his witness comes immediately after the inspired sources of truth, that he was the friend of Apostles, and that, therefore, he was more likely to know their views of Gospel truth, and consequently their meaning in their extant writings, than a modern. ('The Theology of St. Ignatius,' *British Critic*, Jan. 1839; in *Ess*. i, sec. VI)

Now, in the case of St. Ignatius, one remarkable thing is, that, while to a modern Protestant he is so unmeaning, a disciple of Irenaeus, Athanasius, or Cyril of Alexandria, will be in no perplexity at all as to what his words mean, but will see at once a sense, and a deep and sufficient one, in them. If so, thus much would seem to follow: that, whichever party is the more scriptural, anyhow St. Ignatius, the disciple and friend of the sacred writers, is on the side of the Catholics, not of the moderns. ('The Theology of St. Ignatius,' *British Critic*, Jan. 1839; in *Ess*. i, sec. VI)

It would be a great service if some divine would put out the text of these Epistles, with a running comment from the Fathers who come after them. It is hardly too much to say that almost the whole system of Catholic doctrine may be discovered, at least in outline, not to say in parts filled up, in the course of them. ('The Theology of St. Ignatius,' *British Critic*, Jan. 1839; in *Ess*. i, sec. VI)

[I]s any further witness wanting to prove that the Catholic system, not in an inchoate state, not in doubtful dawnings, not in mere tendencies, or in implicit teaching, or in temper, or in surmises, but in a definite, complete, and dogmatic form, was the religion of St. Ignatius; and if so, where in the world did he come by it? How came he to lose, to blot out from his mind, the true Gospel, if this was not it? How came he to possess this, except it be apostolic? ('The Theology of St. Ignatius,' *British Critic*, Jan. 1839; in *Ess*. i, sec. VI)

And if the Catholic system, as a system, is brought so near to the Apostles; if it is proved to have existed as a paramount thought and a practical principle in the minds of their immediate disciples and associates, it becomes a very grave question, on this ground alone, waving altogether the consideration of uninterrupted Catholic consent, and the significant structure and indirect teaching of Scripture, whether the New Testament is not to be interpreted in accordance with that system. If indeed Scripture actually refuses to be so interpreted, then indeed we may be called on to suspend our judgment; but if only its text is *not inconsistent* with the Church system, there is surely greater reason for interpreting it in accordance with it than not; for it is surely more unaccountable that a new Gospel should have possessed the Church, and that, in the persons of its highest authorities, and almost in the lifetime and presence of Apostles, than that their extant writings should not have upon their surface the whole of Scripture truth. ('The Theology of St. Ignatius,' *British Critic*, Jan. 1839; in *Ess.* i, sec. VI)

Ignorance, Invincible

[T]hose who are in a great deal of ignorance may be saved if they are doing their best, and their ignorance invincible. (*SN*, 'Faith,' 31 January 1858)

Those who die in invincible ignorance are not in the place of lost souls; those who are not lost, are either in purgatory or in heaven. (*TT* #71, footnote 6 of 1883)

Images, Use and Veneration of

Again, the Divines at Trent say that 'to Images are to be paid due honour and veneration;' and to those who honour the sacred volume, pictures of friends and the like, as we all do, I do not see that these very words can of themselves afford matter of objection. (*VM* ii, IX. 'Letter to Rev. R. W. Jelf in Explanation of Tract 90,' 1841)

[I]n the New [Covenant], the Third Person of the Holy Trinity has signified His Presence by the appearance of a Dove, and the Second Person has presented His sacred Humanity for worship under the name of the Lamb. (*Dev.*, Part II: ch. 11, sec. 1)

[W]hen an unreligious movement, the first business to destroy these [embellishments] — the Danes, the Reformers, the Huguenots, the French Revolution. As the devil delighted to destroy our Lord's beauty, so the beauty of His Church (even organ and surplice). (*SN*, 'On External Reli-gion,' 18 October 1850)

Protestants actually set up images to represent their heroes, and they show them honour without any misgiving. The very flower and cream of Protestantism used to glory in the statue of King William on College Green, Dublin; ... You might have thought the poor senseless block had life, to see the way people took on about it, and how they spoke of his face, and his arms, and his legs; yet those same Protestants, I say, would at the same time be horrified, had I used 'he' and 'him' of a crucifix, and would call me one of the monsters described in the Apocalypse, did I but honour my living Lord as they their dead king. (*PPC*, Lecture 5)

In England Catholics pray *before* images, not to them. I wonder whether as many as a dozen pray *to* them, but *they* will be the best Catholics, not ordinary ones. The truth is, that sort of affectionate fervour which leads one to confuse an object with its representation, is skin-deep in the South and argues nothing for a worshipper's faith, hope and charity, whereas in a Northern race like ours, with whom ardent devotional feeling is not common, it may be the mark of great spirituality. As to the nature of the feeling itself, and its absolute incongruity with any intellectual intention of addressing the image as an image, I think it is not difficult for any one with an ordinary human heart to understand it. Do we not love the pic-tures which we may have of friends departed? Will not a husband wear in his bosom and kiss the miniature of his wife? Cannot you fancy a man ad-dressing himself to it, as if it were the reality? Think of Cowper's lines on his Mother's picture. 'Those lips are thine,' he says, 'thy own sweet smile I see'—and then 'Fancy shall steep me in Elysian reverie, a momentary dream, *that thou art She.*' And then he goes on to the Picture, 'My Mother,' &c.' (*Ward* i, 652 [Appendix to Ch. 19]; Letter to William Robert Brown-low, 25 October 1863)

Only this I know full well now, and did not know then, that the Catholic Church allows no image of any sort, material or immaterial, no dogmatic symbol, no rite, no sacrament, no Saint, not even the Blessed

Virgin herself, to come between the soul and its Creator. It is face to face, 'solus cum solo,' in all matters between man and his God. He alone creates; He alone has redeemed; before His awful eyes we go in death; in the vision of Him is our eternal beatitude. (*Apo.*, ch. 4)

Very large numbers of men, whom no one would accuse of superstitiously confusing the Divine Object with the Image, still testify of themselves, that they pray much better with a carved or painted representative before them than without one. (*TT* #71, footnote 11 of 1883)

Indulgences

They on the other hand agree with us in maintaining that Christ's death *might,* if God so willed, be applied for the removal even of these specific punishments of sins, which they call *temporal* punishments. (*TT* #79, 1836)

Granting that a certain fixed temporal penalty attached to every act of sin, in such case, it would be conceivable that, as the multitude of Christians did not discharge their total debt in this life, so some extraordinary holy men might more than discharge it. Such are the Prophets, Apostles, Martyrs, Ascetics, and the like, who have committed few sins, and have undergone extreme labours and sufferings, voluntary or involuntary. This being supposed, the question rises, what becomes of the overplus; and then there seems a fitness that what is not needed for themselves, should avail for their brethren who are still debtors. It is accordingly stored, together with Christ's merits, in a kind of treasure-house, to be dispensed according to the occasion, and that at the discretion of the Church. The application of this treasure is called an Indulgence. (*TT* #79, 1836)

Indulgences have sometimes been drawn up in such a form as conveys to a Protestant reader the idea of real absolution, which they always presuppose and never convey. To a person who is not pardoned (and pardoned he cannot be without repentance), an Indulgence does no good whatever; an indulgence supposes the person receiving it to be already absolved and in a state of grace, and then it remits to him the punishment which remains due to his past sins, whatever they are ... an Indulgence has nothing to do with pardon; it presupposes pardon; it is an additional remission upon and after pardon, being the remission of the arrears of suffering due from those who are already pardoned. If on receipt of this Indulgence the recipient rushed into sin, the benefit of the Indulgence would be at least suspended, till he repented, went to confession, gained a new spirit, and was restored to God's favour. If he was found in this state of pardon and grace at the point of death, then it would avail him at the point of death. Then, that pardon which his true repentance would gain him in the sacrament of penance, would be crowned by the further re-mission of punishment through the Indulgence, certainly not otherwise. (*PPC*, Lecture 8)

That our Lord has left to His Church the power of relaxing the temporal punishments due to sin, is a doctrine plain from Scripture, from the continual practice of the Church, and from the Fathers, and it is enjoined on Catholics as *de fide*, as being the decision of the infallible Church ... the merits of the Saints are only the *medium* by which the infinite merits of the Redeemer are applied for the relaxation of the temporal punishment. (*VM* i, Lecture 4; footnotes 4 and 6 from 1877)

The Church has the power of opening another and more certain way, of shortening the suffering in purgatory; she can assign particular works, prayers, etc etc on the performance of which Almighty God shortens that period of suffering which otherwise the repentant sinner would undergo in purgatory. This grant is called an 'indulgence.' An indulgence cannot be gained by a man living in sin—nor is it a pardon of *sin*—but it is a remission of *punishment*, for the repentant sinner, whose sins have already been forgiven. (*LD* xxix, 299; Letter to J. L. Walton, 9 September 1880)

Inquisition / Temporal Punishments

John Wilson, while they tore out his heart said, 'I forgive the Queen, and all that are the cause of my death.' Edward Campion was cruelly torn and rent upon the rack divers times. 'Before he went to the rack, he used to fall down at the rack-house door, upon both knees, to commend himself to God's mercy; and upon the rack he called continually upon God, repeating often the holy name of Jesus. His keeper asked him the next day, how he felt his hands and feet, he answered, 'Not ill, because not at all.' He was hanged and embowelled at Tyburn.' Ralph Sherwin came next; the hangman, taking hold of him with his bloody hands, which had been busy with the bowels of the martyred priest who preceded him, said to him, thinking to terrify him, 'Come, Sherwin, take thou also thy wages.' But the holy man, nothing dismayed, embraced him with a cheerful countenance, and reverently kissed the blood that stuck to his hands; at which the people were much moved. He had been twice racked, and now he was dealt with as his brother before him. Thomas Sherwood, after six months' imprisonment in a dark and filthy hole, was hanged, cut down alive, dismembered, bowelled, and quartered. Alexander Brian had needles thrust under his nails, was torn upon the rack, hanged, and beheaded. George Haydock was suffered to hang but a very little while, when the Sheriff ordered the rope to be cut, and the whole butchery to be performed upon him while he was alive, and perfectly sensible. John Finch was dragged through the streets, his head beating all the way upon the stones; was then thrust into a dark and fetid dungeon, with no bed but the damp floor; was fed sparingly, and on nothing but oxen's liver. Here he was left first for weeks, then for months; till at length he was hanged, and his quarters sent to the four chief towns of Lancashire. Richard White, being cut down alive, pronounced the sacred name of Jesus twice, while the hangman had his hands in his bowels. James Claxton was first put into *little ease*, that is, a place, where he could neither stand, lie, nor sit; there he was for three days, fed on bread and water. Then he was put into the mill to grind; then he was hanged up by the hands, till the blood sprang forth at his fingers' ends: at length he was hanged, dying at the age of twenty-one years. These are the acts, these are the scenes, which Protestants, stopping their ears, and raising their voices, and casting dust into the air, will not let us inflict upon them. No, it is pleasanter to declaim against persecution, and to call the Inquisition a hell, than to consider their own devices, and the work of their own hands. The catalogue reaches to some hundred names. One was killed in this manner in 1577, two in 1578, four in 1581, eleven in 1582, thirteen in 1583 and 1584, nineteen in 1585 and 1586, thirty-nine in 1587 and 1588, and so on at intervals to the end of the seventeenth century; besides the imprisonments and transportations, which can hardly be numbered. What will the Protestants bring against the Holy See comparable to atrocities such as these? not, surely, with any fairness, the burnings in Queen Mary's reign, the acts, as they were, of an English party, inflamed with revenge against their enemies, and opposed by Cardinal Pole, the Pope's Legate, as well as by the ecclesiastics of Spain ... The horrors I have been describing are no anomaly in the history of Protestantism. Whatever theoretical differences it has had on the subject with the Catholic Religion, it has, in matter of fact, ever shown itself a persecuting power. It has persecuted in England, in Scotland, in Ireland, in Holland, in France, in Germany, in Geneva. (*PPC*, Lecture 5)

To take the instance of the 'physical punishment of heretics,' which you refer to, and to confine myself to Scripture. Is not the miraculous infliction of judgments upon blasphemy, lying, profaneness &c. in the Apostles' day a sanction of infliction upon the same by a human hand in the times of the Inquisition? I think it is. Yet on the other hand such infliction is not enjoined, and, in our Lord's words about Elias's bringing fire from heaven, is discouraged. That is, ecclesiastical rulers may punish with the sword, if they *can*, and if it is *expedient*, or *necessary* to do so. The proposition, thus implied (as I think) in Scripture, is all that the modern Church asserts. For I do not know anything more determinate on the subject (as far as my memory goes) than the condemnation (among the Propositiones damnatæ) of Luther's assertion, 'Hereticos comburi est contra voluntatem Spiritus.' Pius the VI. has condemned the general denial of ecclesiastical punishments in the 'auctorem fidei.' ... I hold, till better instructed, that the Church has a right to make laws and to enforce them with temporal punishments; for so I understand Pius the VI.'s contradiction of '*Ecclesiam non habere potestatem salubribus poenis contumaces coercendi atque cogendi.*' But whether such exercise of her powers is suitable to all times and places, is surely answered in the negative by the fact of her concordats, which involve an engagement not to use her full powers in particular states. (*Ward* i, 639 [Appendix to Ch. 18]; Letter to Lord Acton, 19 July 1862)

Jesus: Divinity of

Christ is God: from eternity He was the Living and True God. This is not mentioned expressly in the Epistle for this day, though it is significantly implied there in various ways; but it is all but expressly stated, and that by Himself, in the Gospel. He says there, 'Before Abraham was, I am:' [John viii. 58.] by which words He declares that He did not begin to exist from the Virgin's womb, but had been in existence before. And by using the words *I am*, He seems to allude, as I have already said, to the Name of God, which was revealed to Moses in the burning bush, when he was commanded to say to the children of Israel, 'I *am* hath sent me unto you.' [Exod. iii. 14.] Again: St. Paul says of Christ, that He was 'in the form of God,' and 'thought it not robbery to be equal with God,' yet 'made Himself of no reputation.' In like manner St. John says; 'In the beginning was the Word, and the Word was with God, and the Word was God.' And St. Thomas addressed Him as his Lord and his God; and St. Paul declares that He is 'God over all, blessed for ever;' and the prophet Isaiah, that He is 'the mighty God, the Everlasting Father;' and St. Paul again, that He is 'our great God and Saviour;' and St. Jude, that He is 'our only Sovereign God and Lord.' [Phil. ii. 6, 7. John i. 1; xx. 28. Rom. ix. 5. Isa. ix. 6. Tit. ii. 13. Jude 4.] It is not necessary, surely, to enlarge on this point, which is constantly brought before us in Scripture ... He tells us expressly Himself, 'He that hath seen Me, hath seen the Father;' and 'all men' are to 'honour the Son, even as they honour the Father;' and 'He that honoureth not the Son, honoureth not the Father which hath sent Him.' [John xiv. 9; v. 23.] ... it is surely not so marvellous and mysterious that the Son of God should be God, as that there should be a Son of God at all. (*PS* vi, Sermon 5: 'Christ, the Son of God Made Man,' 26 April 1836)

He was man indeed, but He was more than man: and He did what man does, but then those deeds of His were the deeds of God, — and we can as little separate the deed from the Doer as our arm from our body. (*PS* v, Sermon 2: 'Reverence, a Belief in God's Presence,' 4 November 1838)

We all know it to be an essential and most practical doctrine that the Person of Christ is Divine, and that *into* His Divine Personality He has taken human nature; or, in other words, the Agent, Speaker, Sufferer, Sacrifice, Intercessor, Judge, is God, though God in our flesh; not man with a presence of Divinity. The latter doctrine is Sabellianism, Nestorianism, and Socinianism. ('Milman's View of Christianity,' *British Critic*, Jan. 1841; in *Ess.* ii, sec. XII)

Jesus: Incarnation and Two Natures of

The main purpose of our Saviour's incarnation, as far as we are permitted to know it, was that of reconciling us to God, and purchasing for us eternal life by His sufferings and death. (*US*, Sermon 2: 'The Influence of Natural and Revealed Religion Respectively,' 13 April 1830)

Let it be understood, then, that the Almighty Son of God, who had been in the bosom of the Father from everlasting, became man; became man as truly as He was always God. He was God from God, as the Creed says; that is, as being the Son of the Father, He had all those infinite perfections from the Father which the Father had. He was of one substance with the Father, and was God, because the Father was God. He was truly God, but He became as truly man. He became man, yet so as not to cease in any respect being what He was before. He added a new nature to Himself, yet so intimately, that it was *as if* He had actually left His former self, which He did not. (*PS* vi, Sermon 6: 'The Incarnate Son, a Sufferer and Sacrifice,' 1 April 1836)

This was the new and perfect tabernacle into which He entered; entered, but not to be confined, not to be circumscribed by it. The Most High dwelleth not in temples made with hands; though His own hands 'made it and fashioned it,' still He did not cease to be what He was, because He became man, but was still the Infinite God, manifested in, not altered by the flesh. He took upon Him our nature, as an instrument of His purposes, not as an agent in the work. What is one thing cannot become another; His manhood remained human, and His Godhead remained divine. God became man, yet was still God, having His manhood as an adjunct, perfect in its kind, but dependent upon His Godhead … Still, we must ever remember, that though He was in nature perfect man, He was not man in exactly the same sense in which any one of us is a man. Though man, He was not, strictly speaking, in the English sense of the word, *a* man; He was not such as one of us, and one out of a number. He was man because He had our human nature wholly and perfectly, but His Person is not human like ours, but divine. He who was from eternity, continued one and the same, but with an addition. His incarnation was a 'taking of the manhood into God.' As He had no earthly father, so has He no human personality. We may not speak of Him as we speak of any individual man, acting from and governed by a human intelligence within Him, but He was God, acting not only as God, but now through the flesh also, when He would. He was not a man made God, but God made man … though His Divine Nature was sovereign and supreme when He became incarnate, yet the manhood which He assumed was not kept at a distance from Him (if I may so speak) as a mere instrument, or put on as a mere garment, or entered as a mere tabernacle, but it was really taken into the closest and most ineffable union with Him. He received it into His Divine Essence (if we may dare so to speak) almost as a new attribute of His Person. (*PS* vi, Sermon 5: 'Christ, the Son of God Made Man,' 26 April 1836)

Christ came to make a new world. He came into the world to regenerate it in Himself, to make a new beginning, to be the beginning of the creation of God, to gather together in one, and recapitulate all things in Himself. The rays of His glory were scattered through the world; one state of life had some of them, another others. The world was like some fair mirror, broken in pieces, and giving back no one uniform image of its Maker. But He came to combine what was dissipated, to recast what was shattered in Himself. He began all excellence, and of His fulness have all we received. (*SD*, Sermon 5: 'The Three Offices of Christ,' 25 December 1840)

The Incarnation is the antecedent of the doctrine of Mediation, and the archetype both of the Sacramental principle and of the merits of

Saints. From the doctrine of Mediation follow the Atonement, the Mass, the merits of Martyrs and Saints, their invocation and *cultus*. From the Sacramental principle come the Sacraments properly so called; the unity of the Church, and the Holy See as its type and centre; the authority of Councils; the sanctity of rites; the veneration of holy places, shrines, images, vessels, furniture, and vestments. Of the Sacraments, Baptism is developed into Confirmation on the one hand; into Penance, Purgatory, and Indulgences on the other; and the Eucharist into the Real Presence, adoration of the Host, Resurrection of the body, and the virtue of relics. Again, the doctrine of the Sacraments leads to the doctrine of Justification; Justification to that of Original Sin; Original Sin to the merit of Celibacy. Nor do these separate developments stand independent of each other, but by cross relations they are connected, and grow together while they grow from one ... You must accept the whole or reject the whole; attenuation does but enfeeble, and amputation mutilate. It is trifling to receive all but something which is as integral as any other portion. (*Dev.*, Part I: ch. 2, sec. 3)

Christianity began by considering Matter as a creature of God, and in itself 'very good.' It taught that Matter, as well as Spirit, had become corrupt, in the instance of Adam; and it contemplated its recovery. It taught that the Highest had taken a portion of that corrupt mass upon Himself, in order to the sanctification of the whole; that, as a first fruits of His purpose, He had purified from all sin that very portion of it which He took into His Eternal Person, and thereunto had taken it from a Virgin Womb, which He had filled with the abundance of His Spirit. Moreover, it taught that during His earthly sojourn He had been subject to the natural infirmities of man, and had suffered from those ills to which flesh is heir. It taught that the Highest had in that flesh died on the Cross, and that His blood had an expiatory power; moreover, that He had risen again in that flesh, and had carried that flesh with Him into heaven, and that from that flesh, glorified and deified in Him, He never would be divided. As a first consequence of these awful doctrines comes that of the resurrection of the bodies of His Saints, and of their future glorification with Him; next, that of the sanctity of their relics; further, that of the merit of Virginity; and, lastly, that of the prerogatives of Mary, Mother of God. All these doctrines are more or less developed in the Ante-nicene period, though in very various degrees, from the nature of the case. (*Dev.*, Part II: ch. 10, sec. 1)

What is more wonderful than that God should become man. Real Presence, power of Mary, purgatory, eternal punishment, intercession of saints, election, original sin. The whole Catholic system bound up in it. (*SN*, 'On the Name of Jesus,' 19 January 1851)

Now our Lord, in His own proper nature as God, is infinitely separate from all beings whatever, but He took on Him a created, a human, a frail nature, when He came on earth. He became a child of Adam. He took on Him that fallen nature which He had made perfect at the time that He created [it], but which had lost its perfection, and which anyhow was always [in] its own essence and by itself frail. If angelic natures have, separate from the grace of God, imperfection, much more has man's nature. Our Lord took on Him a nature which in any other (except His mother) but Him would be sure to sin. He took on Himself a nature which nothing but the grace of God could save from running into sin, from that inherent imperfection which attaches to the creature. He [His human nature] could not sin, but the reason why it could not was not because it was intrinsically higher or better than the nature of any other son of fallen Adam, but because the presence of Himself in it, of Himself who was God, rendered it utterly removed from sin and incompatible with it. Still, His human nature was such that, had it not been His, it might have sinned. But it never was by itself, it never had been without Him. From the first moment of its existence He had taken it up into Himself; He had created it for Himself, and thus it was absolutely and eternally secured from all sin. (*SN*, 'During Exposition for Troubles in India,' 11 October 1857)

Though our Lord, as having two natures, had a human as well as a divine knowledge, and though that human knowledge was not only limited because human, but liable to ignorance in matters in which greater knowledge was possible; yet it is the received doctrine, that *in fact* He was not ignorant even in His human nature, according to its capacity, since it

was from the first taken out of its original and natural condition, and 'deified' by its union with the Word. As then ... His manhood was created,
yet He may not be called a creature even in His manhood, and as ... His
flesh was in its abstract nature a servant, yet He is not a servant in fact,
even as regards the flesh; so, though He took on Him a soul which left to
itself would have been partially ignorant, as other human souls, yet as ever
enjoying the Beatific Vision from its oneness with the Word, it never was
ignorant in fact, but knew all things which human soul can know ... It is
the doctrine of the Church that Christ, as man, was perfect in knowledge
from the first, as if ignorance were hardly separable from sin, and were the
direct consequence or accompaniment of original sin. (*Ath.* ii, 'Ignorance
Assumed Economically by Our Lord')

It is the general teaching of the Fathers in accordance with Athan.,
that our Lord would not have been incarnate had not man sinned ...
There were two reasons then for the Incarnation, viz., atonement for sin,
and renewal in holiness, ... These two ends of our Lord's Incarnation, that
He might die for us, and that He might renew us, answer nearly to those
specified in Rom. iv. 25, 'who was delivered for our offences and raised
again for our justification.' (*Ath.* ii, 'The Incarnation')

Jesus: Passion and Suffering of

The passion of our Lord is one of the most imperative and engrossing
subjects of Catholic teaching. It is the great topic of meditations and
prayers; it is brought into continual remembrance by the sign of the
Cross; it is preached to the world in the Crucifix; it is variously honoured by the many houses of prayer, and associations of religious men,
and pious institutions and undertakings, which in some way or other are
placed under the name and the shadow of Jesus, or the Saviour, or the
Redeemer, or His Cross, or His Passion, or His sacred Heart. (*Dev.*, Part
II: ch. 11, sec. 1)

Well, as to the sufferings of the Son of God, they are awful mysteries;
but they need not surprise us, for He comes to suffer. He indeed might

have saved us without suffering, but it was in fact bound up in His coming. He was a combatant—combatants suffer. He was prophesied as a warrior and man of blood. He fought with the devil. He fought with sin, ... no wonder He should suffer ... He alone suffered all who died for all. (SN, 'On the M. Addolorata—The Seven Dolours,' 28 September 1851)

But still He would know and understand, infinitely more than we can, the shame of having a nature which was in itself peccable. And therefore the sins of all His brethren weighed on Him, and were in one sense His, because He partook their nature, had a share in a common possession which was a very shameful possession. In this sense, though most pure, He bore Him a body of death and the sins of the whole world ... in the Garden, when He sweated drops of blood, it was the weight of that fallen nature which He had assumed which made Him weary even unto death. (SN, 'During Exposition for Troubles in India,' 11 October 1857)

Jesus: Redeemer

The fall of Adam has placed a huge obstacle, as a wall or a mountain, between us and God, and Christ has broken it down. He has opened the kingdom of heaven to all who believe. This is why He took flesh and came on earth. (SN, 'Communion with God,' 27 February 1876)

Justification

St. Paul again and again speaks of our justification as being not from without but from within; from God indeed as its origin, but through our own hearts and minds, wills and powers. He attributes it to the influences of the Spirit working in us, and enabling us to perform that obedience to the Law, towards which by ourselves we could not take a single step. (Jfc., ch. 2)

For we must consider that since we are ever falling into sin and incurring God's wrath, we are ever being justified again and again by His grace. Justification is imparted to us continually all through our lives. (Jfc., ch. 4)

Justification comes *through* the Sacraments; is received *by* faith; *consists* in God's inward presence; and *lives* in obedience. (*Jfc.*, ch. 12)

Catholics hold that, whereas faith, as a disposing condition, is prior to justification, love or *charitas* is posterior to it. (*Jfc.*, ch. 10, footnote 6 from 1874)

Justification and Human Free Will and Cooperation (Synergy)

We can do nothing good of ourselves; with God's grace we can do what is good. This is what I have been hitherto saying; but this is not all,—*with* His grace we are gifted not only with the capacity of being led into truth and holiness, but with the power of co-operating with Him. God's grace unfetters the will which by nature is in bondage, and thus restores to us the faculty of accepting or rejecting that grace itself. It enables us to obey, not as instruments merely, but as free agents, who, while they obey, are not constrained to obey, except that they choose to obey; and whose obedience is for that reason more pleasing to God, as proceeding more entirely from themselves, 'not by constraint,' but 'willingly' and 'heartily.' It does not follow from this, that there is any one good thought, word, or deed of ours, which proceeds from ourselves only, and which we present to God *as* ours; but the circumstance that in such acceptable offerings as we render to Him, there has been a cooperation on our part, has proved a reason, over and above those already mentioned, why justification has been said to consist in our services, not in God's imputation; those services forming a concurrent cause of that imputation being ratified. Without such co-operation, that imputation would be void; as the grace of a sacrament is suspended when the recipient is not duly prepared. Hence, St. Peter urges us to 'make our calling and election *sure*;' St. Paul, to '*work out* our own salvation with fear and trembling;' and St. John declares that 'whatsoever we ask, we receive of Him, *because we keep His commandments*, and do those things *that are pleasing in His sight.*' ... He implants in part within us the very thing which in its fulness He imputes to us; ... our concurrence in being justified is a necessary condition of His justifying. (*Jfc.*, ch. 4)

'Work out your own salvation with fear and trembling, *for* it is God which worketh in you both to will and to do of His good pleasure.' [Phil. ii. 13.] God is in you for righteousness, for sanctification, for redemption, through the Spirit of His Son, and you must use His influences, His operations, not as your own (God forbid!), not as you would use your own mind or your own limbs, irreverently, but as His presence in you. All your knowledge is from Him; all good thoughts are from Him; all power to pray is from Him; your Baptism is from Him; the consecrated elements are from Him; your growth in holiness is from Him. You are not your own, you have been bought with a price, and a mysterious power is working in you ... This then is one of the first elements of Christian knowledge and a Christian spirit, to refer all that is good in us, all that we have of spiritual life and righteousness, to Christ our Saviour; to believe that He works in us, or, to put the same thing more pointedly, to believe that saving truth, life, light, and holiness are not *of* us, though they must be *in* us. (*PS* v, Sermon 10: 'Righteousness not of us, but in us,' 19 January 1840)

And this is what is revealed, viz.:—on the one hand, that our salvation depends on ourselves, and on the other, that it depends on God. Did we not depend on ourselves, we should become careless and reckless, nothing we did or did not do having any bearing on our salvation; did we not depend on God, we should be presumptuous and self-sufficient. I began by telling you, my brethren, and I shall proceed in what is to come more distinctly to tell you, that you depend upon God; but such admonitions necessarily imply your dependence upon yourselves also; for, did not your salvation in some sufficient sense depend on yourselves, what would be the use of appealing to you not to *forget* your dependence on God? It is because you have so great a share in your own salvation, that it avails, that it is pertinent, to speak to you of God's part in it. (*Mix.*, Discourse 7: 'Perseverance in Grace')

He co-operates with us in our acting, and thereby enables us to do that which He wills us to do, and carries us on, if our will does but co-operate with His. (*Apo.*, ch. 4)

[W]hen the Roman schools are treating of one point of theology, they are not treating of other points. When the Council of Trent is treating of man, it is not treating of God. Its enunciations are isolated and defective, taken one by one, of course. (*Jfc.*, ch. 2, footnote 1 from 1874)

Justification and Indwelling of the Holy Spirit

In a word, what is it to have His presence within us, but to be His conse-crated Temple? what to be His Temple, but to be set apart from a state of nature, from sin and Satan, guilt and peril? what to be thus set apart, but to be declared and treated as righteous? and what is this but to be justified? (*Jfc.*, ch. 6)

Next, it may be remarked that whatever blessings in detail we ascribe to justification, are ascribed in Scripture to this sacred indwelling. For instance, is justification *remission of sins*? the Gift of the Spirit conveys it, as is evident from the Scripture doctrine about Baptism: 'One Baptism for the remission of sins.' Is justification *adoption* into the family of God? in like manner the Spirit is expressly called the Spirit of adoption, 'the Spirit whereby we cry, Abba, Father.' Is justification *reconciliation* with God? St. Paul says, 'Jesus Christ is in you, unless ye be reprobates.' Is jus-tification *life*? the same Apostle says, 'Christ liveth in me.' Is justification given to *faith*? it is his prayer 'that *Christ* may dwell in' Christian 'hearts by faith.' Does justification lead to holy *obedience*? Our Lord assures us that 'he that abideth in Him and He in him, the same bringeth forth much fruit.' Is it through justification that we rejoice *in hope of the glory* of God? In like manner 'Christ in us' is said to be 'the hope of glory.' Christ then is our righteousness by dwelling in us by the Spirit: He justifies us by entering into us, He continues to justify us by remaining in us. *This* is really and truly our justification, not faith, not holiness, not (much less) a mere imputation; but through God's mercy, the very Presence of Christ. (*Jfc.*, ch. 6)

[T]he connexion really is between justification and renewal. They are both included in that one great gift of God, the indwelling of Christ in

the Christian soul. That indwelling is *ipso facto* our justification and sanctification, as its necessary results. It is the Divine Presence that justifies
us, not faith, as say the Protestant schools, ... The word of justification is
the substantive living Word of God, entering the soul, illuminating and
cleansing it, as fire brightens and purifies material substances. He who
justifies also sanctifies, because it is He. (*Jfc.*, ch. 6)

Justification and Sanctification

The doctrine popular at present connects joy rigidly with justification; as
if *immediately upon* justification, and *before* sanctification, 'joy and peace
in believing' ensued. I really do not understand how a man can read this
most important Psalm [Ps. 51] without perceiving (though I know many
do not perceive it), that we are forgiven *by being*, or *while we are* renewed,
and that the present broad separation of justification and sanctification,
as if they were two gifts, not in idea only two, but in fact, is technical and
unscriptural. (*Jfc.*, ch. 2)

Now it is plain, from St. Paul, that the regenerate please God, not
merely by the imputation of Christ's obedience, but by their own obedience: by their obedience therefore are they justified. If they were justified
only by imputation of Christ's obedience, they could only please him by
virtue of that obedience; but so far as they are enabled to please Him by
what they are and what they do, so far may they be said, through His
secret grace, to justify themselves. For instance, St. Paul says, 'The God
of grace ... make you perfect in every good work to do His will, *working
in you that which is well pleasing in His sight*, through Jesus Christ;' he does
not say, '*imputing to you* what is pleasing.' Christ then does not keep the
power of justification solely in His own hands, but by His Spirit dispenses
it to us in due measure, through the medium of our own doings. He has
imparted to us the capacity of pleasing Him; and to please Him is that in
part, which justification is in fulness, and tends towards justification as its
limit. (*Jfc.*, ch. 2)

[J]ustification, as such, may properly be a *declaration*, though it involves
in fact a *gift* of righteousness. (*Jfc.*, ch. 3)

[L]et us believe the comfortable truth, that the justifying grace of God effects what it declares. 'The Voice of the Lord is mighty in *operation*, the Voice of the Lord is a glorious Voice.' It is not like some idle sound, or a vague rumour coming at random, and tending no whither, but it is 'the Word which goeth forth out of His mouth;' it has a sacramental power, being the instrument as well as the sign of His will. It never can 'return unto Him void, but it accomplishes that which He pleases, and prospers in the thing whereto He sends it.' Imputed righteousness is the coming in of actual righteousness. They whom God's sovereign voice pronounces just, forthwith become in their measure just. He declares a fact, and makes it a fact by declaring it. He imputes, not a name but a substantial Word, which, being 'ingrafted' in our own hearts, 'is able to save our souls.' God's word, I say, effects what it announces. This is its characteristic all through Scripture. (*Jfc.*, ch. 3)

It would seem, then, in all cases, that God's word is the instrument of His deed. When, then, He solemnly utters the command, 'Let the soul be just,' it becomes inwardly just; by what medium or in what manner or degree, is a further question not now to be discussed. (*Jfc.*, ch. 3)

He provided, not gave salvation, when He suffered; and there must be a giving or applying in the case of all those who are to be saved. The gift of life is in us, as truly as it is not of us; it is not only *from* Him but it is *unto* us. This must carefully be borne in mind, for as there are those who consider that life, righteousness, and salvation are of us, so there are others who hold that they are not in us; and as there are many who more or less forget that justification is of God, so there are quite as many who more or less forget that justification must be in man if it is to profit him. And it is hard to say which of the two errors is the greater. (*PS* v, Sermon 10: 'Righteousness not of us, but in us,' 19 January 1840)

[T]hey consider justification to be nothing more than God's *accounting* them righteous, which is just what justification was to the Jews. Justification *is* God's accounting a man righteous; yes, but it is, in the case of the Christian, something more; it is God's *making* him righteous too. As beasts live, and men live, and life is life, and yet life is not the same in man and beast; but in man consists in the presence of a soul; so in somewhat the same way Jews were justified, and Christians are justified, and in the case of both justification means God's accounting men righteous; but in Christians it means not only an accounting, but it involves a making; so that as the presence of a soul is the mode in which God gives man life, so the presence of the Holy Spirit is the mode in which God gives him righteousness. This is that promise of the Spirit of life, because of which the Gospel is called 'a ministration of righteousness.' But the multitude of religious professors at this day whom I speak of, do not admit this; they even protest against the notion. They think justification to be something, not inward, but merely outward; that is, they acknowledge themselves, they claim to be, in the state of the Jews, and though of course they contend that they *are* justified, yet they own that their own justification is not more than an outward or imputative justification. (*PS* vi, Sermon 13: 'Judaism of the Present Day,' 28 February 1841)

Justification by Faith Alone (Falsity of)

If, after all, to believe and to obey be but different characteristics of one and the same state of mind, in what a most serious error are whole masses of men involved at this day, who are commonly considered religious! It is undeniable that there are multitudes who would avow with confidence and exultation that they put obedience only in the second place in their religious scheme, as if it were rather a necessary consequence of faith than requiring a direct attention for its own sake; a something subordinate to it, rather than connatural and contemporaneous with it. It is certain, however startling it is to reflect upon it, that numbers do not in any true sense believe that they shall be judged; they believe in a coming judgment as regards the wicked, but they do not believe that all men, that they themselves personally, will undergo it. I wish from my heart that the persons in question could be persuaded to read Scripture with their own eyes, and take it in a plain and natural way, instead of perplexing themselves with their human systems, and measuring and arranging its inspired declarations by an artificial rule. (*PS* iii, Sermon 6: 'Faith and Obedience,' 21 February 1830)

Luther, not Scripture, says that faith only justifies. (*Jfc.*, ch. 5)

It is the fashion of the day to sever these two from one another, which God has joined, the seal and the impression, justification and renewal. You hear men speak of glorying in the Cross of Christ, who are utter strangers to the notion of the Cross as actually applied to them in water and blood, in holiness and mortification. They think the Cross can be theirs *without* being applied, — without its coming near them, — while they keep at a distance from it, and only gaze at it. They think individuals are justified immediately by the great Atonement, — justified by Christ's death, and not, as St. Paul says, by means of His Resurrection, — justified by what they consider *looking* at His death. Because the Brazen Serpent in the wilderness healed by being looked at, they consider that Christ's Sacrifice saves by the mind's contemplating it. This is what they call casting themselves upon Christ, — coming before Him simply and without self-trust, and being saved by faith. Surely we ought so to *come* to Christ; surely we must believe; surely we must look; but the question is, in what form and manner He *gives* Himself to us; and it will be found that, when He enters into us, glorious as He is Himself, pain and self-denial are His attendants. Gazing on the Brazen Serpent did not heal; but God's invisible communication of the gift of health to those who gazed. So also justification is wholly the work of God; it comes from God to us; it is a power exerted on our souls by Him, as the healing of the Israelites was a power exerted on their bodies. The gift must be brought *near* to us; it is not like the Brazen Serpent, a mere external, material, local sign; it is a spiritual gift, and, as being such, admits of being applied to us individually. Christ's Cross does not justify by being looked at, but by being applied; not by as merely beheld by faith, but by being actually set up within us, and that not by our act, but by God's invisible grace. Men sit, and gaze, and speak of the great Atonement, and think this is appropriating it; not more truly than kneeling to the material cross itself is appropriating it. Men say that faith is an apprehending and applying; faith cannot really apply the Atonement; man cannot make the Saviour of the world his own; the Cross must be brought home to us, not in word, but in power, and this is the work of the Spirit. This is justification; but when imparted to the soul, it draws blood, it heals, it purifies, it glorifies. (*Jfc.*, ch. 5)

Phinehas, the son of Eleazar, was justified by an act of zeal: 'Then stood up Phinehas and executed judgment, and so the plague was stayed. And that was counted unto him for righteousness unto all generations for evermore.' [Ps. cvi. 30, 31.] Zacharias and Elizabeth were 'both righteous before God, walking in all the commandments and ordinances of the Lord blameless.' [Luke i. 6.] Words cannot be stronger to express the justification of these holy persons, than that they were 'blameless and righteous *before God;*' yet this gift is not coupled with faith, but with acts of obedience paid to the special and particular commandments of God. In like manner St. John teaches, that 'walking in the light' justifies us: 'If we walk in the light, as He is in the light, we have fellowship one with another, *and the blood* of Jesus Christ His Son cleanseth us from all sin.' [1 John i. 7; iii. 7.] (*Jfc.*, ch. 12)

[H]ow do we prove the doctrine of justification by faith only? it is nowhere declared in Scripture. St. Paul does but speak of justification by faith, not by faith only, and St. James actually denies that it is by faith only. Yet we think right to infer, that there is a correct sense in which it is by faith only; though an Apostle has in so many words said just the contrary. Is any of the special Church doctrines about the power of Absolution, the Christian Priesthood, or the danger of sin after Baptism, so disadvantageously circumstanced in point of evidence as this, 'articulus,' as Luther called it, 'stantis ut cadentis ecclesiæ'? (*TT* #85, Sep. 1838)

Justification by Faith without the Sacraments is the essence of sectarian and (modern) heretical doctrine. (*Keb.*, 207; Letter of 4 March 1843)

Every theology has its difficulties; Protestants hold justification by faith only, though there is no text in St. Paul which enunciates it, and though St. James expressly denies it; do we therefore call Protestants dishonest? (*Apo.*, ch. 2)

Justification, Infused

And this, surely, is St. John's doctrine as well as St. Paul's, though brought forward by him in the way of warning, rather than encouragement. He declares solemnly in his general Epistle, that 'He that *doeth righteousness* is righteous;' as if doing righteousness was that in which righteousness consists. And then, that there may be no mistake, he adds, '*even as He is righteous.*' What very strong words! implying that our righteousness is a resemblance, and therefore a partial communication or infusion into our hearts, of that super-human righteousness of Christ, which is our true justification. (*Jfc.*, ch. 4)

St. Paul ... says in the fifth chapter of his Epistle to the Romans, 'As by one man's disobedience many were made sinners, so by the obedience of One shall many be made righteous.' He says that by Christ's righteousness we are made righteous; made, not accounted merely ... In the original Greek the word means not merely *made*, but brought into a *state* of righteousness. It is the same word as is used by St. Peter, when he says, 'If these things,' faith, charity, and other graces, 'be in you and abound, they *make* you,' that is, *constitute* you as being 'neither barren nor unfruitful in the knowledge of our Lord Jesus Christ.' ... When, then, St. Paul says that we 'become righteous' by Christ's obedience, he is speaking of our actual state through Christ, of that internal nature, frame, or character, which Christ gives us, nor gives only, but *constitutes* ours. He speaks of our new nature as really righteousness. (*Jfc.*, ch. 5)

Not only is the *word* 'righteous' applied to Christians in Scripture, but the *idea* is again and again, in various ways, forced upon us. We read, for instance, of 'God working *in us* that which is *well-pleasing in His sight;*' of our being 'holy and *without blame before Him* in love;' of Christ, 'who is His image,' 'shining' and 'living' in our hearts; of His 'making us *accepted*' or *gracious* 'in the Beloved;' and of His '*knowing what is the mind of the Spirit*' in our hearts, because 'He *maketh intercession* for the saints *in God's way.*' [Heb. xiii. 21. 2 Cor. iv. 4. Eph. i. 4, 6. Rom. viii. 27.] Such passages, I say, make it clear that acceptableness or graciousness is imparted to us as really as any other excellence belonging to Christ; and if acceptableness be what is meant by righteousness, it follows that the *thing* as well as the *word* righteousness is ours in the sense in which it is Christ's. Christ's righteousness, which is given us, makes us righteous, because it *is* righteousness; it imparts *itself,* and not something else. (*Jfc.,* ch. 5)

Again: we read of 'righteous Abel;' we are told that 'Noah was a just man, and perfect in his generations;' that Job was 'perfect and upright,' that Lot was 'righteous,' that Moses was 'faithful in all God's house,' that Elias was 'a righteous man,' that Daniel was 'righteous' and 'greatly beloved,' that Zacharias and Elizabeth were 'both righteous,' that Joseph was 'a just man,' that Simeon was 'just and devout,' that Joseph of Arimathea was 'a good man and a just,' that St. John the Baptist was 'a just man and an holy,' that Cornelius was 'a just man, and one that feareth God,' that 'the righteous shall shine forth as the sun in the kingdom of their Father,' that 'the righteous' shall go 'into life eternal,' that there shall be 'a resurrection of the just,' that 'the Law lieth not against a just man,' that a 'Bishop must be sober, just, holy, temperate.' We read of the 'spirits of the just made perfect,' of 'the righteous scarcely being saved,' and of 'him who is just becoming more just;' [Matt. xxiii. 35. Heb. xi. 4. Gen. vi. 9. Job. i. 1. 2 Pet. ii. 7, 8. Num. xii. 7. James v. 16. Ezek. xiv. 14. Dan. ix. 23. Luke i. 6. Matt. i. 19. Luke ii. 25. Mark vi. 20. Acts x. 22. Matt. xiii. 43; xxv. 46. Luke xiv. 14. 1 Tim. i. 9. Tit. i. 8. Heb. xii. 23. 1 Pet. iv. 18. Rev. xxii. 11.] but when we would apply these statements to the great evangelical canon, 'The *just* shall live by faith,' as explaining who are the 'just' there spoken of, we are forbidden, on the arbitrary assumption that such texts speak of a sort of Jewish righteousness, even though some of them relate to times before the giving of the Law; or that they mean Christ's imputed righteousness, even though containing in them other epithets which undeniably are personal to us. (*Jfc.,* ch. 5)

St. Paul says, 'Not as the offence, so also is the *gift* ... the *gift* is of many offences *unto* justification.' Here, observe, he distinctly declares that justification is the result of a *gift.* Now the word used for 'gift' in the original, is the very word used elsewhere for extraordinary gifts, such as of healing, of tongues, and of miracles; that is, a definite power or virtue committed to us. Nowhere else does the word occur in Scripture without this meaning; indeed, it necessarily has it from its grammatical form. For instance, St. Paul says, he 'longs to see' the Romans, 'that he may impart unto them *some spiritual gift;*' again, that 'the *gift* of God is eternal life.' He enumerates as gifts, prophecy, ministry, teaching, exhortation, giving, ruling, and showing mercy. Speaking of continence, he says, 'Every man has his proper *gift* from God.' He says, there are 'diversities of *gifts*, but the same Spirit.' He exhorts Timothy 'not to neglect the *gift* that was *in him,*' but to stir up, to re-kindle, 'the gift of God which was in him.' St. Peter too speaks of our 'ministering' our 'gifts as good stewards.' If, then, by a gift is meant a certain faculty or talent, moral, intellectual, or other, justification is some such faculty. It is not a mere change of purpose or dis-position in God towards us, or a liberty, privilege, or (as it may be called) citizenship, accorded to us, but a something lodged within us. [Rom. i. 11; vi. 23; xii. 6-18. 1 Cor. vii. 7; xii. 4. 1 Tim. iv. 14. 2 Tim. i. 6. 1 Pet. iv. 10.] (*Jfc.*, ch. 6)

Again: St Peter says to the multitude, 'Repent and be baptized every one of you in the name of Jesus Christ for the remission of sins, and ye shall receive the *gift* of the Holy Ghost;' [John iv. 10. Acts ii. 38.] can we doubt that this is identical with the abundance of grace and of the *gift* of righteousness of which St. Paul speaks? (*Jfc.*, ch. 6)

Sin, which we derive through Adam, is not a name merely, but a dread-ful reality; and so our new righteousness also is a real and not a merely imputed righteousness. It is real righteousness, because it comes from the Holy and Divine Spirit, who vouchsafes, in our Church's language, to pour His gift into our hearts, and who thus makes us acceptable to God, whereas by nature, on account of original sin, we are displeasing to Him. We are 'not in the flesh, but in the Spirit,' and therefore in a state of *grace*. Again, St. Paul speaks of the 'offering of the Gentiles being *acceptable.*' How acceptable? He proceeds, 'being sanctified by the Holy Ghost.' He speaks of presenting our 'bodies as a living sacrifice, holy, *acceptable* unto God.' He says that Christ has 'saved us, according to His mercy, by the washing of regeneration, and the renewing of the Holy Ghost,' and that we are able thereby to 'walk worthy of the Lord unto all *pleasing*.' [Rom. xv. 16; xii. 1. Tit. iii. 5. Col. i. 10.] (*PS* v, Sermon 11: 'The Law of the Spirit,' 12 January 1840)

Justification (Luther vs. St. Augustine)

The main point in dispute is this; whether or not the Moral Law can in its substance be obeyed and kept by the regenerate. Augustine says, that whereas we are by nature condemned by the Law, we are enabled by the grace of God to perform it unto our justification; Luther, that whereas we are condemned by the Law, Christ has Himself performed it unto our justification;—Augustine, that our righteousness is active; Luther, that it is passive;—Augustine, that it is imparted; Luther, that it is only imputed;—Augustine that it consists in a change of heart; Luther, in a change of state. Luther maintains that God's commandments are impossible to man; Augustine adds, impossible without his grace; —Luther, that the gospel consists of promises only; Augustine that is also a Law;—Luther, that our highest wisdom is, not to know the Law; Augustine says instead, to know and keep it;—Luther says, that the Law and Christ cannot dwell together in the heart; Augustine says, that the Law *is* Christ;—Luther denies, and Augustine maintains that obedience is a matter of conscience;—Luther says, that a man is made a Christian not by working but by hearing; Augustine excludes those works only which are done before grace given;—Luther, that our best deeds are sins; Augustine, that they are really pleasing to God. Luther says, that faith is taken instead of righteousness; Augustine, in earnest of righteousness;—Luther, that faith is essential, because it is a substitute for holiness; Augustine, because it is the commencement of holiness;—Luther says, that faith, as such, renews the heart; Augustine says, a loving faith;—Luther would call faith the tree, and works the fruit; Augustine, rather, the inward life, or grace of God, or love, the tree, and renewal the fruit. The school of Luther accuse their opponents of self-righteousness; and they retort on them the charge of self-indulgence: the one say that directly aiming at good works fosters pride; the other that not doing so sanctions licentiousness. Such are the two views of justification when placed in contrast with each other; and as so placed, I conceive it will be found that the former is false, and the latter is true, but that while the former is an utter perversion of the truth, the latter does in some respects come short of it. What is wanting to complete it we learn from other parts of St. Austin's writings, which supply what Luther, not finding perhaps in the theology in which he had been educated, expressed in his own way. (*Jfc.*, ch. 2)

St. Austin contemplates the whole of Scripture, and harmonizes it into one consistent doctrine; the Protestants, like the Arians, entrench themselves in a few favourite texts. Luther and the rest, men of original minds, spoke as no one spoke before them; St. Austin, with no less originality, was contented to minister to the promulgation of what he had received. They have been founders of sects; St. Austin is a Father in the Holy Apostolic Church. (*Jfc.*, ch. 2)

Laity; the Faithful

[T]he witness of the Christian people for the orthodox truth is not less striking—nay, more so—than that of the Bishops. One or two of the great cities were corrupted as time went on, but the mass of the laity was decided and fervent in its maintenance of the sacred truth that was in jeopardy. The population of Alexandria, Antioch, Edessa, Cæsarea, Rome, and Milan, were even patterns in their profession of the dogma to the distressed, menaced, and hardly-used ecclesiastics. ('Apostolical Tradition,' *British Critic*, Vol. 19, July 1836; in *Ess.* i, sec. III)

In all times the laity have been the measure of the Catholic spirit; they saved the Irish Church three centuries ago, and they betrayed the Church in England. Our rulers were true, our people were cowards. (*PPC*, Lecture 9)

[I]t was, I conceive, quite allowable for a writer, who was not teaching or treating theology, but, as it were, conversing, to say, as in the passage in question, 'In the preparation of a dogmatic definition, the faithful are consulted.' Doubtless their advice, their opinion, their judgment on the question of definition is not asked; but the matter of fact, viz., their belief, *is* sought for, as a testimony to that apostolical tradition, on which alone any doctrine whatsoever can be defined. In like manner, we may 'consult' the liturgies or the rites of the Church; not that they speak, not that they can take any part whatever in the definition, for they are documents or customs; but they are witnesses to the antiquity or universality of the doctrines which they contain, and about which they are 'consulted.' ... the *fidelium sensus* and *consensus* is a branch of evidence which it is natural or it necessary for the Church to regard and consult, before she proceeds to any definition, from its intrinsic cogency; and by consequence, that it ever has been so regarded and consulted ... *the sense of the faithful is not left out of the question* by the Holy See among the preliminary acts of defining a doctrine. (*Con.*, sec. 1)

[T]he body of the faithful is one of the witnesses to the fact of the tradition of revealed doctrine, and because their *consensus* through Christendom is the voice of the Infallible Church. I think I am right in saying that the tradition of the Apostles, committed to the whole Church in its various constituents and functions *per modum unius*, manifests itself variously at various times: sometimes by the mouth of the episcopacy, sometimes by the doctors, sometimes by the people, sometimes by liturgies, rites, ceremonies, and customs, by events, disputes, movements, and all those other phenomena which are comprised under the name of history. It follows that none of these channels of tradition may be treated with disrespect; granting at the same time fully, that the gift of discerning, discriminating, defining, promulgating, and enforcing any portion of that tradition resides solely in the *Ecclesia docens*. One man will lay more stress on one aspect of doctrine, another on another; for myself, I am accustomed to lay great stress on the *consensus fidelium*, ... in controversy about a matter of faith, the consent of all the faithful has such a force in the proof of this side or that, that the Supreme Pontiff *is able and ought* to *rest* upon it, as being the *judgment or sentiment* of the *infallible* Church ... 'consensus' is an *indicium* or *instrumentum* to us of the judgment of that Church which *is* infallible. (*Con.*, sec. 2)

[I]n 1854, the definition [of the Immaculate Conception] took place, and the Pope's Bull containing it made its appearance. In it the Holy Father speaks as he had spoken in his Encyclical, viz., that although he *already* knew the sentiments of the Bishops, still he had wished to know the sentiments of the *people* also: ... And when, before the formal definition, he enumerates the various witnesses to the apostolicity of the doctrine, ... the two, the Church teaching and the Church taught, are put together, as one twofold testimony, illustrating each other, and never to be divided. (*Con.*, sec. 2)

First, I will set down the various ways in which theologians put before us the bearing of the Consent of the faithful upon the manifestation of the tradition of the Church. Its *consensus* is to be regarded: 1. as a testimony to the fact of the apostolical dogma; 2. as a sort of instinct, or [*phronema*], deep in the bosom of the mystical body of Christ; 3. as a direction of the Holy Ghost; 4. as an answer to its prayer; 5. as a jealousy of error, which it at once feels as a scandal ... It is not a little remarkable, that, though, historically speaking, the fourth century is the age of doctors, illustrated, as it was, by the saints Athanasius, Hilary, the two Gregories, Basil, Chrysostom, Ambrose, Jerome, and Augustine, and all of these saints bishops also, except one, nevertheless in that very day the divine tradition committed to the infallible Church was proclaimed and maintained far more by the faithful than by the Episcopate. Here, of course, I must explain:—in saying this, then, undoubtedly I am not denying that the great body of the Bishops were in their internal belief orthodox; nor that there were numbers of clergy who stood by the laity, and acted as their centres and guides; nor that the laity actually received their faith, in the first instance, from the Bishops and clergy; nor that some portions of the laity were ignorant, and other portions at length corrupted, by the Arian teachers, who got possession of the sees and ordained an heretical clergy;—but I mean still, that in that time of immense confusion the divine dogma of our Lord's divinity was proclaimed, enforced, maintained, and (humanly speaking) preserved, far more by the 'Ecclesia docta' than by the 'Ecclesia docens;' that the body of the episcopate was unfaithful to its commission, while the body of the laity was faithful to its baptism; that at one time the Pope, at other times the patriarchal, metropolitan, and other great sees, at other times general councils, said what they should not have said, or did what obscured and compromised revealed truth; while, on the other hand, it was the Christian people who, under Providence, were the ecclesiastical strength of Athanasius, Hilary, Eusebius of Vercellæ, and other great solitary confessors, who would have failed without them. I see, then, in the Arian history a palmary example of a state of the Church, during which, in order to know the tradition of the Apostles, we must have recourse to the faithful ... [T]he voice of tradition may in certain cases express itself, not by Councils, nor Fathers, nor Bishops, but the 'communis fidelium sensus.' ... The body of Bishops failed in the confession of the faith. They spoke variously, one against another; there was nothing, after Nicaea, of firm, unvarying, consistent testimony, for nearly sixty years. There were untrustworthy Councils, unfaithful Bishops; there was weakness, fear of consequences, misguidance, delusion, hallucination, endless, hopeless, extending itself into nearly every corner of the Catholic Church. The comparatively few who remained faithful were discredited and driven into exile; the rest were either deceivers or were deceived. (Con., sec. 3)

In most cases when a definition is contemplated, the laity will have a testimony to give; but if ever there be an instance when they ought to be consulted, it is in the case of doctrines which bear directly upon devotional sentiments. Such is the Immaculate Conception, of which the Rambler was speaking in the sentence which has occasioned these remarks. The faithful people have ever a special function in regard to those doctrinal truths which relate to the Objects of worship. Hence it is, that, while the Councils of the fourth century were traitors to our Lord's divinity, the laity vehemently protested against its impugners. Hence it is, that, in a later age, when the learned Benedictines of Germany and France were perplexed in their enunciation of the doctrine of the Real Presence, Paschasius was supported by the faithful in his maintenance of it. The saints, again, are the object of a religious cultus; and therefore it was the faithful, again, who urged on the Holy See, in the time of John XXII., to declare their beatitude in heaven, though so many Fathers spoke variously. And the Blessed Virgin is preeminently an object of devotion; and therefore it is, I repeat, that though Bishops had already spoken in favour of her absolute sinlessness, the Pope was not content without knowing the feelings of the faithful ... I think certainly that the *Ecclesia docens* is more happy when she has such enthusiastic partisans about her as are here represented, than when she cuts off the faithful from the study of her divine doctrines and the sympathy of her divine contemplations, and requires from them *fides implicita* in her word, which in the educated classes will terminate in indifference, and in the poorer in superstition. (*Con.*, sec. 3)

A great Prelate said to me years ago, when I said that the laity needed instruction, guidance, tenderness, consideration etc etc, 'You do not know them, Dr. N. Our laity are a peaceable body—they are peaceable.' I understand him to mean 'They are grossly ignorant and unintellectual—and we need not consult or consult for them at all.' ... at Rome they treat them according to the tradition of the Middle Ages ... facts alone will slowly make them recognise the fact of what a laity must be in the 19th century, even if it is not, if it is to cope with Protestantism. (*POL;* Letter to Emily Bowles, 1 May 1865)

[T]here has been a tradition among the Italians that the lay mind is barbaric—fierce and stupid—and is destined to be outwitted, and that fine craft is the true weapon of Churchmen. When I say the lay mind, I speak too narrowly—it is the Saxon, Teuton, Scandinavian, French mind. (*Ward* ii, 141; Letter to Henry Wilberforce, 16 April 1867)

I have said the same in the beginning of the *Church of the Fathers*—'I shall offend many men when I say, we must look to the people' etc etc. I said this apropos of St. Ambrose, and based my view upon the Fathers. (*POL;* Letter to Matthew Arnold, 3 December 1871; italics for his book are my own)

One of the chief evils which I deplored in the management of the affairs of the University 20 years ago when I was in Ireland was the absolute refusal, with which my urgent representations were met, that the Catholic laity should be allowed to co-operate with the Archbishops in the work. So far as I can see, there are ecclesiastics all over Europe, whose policy it is to keep the laity at arms-length, and hence the laity have been disgusted and become infidel, and only two parties exist, both ultras in opposite directions. I came away from Ireland with the distressing fear, that in that Catholic country, in like manner, there was to be an antagonism as time went on between the Hierarchy and the educated classes. You will be doing the greatest possible benefit to the Catholic cause all over the world, if you succeed in making the University a middle station at which laity and clergy can meet, so as to learn to understand and yield to each other, and from which, as from a common ground, they may act in union upon an age which is running headlong into infidelity, and however evil in themselves may be the men and the measures which of late years have had so great a success against the Holy See, they will in the Providence of God be made the instruments of good, if they teach us priests that the '*obsequium*' which the laity owe religion is '*rationabile*.'" (*Ward* ii, 397-398; Letter to George Fottrell, 10 December 1873)

Liberalism and Nominalism, Theological

Yet nothing is more common than for men to think that because they are familiar with words, they understand the ideas they stand for. Educated persons despise this fault in illiterate men who use hard words as if they comprehended them. Yet they themselves, as well as others, fall into the same error in a more subtle form, when they think they understand terms used in morals and religion, because such are common words, and have been used by them all their lives. (*PS* i, Sermon 4: 'Secret Faults,' 12 June 1825)

[T]he cold-hearted indifferent spirit of liberalism ... May I be kept from having any thing to do with those who are 'neither hot nor cold.' (*Ble.*, 434; Letter to an Aunt, 24 August 1832)

It is no argument against a practice being right, that it is neglected; rather we are warned against going the broad way of the multitude of men. (*TT* #6, 1833)

The following Tracts were published with the object of contributing something towards the practical revival of doctrines, which, although held by the great divines of our Church, at present have become obsolete with the majority of her members, and are withdrawn from public view even by the more learned and orthodox few who still adhere to them. (*TT*, Advertisement for vol. 1, November 1834)

[E]cclesiastical history, ignorance of which may safely be accounted one of the most deplorable evils of this time ... Those, then, who know nothing whatever of the history of Christianity in past times, whose insight into the course of Providence for 1800 years is confined to some slight acquaintance with chronology, or with the names of such sects and parties as prevail de facto in this day, wilt remain contented with the present platform of things, and will take every event in the ecclesiastical world as it comes, without capacity or anxiety to form any definite judgment about it. To them one opinion about existing matters is as good as another, and none good for much, except it be to afford subject for conversation, or lead to this or that immediate secular result. Ecclesiastical changes or movements are regarded merely as they affect local or personal interests or political parties. (Review of *The Life of Archbishop Laud*, by Charles Webb Le Bas, *British Critic*, vol. 18, April 1836)

Another serious indication and result of the same ignorance is the flippancy with which even religious writers speak of the established forms of orthodoxy, and the labours of the early Fathers to whom we owe their public adoption. Every word in the Creeds is the issue of a long history of controversy and trouble; and till we know that history, we cannot possibly know the value of such expressions, nor the expediency or lawfulness of altering or dispensing with them. Every error, now produced, is the same or all but the same as former errors; and though the fact that an opinion has been anticipated long since, is no argument to its present upholders that it is an error, yet it is a reason why they should not be so very well pleased with themselves, and so very confident that they have wherewith to demolish received doctrines. (Review of *The Life of Archbishop Laud*, by Charles Webb Le Bas, *British Critic*, vol. 18, April 1836)

Is it indeed possible for the run of men, if they are bound to hold that the high doctrines about our Lord are only the private, uninspired inferences of individuals from the Scripture text, to hold also that they are necessary to be believed in order to salvation? Does not, then, as we have said, the theory that Scripture only is to be the guide of Protestants, lead them to a certainty, when it is mastered, to become liberals? ('Apostolical Tradition,' *British Critic*, Vol. 19, July 1836; in *Ess.* i, sec. III)

It has been much the fashion at various times, to speak as if Christianity was becoming better and better understood as time went on, and its professors more enlightened and more virtuous ... that the nineteenth century (i.e. *because* the nineteenth) is superior to the first and second. (Review of *The History of the Christian Church*, by Edward Burton, *British Critic*, vol. 19, July 1836)

The view henceforth is to be, that Christianity does not exist in documents, any more than in institutions; in other words, the Bible will be given up as well as the Church. It will be said that the benefit which Christianity has done to the world, and which its Divine Author meant it should do, was to give an impulse to society, to infuse a spirit, to direct, control, purify, enlighten the mass of human thought and action, but not to be a separate and definite something, whether doctrine or association, existing objectively, integral, and with an identity, and for ever, and with a claim upon our homage and obedience. And all this fearfully coincides with the symptoms in other directions of the spread of a Pantheistic spirit, that is, the religion of beauty, imagination, and philosophy, without constraint moral or intellectual, a religion speculative and self-indulgent. Pantheism, indeed, is the great deceit which awaits the Age to come. (*TT* #85, Sep. 1838)

[T]he religion of this day is destitute of *fear*. Many other instances might be mentioned of very various kinds. For instance, the freedom with which men propose to alter God's ordinances, to suit their own convenience, or to meet the age; their reliance on their private and antecedent notions about sacred subjects; their want of interest and caution in inquiring what God's probable will is; their contempt for any view of the Sacraments which exceeds the evidence of their senses; and their confidence in settling the order of importance in which the distinct articles of Christian faith stand;—all which shows that it is no question of words whether men have fear or not, but that there is a something they really have not, whatever name we give it ... can anything be clearer than that the *want* of fear is nothing else but *want* of faith, and that in consequence we in this age are approaching in religious temper that evil day of which it is said, 'When the Son of Man cometh, shall He find faith on the earth?' [Luke xviii. 8.] (*PS* v, Sermon 2: 'Reverence, a Belief in God's Presence,' 4 November 1838)

As to Liberalism, we think the formularies of the Church will ever, with the aid of a good Providence, keep it from making any serious inroads upon the clergy; besides, it is too cold a principle to prevail with the multitude; so we shall say no more about it. ('Prospects of the Anglican Church,' *British Critic*, April 1839; in *Ess.* i, sec. VII)

As liberals are the bitterest persecutors, so denouncers of controversy are sure to proceed upon the most startling, irritating, blistering methods which the practice of their age furnishes. ('Milman's View of Christianity,' *British Critic*, Jan. 1841; in *Ess.* ii, sec. XII)

Are you aware that the more serious thinkers among us are used, as far as they dare form an opinion, to regard the spirit of Liberalism as the characteristic of the destined Antichrist? ... The spirit of lawlessness came in with the Reformation, and Liberalism is its offspring. (*Apo.*, ch. 4; Letter to a Catholic, 18 June 1841)

[I]f there is any thing which we must avoid ... it is new views in Theology. This consideration has so weighed with myself, that, many as were the misrepresentations which have been published of my Essay on Development, I have written nothing on the subject since I was a Catholic, and shall not without the greatest deliberation and caution. (*LD* xii, 302; Letter to Henry Formby, 19 or 20 October 1848)

[T]he liberalism of the age, after many previous attempts, is apparently at length about to get possession of the [Anglican] Church and Universities of the nation. (*Dif.* i, Lecture 1)

Moreover, I can quite enter into the sentiment with which members of the liberal and infidel school investigate the history and the documents of the early Church. They profess a view of Christianity, truer than the world has ever had; nor, on the assumption of their principles, is there anything shocking to good sense in this profession. They look upon the Christian Religion as something simply human; and there is no reason at all why a phenomenon of that kind should not be better understood, in its origin and nature, as years proceed. (*Dif.* i, Lecture 5)

Liberal Knowledge has a special tendency, ... to impress us with a mere philosophical theory of life and conduct, in the place of Revelation ... Truth has two attributes — beauty and power; and while Useful Knowledge is the possession of truth as powerful, Liberal Knowledge is the apprehension of it as beautiful. Pursue it, either as beauty or as power, to its furthest extent and its true limit, and you are led by either road to the Eternal and Infinite, to the intimations of conscience and the announcements of the Church. Satisfy yourself with what is only visibly or intelligibly excellent, as you are likely to do, and you will make present utility and natural beauty the practical test of truth, and the sufficient object of the intellect. It is not that you will at once reject Catholicism, but you will measure and proportion it by an earthly standard. You will throw its highest and most momentous disclosures into the background, you will deny its principles, explain away its doctrines, re-arrange its precepts, and make light of its practices, even while you profess it. Knowledge, viewed as Knowledge, exerts a subtle influence in throwing us back on ourselves, and making us our own centre, and our minds the measure of all things. This then is the tendency of that Liberal Education, of which a University is the school, viz., to view Revealed Religion from an aspect of its own, — to fuse and recast it, to tune it, as it were, to a different key, and to reset its harmonies, — to circumscribe it by a circle which unwarrantably amputates here, and unduly develops there; and

all under the notion, conscious or unconscious, that the human intellect, self-educated and self-supported, is more true and perfect in its ideas
and judgments than that of Prophets and Apostles, to whom the sights
and sounds of Heaven were immediately conveyed. A sense of propriety,
order, consistency, and completeness gives birth to a rebellious stirring
against miracle and mystery, against the severe and the terrible. This
Intellectualism first and chiefly comes into collision with precept, then
with doctrine, then with the very principle of dogmatism; — a perception of the Beautiful becomes the substitute for faith. In a country which
does not profess the faith, it at once runs, if allowed, into scepticism or
infidelity; but even within the pale of the Church, and with the most
unqualified profession of her Creed, it acts, if left to itself, as an element
of corruption and debility. Catholicism, as it has come down to us from
the first, seems to be mean and illiberal; it is a mere popular religion; it is
the religion of illiterate ages or servile populations or barbarian warriors;
it must be treated with discrimination and delicacy, corrected, softened,
improved, if it is to satisfy an enlightened generation. It must be stereo-
typed as the patron of arts, or the pupil of speculation, or the protégé of
science; it must play the literary academician, or the empirical philan-
thropist, or the political partisan; it must keep up with the age; some or
other expedient it must devise, in order to explain away, or to hide, tenets
under which the intellect labours and of which it is ashamed — its doctrine, for instance, of grace, its mystery of the Godhead, its preaching of
the Cross, its devotion to the Queen of Saints, or its loyalty to the Apostolic See ... first indifference, then laxity of belief, then even heresy will
be the successive results. (*IU*, Part I, Discourse 9: 'Duties of the Church
Towards Knowledge,' 1852)

There are those who hope, there are those who are sure, that in the
incessant investigation of facts, physical, political, and moral, something
or other, or many things, will sooner or later turn up, and stubborn facts
too, simply contradictory of revealed declarations. A vision comes before
them of some physical or historical proof that mankind is not descended
from a common origin, or that the hopes of the world were never consigned to a wooden ark floating on the waters, or that the manifestations

on Mount Sinai were the work of man or nature, or that the Hebrew patriarchs or the judges of Israel are mythical personages, or that St. Peter had no connexion with Rome, or that the doctrine of the Holy Trinity or of the Real Presence was foreign to primitive belief. An anticipation possesses them that the ultimate truths embodied in mesmerism will certainly solve all the Gospel miracles; ... They imagine that the eternal, immutable word of God is to quail and come to nought before the penetrating intellect of man ... [I]t is clear that the tendency of science is to make men indifferentists or sceptics, merely by being exclusively pursued. (*IU*, Part II, ch. 5, sec. 2: 'A Form of Infidelity of the Day,' 1854)

[L]et me state more definitely what the position was which I took up, and the propositions about which I was so confident ... First was the principle of dogma: my battle was with liberalism; by liberalism I mean the anti-dogmatic principle and its developments. This was the first point on which I was certain ... The main principle of the movement is as dear to me now, as it ever was. I have changed in many things: in this I have not. From the age of fifteen, dogma has been the fundamental principle of my religion: I know no other religion; I cannot enter into the idea of any other sort of religion; religion, as a mere sentiment, is to me a dream and a mockery ... What I held in 1816, I held in 1833, and I hold in 1864. Please God, I shall hold it to the end. (*Apo.*, ch. 2)

The most oppressive thought, in the whole process of my change of opinion, was the clear anticipation, verified by the event, that it would issue in the triumph of Liberalism. Against the Anti-dogmatic principle I had thrown my whole mind; yet now I was doing more than any one else could do, to promote it. I was one of those who had kept it at bay in Oxford for so many years; and thus my very retirement was its triumph. The men who had driven me from Oxford were distinctly the Liberals; it was they who had opened the attack upon Tract 90, and it was they who would gain a second benefit, if I went on to abandon the Anglican Church. But this was not all. As I have already said, there are but two alternatives, the way to Rome, and the way to Atheism: Anglicanism is the halfway house on the one side, and Liberalism is the halfway house on the other. How many men were there, as I knew full well, who would not follow me now in my advance from Anglicanism to Rome, but would at once leave Anglicanism and me for the Liberal camp. (*Apo.*, ch. 4)

I am not going to criticize here that vast body of men, in the mass, who at this time would profess to be liberals in religion; and who look towards the discoveries of the age, certain or in progress, as their informants, direct or indirect, as to what they shall think about the unseen and the future. The Liberalism which gives a colour to society now, is very different from that character of thought which bore the name thirty or forty years ago. Now it is scarcely a party; it is the educated lay world ... At present it is nothing else than that deep, plausible scepticism, of which I spoke above, as being the development of human reason, as practically exercised by the natural man. (*Apo.*, ch. 5)

Liberty of thought is in itself a good; but it gives an opening to false liberty. Now by Liberalism I mean false liberty of thought, or the exercise of thought upon matters, in which, from the constitution of the human mind, thought cannot be brought to any successful issue, and therefore is out of place. Among such matters are first principles of whatever kind; and of these the most sacred and momentous are especially to be reckoned the truths of Revelation. Liberalism then is the mistake of subjecting to human judgment those revealed doctrines which are in their nature beyond and independent of it, and of claiming to determine on intrinsic grounds the truth and value of propositions which rest for their reception simply on the external authority of the Divine Word. (*Apo.*, Note A: 'Liberalism')

As to the prospects of the Church, as to which you ask my opinion, you know old men are generally desponding—but my apprehensions are not new, but above 50 years standing. I have all that time thought that a time of wide-spread infidelity was coming, and through all those years the waters have in fact been rising as a deluge. I look for the time, after my life, when only the tops of the mountains will be seen like islands in the waste of waters. I speak principally of the Protestant world—but great actions and successes must be achieved by the Catholic leaders, great wisdom as well as courage must be given them from on high, if Holy Church is to (be) kept safe from this awful calamity, and, though any trial which came upon her would but be temporary, it may be fierce in the extreme while it lasts. (*Ward* ii, 416; Letter to Mrs. Maskell, 6 January 1877)

And, I rejoice to say, to one great mischief I have from the first opposed myself. For thirty, forty, fifty years I have resisted to the best of my powers the spirit of Liberalism in religion. Never did Holy Church need champions against it more sorely than now, when, alas! it is an error overspreading, as a snare, the whole earth; and on this great occasion, when it is natural for one who is in my place to look out upon the world, and upon Holy Church as in it, and upon her future, it will not, I hope, be considered out of place, if I renew the protest against it which I have made so often. Liberalism in religion is the doctrine that there is no positive truth in religion, but that one creed is as good as another, and this is the teaching which is gaining substance and force daily. It is inconsistent with any recognition of any religion, as *true*. It teaches that all are to be tolerated, for all are matters of opinion. Revealed religion is not a truth, but a sentiment and a taste; not an objective fact, not miraculous; and it is the right of each individual to make it say just what strikes his fancy. Devotion is not necessarily founded on faith. Men may go to Protestant Churches and to Catholic, may get good from both and belong to neither. They may fraternise together in spiritual thoughts and feelings, without having any views at all of doctrines in common, or seeing the need of them. Since, then, religion is so personal a peculiarity and so private a possession, we must of necessity ignore it in the intercourse of man with man. If a man puts on a new religion every morning, what is that to you? It is as impertinent to think about a man's religion as about his sources of income or his management of his family. Religion is in no sense the bond of society. (*Ward* ii, 460; 'Biglietto Speech' upon becoming a Cardinal, 12 May 1879)

I ... am as fierce in my heart now as ever against Liberalism. (*LD* xxix, 207; Letter to T. W. Allies, 30 November 1879)

Liturgy

The Mass must not be said without a Missal under the priest's eye; nor in any language but that in which it has come down to us from the early hierarchs of the Western Church. (*IU*, Part II, ch. 6: 'University Preaching,' 1855)

Mary: Assumption of

It was surely fitting then, it was becoming, that she should be taken up into heaven and not lie in the grave till Christ's second coming, who had passed a life of sanctity and of miracle such as hers … Who can conceive, my brethren, that God should so repay the debt, which He condescended to owe to His Mother, for the elements of His human body, as to allow the flesh and blood from which it was taken to moulder in the grave? … Why should she share the curse of Adam, who had no share in his fall? 'Dust thou art, and into dust thou shalt return,' was the sentence upon sin; she then, who was not a sinner, fitly never saw corruption. She died, then, as we hold, because even our Lord and Saviour died … [B]y the grace of Christ which in her had anticipated sin, which had filled her with light, which had purified her flesh from all defilement, she was also saved from disease and malady, and all that weakens and decays the bodily frame. Original sin had not been found in her … If the Mother of Emmanuel ought to be the first of creatures in sanctity and in beauty; if it became her to be free from all sin from the very first, and from the moment she received her first grace to begin to merit more; and if such as was her beginning, such was her end, her conception immaculate and her death an assumption. (*Mix.*, Discourse 18: 'On the Fitness of the Glories of Mary')

[I]t is a pious belief that she died from love. This alone could kill that body. It was a *contest* between body and soul. The body so strong, the soul so desirous to see God. No disease could kill that body. What killed it? The soul, that it might get to heaven … Hence [it was] fitting that, when she did get loose, her Son should not let the body be so overmatched and overcome, but at once that the soul had got the victory, He raised up the body without corruption. (*SN*, 'On Our Lady as in the Body,' 15 August 1852)

I do believe it, tho' the Church has not defined it … It is to me impossible to hold what we hold about Mary, as the Second Eve, and the Mother of God, and yet deny her Assumption, though we have no direct proof of it. (*LD* xxix, 6; Letter to Robert Charles Jenkins, 11 January 1879)

As soon as we apprehend by faith the great fundamental truth that Mary is the Mother of God, other wonderful truths follow in its train; and one of these is that she was exempt from the ordinary lot of mortals, which is not only to die, but to become earth to earth, ashes to ashes, dust to dust. Die she must, and die she did, as her Divine Son died, for He was man; but various reasons have approved themselves to holy writers, why, although her body was for a while separated from her soul and consigned to the tomb, yet it did not remain there, but was speedily united to her soul again, and raised by our Lord to a new and eternal life of heavenly glory. And the most obvious reason for so concluding is this—that *other* servants of God have been raised from the grave by the power of God, and it is not to be supposed that our Lord would have granted any such privilege to anyone else without also granting it to His own Mother. We are told by St. Matthew, that after our Lord's death upon the Cross 'the graves were opened, and many bodies of the saints that had slept'—that is, slept the sleep of death, 'arose, and coming out of the tombs after His Resurrection, came into the Holy City, and appeared to many.' St. Matthew says, '*many* bodies of the Saints'—that is, the holy Prophets, Priests, and Kings of former times—rose again in anticipation of the last day. Can we suppose that Abraham, or David, or Isaias, or Ezechias, should have been thus favoured, and not God's own Mother? Had she not a claim on the love of her Son to have what any others had? Was she not nearer to Him than the greatest of the Saints before her? And is it conceivable that the law of the grave should admit of relaxation in their case, and not in hers? Therefore we confidently say that our Lord, having preserved her from sin and the consequences of sin by His Passion, lost no time in pouring out the full merits of that Passion upon her body as well as her soul.

(*MD*, 'Meditations on the Litany of Loretto, for the Month of May: IV. On the Assumption,' for May 24)

Another consideration which has led devout minds to believe the Assumption of our Lady into heaven after her death, without waiting for the general resurrection at the last day, is furnished by the doctrine of her Immaculate Conception. By her Immaculate Conception is meant, that not only did she never commit any sin whatever, even venial, in thought, word, or deed, but further than this, that the guilt of Adam, or what is called original sin, never was her guilt, as it is the guilt attaching to all other descendants of Adam. By her Assumption is meant that not only her soul, but her body also, was taken up to heaven upon her death, so that there was no long period of her sleeping in the grave, as is the case with others, even great Saints, who wait for the last day for the resurrection of their bodies. One reason for believing in our Lady's Assumption is that her Divine Son loved her too much to let her body remain in the grave. A second reason — that now before us — is this, that she was not only dear to the Lord as a mother is dear to a son, but also that she was so transcendently holy, so full, so overflowing with grace. Adam and Eve were created upright and sinless, and had a large measure of God's grace bestowed upon them; and, in consequence, their bodies would never have crumbled into dust, had they not sinned; upon which it was said to them, 'Dust thou art, and unto dust thou shalt return.' If Eve, the beautiful daughter of God, never would have become dust and ashes unless she had sinned, shall we not say that Mary, having never sinned, retained the gift which Eve by sinning lost? What had Mary done to forfeit the privilege given to our first parents in the beginning? Was her comeliness to be turned into corruption, and her fine gold to become dim, without reason assigned? Impossible. Therefore we believe that, though she died for a short hour, as did our Lord Himself, yet, like Him, and by His Almighty power, she was raised again from the grave. (*MD*, 'Meditations on the Litany of Loretto, for the Month of May: IV. On the Assumption,' for May 25)

[I]f her body was not taken into heaven, where is it? how comes it that it is hidden from us? why do we not hear of her tomb as being here or there? why are not pilgrimages made to it? why are not relics producible of her, as of the saints in general? Is it not even a natural instinct which makes us reverent towards the places where our dead are buried? We bury our great men honourably. St. Peter speaks of the sepulchre of David as known in his day, though he had died many hundred years before. When our Lord's body was taken down from the Cross, He was placed in an honourable tomb. Such too had been the honour already paid to St. John Baptist, his tomb being spoken of by St. Mark as generally known. Christians from the earliest times went from other countries to Jerusalem to see the holy places. And, when the time of persecution was over, they paid still more attention to the bodies of the Saints, as of St. Stephen, St. Mark, St. Barnabas, St. Peter, St. Paul, and other Apostles and Martyrs. These were transported to great cities, and portions of them sent to this place or that. Thus, from the first to this day it has been a great feature and characteristic of the Church to be most tender and reverent towards the bodies of the Saints. Now, if there was anyone who more than all would be preciously taken care of, it would be our Lady. Why then do we hear nothing of the Blessed Virgin's body and its separate relics? Why is she thus the *hidden* Rose? Is it conceivable that they who had been so reverent and careful of the bodies of the Saints and Martyrs should neglect her—her who was the Queen of Martyrs and the Queen of Saints, who was the very Mother of our Lord? It is impossible. (*MD*, 'Meditations on the Litany of Loretto, for the Month of May: IV. On the Assumption,' for May 26)

Mary, Blessed Virgin (General)

In her the destinies of the world were to be reversed, and the serpent's head bruised. On her was bestowed the greatest honour ever put upon any individual of our fallen race. God was taking upon Him her flesh, and humbling Himself to be called her offspring;—such is the deep mystery! (*PS* ii, Sermon 12: 'The Reverence Due to the Virgin Mary,' 25 March 1832)

Nay, may we not say that our Lord Himself had commenced His ministry, that is, bade farewell to His earthly home, at a feast? for it was at the marriage entertainment at Cana of Galilee that He did His first miracle, and manifested forth His glory. He was in the house of friends, He was surrounded by intimates and followers, and He took a familiar interest in the exigencies of the feast. He supplied a principal want which was interfering with their festivity. It was His contribution to it. By supplying it miraculously He showed that He was beginning a new life, the life of a Messenger from God, and that that feast was the last scene of the old life. And, moreover, He made use of one remarkable expression, which seems to imply that this change of condition really was in His thoughts, if we may dare so to speak of them, or at all to interpret them. For when His Mother said unto Him, 'They have no wine,' He answered, 'What have I to do with thee?' [John ii. 3, 4.] He had had to do with her for thirty years. She had borne Him, she had nursed Him, she had taught Him. And when He had reached twelve years old, at the age when the young may expect to be separated from their parents, He had only become more intimately one with them, for we are told that 'He went down with them, and came to Nazareth, and was subject unto them.' [Luke ii. 51.] Eighteen years had passed away since this occurred. St. Joseph (as it seems) had been taken to his rest. Mary remained; but from Mary, His Mother, He must now part, for the three years of His ministry. He had gently intimated this to her at the very time of His becoming subject to her, intimated that His heavenly Father's work was a higher call than any earthly duty. 'Wist ye not,' He said, when found in the Temple, 'that I must be about My Father's business?' [Luke ii. 49.] The time was now come when this was to be fulfilled, and, therefore, when His Mother addressed Him at the marriage feast, He answered, 'What have I to do with thee?' What is between Me and thee, My Mother, any longer? 'The time is fulfilled, and the Kingdom of God is at hand.' [Mark i. 15.] ... Observe, He said to His Mother, 'What have I to do with thee? Mine hour is not yet come.' Perhaps this implies that *when* His hour was come, then He *would* have to do with her again as before; and such really seems to be the meaning of the passage. 'What have I to do with thee *now*? I have had, I shall have; but what have I to do with thee now as before? what as yet? what *till* My hour is come?' (*SD*, Sermon 3: 'Our Lord's Last Supper and His First,' 26 February 1843)

I have ever been under her shadow, if I may say it. (*LD* xii, 153; Letter to Henry Wilberforce, 12 January 1848)

I fully grant that *devotion* towards the blessed Virgin has increased among Catholics with the progress of centuries; I do not allow that the *doctrine* concerning her has undergone a growth, for I believe that it has been in substance one and the same from the beginning. (*Dif.* ii, Letter to Pusey, ch. 3, 1865)

I cannot help hoping that your own reading of the Fathers will on the whole bear me out in the above account of their teaching concerning the Blessed Virgin. Anglicans seem to me simply to overlook the strength of the argument adducible from the works of those ancient doctors in our favour; and they open the attack upon our medieval and modern writers, careless of leaving a host of primitive opponents in their rear ... When they found you with the Fathers calling her Mother of God, Second Eve, and Mother of all Living, the Mother of Life, the Morning Star, the Mystical New Heaven, the Sceptre of Orthodoxy, the All-undefiled Mother of Holiness, and the like, they would have deemed it a poor compensation for such language, that you protested against her being called a Co-redemptress or a Priestess. (*Dif.* ii, Letter to Pusey, ch. 4, 1865)

I cannot allow that the Blessed Virgin has the first place in our Churches. On the contrary, it is the Blessed Sacrament which we believe and know to be the actual presence of the Eternal Son. (*LD* xxxii, 429; Letter to the Rev. J. R. Young, 18 May 1881)

She is the first of creatures, the most acceptable child of God, the dearest and nearest to Him ... Mary is not only the acceptable handmaid of the Lord. She is also Mother of His Son, and the Queen of all Saints. (*MD*, 'Meditations on the Litany of Loretto, for the Month of May,' for May 2)

Mary: Devotion to; Veneration of

Next, it must be observed, that the tone of the devotion paid to the Blessed Mary is altogether distinct from that which is paid to her Eternal Son, and to the Holy Trinity, as we must certainly allow on inspection of the Catholic services. The supreme and true worship paid to the

Almighty is severe, profound, awful, as well as tender, confiding, and dutiful. Christ is addressed as true God, while He is true Man; as our Creator and Judge, while He is most loving, gentle, and gracious. On the other hand, towards St. Mary the language employed is affectionate and ardent, as towards a mere child of Adam; though subdued, as coming from her sinful kindred. How different, for instance, is the tone of the *Dies Irae* from that of the *Stabat Mater* ... Nor does it avail to object that, in this contrast of devotional exercises, the human will supplant the Divine, from the infirmity of our nature; for, I repeat, the question is one of fact, whether it has done so. And next it must be asked, whether the character of much of the Protestant devotion towards our Lord has been that of adoration at all; and not rather such as we pay to an excellent human being, that is, no higher devotion than that which Catholics pay to St. Mary, differing from it, however, in often being familiar, rude, and earthly. Carnal minds will ever create a carnal worship for themselves; and to forbid them the service of the Saints will have no tendency to teach them the worship of God. (*Dev.*, Part II: ch. 11, sec. 2)

[M]y former objections against the Devotions to our Lady were twofold—1. as being not in the Fathers—2. as interfering with the supreme worship of God. Both, I have considered, and removed (as I think) in my Essay on Development. (*LD* xii, 194-195; Letter to Mrs. George Ryder, 28 March 1848)

[D]*evotion* to the Most Blessed Mother of God is not imperatively required of all. It is a gift which God gives to those whom He will. I do not see therefore that a person ought to force himself into the use of particular manuals or exercises which do not come natural to him. (*LD* xii, 217; Letter to the Marquise de Salvo, 11 June 1848)

[D]evotion to the Blessed Virgin is *the* ordinary way to heaven, and the absence of it is at least a bad symptom of the *state* of our faith ... I will not allow that the doctrine is not in Scripture; indeed in a covert way, under image and allusion, it is there with wonderful fulness. (*LD* xii, 333-334; Letter to Catherine Ward, 18 November 1848)

That Mary is the Mother of God is a point of faith—that Mary is to be honoured and exalted in this or that way is a point of devotion. The latter is the consequence indeed of the former, but a consequence which follows with various intensity, in various degrees and in various modes, in various minds ... God is to be worship[ed] with an honour of His own, infinitely distinct from any honour we give His creatures, even Mary, the first of them. (*POL*; Letter to Mrs. William Froude, 2 January 1855)

I had a true devotion [as an Anglican] to the Blessed Virgin, in whose College I lived, whose Altar I served, and whose Immaculate Purity I had in one of my earliest printed Sermons made much of. (*Apo.*, ch. 4)

Such devotional manifestations in honour of our Lady had been my great *crux* as regards Catholicism; I say frankly, I do not fully enter into them now; I trust I do not love her the less, because I cannot enter into them. They may be fully explained and defended; but sentiment and taste do not run with logic: they are suitable for Italy, but they are not suitable for England. (*Apo.*, ch. 4)

[A] great author, or public man, may be acknowledged as such for a course of years; yet there may be an increase, an ebb and flow, and a fashion, in his popularity. And if he takes a lasting place in the minds of his countrymen, he may gradually grow into it, or suddenly be raised to it. The idea of Shakespeare as a great poet, has existed from a very early date in public opinion; and there were at least individuals then who understood him as well, and honoured him as much, as the English people can honour him now; yet, I think, there is a national devotion to him in this day such as never has been before ... The sun in the spring-time will have to shine many days before he is able to melt the frost, open the soil, and bring out the leaves; yet he shines out from the first notwithstanding, though he makes his power felt but gradually. It is one and the same sun, though his influence day by day becomes greater; and so in the Catholic Church it is the one Virgin Mother, one and the same from first to last, and Catholics may have ever acknowledged her; and yet, in spite of that acknowledgment, their devotion to her may be scanty in one time and place, and overflowing in another. (*Dif.* ii, Letter to Pusey, ch. 3, 1865)

Now I do not deny of course, that under the image of the Woman, the Church is signified; but what I would maintain is this, that the Holy Apostle would not have spoken [in Revelation 12] of the Church under this particular image, *unless* there had existed a blessed Virgin Mary, who was exalted on high, and the object of veneration to all the faithful. No one doubts that the 'man-child' spoken of is an allusion to our Lord: why then is not 'the Woman' an allusion to His Mother? This surely is the obvious sense of the words; of course they have a further sense also, which is the scope of the image; doubtless the Child represents the children of the Church, and doubtless the Woman represents the Church; this, I grant, is the real or direct sense, but what is the sense of the symbol under which that real sense is conveyed? [W]ho are the Woman and the Child? I answer, they are not personifications but Persons. This is true of the Child, therefore it is true of the Woman. But again: not only Mother and Child, but a serpent is introduced into the vision. Such a meeting of man, woman, and serpent has not been found in Scripture, since the beginning of Scripture, and now it is found in its end. Moreover, in the passage in the Apocalypse, as if to supply, before Scripture came to an end, what was wanting in its beginning, we are told, and for the first time, that the serpent in Paradise was the evil spirit. If the dragon of St. John is the same as the serpent of Moses, and the man-child is 'the seed of the woman,' why is not the woman herself she, whose seed the man-child is? And, if the first woman is not an allegory, why is the second? if the first woman is Eve, why is not the second Mary? . . . If the Woman ought to be some real person, who can it be whom the Apostle saw, and intends, and delineates, but that same Great Mother to whom the chapters in the Proverbs are accommodated? And let it be observed, moreover, that in this passage, from the allusion made in it to the history of the fall, Mary may be said still to be represented under the character of the Second Eve. I make a farther remark: it is sometimes asked, Why do not the sacred writers mention our Lady's greatness? I answer, she was, or may have been alive, when the Apostles and Evangelists wrote; — there was just one book of Scripture certainly written after her death, and that book does (so to say) canonize and crown her. But if all this be so, if it is really the Blessed Virgin whom Scripture represents as clothed with the sun, crowned with the stars of heaven, and with the moon as her footstool, what height of glory may we not attribute to her? and what are we to say of those who, through ignorance, run counter to the voice of Scripture, to the testimony of the Fathers, to the traditions of East and West, and speak and act contemptuously towards her whom her Lord delighteth to honour? (*Dif.* ii, Letter to Pusey, ch. 3, 1865)

Such was the origin of that august *cultus* which has been paid to the Blessed Mary for so many centuries in the East and in the West. That in times and places it has fallen into abuse, that it has even become a superstition, I do not care to deny; for, as I have said above, the same process which brings to maturity carries on to decay, and things that do not admit of abuse have very little life in them. This of course does not excuse such excesses, or justify us in making light of them, when they occur ... Now I say plainly, I never will defend or screen any one from your just rebuke, who, through false devotion to Mary, forgets Jesus. But I should like the fact to be proved first; I cannot hastily admit it. There is this broad fact the other way;—that, if we look through Europe, we shall find, on the whole, that just those nations and countries have lost their faith in the divinity of Christ, who have given up devotion to His Mother, and that those on the other hand, who had been foremost in her honour, have retained their orthodoxy ... In the Catholic Church Mary has shown herself, not the rival, but the minister of her Son; she has protected Him, as in His infancy, so in the whole history of the Religion ... The Mass again conveys to us the same lesson of the sovereignty of the Incarnate Son; it is a return to Calvary, and Mary is scarcely named in it ... When then, my dear Pusey, you read anything extravagant in praise of our Lady, is it not charitable to ask, even while you condemn it in itself, did the author write nothing else? Had he written on the Blessed Sacrament? had he given up 'all for Jesus?' ... In like manner it seems to me a simple purism, to insist upon minute accuracy of expression in devotional and popular writings. However, the *Raccolta*, as coming from responsible authority, for the most part observes it. It commonly uses the phrases 'gain for us by thy prayers,' 'obtain for us,' 'pray to Jesus for me,' 'speak for me, Mary,' 'carry thou our prayers,' 'ask for us grace;' 'intercede for the people of God,' and the like,

marking thereby with great emphasis that she is nothing more than an Advocate, and not a source of mercy. Nor do I recollect in this book more than one or two ideas to which you would be likely to raise an objection. The strongest of these is found in the Novena before her Nativity, in which, *apropos* of her Birth, we pray that she 'would come down again, and be reborn spiritually in our souls;'—but it will occur to you that St. Paul speaks of his wish to impart to his converts, 'not only the gospel, but his own soul;' and writing to the Corinthians, he says he has 'begotten them by the gospel,' and to Philemon, that he had 'begotten Onesimus, in his bonds;' whereas St. James, with greater accuracy of expression, says 'of His own will hath God begotten us with the word of truth.' Again, we find the petitioner saying to the Blessed Mary, 'In thee I place all my hope;' but this is explained by another passage, 'Thou art my best hope after Jesus.' Again, we read elsewhere, 'I would I had a greater love for thee, since to love thee is a great mark of predestination;' but the prayer goes on, 'Thy Son deserves of us an immeasurable love; pray that I may have this grace, a great love for Jesus,' and further on, 'I covet no good of the earth, but to love my God alone.' … to say that prayer (and the Blessed Virgin's prayer) is omnipotent, is a harsh expression in every-day prose; but, if it is explained to mean that there is nothing which prayer may not obtain from God, it is nothing else than the very promise made us in Scripture. (*Dif.* ii, Letter to Pusey, ch. 5, 1865)

[N]or do I dispute the right of whoso will to use devotions to the Blessed Virgin which seem to me unnatural and forced … the Church of Rome is severe on freethinkers, and indulgent towards devotees. (*Ward* ii, 92; Letter to Edward B. Pusey, 5 September 1865)

It is still more difficult at once to praise her, and to dispraise some of her imprudent votaries. (*Ward* ii, 113; Letter to Mother Mary Imelda Poole, 2 April 1866)

It is at first strange that these instances of special exemptions should be named by early writers, without our Lady also being mentioned; or rather it would be strange, unless we bore in mind how little is said of her

at all by Scripture or the Fathers up to the Council of Ephesus, A.D. 431. It would seem as if, till our Lord's glory called for it, it required an effort for the reverent devotion of the Church to speak much about her or to make her the subject of popular preaching; but, when by her manifestation a right faith in her Divine Son was to be secured, then the Church was to be guided in a contrary course. It must be recollected that there was a *disciplina arcani* in the first centuries, and, if it was exercised, as far as might be, as regards the Holy Trinity and the Eucharist, so would it be as regards the Blessed Virgin. (*Ath.* ii, 'The Blessed Mary')

[T]he preaching of Mary to the children of the Church, and the devotion paid to her by them, has *grown*, grown gradually, with successive ages. Not so much preached about her in *early* times as in *later*. First she was preached as the Virgin of Virgins—then as the Mother of God—then as glorious in her Assumption—then as the Advocate of sinners—then as Immaculate in her Conception. (*MD*, 'Meditations on the Litany of Loretto, for the Month of May: I. On the Immaculate Conception,' for May 4)

Look at the Protestant countries which threw off all devotion to her three centuries ago, under the notion that to put her from their thoughts would be exalting the praises of her Son. Has that consequence really followed from their profane conduct towards her? Just the reverse—the countries, Germany, Switzerland, England, which so acted, have in great measure ceased to worship Him, and have given up their belief in His Divinity while the Catholic Church, wherever she is to be found, adores Christ as true God and true Man, as firmly as ever she did; and strange indeed would it be, if it ever happened otherwise. (*MD*, 'Meditations on the Litany of Loretto, for the Month of May: IV. On the Assumption,' for May 27)

Mary: Holiness and Immaculate Conception

Who can estimate the holiness and perfection of her, who was chosen to be the Mother of Christ? If to him that hath, more is given, and holiness

and Divine favour go together (and this we are expressly told), what must have been the transcendent purity of her, whom the Creator Spirit condescended to overshadow with His miraculous presence? What must have been her gifts, who was chosen to be the only near earthly relative of the Son of God, the only one whom He was bound by nature to revere and look up to; the one appointed to train and educate Him, to instruct Him day by day, as He grew in wisdom and in stature? This contemplation runs to a higher subject, did we dare follow it; for what, think you, was the sanctified state of that human nature, of which God formed His sinless Son; knowing as we do, 'that which is born of the flesh is flesh,' and that 'none can bring a clean thing out of an unclean?' [1 John iii. 6. Job xiv. 4.] (*PS* ii, Sermon 12: 'The Reverence Due to the Virgin Mary,' 25 March 1832)

Nay: do they not already lay this down as a general principle, that, to suppose He diffuses from His Person heavenly virtue, is a superstition? … on what other ground do they deny that the Blessed Virgin, whom all but heretics have ever called the Mother of God, was most holy in soul and body, from her ineffable proximity to God? He who gave to the perishing and senseless substances of wool or cotton that grace of which it was capable, should not He rather communicate of His higher spiritual perfections to her in whose bosom He lay, …? (*TT* #85, Sep. 1838)

She who was chosen to be the Mother of God was also chosen to be *gratia plena*, full of grace. This you see is an explanation of those high doctrines which are received among Catholics concerning the purity and sinlessness of the Blessed Virgin. St. Augustine will not listen to the notion that she ever committed sin, and the Holy Council of Trent declares that by special privilege she through all her life avoided all, even venial sin. And at this time you know it is the received belief of Catholics that she was not conceived in original sin, and that her conception was immaculate … Before the Blessed Mary could be Mother of God, and in order to her being Mother, she was set apart, sanctified, filled with grace, and made meet for the presence of the Eternal. (*FP*, Sermon 7: 'Our Lady in the Gospel,' 26 March 1848)

It was fitting, for His honour and glory, that she, who was the instrument of His bodily presence, should first be a miracle of His grace; it was fitting that she should triumph, where Eve had failed, and should 'bruise the serpent's head' by the spotlessness of her sanctity. In some respects, indeed, the curse was not reversed; Mary came into a fallen world, and resigned herself to its laws; she, as also the Son she bore, was exposed to pain of soul and body, she was subjected to death; but she was not put under the power of sin. As grace was infused into Adam from the first moment of his creation, so that he never had experience of his natural poverty, till sin reduced him to it; so was grace given from the first in still ampler measure to Mary, and she never incurred, in fact, Adam's deprivation … If Adam might have kept himself from sin in his first state, much more shall we expect immaculate perfection in Mary … in this very day, should God so will, she will win at length her most radiant crown, and, without opposing voice, and amid the jubilation of the whole Church, she will be hailed as immaculate in her conception. (*Mix.*, Discourse 17: 'The Glories of Mary for the Sake of Her Son')

We should be prepared then, my brethren, to believe that the Mother of God is full of grace and glory, from the very fitness of such a dispensation, even though we had not been taught it; and this fitness will appear still more clear and certain when we contemplate the subject more steadily. Consider then, that it has been the ordinary rule of God's dealings with us, that personal sanctity should be the attendant upon high spiritual dignity of place or work. The angels, who, as the word imports, are God's messengers, are also perfect in holiness; 'without sanctity, no one shall see God;' no defiled thing can enter the courts of heaven; and the higher its inhabitants are advanced in their ministry about the throne, the holier are they, and the more absorbed in their contemplation of that Holiness upon which they wait. The Seraphim, who immediately surround the Divine Glory, cry day and night, 'Holy, Holy, Holy, Lord God of Hosts.' So is it also on earth; the prophets have ordinarily not only gifts but graces; they are not only inspired to know and to teach God's will, but inwardly converted to obey it … in like manner Job, Elias, Isaias, Jeremias, Daniel, and above them all St. John Baptist, and then again St. Peter, St. Paul, St.

John, and the rest, are all especial instances of heroic virtue, and patterns to their brethren ... St. John Baptist was sanctified by the Spirit before his birth; shall Mary be only equal to him? is it not fitting that her privilege should surpass his? is it wonderful, if grace, which anticipated his birth by three months, should in her case run up to the very first moment of her being, outstrip the imputation of sin, and be beforehand with the usurpation of Satan? Mary must surpass all the saints; the very fact that certain privileges are known to have been theirs persuades us, almost from the necessity of the case, that she had the same and higher. Her conception was immaculate, in order that she might surpass all saints in the date as well as the fulness of her sanctification. (*Mix.*, Discourse 18: 'On the Fitness of the Glories of Mary')

Immaculate in her conception—so sweet, so musical, etc. She holds up to us what man is intended to be, as a type, the most perfect submission of his powers to grace ... Christ the source, Mary the work of grace. (*SN*, 'On Man as Disobedient by Sin as Contrasted with Mary,' 9 December 1849)

This age [is] an impure age. Hence [the] Blessed Virgin Mary [is] attacked. Hence [the devotion to] the Immaculate Conception is so apposite. (*SN*, 'The Immaculate Conception the Antagonist of an Impure Age,' Dec. 1851)

Genesis iii. We cannot be surprised at our Lady's Immaculate Conception. The reason is so plain that it seems axiomatic, nor, though it has been a point of controversy, do I think any holy person in any age has ever really denied it; if they seemed to do so, it was something else they opposed. Has not God required holiness wherever He has come?—(1) burning bush [Ex. 3:5] (2) 'Be ye holy, for,' etc. [Lev. 20:7] (3) priests' purifications; (4) consecration of Temple and tabernacle; (5) without sanctity, no one, etc.; (6) Confession before Communion. If, then, our Lady was to hold God, etc. Still more, if from her flesh, etc. Hence, though the Church has never proposed it as a point of faith, it is not difficult to conceive it should be one, and there has been a growing wish that the Church

could find that it was part of the original dogma. Indeed, it is almost saying what has been said in other words, for if no venial sin, must there not
be Immaculate Conception? Now to explain what the doctrine is. Eve,
as Adam, had been not only created, but constituted holy, grace given,
etc. Eve was without sin from the first, filled with grace from the first ...
She was to conquer. How would this be the case, unless Mary had at least
the gifts which Eve had? We believe, then, that Mary had this sanctifying
grace from the moment she began to be ... Do you not see that there cannot be a more insufferable penance than to be thus perfectly holy, yet in
this unholy world? (*SN*, 'On the Peculiarities and Consequent Sufferings
of Our Lady's Sanctity,' 8 December 1853)

This year, as you know, the Pope, in the midst of the bishops of the
world, has defined the Immaculate Conception, viz., that Mary had nothing to do with sin. We were sure that it was so. We could not believe it was
not. We could not believe it had not been revealed. We thought it had,
but the Church did not say it was, etc. (*SN*, 'Christmas Joy,' 25 December
1854)

Let me take the doctrine which Protestants consider our greatest difficulty, that of the Immaculate Conception. Here I entreat the reader to
recollect my main drift, which is this. I have no difficulty in receiving the
doctrine; and that, because it so intimately harmonizes with that circle
of recognised dogmatic truths, into which it has been recently received;
... there is no burden at all in holding that the Blessed Virgin was conceived without original sin; indeed, it is a simple fact to say, that Catholics
have not come to believe it because it is defined, but that it was defined
because they believed it. So far from the definition in 1854 being a tyran-
nical infliction on the Catholic world, it was received every where on its
promulgation with the greatest enthusiasm. It was in consequence of the
unanimous petition, presented from all parts of the Church to the Holy
See, in behalf of an *ex cathedrâ* declaration that the doctrine was Apostolic, that it was declared so to be. I never heard of one Catholic having
difficulties in receiving the doctrine, whose faith on other grounds was
not already suspicious. (*Apo.*, ch. 5)

I ask you, have you any intention to deny that Mary was as fully en-dowed as Eve? is it any violent inference, that she, who was to co-operate in the redemption of the world, at least was not less endowed with power from on high, than she who, given as a help-mate to her husband, did in the event but cooperate with him for its ruin? If Eve was raised above hu-man nature by that indwelling moral gift which we call grace, is it rash to say that Mary had even a greater grace? And this consideration gives sig-nificance to the Angel's salutation of her as 'full of grace,' — an interpre-tation of the original word which is undoubtedly the right one, as soon as we resist the common Protestant assumption that grace is a mere external approbation or acceptance, answering to the word 'favour,' whereas it is, as the Fathers teach, a real inward condition or superadded quality of soul. And if Eve had this supernatural inward gift given her from the first moment of her personal existence, is it possible to deny that Mary too had this gift from the very first moment of her personal existence? I do not know how to resist this inference: — well, this is simply and literally the doctrine of the Immaculate Conception. I say the doctrine of the Immaculate Conception is in its substance this, and nothing more or less than this (putting aside the question of degrees of grace); and it really does seem to me bound up in the doctrine of the Fathers, that Mary is the second Eve. It is indeed to me a most strange phenomenon that so many learned and devout men stumble at this doctrine; and I can only account for it by supposing that in matter of fact they do not know what we mean by the Immaculate Conception; ... I do not see how any one who holds with Bull the Catholic doctrine of the supernatural endowments of our first parents, has fair reason for doubting our doctrine about the Blessed Virgin. It has no reference whatever to her parents, but simply to her own person; it does but affirm that, together with the nature which she inherited from her parents, that is, her own nature, she had a superadded fulness of grace, and that from the first moment of her existence. Sup-pose Eve had stood the trial, and not lost her first grace; and suppose she had eventually had children, those children from the first moment of their existence would, through divine bounty, have received the same privilege that she had ever had; that is, as she was taken from Adam's side, in a garment, so to say, of grace, so they in turn would have received what may be called an immaculate conception. They would have then been conceived in grace, as in fact they are conceived in sin. What is there difficult in this doctrine? What is there unnatural? Mary may be called, as it were, a daughter of Eve unfallen. You believe with us that St. John Baptist had grace given to him three months before his birth, at the time that the Blessed Virgin visited his mother. He accordingly was *not* immaculately conceived, because he was alive before grace came to him; but our Lady's case only differs from his in this respect, that to her the grace of God came, not three months merely before her birth, but from the first moment of her being, as it had been given to Eve ... they fancy that we ascribe a different nature from ours to the Blessed Virgin, different from that of her parents, and from that of fallen Adam. We hold nothing of the kind; we consider that in Adam she died, as others; that she was included, together with the whole race, in Adam's sentence; that she incurred his debt, as we do; but that, for the sake of Him who was to redeem her and us upon the Cross, to her the debt was remitted by anticipation, on her the sentence was not carried out, except indeed as regards her natural death, for she died when her time came, as others. All this we teach, but we deny that she had original sin; ... Mary could not merit, any more than they, the restoration of that grace; but it was restored to her by God's free bounty, from the very first moment of her existence, and thereby, in fact, she never came under the original curse, which consisted in the loss of it. And she had this special privilege, in order to fit her to become the Mother of her and our Redeemer, to fit her mentally, spiritually for it; so that, by the aid of the first grace, she might so grow in grace, that, when the Angel came and her Lord was at hand, she might be 'full of grace,' prepared as far as a creature could be prepared, to receive Him into her bosom. I have drawn the doctrine of the Immaculate Conception, as an immediate inference, from the primitive doctrine that Mary is the second Eve. The argument seems to me conclusive ... If controversy had in earlier days so cleared the subject as to make it plain to all, that the doctrine meant nothing else than that in fact in her case the general sentence on mankind was not carried out, and that, by means of the indwelling in her of divine grace from the first moment of her being (and this is all the decree of 1854 has declared), I cannot believe that the doctrine would have ever been opposed. (*Dif*. ii, Letter to Pusey, ch. 3, 1865)

That 'Mary is the new Eve,' ... is an explicit tradition; and by the force of it follow two others, which are implicit: — first (considering the condition of Eve in paradise), that Mary had no part in sin, and indefinitely large measures of grace; secondly (considering the doctrine of merits), that she has been exalted to glory proportionate to that grace. (*Dif*. ii, Letter to Pusey, Note III, 1865)

Step after step was taken *towards* it. The Church patiently waited till all was ripe — No Council was necessary — the theological opinion [Immaculate Conception] grew into a dogma, as it were, spontaneously. (*POL*; Letter to Reginald Buckler, O.P., 15 April 1870)

That the Immaculate Conception was in the *depositum* seems to me clear, as soon as it is understood what the doctrine is. I have drawn out the argument in my 'Letter to Dr. Pusey.' The Fathers from the beginning call Mary the Second Eve. This has been the dogma proclaimed by the earliest Fathers. There are three especially witnesses to [it] in three or four or five countries widely separated. St. Justin Martyr speaks for Syria, St. Irenaeus for Asia Minor and Gaul, and Tertullian for Rome and Africa. Nothing is included in the doctrine of the Immaculate Conception which is not included in the Eve character of Mary — nay, not so much, for Eve in Paradise did not need redemption, but Mary was actually redeemed by the blood of her Son so much as any of us, and the grace she had was not like Eve's grace in Paradise, but simply a purchased grace. (*Ward* ii, 376-377; Letter to Mrs. William Froude, March 1871)

Mary's redemption was determined in that special manner which we call the Immaculate Conception. It was decreed, not that she should be *cleansed* from sin, but that she should, from the first moment of her being, be *preserved* from sin; so that the Evil One never had any part in her. Therefore she was a child of Adam and Eve as if they had never fallen; she did not share with them their sin; she inherited the gifts and graces (and more than those) which Adam and Eve possessed in Paradise. This is her prerogative, and the foundation of all those salutary truths which are revealed to us concerning her. Let us say then with all holy souls, *Virgin most pure, conceived without original sin, Mary, pray for us.* (MD, 'Meditations on the Litany of Loretto, for the Month of May: I. On the Immaculate Conception,' for May 3)

What is the highest, the rarest, the choicest prerogative of Mary? It is that she was without sin. When a woman in the crowd cried out to our Lord, 'Blessed is the womb that bare Thee!' He answered, 'More blessed are they who hear the word of God and keep it.' Those words were fulfilled in Mary. She was filled with grace *in order* to be the Mother of God. But it was a higher gift than her maternity to be thus sanctified and thus pure. Our Lord indeed would not have become her son *unless* He had first sanctified her; but still, the greater blessedness was to have that perfect sanctification. *This* then is why she is the *Virgo Prædicanda*; she is deserving to be preached abroad because she never committed any sin, even the least; because sin had no part in her; because, through the fulness of God's grace, she never thought a thought, or spoke a word, or did an action, which was displeasing, which was not most pleasing, to Almighty God; because in her was displayed the greatest triumph over the enemy of souls. Wherefore, when all seemed lost, in order to show what He could do for us all by dying for us; in order to show what human nature, His work, was capable of becoming; to show how utterly He could bring to naught the utmost efforts, the most concentrated malice of the foe, and reverse all the consequences of the Fall, our Lord began, even before His coming, to do His most wonderful act of redemption, in the person of her who was to be His Mother. By the merit of that Blood which was to be shed, He interposed to hinder her incurring the sin of Adam, before He had made on the Cross atonement for it. And therefore it is that we *preach* her who is the subject of this wonderful grace. (MD, 'Meditations on the Litany of Loretto, for the Month of May: I. On the Immaculate Conception,' for May 4)

Even created excellence is fearful to think of when it is so high as Mary's. As to the great *Creator*, when Moses desired to see His glory, He

Himself says about Himself, 'Thou canst not see My face, for man shall not see Me and live;' and St. Paul says, 'Our God is a consuming fire.' And when St. John, holy as he was, saw only the *Human Nature* of our Lord, as He is in Heaven, 'he fell at His feet as dead.' And so as regards the appearance of angels. The holy Daniel, when St. Gabriel appeared to him, 'fainted away, and lay in a consternation, with his face close to the ground.' When this great archangel came to Zacharias, the father of St. John the Baptist, he too was troubled, and fear fell upon him.' But it was otherwise with Mary when the same St. Gabriel came to her. She was overcome indeed, and troubled at his *words*, because, humble as she was in her own opinion of herself, he addressed her as 'Full of grace,' and 'Blessed among women;' but she was able to bear the sight of him. Hence we learn two things: first, how great a holiness was Mary's, seeing she could endure the presence of an angel, whose brightness smote the holy prophet Daniel even to fainting and almost to death; and secondly, since she is so much holier than that angel, and we so much less holy than Daniel, what great reason we have to call her the *Virgo Admirabilis*, the Wonderful, the Awful Virgin, when we think of her ineffable purity! (*MD*, 'Meditations on the Litany of Loretto, for the Month of May: I. On the Immaculate Conception,' for May 5)

How are we sure that our Lady, when she was on earth, attracted people round her, and made them love her merely because she was holy?—considering that holy people sometimes have not that gift of drawing others to them. To explain this point we must recollect that there is a vast difference between the state of a soul such as that of the Blessed Virgin, which has *never* sinned, and a soul, however holy, which has *once* had upon it Adam's sin; for, even after baptism and repentance, it suffers necessarily from the spiritual wounds which are the consequence of that sin. Holy men, indeed, never commit *mortal* sin; nay, sometimes have never committed even one mortal sin in the whole course of their lives. But Mary's holiness went beyond this. She never committed even a *venial* sin, and this special privilege is not known to belong to anyone but Mary. Now, whatever want of amiableness, sweetness, attractiveness, really exists in holy men arises from the *remains* of sin in them, or again from the want of a holiness powerful enough to overcome the defects of nature, whether of soul or body; but, as to Mary, her holiness was such, that if we saw her, and heard her, we should not be able to tell to those who asked us anything about her except simply that she was angelic and heavenly. Of course her face was most beautiful; but we should not be able to recollect whether it was beautiful or not; we should not recollect any of her features, because it was her beautiful sinless soul, which looked through her eyes, and spoke through her mouth, and was heard in her voice, and compassed her all about; when she was still, or when she walked, whether she smiled, or was sad, her sinless soul, this it was which would draw all those to her who had any grace in them, any remains of grace, any love of holy things. There was a divine music in all she said and did—in her mien, her air, her deportment, that charmed every true heart that came near her. Her innocence, her humility and modesty, her simplicity, sincerity, and truthfulness, her unselfishness, her unaffected interest in everyone who came to her, her purity—it was these qualities which made her so lovable; and were we to see her now, neither our first thought nor our second thought would be, what she could do for us with her Son (though she can do so much), but our first thought would be, 'Oh, how beautiful!' and our second thought would be, 'Oh, what ugly hateful creatures are we!' (MD, 'Meditations on the Litany of Loretto, for the Month of May: I. On the Immaculate Conception,' for May 7)

We see then the force of our Lady's title, when we call her 'Holy Mary.' When God would prepare a human mother for His Son, this was why He began by giving her an immaculate conception. He began, not by giving her the gift of love, or truthfulness, or gentleness, or devotion, though according to the occasion she had them all. But He began His great work before she was born; before she could think, speak, or act, by making her holy, and thereby, while on earth, a citizen of heaven. 'Tota pulchra es, Maria!' Nothing of the deformity of sin was ever hers. Thus she differs from all saints. There have been great missionaries, confessors, bishops, doctors, pastors. They have done great works, and have taken with them numberless converts or penitents to heaven. They have suffered much, and have a superabundance of merits to show. But Mary in this way resembles her Divine Son, viz., that, as He, being God, is separate by holiness from all creatures, so she is separate from all Saints and Angels, as being *'full of grace.'* (MD, 'Meditations on the Litany of Loretto, for the Month of May: I. On the Immaculate Conception,' for May 9)

Does not the objector consider that *Eve* was created, or born, *without* original sin? Why does not *this* shock him? Would he have been inclined to *worship* Eve in that first estate of hers? Why, then, Mary? Does he not believe that St. John Baptist had the grace of God—i.e., was regenerated, even before his birth? What do we believe of Mary, but that grace was given her at a still earlier period? *All* we say is, that grace was given her from the first moment of her existence. We do not say that she did not owe her salvation to the death of her Son. Just the contrary, we say that she, of all mere children of Adam, is in the truest sense the fruit and the purchase of His Passion. He has done for her more than for anyone else. To others He gives grace and regeneration at a *point* in their earthly existence; to her, from the very beginning. We do not make her *nature* different from others. Though, as St. Austin says, we do not like to name her in the same breath with mention of sin, yet, certainly she *would* have been a frail being, like Eve, *without* the grace of God. A more abundant gift of grace made her what she was from the first. It was not her *nature* which secured her perseverance, but the excess of grace which hindered Nature acting as Nature ever will act. There is no difference in *kind* between her and us, though an inconceivable difference of *degree*. She and we are both simply saved by the grace of Christ. Thus, sincerely speaking, I really do not see *what* the difficulty is, and should like it set down distinctly in words. I will add that the above statement is no private statement of my own. I never heard of any Catholic who ever had any other view. I never heard of any other put forth by anyone ... Now, as to the doctrine of the Immaculate Conception, it was *implied* in early times, and never *denied*. In the Middle Ages it *was* denied by St. Thomas and by St. Bernard, but they took the phrase in a different sense from that in which the Church now takes it. They understood it with reference to our Lady's mother, and thought it contradicted the text, 'In sin hath my mother conceived me'—whereas *we* do not speak of the Immaculate Conception except as relating to Mary; and the other doctrine (which St. Thomas and St. Bernard did oppose) *is* really heretical ... Consider what I have said. Is it, after all, *certainly* irrational? is it *certainly* against Scripture? is it *certainly* against the primitive Fathers? is it *certainly* idolatrous? I cannot help smiling as I put the questions. Rather, may not *something* be said for it from reason, from piety, from antiquity, from the inspired text? You may see no reason at all to believe the voice of the Church; you may not yet have attained to faith in it—but what on earth this doctrine has to do with *shaking* your faith in her, if you have faith, or in sending you to the right-about if you are beginning to think she *may* be from God, is more than my mind can comprehend. Many, many doctrines are far harder than the Immaculate Conception. The doctrine of Original Sin is indefinitely harder. Mary just has *not* this difficulty. It is *no* difficulty to believe that a soul is united to the flesh *without* original sin; the great mystery is that any, that millions on millions, are born with it. Our teaching about Mary has just one difficulty less than our teaching about the state of mankind generally. I say it distinctly—there may be many excuses at the last day, good and bad, for not being Catholics; *one* I cannot conceive: 'O Lord, the doctrine of the Immaculate Conception was so derogatory to Thy grace, so inconsistent with Thy Passion, so at variance with Thy word in Genesis and the Apocalypse, so unlike the teaching of Thy first Saints and Martyrs, as to give me a *right* to reject it at all risks, and Thy Church for teaching it. It is a doctrine as to which my private judgment is fully justified in opposing the Church's judgment. And this is my plea for living and dying a Protestant.' (*MD*, 'Memorandum on the Immaculate Conception')

Mary: Intercessor, Mediatrix, and Spiritual Mother

St. Justin, St. Irenaeus, and others, had distinctly laid it down, that she not only had an office, but bore a part, and was a voluntary agent, in the actual process of redemption, as Eve had been instrumental and responsible in Adam's fall. They taught that, as the first woman might have foiled the Tempter and did not, so, if Mary had been disobedient or unbelieving on Gabriel's message, the Divine Economy would have been frustrated. And certainly the parallel between 'the Mother of all living' and the Mother of the Redeemer may be gathered from a comparison of the first chapters of Scripture with the last. (*Dev.*, Part II: ch. 10, sec. 4)

[I]nterest your dear Mother, the Mother of God, in your success; pray to her earnestly for it; she can do more for you than any one else. Pray her by the pain she suffered, when the sharp sword went through her, pray her, by her own perseverance, which was in her the gift of the same God of whom you ask it for yourselves. God will not refuse you, He will not refuse her, if you have recourse to her succour. It will be a blessed thing, in your last hour, when flesh and heart are failing, in the midst of the pain, the weariness, the restlessness, the prostration of strength, and the exhaustion of spirits, which then will be your portion, it will be blessed indeed to have her at your side, more tender than an earthly mother, to nurse you and to whisper peace. It will be most blessed, when the evil one is making his last effort, when he is coming on you in his might to pluck you away from your Father's hand, if he can—it will be blessed indeed if Jesus, if Mary and Joseph are then with you, waiting to shield you from his assaults and to receive your soul. (*Mix.*, Discourse 7: 'Perseverance in Grace')

Put yourself ever fully and utterly into Mary's hands, and she will nurse you and bring you forward. She will watch over you as a mother over a sick child. (*POL*; Letter to Miss Mary Holmes, 31 July 1850)

Much is said by Protestants against our Lady's power, but our Lady's power is nothing else than the greatest exemplification of the power of prayer. We don't give her power of atonement, etc., but simply prayer, as we give ourselves; we in a degree, she in fulness. Now I can understand persons scrupling at the power of prayer *altogether*; but why, that there should be one instance [*i.e.* great exemplification] of it? We do not introduce a mystery, but realise it. The great mystery is that prayer should have influence. (*SN*, 'On the Doctrine of Prayer as Reconciling Us to the Catholic Teaching About Our Blessed Lady,' 11 August 1850)

The lawyers, again, as I noticed in my first Lecture, speak of the 'Omnipotence of Parliament;' I never will be so unjust to them as to take them literally. I am perfectly sure that it never entered into the head of any Speaker, or Prime Minister, or Serjeant-at-arms, to claim any super-human prerogative for the Two Houses. Those officials all feel intensely, I am sure, that they are but feeble and fallible creatures, and would laugh at any one who shuddered at their use of a phrase which has a parliamentary sense as well as a theological. Now I only claim to be heard in turn with the same candour which I exemplify so fully, when I speak myself of the omnipotence of the Blessed Virgin. When such an expression is used by a Catholic, he would be as indignant as a member of Parliament to find it perverted by an enemy from the innocent sense in which he used it. Parliament is omnipotent, as having the power to do what it will, not in France, or in Germany, or in Russia, much less all over the earth, much less in heaven, but within the United Kingdom; and in like manner the Blessed Virgin is called omnipotent, as being able to gain from God what she desires by the medium of prayer. Prayer is regarded as omnipotent in Scripture, and she in consequence, as being the chief intercessor among creatures, is considered omnipotent too. And the same remark applies to a great number of other words in Catholic theology. (*PPC*, Lecture 8)

The point urged against the Protestant is this—That, whereas every science, polity, institution, religion, uses the words and phrases which it employs in *a sense of its own,* or a *technical* sense, Englishmen, allowing and exemplifying this very principle in the case of their own Constitution, will not allow it to the divines of the Catholic Church. *E.g.,* the 'Omnipotence of Parliament' is a phrase of English law, in which the word *omnipotence* is taken otherwise than when it is ascribed to Almighty God; and so, too, when used by Catholic divines of the Blessed Virgin. If any one exclaims against its adoption, in the latter case, by Catholics, let him also protest against its adoption, in the former case, by English lawyers; if he rejects explanations, distinctions, limitations, in the latter case, and calls them lame, subtle, evasive, &c., let him do so in the former case also; whereas Protestants denounce such explanations as offered by Catholics, and take a pride in them as laid down by English lawyers. (*PPC*, Note 1)

It is like the divine works to turn things to *account*. Thus, though she subserved the Redeemer, she also subserves the redeemed. Hers is a *ministry* to us, and it was to Him originally ... Thus she is the fount of mercy, as a magistrate of justice, etc. Hence Protestant absurdity of saying [that] we rate her more merciful than Christ. Christ is the judge also. Show what is meant by it. Can a ring be merciful? ... Gen. iii., Apoc. xii. — *Advocata* with clients; mother of all living. 'Behold thy mother,' John xix. 27. (*SN*, 'On the Patrocinium B.V.M.,' 26 October 1851)

We have a friend in court. She is the great work of God's love. (*SN*, 'Rejoicing with Mary,' 20 August 1854)

She is the great advocate of the Church. By which is not meant Atonement, of course. We know perfectly that she was saved by her Son. But she is His greatest work, and He has exalted her to this special office. (*SN*, 'Our Lady the Fulfilling of the Revealed Doctrine of Prayer,' 19 August 1855)

[T]here were three parties concerned, — the serpent, the woman, and the man; and at the time of their sentence, an event was announced for a distant future, in which the three same parties were to meet again, the serpent, the woman, and the man; but it was to be a second Adam and a second Eve, and the new Eve was to be the mother of the new Adam. 'I will put enmity between thee and the woman, and between thy seed and her seed.' The Seed of the woman is the Word Incarnate, and the Woman, whose seed or son He is, is His mother Mary. This interpretation, and the parallelism it involves, seem to me undeniable; but at all events (and this is my point) the parallelism is the doctrine of the Fathers, from the earliest times; and, this being established, we are able, by the position and office of Eve in our fall, to determine the position and office of Mary in our restoration ... As Eve failed in these virtues, and thereby brought on the fall of the race in Adam, so Mary by means of the same had a part in its restoration ... not to go beyond the doctrine of the Three Fathers [Justin, Tertullian, Irenaeus], they unanimously declare that she was *not* a mere instrument in the Incarnation, such as David, or

Judah, may be considered; they declare she co-operated in our salvation not merely by the descent of the Holy Ghost upon her body, but by specific holy acts, the effect of the Holy Ghost within her soul; that, as Eve forfeited privileges by sin, so Mary earned privileges by the fruits of grace; that, as Eve was disobedient and unbelieving, so Mary was obedient and believing; that, as Eve was a cause of ruin to all, Mary was a cause of salvation to all; that as Eve made room for Adam's fall, so Mary made room for our Lord's reparation of it; and thus, whereas the free gift was not as the offence, but much greater, it follows that, as Eve co-operated in effecting a great evil, Mary co-operated in effecting a much greater good ... Having then adduced these Three Fathers of the second century, I have at least got so far as this: viz., that no one, who acknowledges the force of early testimony in determining Christian truth, can wonder, no one can complain, can object, that we Catholics should hold a very high doctrine concerning the Blessed Virgin, unless indeed stronger statements can be brought for a contrary conception of her, either of as early, or at least of a later date. But, as far as I know, no statements can be brought from the ante-Nicene literature, to invalidate the testimony of the Three Fathers concerning her; and little can be brought against it from the fourth century, while in that fourth century the current of testimony in her behalf is as strong as in the second; and, as to the fifth, it is far stronger than in any former time, both in its fulness and its authority. (*Dif.* ii, Letter to Pusey, ch. 3, 1865)

If, as St. Irenaeus says, she acted the part of an Advocate, a friend in need, even in her mortal life, if as St. Jerome and St. Ambrose say, she was on earth the great pattern of Virgins, if she had a meritorious share in bringing about our redemption, if her maternity was gained by her faith and obedience, if her Divine Son was subject to her, and if she stood by the Cross with a mother's heart and drank in to the full those sufferings which it was her portion to gaze upon, it is impossible that we should not associate these characteristics of her life on earth with her present state of blessedness; and this surely she anticipated, when she said in her hymn that all 'generations should call her blessed.' (*Dif.* ii, Letter to Pusey, ch. 3, 1865)

I consider it impossible then, for those who believe the Church to be one vast body in heaven and on earth, in which every holy creature of God has his place, and of which prayer is the life, when once they recognise the sanctity and dignity of the Blessed Virgin, not to perceive immediately, that her office above is one of perpetual intercession for the faithful militant, and that our very relation to her must be that of clients to a patron, and that, in the eternal enmity which exists between the woman and the serpent, while the serpent's strength lies in being the Tempter, the weapon of the Second Eve and Mother of God is prayer. As then these ideas of her sanctity and dignity gradually penetrated the mind of Christendom, so did that of her intercessory power follow close upon them and with them. From the earliest times that mediation is symbolized in those representations of her with up-lifted hands, which, whether in plaster or in glass, are still extant in Rome ... She is the great exemplar of prayer in a generation, which emphatically denies the power of prayer *in toto,* which determines that fatal laws govern the universe, that there cannot be any direct communication between earth and heaven, that God cannot visit His own earth, and that man cannot influence His providence. (*Dif.* ii, Letter to Pusey, ch. 3, 1865)

He alone has an entrance into our soul, reads our secret thoughts, speaks to our heart, applies to us spiritual pardon and strength. On Him we solely depend. He alone is our inward life; He not only regenerates us, but (to use the words appropriated to a higher mystery) *semper gignit;* He is ever renewing our new birth and our heavenly sonship. In this sense He may be called, as in nature, so in grace, our real Father. Mary is only our mother by divine appointment, given us from the Cross; her presence is above, not on earth; her office is external, not within us. Her name is not heard in the administration of the Sacraments. Her work is not one of ministration towards us; her power is indirect. It is her prayers that avail, and her prayers are effectual by the *fiat* of Him who is our all in all. Nor need she hear us by any innate power, or any personal gift; but by His manifestation to her of the prayers which we make to her. When Moses was on the Mount, the Almighty told him of the idolatry of his people at the foot of it, in order that he might intercede for them; and thus it is the

Divine Presence which is the intermediating Power by which we reach her and she reaches us. (*Dif.* ii, Letter to Pusey, ch. 4, 1865)

Our Lord died for those heathens who did not know Him; and His Mother intercedes for those Christians who do not know her; and she intercedes according to His will, and, when He wills to save a particular soul, she at once prays for it. I say, He wills indeed according to her prayer, but then she prays according to His will. Though then it is natural and prudent for those to have recourse to her, who from the Church's teaching know her power, yet it cannot be said that devotion to her is a *sine-quâ-non* of salvation. (*Dif.* ii, Letter to Pusey, ch. 5, 1865)

[W]hen it was said that 'the Blessed Virgin's servants have an assurance that they shall be saved,' this was not meant to deny that her 'servants' must love God and believe the Creed, live good lives and die holy deaths in order to deserve that title, or that 'without holiness no one shall see God.' (*TT* #71, footnote 18 of 1883)

[S]he had a place in the economy of Redemption; it is fulfilled in her spirit and will, as well as in her body. Eve had a part in the fall of man, though it was Adam who was our representative, and whose sin made us sinners. It was Eve who began, and who tempted Adam. Scripture says: 'The woman saw that the tree was good to eat, and fair to the eyes, and delightful to behold; and she took of the fruit thereof, and did eat, and gave to her husband, and he did eat.' It was fitting then in God's mercy that, as the woman began the *destruction* of the world, so woman should also begin its *recovery*, and that, as Eve opened the way for the fatal deed of the first Adam, so Mary should open the way for the great achievement of the second Adam, even our Lord Jesus Christ, who came to save the world by dying on the cross for it. Hence Mary is called by the holy Fathers a second and a better Eve, as having taken that first step in the salvation of mankind which Eve took in its ruin. (*MD*, 'Meditations on the Litany of Loretto, for the Month of May: II. On the Annunciation,' for May 13)

[S]he has, more than anyone else, more than all Angels and Saints, this great, prevailing gift of prayer. No one has access to the Almighty as His Mother has; none has merit such as hers. Her Son will deny her nothing that she asks; and herein lies her power. While she defends the Church, neither height nor depth, neither men nor evil spirits, neither great monarchs, nor craft of man, nor popular violence, can avail to harm us; for human life is short, but Mary reigns above, a Queen for ever. (*MD*, 'Meditations on the Litany of Loretto, for the Month of May: IV. On the Assumption,' for May 28)

Our reading is, 'She shall bruise thy head.' Now, this fact alone of our reading, 'She shall bruise,' has some weight, for *why* should not, perhaps, our reading be the right one? But take the comparison of Scripture with Scripture, and see how the whole hangs together as we interpret it. A war between a woman and the serpent is spoken of in Genesis. *Who* is the serpent? Scripture nowhere says till the twelfth chapter of the Apocalypse. There at last, for the first time, the 'Serpent' is interpreted to mean the Evil Spirit. Now, *how* is he introduced? Why, by the vision *again* of a Woman, his enemy—and just as, in the first vision in Genesis, the Woman has a 'seed,' so here a 'Child.' Can we help saying, then, that the Woman is Mary in the third of Genesis? And if so, and our reading is right, the first prophecy ever given contrasts the Second Woman with the First—Mary with Eve, just as St. Justin, St. Irenaeus, and Tertullian do. Moreover, see the direct bearing of this upon the Immaculate Conception. There was *war* between the woman and the Serpent. This is most emphatically fulfilled if she had nothing to do with sin—for, so far as any one sins, he has an alliance with the Evil One. (*MD*, 'Memorandum on the Immaculate Conception')

Mary: Mother of God (*Theotokos*)

I have said that there was in the first ages no public and ecclesiastical recognition of the place which St. Mary holds in the Economy of grace; this was reserved for the fifth century, as the definition of our Lord's proper Divinity had been the work of the fourth ... In order to do honour to Christ, in order to defend the true doctrine of the Incarnation, in order to secure a right faith in the manhood of the Eternal Son, the Council of Ephesus [431] determined the Blessed Virgin to be the Mother of God. Thus all heresies of that day, though opposite to each other, tended in a most wonderful way to her exaltation; and the School of Antioch, the fountain of primitive rationalism, led the Church to determine first the conceivable greatness of a creature, and then the incommunicable dignity of the Blessed Virgin. (*Dev.*, Part I: ch. 4, sec. 2)

It has been anxiously asked, whether the honours paid to St. Mary, which have grown out of devotion to her Almighty Lord and Son, do not, in fact, tend to weaken that devotion; and whether, from the nature of the case, it is possible so to exalt a creature without withdrawing the heart from the Creator ... the question is one of fact, not of presumption or conjecture. The abstract lawfulness of the honours paid to St. Mary, and their distinction in theory from the incommunicable worship paid to God, are points which have already been dwelt upon; but here the question turns upon their practicability or expedience, which must be determined by the fact whether they are practicable, and whether they have been found to be expedient. Here I observe, first, that, to those who admit the authority of the Fathers of Ephesus, the question is in no slight degree answered by their sanction of the [*Theotokos*] or 'Mother of God,' as a title of St. Mary, and as given in order to protect the doctrine of the Incarnation, and to preserve the faith of Catholics from a specious Humanitarianism. And if we take a survey at least of Europe, we shall find that it is not those religious communions which are characterized by devotion towards the Blessed Virgin that have ceased to adore her Eternal Son, but those very bodies, (when allowed by the law,) which have renounced devotion to her. The regard for His glory, which was professed in that keen jealousy of her exaltation, has not been supported by the event. They who were accused of worshipping a creature in His stead, still worship Him; their accusers, who hoped to worship Him so purely, they, wherever obstacles to the development of their principles have been removed, have ceased to worship Him altogether. (*Dev.*, Part II: ch. 11, sec. 2)

[I]t has been held from the first, and defined from an early age, that Mary is the Mother of God. She is not merely the Mother of our Lord's manhood, or of our Lord's body, but she is to be considered the Mother of the Word Himself, the Word incarnate. God, in the person of the Word, the Second Person of the All-glorious Trinity, humbled Himself to become her Son. (*Mix.*, Discourse 18: 'On the Fitness of the Glories of Mary')

[T]he Mother of God has ever been the bulwark of our Lord's divinity. And it is that which heretics have ever opposed, for it is the great witness that the doctrine of God being man is true ... The *third* ground was at the Reformation—bolder—that it [i.e., Catholic teaching about our Lady] was idolatry, etc., Satan hoping so to destroy the belief in our Lord's divinity. Here again false reverence, so they abolished the honour of our Lady out of tenderness to Christ's divinity! Look at the issue. The truth is, the doctrine of our Lady keeps us from a dreaming, unreal way. If no mother, no history, how did He come here, etc? He is from heaven. It startles us and makes us think what we say when we say Christ is God; not merely like God, inhabited by, sent by God, but really God; so really, that she is the mother of God because His mother. (*SN*, 'Maternity of Mary,' 14 October 1849)

[S]he is Mother of her Creator. It is this awful title, which both illustrates and connects together the two prerogatives of Mary, on which I have been lately enlarging, her sanctity and her greatness. It is the issue of her sanctity; it is the origin of her greatness. What dignity can be too great to attribute to her who is as closely bound up, as intimately one, with the Eternal Word, as a mother is with a son? What outfit of sanctity, what fulness and redundance of grace, what exuberance of merits must have been hers, when once we admit the supposition, which the Fathers justify, that her Maker really did regard those merits, and take them into account, when He condescended 'not to abhor the Virgin's womb'? Is it surprising then that on the one hand she should be immaculate in her Conception? or on the other that she should be honoured with an Assumption, and exalted as a queen with a crown of twelve stars, with the rulers of day and night to do her service? Men sometimes wonder that we call her Mother of life, of mercy, of salvation; what are all these titles compared to that one name, Mother of God? ... This being the faith of the Fathers about the Blessed Virgin, we need not wonder that it should in no long time be transmuted into devotion. No wonder if their language should become unmeasured, when so great a term as 'Mother of God' had been formally set down as the safe limit of it. No wonder if it should be stronger and stronger as time went on, since only in a long period could the fulness of its import be exhausted. (*Dif.* ii, Letter to Pusey, ch. 3, 1865)

I say then, when once we have mastered the idea, that Mary bore, suckled, and handled the Eternal in the form of a child, what limit is conceivable to the rush and flood of thoughts which such a doctrine involves? What awe and surprise must attend upon the knowledge, that a creature has been brought so close to the Divine Essence? ... a second range of thoughts was opened on mankind, unknown before, and unlike any other, as soon as it was understood that that Incarnate God had a mother. The second idea is perfectly distinct from the former, and does not interfere with it. He is God made low, she is a woman made high. (*Dif.* ii, Letter to Pusey, ch. 4, 1865)

Christians were accustomed from the first to call the Blessed Virgin 'The Mother of God,' because they saw that it was impossible to deny her that title without denying St. John's words, 'The Word' (that is, God the Son) 'was made flesh.' And in no long time it was found necessary to proclaim this truth by the voice of an Ecumenical Council of the Church. For, in consequence of the dislike which men have of a mystery, the error sprang up that our Lord was not really God, but a man, differing from us in this merely — that God dwelt in Him, as God dwells in all good men, only in a higher measure; as the Holy Spirit dwelt in Angels and Prophets, as in a sort of Temple; or again, as our Lord now dwells in the Tabernacle in church. And then the bishops and faithful people found there was no other way of hindering this false, bad view being taught but by declaring distinctly, and making it a point of faith, that Mary was the Mother, not of man only, but of God. And since that time the title of Mary, as *Mother of God*, has become what is called a dogma, or article of faith, in the Church. But this leads us to a larger view of the subject. Is this title as given to Mary more wonderful than the doctrine that God, without ceasing to be God, should become man? Is it more mysterious that Mary should be Mother of God, than that *God* should be *man*? Yet the latter, as I have said, is the elementary truth of revelation, witnessed by Prophets, Evangelists, and Apostles all through Scripture. (*MD*, 'Meditations on the Litany of Loretto, for the Month of May: II. On the Annunciation,' for May 14)

Mary, Perpetual Virginity of

Again, our divines, such as Bramhall, Bull, Pearson, and Patrick, believed that the Blessed Mary was 'Ever-Virgin,' as the Church has called her; but Tradition was their only informant on the subject. Thus there are true Traditions still remaining to us, independent of Scripture. (*VM* i, ch. 11)

[T]here is a natural instinct in pious Protestants which shrinks from the notion that the Blessed Virgin had children after the miraculous conception of our Lord. (*LD* xxx, 144; Letter to Richard Frederick Clarke, S.J., 5 November 1882; words beginning with 'which' are from the first draft of the letter: footnote 2)

Mary, Queen of Heaven

If the Creator comes on earth in the form of a servant and a creature, why may not His Mother, on the other hand, rise to be the Queen of heaven, and be clothed with the sun, and have the moon under her feet? (*Mix.*, Discourse 17: 'The Glories of Mary for the Sake of Her Son')

Mass, Sacrifice of

Much less dare I be so irreverent as to determine that His flesh and blood are there as they were on Calvary ... a spiritual body may be present, the bread and wine still remaining. Therefore it seems safe and according to Scripture to say He is present *in* the bread and wine — but unnecessary and irreverent to insist on our saying that the bread and wine are *changed* into that flesh and blood which were on the Cross. (*POL*; Letter to Mrs. William Wilberforce, 17 November 1834)

Is it so strange then, so contrary to the Scripture account of the institution, that the Lord's Supper should also be a Sacrifice ... all Anglo-Catholics profess to prove the sacrificial character of the Lord's Supper from Scripture. (*TT* #85, Sep. 1838)

[T]he Holy Eucharist is a 'communication of the body and blood of Christ,' ... a mysterious representation of His meritorious Sacrifice. (*TT* #85, Sep. 1838)

Again, after, not teaching, but reminding them about the Lord's Supper, he adds, '*the rest* will I set in order when I come.' [1 Cor. 11:34] When then we find the Church has always considered that Holy Sacrament to be not only a feast or supper, but in its fulness to contain a sacrifice, and to require a certain liturgical form, how does this contradict the inspired text, which plainly signifies that something else *is* to come besides what it has said itself? So far from its being strange that the Church brings out and fills up St. Paul's outline, it would be very strange if it did not. Yet it is not unusual to ascribe these additional details to priestcraft, and without proof to call them corruptions and innovations. (*TT* #85, Sep. 1838)

[T]he Holy Eucharist is also ... a pleading before Him the merits of Christ's death, ... a propitiatory offering. (*TT* #85, Sep. 1838)

[T]hat the Eucharist is a Sacrifice is declared or implied by St. Clement of Rome, St. Paul's companion, by St. Justin, by St. Irenaeus, by Tertullian, by St. Cyprian, and others. On the other hand, the Acts of the Apostles are perhaps alluded to by St. Polycarp, but are first distinctly noticed by St. Irenaeus, then by three writers who came soon after (St. Clement of Alexandria, Tertullian, and the Letter from the Church of Lyons), and then not till the end of the two hundred years from St. John's death. Which has the best evidence, the Book of Acts, or the doctrine of the Eucharistic Sacrifice? (*TT* #85, Sep. 1838)

The Eucharist is a proper Sacrifice made by the Priest as Christ's representative, but only as such. (*Keb.*, 207; Letter of 4 March 1843)

[A]ccording to the lawyer's phrase, the doctrines etc of the Catholic Church (e.g., the Mass) go back in time such that the memory of man 'knoweth not' any thing different. It is the strongest ground in law. After being used to the Mass, it comes upon one, 'How can any one ever fancy that the Mass is in the English Church!' (LD xi, 175-176; Letter to Henry Wilberforce, 8 June 1846)

[T]he Holy Mass, in which He who once died for us upon the Cross, brings back and perpetuates, by His literal presence in it, that one and the same sacrifice which cannot be repeated. (GA, Part II, ch. 10, sec. 2)

Our Lord not only offered Himself as a Sacrifice on the Cross, but He makes Himself a perpetual, a daily sacrifice, to the end of time. In the Holy Mass that One Sacrifice on the Cross once offered is renewed, continued, applied to our benefit. He seems to say, My Cross was raised up 1800 years ago, and only for a few hours—and very few of my servants were present there—but I intend to bring millions into my Church. For their sakes then I will perpetuate my Sacrifice, that each of them may be as though they had severally been present on Calvary. I will offer Myself up day by day to the Father, that every one of my followers may have the opportunity to offer his petitions to Him, sanctified and recommended by the all-meritorious virtue of my Passion. Thus I will be a Priest for ever, after the order of Melchisedech—My priests shall stand at the Altar—but not they, but I rather, will offer. I will not let them offer mere bread and wine, but I myself will be present upon the Altar instead, and I will offer up myself invisibly, while they perform the outward rite. And thus the Lamb that was slain once for all, though He is ascended on high, ever remains a victim from His miraculous presence in Holy Mass under the figure and appearance of mere earthly and visible symbols. (MD, 'Twelve Meditations and Intercessions for Good Friday: 12. Jesus Our Daily Sacrifice')

I adore Thee, O my Lord God, with the most profound awe for thy passion and crucifixion, in sacrifice for our sins. Thou didst suffer incommunicable sufferings in Thy sinless soul. Thou wast exposed in Thy innocent body to ignominious torments, to mingled pain and shame. Thou wast stripped and fiercely scourged, Thy sacred body vibrating under the heavy flail as trees under the blast. Thou wast, when thus mangled, hung up upon the Cross, naked, a spectacle for all to see Thee quivering and dying. What does all this imply, O Mighty God! What a depth is here which we cannot fathom! My God, I know well, Thou couldst have saved us at Thy word, without Thyself suffering; but Thou didst choose to purchase us at the price of Thy Blood. I look on Thee, the Victim lifted up on Calvary, and I know and protest that that death of Thine was an expiation for the sins of the whole world. I believe and know, that Thou alone couldst have offered a meritorious atonement; for it was Thy Divine Nature which gave Thy sufferings worth. Rather then than I should perish according to my deserts, Thou wast nailed to the Tree and didst die. Such a sacrifice was not to be forgotten. It was not to be — it could not be — a mere event in the world's history, which was to be done and over, and was to pass away except in its obscure, unrecognised effects. If that great deed was what we believe it to be, what we know it is, it must remain present, though past; it must be a standing fact for all times. Our own careful reflection upon it tells us this; and therefore, when we are told that Thou, O Lord, though Thou hast ascended to glory, hast renewed and perpetuated Thy sacrifice to the end of all things, not only is the news most touching and joyful, as testifying to so tender a Lord and Saviour, but it carries with it the full assent and sympathy of our reason. Though we neither could, nor would have dared, anticipate so wonderful a doctrine, yet we adore its very suitableness to Thy perfections, as well as its infinite compassionateness for us, now that we are told of it. Yes, my Lord, though Thou hast left the world, Thou art daily offered up in the Mass; and, though Thou canst not suffer pain and death, Thou dost still subject Thyself to indignity and restraint to carry out to the full Thy mercies towards us. Thou dost humble Thyself daily; for, being infinite, Thou couldst not end Thy humiliation while they existed for whom Thou didst submit to it. So Thou remainest a Priest for ever. (*MD*, Part III, sec. XIV: 'The Holy Sacrifice: (1) The Mass')

Merit

[T]here are two things we cannot merit — the first grace and the last. As to the first grace, it is plainly God's free bounty which has made us

Christians. As to the last, it is God's free bounty, in spite of the accumulation of merits. No extent of merit is sufficient to gain perseverance — the just may fall, however holy, etc. Think of Solomon; think of Judas. It is a special gift to die in grace. (*SN*, 'Final Perseverance,' 20 October 1872)

Theology lays down the undeniable truth (as derived from such passages as 'God is not *unjust* to forget your work,' &c. Heb. vi. 10,) that our good works have merit and are a ground of confidence for us in God's judgment of us. This dogma shocks good Protestants, who think that, in the case of an individual Catholic, it is the mark of a self-righteous spirit, and incompatible with his renunciation of his own desert and with a recourse to God's mercy. But they confuse an intellectual view with a personal sentiment. Now it is well known that Bellarmine has written on Justification, and of course in his treatise he insists, as a theologian must, on the doctrine of merit; but it also happens he is led on, as if he was praying or preaching or giving absolution, to drop some few words, beyond the limits of his science, about his own or his brethren's unworthiness and need of pardon and grace. That is, he has happened to let his devout nature betray itself between the joints of his theological harness. He says, 'On account of the uncertainty of our own righteousness and the danger of vain-glory, *it is safest* to place our *whole* trust in the *sole* mercy and goodness of God.' (VM i, Preface to the Third Edition, 1877)

The main feature in modern Catholic teaching, as distinct from *that* of Antiquity, is the doctrine of the 'Treasure of Merits,' but the thing is in the Fathers, though not the phrase. This doctrine is founded on the article of the creed, the Communion of Saints, according to which the Christian body is like an expedition of pilgrims, helping each other with all their powers and in every way by temporal aid and spiritual, with prayers, good works, sufferings, as they go forward towards heaven, and that, up to the hour of death, when each shall stand by himself and 'bear his own burden.' Beginning with this great doctrine, we teach that the Church has the prerogative of effecting the remission, in whole or part in each case, of such punishments as are still due for venial sin or for forgiven mortal sin, not only by the Eucharistic Sacrifice, &c., but also by setting against them, or rather, pleading with God, that infinite treasure of merits which our Lord has wrought out, first in His own Person, next through the grace which He has given to His saints. I say, 'next,' for this treasure consists essentially of His own merits, not of His Saints;' and includes theirs, only as it includes also those of good men on earth. Moreover, its benefits cannot be given in any measure, great or small, except in regard of the punishment of past sins, already repented of and forgiven. (VM i, Lecture 3; footnote 27 from 1877)

Miracles

A miracle may be considered as an event inconsistent with the constitution of nature, that is, with the established course of things in which it is found. Or, again, an event in a given system which cannot be referred to any law, or accounted for by the operation of any principle, in that system. It does not necessarily imply a violation of nature, as some have supposed,—merely the interposition of an external cause, which, we shall hereafter show, can be no other than the agency of the Deity ... To consider them as mere exceptions to physical order, is to take a very incomplete view of them. It is to degrade them from the station which they hold in the plans and provisions of the Divine Mind, and to strip them of their real use and dignity. (Mir., Essay One: 'The Miracles of Scripture,' 1826)

In proof of miraculous occurrences, we must have recourse to the same kind of evidence as that by which we determine the truth of historical accounts in general. For though Miracles, in consequence of their extraordinary nature, challenge a fuller and more accurate investigation, still they do not admit an investigation conducted on different principles,—Testimony being the main assignable medium of proof for past events of any kind. (Mir., Essay One: 'The Miracles of Scripture,' 1826)

Yet, while we reasonably object to gross ignorance or besotted credulity in witnesses for a miraculous story, we must guard against the opposite extreme of requiring the testimony of men of science and general knowledge. Men of philosophical minds are often too fond of inquiring into the causes and mutual dependence of events, of arranging, theorizing, and refining, to be accurate and straightforward in their account of extraordinary occurrences. Instead of giving a plain statement of facts, they are insensibly led to correct the evidence of their senses with a view to account for the strange phenomenon; as Chinese painters, who, instead of drawing in perspective, give lights and shadows their supposed meaning, and depict the prospect as they think it should be, not as it is. As Miracles differ from other events only when considered relatively to a general system, it is obvious that the same persons are competent to attest miraculous facts who are suitable witnesses of corresponding natural ones. If a peasant's testimony be admitted to the phenomenon of meteoric stones, he may evidence the fact of an unusual and unaccountable darkness. A physician's certificate is not needed to assure us of the illness of a friend; nor is it necessary for attesting the simple fact that he has instantaneously recovered. It is important to bear this in mind, for some writers argue as if there were something intrinsically defective in the testimony given by ignorant persons to miraculous occurrences. To say that unlearned persons are not judges of the fact of a miraculous event, is only so far true as all testimony is fallible and liable to be distorted by predjudice. Every one, not only superstitious persons, is apt to interpret facts in his own way; if the superstitious see too many prodigies, men of science may see too few. (Mir., Essay One: 'The Miracles of Scripture,' 1826)

[M]iracles, according to the common saying, are not wrought to convince Atheists, and, when they claim to be evidence of a Revelation, presuppose the being of an Intelligent Agent to whom they may be referred. (US, Sermon 10: 'Faith and Reason, Contrasted as Habits of Mind,' Jan. 1839)

It may be advisable to state in the commencement the conclusions to which the remarks which follow will be found to tend; they are such as these: — that Ecclesiastical Miracles, that is, Miracles posterior to the Apostolic age, are on the whole different in object, character, and evidence, from those of Scripture on the whole, so that the one series or family ought never to be confounded with the other; yet that the former are not therefore at once to be rejected; that there was no Age of Miracles, after which miracles ceased; that there have been at all times true miracles and false miracles, true accounts and false accounts; that no authoritative guide is supplied to us for drawing the line between the two; that some of the miracles reported were true miracles; that we cannot be certain how many were not true; and that under these circumstances the decision in particular cases is left to each individual, according to his opportunities of judging. (*Mir.*, Essay Two: 'The Miracles of Early Ecclesiastical History,' 1843)

[T]he view here taken of the primitive miracles is applicable in defence of those of the medieval period also. If the occurrence of miraculous interpositions depends upon the presence of the Catholic Church, and if that Church is to remain on earth until the end of the world, it follows, of course, that what will be vouchsafed to Christians at all times, was vouchsafed to them in the middle ages inclusively. Whether this or that alleged miracle be in fact what it professes to be, must be determined, as in the instances already taken, by the particular case; but it stands to reason, that, where the views and representations drawn out in the foregoing pages are admitted, no prejudice will attend the medieval miracles at first hearing, though no distinct opinion can be formed about them before examination. (*Mir.*, Essay Two: 'The Miracles of Early Ecclesiastical History,' 1843)

Protestants are most inconsistent and one-sided, in *refusing to go into the evidence* for ecclesiastical miracles, which, on the first blush of the matter, are not stranger than those miracles of Scripture which they happily profess to admit. (*PPC*, Note 2)

Catholics believe that miracles happen in any age of the Church, though not for the same purposes, in the same number, or with the same evidence, as in Apostolic times. The Apostles wrought them in evidence of their divine mission; and with this object they have been sometimes wrought by Evangelists of countries since, as even Protestants allow ... As they are granted to Evangelists, so are they granted, though in less measure and evidence, to other holy men; and as holy men are not found equally at all times and in all places, therefore miracles are in some places and times more than in others. And since, generally, they are granted to faith and prayer, therefore in a country in which faith and prayer abound, they will be more likely to occur, than where and when faith and prayer are not; so that their occurrence is irregular. And further, as faith and prayer obtain miracles, so still more commonly do they gain from above the ordinary interventions of Providence; and, as it is often very difficult to distinguish between a providence and a miracle ... I frankly confess that the present advance of science tends to make it probable that various facts take place, and have taken place, in the order of nature, which hitherto have been considered by Catholics as simply supernatural. Though I readily make this admission, it must not be supposed in consequence that I am disposed to grant at once, that every event was natural in point of fact, which *might* have taken place by the laws of nature; for it is obvious, no Catholic can bind the Almighty to act only in one and the same way, or to the observance always of His own laws ... In a given case, then, the possibility of assigning a human cause for an event does not *ipso facto* prove that it is not miraculous ... Questions of fact cannot be disproved by analogies or presumptions; the inquiry must be made into the particular case in all its parts, as it comes before us. (*Apo.*, Note B: 'Ecclesiastical Miracles')

Unbelievers use the antecedent argument from the order of nature against our belief in miracles. Here, if they only mean that the fact of that system of laws, by which physical nature is governed, makes it antecedently improbable that an exception should occur in it, there is no objection to the argument; but if, as is not uncommon, they mean that the fact of an established order is absolutely fatal to the very notion of an exception, they are using a presumption as if it were a proof. They are saying, — What has happened 999 times one way cannot possibly happen on the 1000th time another way, because what has happened 999 times one way is likely to happen in the same way on the 1000th. But unlikely things do happen sometimes. If, however, they mean that the existing order of nature constitutes a physical necessity, and that a law is an unalterable fact, this is to assume the very point in debate, and is much more

than asserting its antecedent probability. Facts cannot be proved by presumptions, yet it is remarkable that in cases where nothing stronger than
presumption was even professed, scientific men have sometimes acted as
if they thought this kind of argument, taken by itself, decisive of a fact
which was in debate. (GA, Part II, ch. 9, sec. 3)

I take this paper-knife, I push the inkstand with it. Here is distinctly,
through the action of my free will an interference with the laws of nature.
If these laws were left to themselves, the knife would remain still and the
inkstand unmoved. Take a stronger case, I fire a gunpowder train. See
what a tremendous effect I produce in changing the ordinary course of
nature. Now, surely it is little to grant that if there *be* a God, He can do
what I can do; and yet, so far as we know, a miracle amounts to no more
than this ... I only contend that what man can do God can do. (*Ward* ii,
494-495; personal conversation recorded by the author, Wilfrid Ward, 31
January 1885)

Mortification and Self-Denial

Fasting is clearly a Christian duty, as our Saviour implies in His Sermon
on the Mount. Now what is fasting but a refraining from what is lawful;
not merely from what is sinful, but what is innocent?—from that bread
which we might lawfully take and eat with thanksgiving, but which at
certain times we do not take, in order to deny ourselves. Such is Christian
self-denial,—not merely a mortification of what is sinful, but an absti-
nence even from God's blessings. (*PS* vii, Sermon 7: 'The Duty of Self-
Denial,' 28 March 1830)

If we take the example of the Holy men of Scripture as our guide,
certainly bodily privation and chastisement are a very essential duty of
all who wish to serve God, and prepare themselves for His presence. First,
we have the example of Moses. His recorded Fasts were miraculous; still
they were Fasts, and the ordinance was recommended to the notice of all
believers afterwards, by the honour put upon it ... Fasting is connected
with moral acts, humiliation, prayer, meditation, which are equally binding on us as on the Jews. Man is now what he was then; and if affliction

of the flesh was good then, it is now … Elijah and Daniel, were without express command singularly austere and self-afflicting men … St. Peter was fasting, when he had the vision which sent him to Cornelius: Acts x. 10. The prophets and teachers at Antioch were fasting, when the Holy Ghost revealed to them His purpose about Saul and Barnabas: Acts iii. 2, 3. Vide also Acts xiv. 23. 2 Cor. vi. 5. xi. 27. (*TT* #21, 1834)

Surely the same feeling which would make men condemn an austere life now, if individuals attempted it, which makes them, when they read of such instances in the early Church, condemn it, would lead the same parties to condemn it in St. John [the Baptist], were they not bound by religious considerations. (*TT* #85, Sep. 1838)

Let us set it down then, as a first principle in religion, that all of us must come to Christ, in some sense or other, through things naturally unpleasant to us; it may be even through bodily suffering, such as the Apostles endured, or it may be nothing more than the subduing of our natural infirmities and the sacrifice of our natural wishes; it may be pain greater or pain less, on a public stage or a private one; but, till the words 'yoke' and 'cross' can stand for something pleasant, the bearing of our yoke and cross is something not pleasant; and though rest is promised as our reward, yet the way to rest must lie through discomfort and distress of heart … This is the especial object which is set before us, to become holy as He who has called us is holy, and to discipline and chasten ourselves in order that we may become so; and we may be quite sure, that unless we chasten ourselves, God will chasten us. If we judge ourselves, through His mercy we shall not be judged of Him; if we do not afflict ourselves in light things, He will afflict us in heavy things; if we do not set about changing ourselves by gentle measures, He will change us by severe remedies. (*PS* vii, Sermon 8: 'The Yoke of Christ,' 24 February 1839)

Mystery (Biblical, Theological)

It is indeed a remarkable circumstance, that the very revelation that brings us *practical and useful knowledge* about our souls, in the very *act of doing* so, nay (as it would seem), in *consequence of* doing so, brings us mysteries. We gain spiritual light at the price of intellectual perplexity; a blessed exchange doubtless, (for which is better, to be well and happy within ourselves, or to know what is going on at the world's end?) still at the price of perplexity ... It seems, then, that difficulties in revelation are especially given to prove *the reality of our faith* ... They are stumbling-blocks to proud and unhumbled minds, and were intended to be such. Faith is unassuming, modest, thankful, obedient. It receives with reverence and love whatever God gives, when convinced it is His gift. But when men do not feel rightly their need of His redeeming mercy, their lost condition and their inward sinfulness, when, in fact, they do not seek Christ in good earnest, in order to gain something, and do something, but as a matter of curiosity, or speculation, or form, *of course* these difficulties will become great objections in the way of their receiving His word simply. And I say these difficulties were intended to be such by Him who 'scattereth the proud in the imagination of their hearts.' ... [O]ur Lord's conduct through His ministry is a continued example of this. He spoke in parables, that they might see and hear, yet not understand, — a righteous detection of insincerity; whereas the same difficulties and obscurities, which offended irreligious men, would but lead the humble and meek to seek for more light, for information as far as it was to be obtained, and for resignation and contentedness, where it was not given. (*PS* i, Sermon 16: 'The Christian Mysteries,' 14 June 1829)

Every science has its difficulties at first; why then should the science of living well be without them? (*PS* i, Sermon 18: 'Obedience the Remedy for Religious Perplexity,' 14 November 1830)

What was hidden altogether before Christ came, could not be a mystery; it became a Mystery, then for the first time, by being disclosed at His coming. What had never been dreamed of by 'righteous men,' before Him, when revealed, as *being* unexpected, if for no other reason, would be strange and startling. And such unquestionably is the meaning of St. Paul, when he uses the word; for he applies it, not to what was passed and over, but to what was the then state of the doctrine revealed. Thus in the text,

1 Cor. xv. 51, 52, 'Behold I show you a Mystery; we shall not all sleep, but we shall all be changed, in a moment, in the twinkling of an eye, at the last trump.' ... In like manner when St. Paul speaks of the election of the Gentiles as a Mystery revealed, the facts of the case show that it was still a mystery, and therefore but revealed to be a mystery, not a secret explained. (*TT* #73, 1836)

St. Paul glories in the doctrine of Christ crucified, as being a *strange* doctrine and a *stumbling-block*. St. John states the doctrine of the Incarnation, in the first chapter of his Gospel, as a heavenly truth, which was too glorious for men, and believed in only by the few, and by which the Father, indeed, was manifested, but which *shone in darkness*. (*TT* #73, 1836)

Christ enunciates a solemn *Mystery* for Nicodemus to receive in *faith*; that Nicodemus so understands His words, and hesitates at it; that our Lord reproves him for hesitating, tells him that there are even higher Mysteries than that He had set forth, and proceeds to instance that of the Incarnation ... The latter part, particularly the conclusion, of the sixth chapter of the same Gospel, would afford another instance in point. (*TT* #73, 1836)

For though the death of Christ manifests God's *hatred of sin*, as well as His love for man, (inasmuch as it was sin that made His death necessary, and the greater the sacrifice the greater must have been the evil that caused it,) yet *how* His death expiated our sins, and what satisfaction it was to God's *justice*, are surely subjects quite above us ... it is an event ever *mysterious* on account of its necessity, ... But Rationalism would account for everything. (*TT* #73, 1836)

[T]he Church Catholic has ever taught (as in her Creeds) that there are facts revealed to us, not of this world, not of time, but of eternity, and that absolutely and independently; not merely embodied and indirectly conveyed in a certain historical course, not subordinate to the display of the Divine Character, not revealed merely relatively to us, but primary objects of our faith, and essential in themselves, whatever dependence or influence they may have upon other doctrines, or upon the course of the Dispensation. In a word, it has taught the existence of *Mysteries* in religion, for such emphatically must truths ever be which are external to this world, and existing in eternity. (*TT* #73, 1836)

First, one great perplexity is caused to a reflecting mind by not knowing whether a particular point is a mystery or not; or, in other words, whether it ought to attempt to answer objections urged against it, or to acknowledge at once and from the first that they are unanswerable. It is a great comfort to a man to know that he ought not to lose time on a point, or to fidget himself, but to say to himself or to others at once, 'It is unanswerable, it is beyond us, it is above reason, it is one of the things which we must take upon faith.' ... mysteriousness does not lie in any thing substantive, but in our mode of viewing what is substantive. We do not see how a certain relation is possible, viz., that one thing should ever be approaching another, and yet never meet it. We cannot frame to ourselves an idea imagining this relation; but at the same time each of the two conclusions, taken by itself, is perfectly intelligible. And in like manner as regards the supernatural doctrine of the Holy Trinity. That the Father is God, is in form an intelligible proposition; and so also, that the Word is God; and again, that the Holy Ghost is God. Again, it is sufficiently clear what we mean when we say that there is only one God: but take all four propositions together, and you have the Mystery. It lies in the impossibility of any human intelligence being able to perceive how propositions can be all true, which seem to it destructive of each other, that is, as self-destructive as the above mathematical dictum that a line is always approaching what it never reaches. Theologians cannot comprehend these relations more than we can; but they can give *names* to them. They cannot understand the distinction between God and the Word, or between Father and Son, more than the dullest clodhopper; but they can distinguish them from each other in scientific language. The name which they have given, — given under a supernatural guidance, — is just as unintelligible as the truth itself is incomprehensible. We gain nothing by it in the way of explanation, but it is a *recognition* on their part that there *is* a mystery — that is the first gain; next, it is a declaration *in what* point or points the mystery lies; and thirdly, it does for the mystery what the symbol *x* does for an unknown quantity, — it enables the mind to use it freely, to recognise it whenever it comes up again in the course of investigation, and to speak of it and discuss it with others. The term which we introduce as regards the doctrine of the Holy Trinity is the word *Person*. It expresses, it does not explain, the point of mystery. We know nothing more than before; but we have located the mystery, and may shut up the subject. (*Rambler*, May 1859; Correspondence; Questions and Answers)

Scripture is necessarily full of economies, when speaking of heavenly things, because there is no other way of introducing into our minds even a rude idea, even any idea at all, of matters so utterly out of our experience ... Thus we read, 'God is a consuming fire;' now fire is a material substance, and cannot literally belong to the Divine Nature; but it is the only, or at least the truest, mode in which His nature, in a certain relation to us, can be brought home to us, and we must accept it and believe it as a substantial truth, in spite of its not being the whole truth or the exact impress of the truth ... mystery is the necessary note of divine revelation, that is, mystery subjectively to the human mind ... Scripture is full of mysteries, but they are mysteries of *fact*, not of words. Its dark sayings or aenigmata are such, because in the nature of things they cannot be expressed clearly. (*Ath.* ii, 'Economical Language')

What in fact do we know of pure spirit? What do we know of the infinite? Of the latter just a little, by means of mathematical science, that is, under the conditions of number, quantity, space, distance, direction, and shape; just enough to tell us how little we know, and how little we are able to draw arguments and inferences when infinites are in question. Mathematical science tells us that one and one infinite do not, put together, make two; that there may be innumerable infinites, and that all put together are not greater than one of them; that there are orders of infinites. It is plain we are utterly unable to determine what is possible and what is impossible in this high region of realities ... Nor in its doctrine of infinites only, does mathematical science illustrate the mysteries of Theology. Geometry, for instance, may be used to a certain point as an exponent of algebraical truth; but it would be irrational to deny the wider revelations of algebra, because they do not admit of a geometrical expression. The fourth power of a quantity may be received as a fact, though a fourth dimension in space is inconceivable. Again, a polygon or an ellipse is a figure different in kind from a circle; yet we may tend towards a conception of the latter by using what we know of either of the former. Thus it is by economical expedients that we teach and transmit the mysteries of religion, separating them into parts, viewing them in aspects, adumbrating them by analogies, and so approximating to them by means of words which say too much or too little. And if we consent to such ways of thought in our scientific treatment of 'earthly things,' is it wonderful that we should be forced to them in our investigation of 'heavenly'? (*Ath*. ii, 'The Holy Trinity in Unity')

Ordination; Holy Orders

For if ordination is a divine ordinance, it must be necessary; and if it is not a divine ordinance, how dare we use it? (*TT* #1, 1833)

Original Sin; The Fall of Man

This is one kind of knowledge, and most miserable doubtless, which we have gained by the fall, to know sin by experience; — not to gaze at it with awe as the Angels do, or as children when they wonder how there can be wicked men in the world, but to admit it into our hearts. Alas! ever since the fall this has been more or less the state of the natural man, to live in sin; and though here and there, under the secret stirrings of God's grace, he has sought after God and obeyed Him, it has been in a grovelling sort, like worms working their way upwards through the dust of the earth, turning evil against itself, and unlearning it from having known it. (*PS* v, Sermon 8: 'The State of Innocence,' 11 February 1838)

Now of the sins which stain us, though without such a consent of the will as to forfeit grace, I must mention first original sin. How it is that we are born under a curse which we did not bring upon us, we do not know; it is a mystery; but when we become Christians, that curse is removed. We are no longer under God's wrath; our guilt is forgiven us, but still the infection of it remains. I mean, we still have an evil principle within us, dishonouring our best services. How far, by God's grace, we are able in time to chastise, restrain, and destroy this infection, is another question; but still it is not removed at once by Baptism, and if not, surely it is a most grievous humiliation to those who are striving to 'walk worthy of the Lord unto all pleasing.' [Col. i. 10.] It is involuntary, and therefore does not cast us out of grace; yet in itself it is very miserable and very humbling: and every one will discover it in himself, if he watches himself narrowly. I mean, what is called the old Adam, pride, profaneness, deceit, unbelief, selfishness, greediness, the inheritance of the Tree of the knowledge of good and evil; (*PS* v, Sermon 15: 'Sins of Infirmity,' 1 April 1838)

What then human nature *tends* to, is very plain, and according to the end, so I say must be the beginning. If the end is evil, so is the beginning; if the termination is astray, the first direction is wrong. 'Out of the abundance of the heart the mouth speaketh,' and the hand worketh; and such as is the work and the word, such is the heart. Nothing then can be more certain, if we go by Scripture, not to speak of experience, than that the present nature of man is evil, and not good; that evil things come from it, and not good things. If good things come from it, they are the exception, and therefore not of it, but in it merely; first given to it, and then coming from it; not of it by nature, but in it by grace. (*PS* v, Sermon 10: 'Righteousness not of us, but in us,' 19 January 1840)

[T]he recognition of Original Sin, considered as the consequence of Adam's fall, was, both as regards general acceptance and accurate understanding, a gradual process, not completed till the time of Augustine and Pelagius ... we have here an instance of a doctrine held back for a time by circumstances, yet in the event forcing its way into its normal shape, and at length authoritatively fixed in it, that is, of a doctrine held implicitly, then asserting itself, and at length fully developed. (*Dev.*, Part I: ch. 4, sec. 1)

[W]hen man cast off God, his passions and affections rebelled against his reason, and his body against his soul. (*SN*, 'State of Original Sin,' 3 March 1861)

And so I argue about the world;—*if* there be a God, *since* there is a God, the human race is implicated in some terrible aboriginal calamity. It is out of joint with the purposes of its Creator. This is a fact, a fact as true as the fact of its existence; and thus the doctrine of what is theologically called original sin becomes to me almost as certain as that the world exists, and as the existence of God. (*Apo.*, ch. 5)

Our doctrine of original sin is not the same as the Protestant doctrine. 'Original sin,' with us, cannot be called sin, in the mere ordinary sense of the word 'sin;' it is a term denoting Adam's sin as transferred to us, or the state to which Adam's sin reduces his children; but by Protestants it seems to be understood as sin, in much the same sense as actual sin. We, with the Fathers, think of it as something negative, Protestants as something positive. Protestants hold that it is a disease, a radical change of nature, an active poison internally corrupting the soul, infecting its primary elements, and disorganising it; ... by original sin we mean, as I have already said, something negative, viz., this only, the *deprivation* of that supernatural unmerited grace which Adam and Eve had on their first formation,—deprivation and the consequences of deprivation. (*Dif.* ii, Letter to Pusey, ch. 3, 1865)

Since the fall of Adam all mankind, his descendants, are conceived and born in sin. 'Behold,' says the inspired writer in the Psalm *Miserere*—'Behold, I was conceived in iniquity, and in sin did my mother conceive me.' That sin which belongs to every one of us, and is ours from the first moment of our existence, is the sin of unbelief and disobedience, by which Adam lost Paradise. We, as the children of Adam, are heirs to the consequences of his sin, and have forfeited in him that spiritual robe of grace and holiness which he had given him by his Creator at the time that he was made. In this state of forfeiture and disinheritance we are all of us conceived and born; and the ordinary way by which we are taken out of it is the Sacrament of Baptism. (MD, 'Meditations on the Litany of Loretto, for the Month of May: I. On the Immaculate Conception,' for May 3)

Orthodoxy

He who makes orthodoxy consist in any thing but truth in *faith* and *morals*, or thinks that there is exclusive truth, necessary for us, except in faith and morals, goes far towards being a heretic himself—and I have no confidence *whatever* in such theorists. (POL; Letter to Miss Mary Holmes, 7 April 1850)

Papal Infallibility

In June and July 1839, near four years ago, I read the Monophysite Controversy, and it made a deep impression on me, which I was not able to shake off, that the Pope had a certain gift of infallibility, and that communion with the See of Rome was the divinely intended means of grace and illumination. I do not know how far I fully recognised this at the moment; but towards the end of the same Long Vacation I considered attentively the Donatist history, and became quite excited. It broke upon me that we were in a state of schism. Since that, all history, particularly that of Arianism, has appeared to me in a new light; confirmatory of the same doctrine. (*Keb.*, 219; Letter to John Keble, 4 May 1843)

[T]he one essential question is whether the recognised organ of teaching, the Church herself, acting through Pope or Council as the oracle of heaven, has ever contradicted her own enunciations. If so, the hypothesis which I am advocating is at once shattered; but, till I have positive and distinct evidence of the fact, I am slow to give credence to the existence of so great an improbability. (*Dev.*, Part I: ch. 3, sec. 2)

As to what Catholics say to the charge of 'Pope against Pope, and Council against Council' it is (I suppose) this—that in a very large system you necessarily must have great apparent anomalies—*as in Scripture* (a parallel which might be effectively worked out) and that *you must begin by expecting* this, and making allowance for it — that some things perhaps must ever be difficulties, (as there are insolvable difficulties in Scripture.) but that on the whole, and in proportion as persons come *nearer* to the system, there is a *growing evidence* of consistency. (*LD* xi, 69; Letter to Mrs. Elizabeth Anstice, 18 December 1845)

[A]nd in like manner His Church also after Him, though full of divine gifts, the Immaculate Spouse, the Oracle of Truth, the Voice of the Holy Ghost, infallible in matters of faith and morals, whether in the chair of her Supreme Pontiff, or in the unity of her Episcopate. (*SVO*, Sermon 12: 'The Mission of St. Philip Neri, Part 1,' 15 January 1850)

Here, too, is vividly brought out before you what we mean by Papal infallibility, or rather what we do not mean by it: you see how the Pope was open to any mistake, as others may be, in his own person, true as it is, that whenever he spoke *ex cathedrâ* on subjects of revealed truth, he spoke as its divinely-ordained expounder ... Popes, then, though they are infallible in their office, as Prophets and Vicars of the Most High, and though they have generally been men of holy life, and many of them actually saints, have the trials, and incur the risks of other men. Our doctrine of infallibility means something very different from what Protestants think it means. (*PPC*, Lecture 8)

'[T]he king can do no wrong' has *a* sense in constitutional law, though not the sense which the words would suggest to a foreigner who heard them for the first time; and 'the Pope is infallible' has its own sense in theology, but not that which the words suggest to a Protestant, who takes the words in their ordinary meaning. And, as it is the way with Protestants to maintain that the Pope's infallibility is intended by us as a guarantee of his private and personal exemption from theological error, nay, even from moral fault of every kind; so a foreigner, who knew nothing of England, were he equally impatient, prejudiced, and indocile, might at first hearing confound the maxim, 'the king can do no wrong,' with the dogma of some Oriental despotism or theocracy. (*PPC*, Note 1)

But why should the Pope, acting, not as a theologian, but, as I may say, as a politician, trouble us? ... Father Perrone, when defending the Pope's infallibility ... speaks of Pope Honorius as committing himself to 'an ill advised and imprudent' measure; as 'over credulous;' as 'condemned by the 6th Ecumenical Council' on account of his 'imprudent' command, and 'ill advised dissimulation' etc etc. Indeed, where should we be, if we thought it a duty to defend all the acts of all the Popes? (*LD* xxxii, 260-261; Letter to Lady Georgiana Fullerton, 21 October 1864)

It is to the Pope in Ecumenical Council that we look, as to the normal seat of Infallibility. (*Apo.*, ch. 5)

[B]y reason of the very power of the Popes they have commonly been slow and moderate in their use of it. (*Apo.*, ch. 5)

As to the Infallibility of the Pope, I see nothing against it, or to dread in it,—for I am confident that it *must* be so limited practically that it will leave things as they are. (*Ward* ii, 101; Letter to Edward B. Pusey, 17 November 1865)

As to writing a volume on the Pope's infallibility, it never so much as entered into my thoughts ... And I should have nothing to say about it. I have ever thought it likely to be true, never thought it certain. I think too, its definition inexpedient and unlikely; but I should have no difficulty accepting it, were it made. And I don't think my reason will ever go forward or backward in the matter. (*POL*; Letter to William G. Ward, 18 February 1866)

And so, as to the Church's teaching about the Holy See, before the Council of Florence, about which you ask (supposing the following point was not already defined, which I do not know) it might be pious to believe, and a defect in piety (in educated men) not to believe that the Pope was '*totius Ecclesiae Doctor,*' because it was clear the Church held it, and probable that she might and would define it; and it is this spirit of piety which holds together the whole Church. We embrace and believe what we find universally received, till a question arises about any particular point. Thus, as to our Lord's perfect knowledge in His Human Nature, we might always have admitted it without a question through *piety* to the general voice—then, when the controversy arose, we might ask ourselves if it *had* been defined, examine the question for ourselves and end the examination by (wrongly but allowably) doubting of it; but then *when* the definition was published in its favour, we should submit our minds to the obedience of faith … Applying this principle to the Pope's Infallibility, (N.B. this of course is mine own opinion only, *meo periculo*) a man will find it a religious duty to *believe* it *or* may safely *disbelieve* it, in *proportion* as he thinks it probable or improbable that the Church might or will define it, or does hold it, and that it is the doctrine of the Apostles. For myself, (still to illustrate what I mean, not as arguing) I think that the Church *may* define it (i.e. it possibly may turn out to belong to the original *depositum*), but that she will not ever define it; and again I do not see that she can be said to hold it. She never can simply *act* upon it, (being undefined, as it is) and I believe never has;—moreover, on the other hand, I think there is a good deal of evidence, on the very surface of history and the Fathers in its favour. On the whole then I hold it; but I should account it no sin if, on the grounds of reason, I doubted it. (*Ward* ii, 220-221; Letter to Edward B. Pusey, 23 March 1867)

There is a great attempt by W. G. Ward, Dr. Murray of Maynooth, and Father Schrader, the Jesuit of Rome and Vienna, to bring in a new theory of Papal Infallibility, which would make it a mortal sin, to be visited by damnation, not to hold the Temporal Power necessary to the Papacy. No one answers them and multitudes are being carried away,—the Pope, I should fear, gives ear to them, and the consequence is there is a very extreme prejudice in the highest quarters at Rome against such as me. (*Ward* ii, 152-153; Letter to James Robert Hope-Scott, 11 April 1867)

For myself, I have never taken any great interest in the question of the limits and seat of infallibility. I was converted simply because the Church was to last to the end, and that no communion answered to the Church of the first ages but the Roman Communion, both in substantial likeness and in actual descent. And as to faith, my great principle was: *'securus judicat orbis terrarum.'* So I say now—and in all these questions of detail I say to myself, I believe whatever the Church teaches as the voice of God—and this or that particular inclusively, if she teaches this—it is this *fides implicita* which is our comfort in these irritating times. And I cannot go beyond this—I see arguments here, arguments there—I incline one way today another tomorrow—on the whole I more than incline in one direction—but I do not dogmatise—and I detest any dogmatism where the Church has not clearly spoken ... I have only an opinion at best (not faith) that the Pope *is* infallible ... if it be true after all and divine, my faith in it is included in the *implicita fides* which I have in the Church. (*Ward* ii, 234-235; Letter to Henry Wilberforce, 21 July 1867)

I say with Cardinal Bellarmine whether the Pope be infallible or not in any pronouncement, anyhow he is to be obeyed. No good can come from disobedience. His facts and his warnings may be all wrong; his deliberations may have been biassed. He may have been misled. Imperiousness and craft, tyranny and cruelty, may be patent in the conduct of his advisers and instruments. But when he speaks formally and authoritatively he speaks as our Lord would have him speak, and all those imperfections and sins of individuals are overruled for that result which our Lord intends (just as the action of the wicked and of enemies to the Church are overruled) and therefore the Pope's word stands, and a blessing goes with obedience to it, and no blessing with disobedience. (*Ward* ii, 193; Letter to Lady Simeon, 10 November 1867)

I certainly did not know how strong a case could be made out against Pope Honorius. But with all its power, I do not find that it seriously interferes with my own view of Papal Infallibility ... I hold the Pope's Infallibility, not as a dogma, but as a theological opinion; that is, not as a certainty, but as a probability ... To my mind the balance of probabilities is still in favour of it. There are vast difficulties, taking facts as they are, in the way of denying it ... Anyhow the doctrine of Papal Infallibility must be fenced round and limited by *conditions*. (*Ward* ii, 236; Letter to Peter le Page Renouf, 21 June 1868)

The Pope's infallibility implies nothing of the kind [i.e., inspiration]. His state of mind is not unlike that of other men. He has no inward gift—but an external assistance or providence such, that, if he is going wrong, he is stopped—and his ultimate decision (*ex cathedrâ*, and *in revus fidei et morum* ['in matters of faith and morals']) is overruled so as not to swerve from, to be consistent with, to be the oracle of, the *Verbum Dei* ['Word of God'] ... thus Liberius, thus Honorius, (as those say who hold the Pope's Infallibility,) were *all but* authoritatively declaring false doctrine, but were balked, stopped, silenced, whether they would or no, before they had committed themselves ... And so a Pope's declaration may be political, brought about by the persuasion of a party or clique, or of some foreign sovereign, but still he cannot go beyond the will and irresistible power of Him whose Vicar he is. (*LD* xxxii, 292-293; Letter to an Unknown Correspondent, 12 February 1869)

When we are all at rest, and have no doubts, and at least practically, not to say doctrinally, hold the Holy Father to be infallible, suddenly there is thunder in the clear sky, ... As to myself personally, please God, I do not expect any trial at all; but I cannot help suffering with the various souls which are suffering, and I look with anxiety at the prospect of having to defend decisions, which may not be difficult to my private judgment ... If it is God's will that the Pope's infallibility should be defined, then it is His blessed will to throw back 'the times and the moments' of that triumph which He has destined for His Kingdom; and I shall feel I have but to bow my head to His adorable, inscrutable Providence. (*LD* xxv, 18-19; Letter to Bishop William B. Ullathorne, 28 January 1870; also in *POL*, 180-181)

If it be God's will that some definition in favour of the Pope's infallibility is passed, I then should at once submit—but up to that very moment I shall pray most heartily and earnestly against it. Any how, I cannot bear to think of the tyrannousness and cruelty of its advocates. (*Ward* ii, 289; Letter to Bishop David Moriarty of Kerry, 20 March 1870)

One can but go by one's best light. Whoever is infallible, I am not; but I am bound to argue out the matter and to act as if I were, till the Council decides; and then, if God's Infallibility is against me, to submit at once, still not repenting of having taken the part which I felt to be right, any more than a lawyer in Court may repent of believing in a cause and advocating a point of law, which the Bench of Judges ultimately give against him. We can but do our best. (*Ward* ii, 295; Letter to Robert Whitty, S.J., 12 April 1870)

My rule is to act according to my best light as if I was infallible before the Church decides; but to accept and submit to God's Infallibility, when the Church has spoken. The Church has not yet spoken. (*POL*; Letter to Reginald Buckler, O.P., 15 April 1870)

Anxious as I am, I will not believe that the Pope's Infallibility can be defined at the Council till I see it actually done. Seeing is believing. We are in God's Hands — not in the hands of men, however high-exalted. Man proposes, God disposes. When it is actually done, I will accept it as His act; but, till then, I will believe it impossible. One can but act according to one's best light. Certainly, we at least have no claim to call ourselves infallible; still it is our duty to act as if we were, to act as strongly and vigorously in the matter, as if it were impossible we could be wrong, to be full of hope and of peace, and to leave the event to God. This is right, isn't it? (*Ward* ii, 293; Letter to Ambrose Phillipps de Lisle, April or May [?] 1870)

I saw the new Definition yesterday, and am pleased at its moderation — that is, if the doctrine in question is to be defined at all. The terms are vague and comprehensive; and, personally, I have no difficulty in admitting it. The question is, does it come to me with the authority of an Ecumenical Council? Now the *primâ facie* argument is in favour of its having that authority. The Council was legitimately called; it was more largely attended than any Council before it; and innumerable prayers from the whole of Christendom, have preceded and attended it, and merited a happy issue of its proceedings ... if the definition is consistently received by the whole body of the faithful, as valid, or as the expression of a truth, then too it will claim our assent by the force of the great dictum, 'Securus judicat orbis terrarum.' This indeed is a broad principle by which all acts of the rulers of the Church are ratified. But for it, we might reasonably question some of the past Councils or their acts. (*Dif.* ii, Letter to the Duke of Norfolk, ch. 8, 1875; Letter to Ambrose Phillipps de Lisle, 24 July 1870)

[T]here are other means by which I can be brought under the obligation of receiving a doctrine as a dogma. If I am clear that there is a primitive and uninterrupted tradition, as of the divinity of our Lord; or where a high probability drawn from Scripture or Tradition is partially or probably confirmed by the Church. Thus a particular Catholic might be so nearly sure that the promise to Peter in Scripture proves that the infallibility of Peter is a necessary dogma, as only to be kept from holding it as such by the absence of any judgment on the part of the Church, so that the present unanimity of the Pope and 500 Bishops, even though not sufficient to constitute a formal Synodal act, would at once put him in the position, and lay him under the obligation, of receiving the doctrine as a dogma, that is, to receive it with its anathema. Or again, if nothing definitely sufficient from Scripture or Tradition can be brought to contradict a definition, the fact of a legitimate Superior having defined it, may be an obligation in conscience to receive it with an internal assent. For myself, ever since I was a Catholic, I have held the Pope's infallibility as a matter of theological opinion; at least, I see nothing in the Definition which necessarily contradicts Scripture, Tradition, or History; and the 'Doctor Ecclesiæ' (as the Pope is styled by the Council of Florence) bids me accept it. In this case, I do not receive it on the word of the Council, but on the Pope's self-assertion. And I confess, the fact that all along for so many centuries the Head of the Church and Teacher of the faithful and Vicar of Christ has been allowed by God to assert virtually his own infallibility, is a great argument in favour of the validity of his claim. Another ground for receiving the dogma, still not upon the direct authority of the Council, or with acceptance of the validity of its act *per se*, is the consideration that our Merciful Lord would not care so little for His elect people, the multitude of the faithful, as to allow their visible Head, and such a large number of Bishops to lead them into error, and an error so serious, if an error it be. This consideration leads me to accept the doctrine as a dogma, indirectly indeed from the Council, but not so much from a Council, as from the Pope and a very large number of Bishops. The question is not whether they had a right to impose, or even were right in imposing the dogma on the faithful; but whether, having done so, I have not an obligation to accept it, according to the maxim, 'Fieri non debuit, factum valet.' (*Dif*. ii, Letter to the Duke of Norfolk, ch. 8, 1875; Letter of 27 July 1870)

I agree with you that the wording of the Dogma has nothing very difficult in it. It expresses what, as an opinion, I have ever held myself with a host of other Catholics ... the greater part of the Church has long thought that the Pope has the power which he and the Bishops of the majority have declared *is* his; and that, if the Church is the work and ordinance of God, we must have a little faith in Him and be assured that He will provide that there is no abuse of the Pope's power. Your friend must not *assume*, before the event, that his power will be abused. (*Ward* ii, 310-311; Letter to O'Neill Daunt, 7 August 1870)

It is too soon to give an opinion about the definition. I want to know what the Bishops of the minority say on the subject, and what they mean to do. As I have ever believed as much as the definition says, I have a difficulty in putting myself into the position of mind of those who have not. As far as I see, no one is bound to believe it at this moment, certainly not till the end of the Council. This I hold in spite of Dr. Manning. At the same time, since the Pope has pronounced the definition, I think it safer to accept it at once. I very much doubt if at this moment—before the end of the Council, I could get myself publicly to say it was *de fide*, whatever came of it—though I believe the doctrine itself ... The Pope is infallible *in actu*, not *in habitu*—in his particular pronouncements *ex cathedrâ*, not in his state of illumination, as an Apostle might be, which would be inspiration. (*Ward* ii, 308-309; Letter to Mrs. William Froude, 8 August 1870)

For myself, I have at various times in print professed to hold the Pope's Infallibility; your difficulty is not mine—but still I deeply lament the violence which has been used in this matter. However, there is a deeper question behind. When you became a Catholic, you ought to have understood that the voice of the Church is the voice of God. The Church defines nothing that was not given to the Apostles in the beginning, but that sacred deposit cannot be fully brought forward and dispensed except in the course of ages. It is not any argument against the Pope's Infallibility, that it was not defined as a truth till the 19th century. Don't set yourself against the doctrine. Very little was passed, much less than its advocates wished — they are disappointed. Nothing is defined as to *what acts* are *ex cathedrâ*, nor to what things infallibility extends. Some people think the decree lessens the Pope's *actual* power. (*LD* xxv, 216; Letter to Mrs. Margaret A. Wilson, 20 October 1870; also in *POL*; 185-186)

The Church is the Mother of high and low, of the rulers as well as of the ruled. *Securus judicat orbis terrarum.* If she declares by her various voices that the Pope is infallible in certain matters, in those matters infallible he is. What Bishops and people say all over the earth, that is the truth, whatever complaint we may have against certain ecclesiastical proceedings. Let us not oppose ourselves to the universal voice. (*Ward* ii, 376; Letter to Père Hyacinthe, 24 November 1870)

[C]ertainly the Pope is not infallible beyond the Deposit of Faith originally given — though there is a party of Catholics who, I suppose to frighten away converts, wish to make out that he is giving forth infallible utterances every day … John the XXII. is nothing to the purpose. He put nothing forward in any formal way, and, I think, repented of his private sentiments before his death. Of course, if he had been called upon to speak *ex cathedrâ*, he would (humanly speaking) have defined an error, but he did not. And this will just illustrate what is meant by the gift of infallibility. As Balaam wished to curse, but opened his mouth with blessings, so a Pope may all his life be in error, but if he attempts to put it forth, he will be cut off, or be deterred, or find himself saying what he did not mean to say. I have no hesitation in saying that, to all appearance, Pius IX. wished to say a great deal more (that is that the Council should say a great deal more) than it did, but a greater Power hindered it. A Pope is not inspired; he has not an inherent gift of divine knowledge. When he speaks *ex cathedrâ*, he may say little or much, but he is simply protected from saying what is untrue … As to St. Cyprian's quarrel with the Pope, strong letters came from the Pope to him. He certainly did not think the Pope infallible in those letters. I cannot tell without hunting them up, whether they look like *ex cathedrâ* letters. I should think not. I doubt very much whether the point of the Infallibility of the Pope was clearly understood, as a dogma, by the Popes themselves at that time; but then I also doubt whether the Infallibility of a General Council was at that time understood either, for no General Council as yet had been. The subject was what Vincentius calls 'obscurely held.' The Popes acted as if they were infallible in doctrine—with a very high hand, peremptorily, magisterially, fiercely. But, when we come to the question of the *analysis* of such conduct, I think they had as vague ideas on the subject as many of the early Fathers had upon portions of the doctrine of the Holy Trinity. *They acted in a way which needed infallibility as its explanation.* (Ward ii, 376, 378-379; Letter to Mrs. William Froude, March 1871)

As to the definition, I grieve you should have been tried with it. The dogma has been *acted on* by the Holy See for centuries—the only difference is that now it is actually *recognised*. I know this is a difference—for at first sight it would seem to invite the Pope to use his now recognised power. But we must have a little faith. Abstract propositions avail little—theology surrounds them with a variety of limitations, explanations, etc. No truth stands by itself—each is kept in order and harmonized by other truths. The dogmas relative to the Holy Trinity and the Incarnation were not struck off all at once—but piecemeal—one Council did one thing, another a second—and so the whole dogma was built up. And the first portion of it looked extreme—and controversies rose upon it—and these controversies led to the second, and third Councils, and they did not *reverse* the first, but *explained* and *completed* what was first done. So will it be now. Future Popes will explain and in one sense limit their own power. This would be unlikely, if they merely acted as men, but God will overrule them. Pius has been overruled—I believe he wished a much more stringent dogma than he has got. Let us have faith and patience. (*Ward* ii, 379; Letter to Miss Mary Holmes, 15 May 1871)

As little as possible was passed at the Council—nothing about the Pope which I have not myself always held. But it is impossible to deny that it was done with an imperiousness and overbearing wilfulness, which has been a great scandal. (*Ward* ii, 380; Letter to Mrs. William Froude, c. Oct. 1871)

Divine Providence has allowed the act of last year for some good purpose, and we must submit to His will. For myself, I see the doctrine implied in the conduct of the Roman See, nay of the Catholic Church, from the first, but I am not of course blind to the difficulties in detail which it has to encounter. The dogma seems to me as mildly framed as it could be—or nearly so. That the Pope was infallible in General Council, or when speaking with the Church, all admitted, even Gallicans. They admitted, I think I may say, that his word *ex cathedrâ* was infallible, if the Bishops did no more than keep silence. All that is passed last year, that in some sense he may speak per se, and his speech may be infallible ... All these questions are questions for the theological school—and theologians will, as time goes on, settle the force of the wording of the dogma, just as the courts of law solve the meaning and bearing of the Acts of Parliament. I don't think it should interfere, whatever perplexity it may cause, with the great fact that the Catholic Church (so called) is the Church of the Apostles, the one fold of Christ. (*Ward* ii, 556 [Appendix to Ch. 31]; Letter to Sir William Henry Cope, 10 December 1871)

[A]s regards the force, limits, and consequents of the recent definitions, we have as yet nothing better to guide us, from the necessity of the case, than the Dublin Review and the Civilta Cattolica. We have yet to learn what is precisely meant by 'inspiration,' as applied to a book, and in what cases and under what conditions the Pope is infallible. Not to say that the Council is not yet finished. (*POL*; Letter to Lord Howard of Glossop, 27 April 1872)

I cannot allow such language as Mr. Capes uses of me in yesterday's Guardian to pass unnoticed, nor can I doubt that you will admit my answer to it. I thank him for having put into print what doubtless has often been said behind my back; I do not thank him for the odious words, which he has made the vehicle of it. I will not dirty my ink by repeating them; but the substance, mildly stated, is this: — that I have all along considered the doctrine of the Pope's Infallibility to be contradicted by the facts of Church History, and that though convinced of this, I have in consequence of the Vatican Council forced myself to do a thing that I never fancied would befall me when I became a Catholic: — viz.: forced myself by some unintelligible quibble to fancy myself believing what really after all in my heart I could not and did not believe, and that this operation and its result had given me a considerable amount of pain. I could say much, and quote much from what I have written in comment upon this nasty view of me. But, not to take up too much of your room, I will, in order to pluck it up 'by the very roots' (to use his own expression) quote one out of various passages, in which, long before the Vatican Council was dreamed of, at least by me, I enunciated absolutely the doctrine of the Pope's Infallibility. It is in my 'Discourses on University Education,' delivered in Dublin in 1852. It runs as follows: —

'Deeply do I feel, ever will I protest, for I can appeal to the ample testimony of history to bear me out, that in questions of right and wrong, there is nothing really strong in the whole world, nothing decisive and operative, but the voice of Him, to whom have been committed the Keys of the Kingdom, and the oversight of Christ's flock. That voice is now, as ever it has been, a real authority, infallible when it teaches, prosperous when it commands, ever taking the lead wisely and distinctly in its own province, adding certainty to what is probable, and persuasion to what is certain. Before it speaks, the most saintly may mistake; and after it has spoken, the most gifted must obey ... If there ever was a power on earth who had an eye for the times, who has confined himself to the practicable, and has been happy in his anticipations, whose words have been deeds, and whose commands prophecies, such is he in the history of ages, who sits on from generation to generation in the chair of the Apostles, as the Vicar of Christ, and Doctor of the Church. Has he failed in his successes up to this hour? Did he, in our Fathers' day, fail in his struggle with Joseph of Germany, and his confederates; with Napoleon — a greater name — and his dependent Kings, that though in another kind of fight he should fail in ours? What grey hairs are on the head of Judah, whose youth is renewed like the eagle's, whose feet are like the feet of harts, and underneath the everlasting arms?' pp. 27-28.

I could quote to the same purpose passages from my 'Essay on Development' 1845: 'Loss and Gain' 1847: 'Discourses to mixed Congregations' 1849: 'Position of Catholics' 1851: 'Church of the Fathers' 1857. I underwent then, no change of mind as regards the truth of the doctrine of the Pope's infallibility in consequence of the Council. It is true I was deeply, though not personally, pained both by the fact, and by the circumstances of the definition; and when it was in contemplation, I wrote a most confidential letter, which was surreptitiously gained and published, but of which I have not a word to retract. The feelings of surprise and concern expressed in that letter have nothing to do with a screwing one's conscience to profess what one does not believe, which is Mr. Capes' pleasant account of me. He ought to know better. (*Ward* ii, 558-559; Letter to the *Guardian*, 12 September 1872, in reply to John Moore Capes)

[T]he Apostles were inspired — the Pope is not. What he 'defines' or explains in Catholic doctrine is gained by him by human means such as the advice of theologians, etc., — but in the last step, a Divine Hand is over him, keeping him *in tether*, so that he cannot go beyond the truth of revelation. He has no habit on what is called 'donum infusum' of infallibility, but when he speaks *ex cathedrâ* he is restrained *pro re nata, pro hac vice* ... the recent definition says that the Pope has that infallibility which the Church has — but as Perrone says above 'Never have Catholics taught that the gift is an inspiration.' (*Ward* ii, 558 [Appendix to Ch. 31]; Letter to Arthur Arnold, 22 September 1872)

I would say that you are quite right in saying that 'the Church cannot delegate her magisterium to another,' and therefore cannot make the Pope infallible. The Council has done nothing of the kind — no Council does more than *declare* the Apostolic truth. The early Councils declared that it was true that Almighty God was a Trinity in Unity — they did not *make* the Trinity in Unity — and the Vatican Council does not *make* the Pope infallible but declares that, when he teaches the revealed doctrine, God from the beginning has made him infallible ... It has been his pleasure to protect his own revelation, by committing the true teaching of it to the Church and to the Pope. They are infallible when they teach, because God made them so — they are not infallible except when they teach because God has not given them that gift at other times. (*LD* xxxii, 348; Letter to Henry Stacke, 9 February 1875)

The wisdom of God, which has its own times and seasons for every thing, has determined that the Pope's infallibility in teaching should be defined in the 19th century ... The Pope speaks to the world as Supreme Pastor, *when* he speaks *ex cathedrâ;* the Vatican Council has set down explicitly the conditions of an *ex cathedrâ* enunciation. 'A Bull, or Encyclical, or Allocution,' are not 'solemn enough.' He must speak under the various conditions necessary for an *ex cathedrâ* utterance. The Pope is not infallible in his excommunications. (*LD* xxxii, 349; Letter to Henry Stacke, 12 February 1875)

I have ever felt from experience that no one would believe me in earnest if I spoke calmly, when again and again I denied the repeated report that I was on the point of coming back to the Church of England. I have uniformly found that, if I simply denied it, this only made the newspapers repeat the report more confidently — but, if I said something sharp, they abused me for scurrility against the Church I had left, but they believed me ... Within the last few years I have been obliged to adopt a similar course towards those who said I could not receive the Vatican Decrees. I sent a sharp letter to the Guardian and of course the Guardian called me names, but it believed me — and did not allow the offence of its correspondent to be repeated. (*POL;* Letter to Sir William Henry Cope, 13 February 1875)

For myself, I did not call it inopportune, for times and seasons are known to God alone, and persecution may be as opportune, though not so pleasant as peace; nor, in accepting as a dogma what I had ever held as a truth, could I be doing violence to any theological view or conclusion of my own; nor has the acceptance of it any logical or practical effect whatever, as I consider, in weakening my allegiance to Queen Victoria. (*Dif.* ii, Letter to the Duke of Norfolk, ch. 1, 1875)

Only a few weeks ago it was stated categorically by some anonymous correspondent of a Liverpool paper, with reference to the prospect of my undertaking the task on which I am now employed, that it was, 'in fact understood that at one time Dr. Newman was on the point of uniting with Dr. Dollinger and his party, and that it required the earnest persuasion of several members of the Roman Catholic Episcopate to prevent him from taking that step,'—an unmitigated and most ridiculous untruth in every word of it, nor would it be worth while to notice it here, except for its connexion with the subject on which I am entering. But the explanation of such reports about me is easy. They arise from forgetfulness on the part of those who spread them, that there are two sides of ecclesiastical acts, that right ends are often prosecuted by very unworthy means, and that in consequence those who, like myself, oppose a line of action, are not necessarily opposed to the issue for which it has been adopted ... What I felt deeply, and ever shall feel, while life lasts, is the violence and cruelty of journals and other publications, which, taking as they professed to do the Catholic side, employed themselves by their rash language (though, of course, they did not mean it so), in unsettling the weak in faith, throwing back inquirers, and shocking the Protestant mind ... So much as to my posture of mind before the Definition. (*Dif.* ii, Letter to the Duke of Norfolk, ch. 8, 1875)

This letter [of 27 July 1870, above], written before the minority had melted away, insists on this principle, that a Council's definition would have a virtual claim on our reception, even though it were not passed *conciliariter*, but in some indirect way; the great object of a Council being in some way or other to declare the judgment of the Church. I think the Third Ecumenical will furnish an instance of what I mean. There the question in dispute was settled and defined, even before certain constituent portions of the Episcopal body had made their appearance; and this, with a protest of sixty-eight of the Bishops then present against the opening of the Council. When the expected party arrived, these did more than protest against the definition which had been carried; they actually anathematized the Fathers who carried it, and in this state of disunion the Council ended. How then was its definition valid? In consequence of after events, which I suppose must be considered complements, and integral portions of the Council. The heads of the various parties entered into correspondence with each other, and at the end of two years their differences with each other were arranged. There are those who have no belief in the authority of Councils at all, and feel no call upon them to discriminate between one Council and another; but Anglicans, who are so fierce against the Vatican, and so respectful towards the Ephesine, should consider what good reason they have for swallowing the third Council, while they strain out the nineteenth. The Council of Ephesus furnishes us with another remark, bearing upon the Vatican. It was natural for men who were in the minority at Ephesus to think that the faith of the Church had been brought into the utmost peril by the definition of the Council which they had unsuccessfully opposed. They had opposed it on the conviction that the definition gave great encouragement to religious errors in the opposite extreme to those which it condemned; and, in fact, I think that, humanly speaking, the peril was extreme. The event proved it to be so, when twenty years afterwards another Council was held under the successors of the majority at Ephesus and carried triumphantly those very errors whose eventual success had been predicted by the minority. But Providence is never wanting to His Church. St. Leo, the Pope of the day, interfered with this heretical Council, and the innovating party was stopped in its career. Its acts were cancelled at the great Council of Chalcedon, the Fourth Ecumenical, which was held under the Pope's guidance, and which, without of course touching the definition of the Third, which had been settled once for all, trimmed the balance of doctrine by completing it, and excluded for ever from the Church those errors which seemed to have received some sanction at Ephesus. (*Dif.* ii, Letter to the Duke of Norfolk, ch. 8, 1875)

And I have one remark to make upon the argumentative method by which the Vatican Council was carried on to its definition. The *Pastor*

Æternus refers to various witnesses as contributing their evidence towards the determination of the contents of the *depositum*, such as Tradition, the Fathers and Councils, History, but especially Scripture … it lays an especial stress on three passages of Scripture in particular—viz., 'Thou art Peter,' &c., Matthew xvi. 16-19; 'I have prayed for thee,' &c., Luke xxii. 32, and 'Feed My sheep,' &c., John xxi. 15-17 … What has the long history of the contest for and against the Pope's infallibility been, but a growing insight through centuries into the meaning of those three texts, to which I just now referred, ending at length by the Church's definitive recognition of the doctrine thus gradually manifested to her? (*Dif.* ii, Letter to the Duke of Norfolk, ch. 8, 1875)

The Church has the office of teaching, and the matter of that teaching is the body of doctrine, which the Apostles left behind them as her perpetual possession. If a question arises as to what the Apostolic doctrine is on a particular point, she has infallibility promised to her to enable her to answer correctly. And, as by the teaching of the Church is understood, not the teaching of this or that Bishop, but their united voice, and a Council is the form the Church must take, in order that all men may recognise that in fact she is teaching on any point in dispute, so in like manner the Pope must come before us in some special form or posture, if he is to be understood to be exercising his teaching office, and that form is called *ex cathedrâ*. This term is most appropriate, as being on one occasion used by our Lord Himself. When the Jewish doctors taught, they placed themselves in Moses' seat, and spoke *ex cathedrâ*; and then, as He tells us, they were to be obeyed by their people, and that, whatever were their private lives or characters. 'The Scribes and Pharisees,' He says, 'are seated on the chair of Moses: all things therefore whatsoever they shall say to you, observe and do; but according to their works do you not, for they say and do not.' The forms, by which a General Council is identified as representing the Church herself, are too clear to need drawing out; but what is to be that moral *cathedrâ*, or teaching chair, in which the Pope sits, when he is to be recognised as in the exercise of his infallible teaching? the new definition answers this question. He speaks *ex cathedrâ*, or infallibly, when he speaks, first, as the Universal Teacher; secondly, in the name and with the authority of the Apostles; thirdly, on a point of faith or morals; fourthly, with the purpose of binding every member of the Church to accept and believe his decision. (*Dif.* ii, Letter to the Duke of Norfolk, ch. 9, 1875)

[I]t can hardly be doubted that there were those in the Council who were desirous of a stronger definition; and the definition actually made, as being moderate, is so far the victory of those many bishops who considered any definition on the subject inopportune. And it was no slight fruit of their proceedings in the Council, if a definition was to be, to have effected a moderate definition. (*Dif.* ii, Letter to the Duke of Norfolk, Postscript, 1875)

He can decide a point infallibly which never came before any council. (*LD* xxxii, 367; Letter to William Maskell, 15 February 1876)

The Pope (or the Church) is not infallible in action, but in doctrinal utterances. (*VM* i, Lecture 2; footnote 1 from 1877)

There were circumstances in the mode of conducting the Vatican Council which I could not like, but its definition of the Pope's Infallibility was nothing short of the upshot of numberless historical facts looking that way, and of the multitudinous mind of theologians acting upon them. (*LD* xxix, 118; Letter to William Froude, 29 April 1879)

Of course the Vatican Council has distinctly adopted as *de fide* what from the beginning was taught in the Church, though not defined. (*LD* xxx, 101; Letter to Henry Bittleston [2], 14 June 1882)

Papal Sins, Limitations, and Lack of Impeccability

No Pope can make evil good. No Pope has any power over those eternal moral principles which God has imprinted on our hearts and consciences … Whether, in matter of fact, Pope Gregory XIII had a share in the guilt of the St Bartholomew massacre, must be proved to me, before I believe it. It is commonly said in his defence, that he had an untrue, one-sided account of the matter presented to him, and acted on misinformation. This involves a question of fact, which historians must decide. But, even if they decide against the Pope, his infallibility is in no respect compromised. Infallibility is not impeccability. Even Caiphas prophesied; and Gregory XIII was not quite Caiphas. (*POL*; Letter to the Editor of *The Times*, 9 September 1872)

As to your difficulty about Popes being bad men is not Caiphas a better parallel than Judas [?]. (*LD* xxx, 264; Letter to Richard Holt Hutton, 12 October 1883)

Papal Supremacy and Petrine Primacy

I found the Eastern Church under the superintendence (as I may call it) of Pope Leo. I found that *he* had made the Fathers of the Council to unsay their decree and pass another ... I found that Pope Leo based his authority upon St Peter. I found the Fathers of the Council crying out 'Peter hath spoken by the mouth of Leo,' when they altered their decree. (*Ble.*, 244; Letter to Mrs. William Froude, 5 April 1839)

But now comes this difficulty; ... it would certainly seem as if St. Augustine ... held a doctrine more nearly approaching to the Roman, as though the principle of unity lay, *not* in each individual bishop, but in the body of the Church, or, if in any one bishop, in the Pope; and as though the union of Church with Church were *not* a mere accident, but of the essence of ecclesiastical unity — not for the sake of convenience or piety, but as a sacramental form; and as though schism were separation from this one whole body, and from this or that bishop only as far as he was the organ or representative of all bishops, that is, of the Bishop of Rome. ('Catholicity of the Anglican Church,' *British Critic*, Jan. 1840; in *Ess.* ii, sec. X)

I certainly do think the Pope the Head of the Church. Nay I thought all churchmen so thought; only they said that his doctrine, tyranny etc.

suspended his just powers here. (*Keb.*, 198; 'Notes' of a Letter to Edward B. Pusey, 16 October 1842)

St. Peter had the keys of this Church or kingdom, or the power of admitting into it, and excluding from it: and besides that, an awful power of binding and loosing. (*SD*, Sermon 16: 'The Christian Church an Imperial Power,' 27 November 1842)

The fact, to which the Monophysite controversy had opened my eyes, that antagonists of Rome, and Churches in isolation, were always wrong in primitive times, and which I had felt to be a *presumption* against ourselves, this article went on to maintain as a *recognised principle and rule* in those same ages. It professed that the *fact* of isolation and opposition was *always taken* as a *sufficient* condemnation of bodies so cicumstanced ... the *fact* of separation was reckoned anciently as decisive against the body separated. (*Ble.*, 245; Letter to Mrs. William Froude, 9 April 1844)

Again it has pressed most strongly upon me that we pick and choose our doctrines. There is more, I suspect, in the first four centuries, or as much, for the Pope's Supremacy, than for the Real Presence, or the authenticity of certain books of Scripture. (*Ble.*, 391; Letter to Edward B. Pusey, 14 March 1845)

And do not the same ancient Fathers bear witness to another doctrine, which you disown? Are you not as a hypocrite, listening to them when you will, and deaf when you will not? How are you casting your lot with the Saints, when you go but half-way with them? For of whether of the two do they speak the more frequently, of the Real Presence in the Eucharist, or of the Pope's supremacy? You accept the lesser evidence, you reject the greater. In truth, scanty as the Ante-nicene notices may be of the Papal Supremacy, they are both more numerous and more definite than the adducible testimonies in favour of the Real Presence. The testimonies to the latter are confined to a few passages ... a cumulative argument rises from them in favour of the ecumenical and the doctrinal authority of Rome, stronger than any argument which can be drawn from the same period for the doctrine of the Real Presence ... If it be said that the Real Presence appears, by the Liturgies of the fourth or fifth century, to have been the doctrine of the earlier, since those very forms probably existed from the first in Divine worship, this is doubtless an important truth; but then it is true also that the writers of the fourth and fifth centuries fearlessly assert, or frankly allow that the prerogatives of Rome were derived from apostolic times, and that because it was the See of St. Peter. (*Dev.*, Part I: Introduction)

While Apostles were on earth, there was the display neither of Bishop nor Pope; their power had no prominence, as being exercised by Apostles. In course of time, first the power of the Bishop displayed itself, and then the power of the Pope ... St. Peter's prerogative would remain a mere letter, till the complication of ecclesiastical matters became the cause of ascertaining it. While Christians were 'of one heart and one soul,' it would be suspended; love dispenses with laws. Christians knew that they must live in unity, and they were in unity; in what that unity consisted, how far they could proceed, as it were, in bending it, and what at length was the point at which it broke, was an irrelevant as well as unwelcome inquiry. Relatives often live together in happy ignorance of their respective rights and properties, till a father or a husband dies; and then they find themselves against their will in separate interests, and on divergent courses, and dare not move without legal advisers ... When the Church, then, was thrown upon her own resources, first local disturbances gave exercise to Bishops, and next ecumenical disturbances gave exercise to Popes; and whether communion with the Pope was necessary for Catholicity would not and could not be debated till a suspension of that communion had actually occurred. It is not a greater difficulty that St. Ignatius does not write to the Asian Greeks about Popes, than that St. Paul does not write to the Corinthians about Bishops. And it is a less difficulty that the Papal supremacy was not formally acknowledged in the second century, than that there was no formal acknowledgment on the part of the Church of the doctrine of the Holy Trinity till the fourth. No doctrine is defined till it is violated. And, in like manner, it was natural for Christians to direct their course in matters of doctrine by the guidance of mere floating, and, as it were, endemic tradition, while it was fresh and strong; but in proportion as it languished, or was broken in particular places, did it become necessary to fall back upon its special homes, first the Apostolic Sees, and then the See of St. Peter. Moreover, an international bond and a common authority could not be consolidated, were it ever so certainly provided, while persecutions lasted. If the Imperial Power checked the development of Councils, it availed also for keeping back the power of the Papacy. The Creed, the Canon, in like manner, both remained undefined. The Creed, the Canon, the Papacy, Ecumenical Councils, all began to form, as soon as the Empire relaxed its tyrannous oppression of the Church. And as it was natural that her monarchical power should display itself when the Empire became Christian, so was it natural also that further developments of that power should take place when that Empire fell ... a new power had to be defined; as St. Paul had to plead, nay, to strive for his apostolic authority, and enjoined St. Timothy, as Bishop of Ephesus, to let no man despise him: so Popes too have not therefore been ambitious because they did not establish their authority without a struggle ... supposing the power to be divinely bestowed, yet in the first instance more or less dormant, a history could not be traced out more probable, more suitable to that hypothesis, than the actual course of the controversy which took place age after age upon the Papal supremacy. It will be said that all this is a theory. Certainly it is: it is a theory to account for facts as they lie in the history, to account for so much being told us about the Papal authority in early times, and not more; a theory to reconcile what is and what is not recorded about it; and, which is the principal point, a theory to connect the words and acts of the Ante-nicene Church with that antecedent probability of a monarchical principle in the Divine Scheme, and that actual exemplification of it in the fourth century, which forms their presumptive interpretation. All depends on the strength of that presumption. Supposing there be otherwise good reason for saying that the Papal Supremacy is part of Christianity, there is nothing in the early history of the Church to contradict it. It follows to inquire in what this presumption consists? It has, as I have said, two parts, the antecedent probability of a Popedom, and the actual state of the Post-nicene Church. The former of these reasons has unavoidably been touched upon in what has preceded. It is the absolute need of a monarchical power in the Church which is our ground for anticipating it. A political body cannot exist without government, and the larger is the body the more concentrated must the government be. If the whole of Christendom is to form one Kingdom, one head is essential; at least this is the experience of eighteen hundred years. As the Church grew into form, so did the power of the Pope develope; and wherever the Pope has been renounced, decay and division have been the consequence. We know of no other way of preserving the *Sacramentum Unitatis*, but a centre of unity. (*Dev.*, Part I: ch. 4, sec. 3)

[W]e are met by certain announcements in Scripture, more or less obscure and needing a comment, and claimed by the Papal See as having their fulfilment in itself. Such are the words, 'Thou art Peter, and upon this rock I will build My Church; and the gates of hell shall not prevail against it, and I will give unto Thee the Keys of the Kingdom of Heaven.' Again: 'Feed My lambs, feed My sheep.' And 'Satan hath desired to have you; I have prayed for thee, and when thou art converted, strengthen thy brethren.' Such, too, are various other indications of the Divine purpose as regards St. Peter, too weak in themselves to be insisted on separately, but not without a confirmatory power; such as his new name, his walking on the sea, his miraculous draught of fishes on two occasions, our Lord's preaching out of his boat, and His appearing first to him after His resurrection. It should be observed, moreover, that a similar promise was made by the patriarch Jacob to Judah: 'Thou art he whom thy brethren shall praise: the sceptre shall not depart from Judah till Shiloh come;' yet this promise was not fulfilled for perhaps eight hundred years, during which long period we hear little or nothing of the tribe descended from him. In like manner, 'On this rock I will build My Church,' 'I give unto thee the Keys,' 'Feed My sheep,' are not precepts merely, but prophecies and promises, promises to be accomplished by Him who made them, prophecies to be fulfilled according to the need, and to be interpreted by the event,—by the history, that is, of the fourth and fifth centuries, though they had a partial fulfilment even in the preceding period, and a still more noble development in the middle ages. (*Dev.*, Part I: ch. 4, sec. 3)

The Emperor Gratian, in the fourth century, had ordered that the Churches which the Arians had usurped should be restored (not to those who held 'the Catholic faith,' or 'the Nicene Creed,' or were 'in communion with the *orbis terrarum*') but 'who chose the communion of Damasus,' the then Pope. (*Dev.*, Part II: ch. 6, sec. 3)

Such was the state of Eastern Christendom in the year 449; a heresy, appealing to the Fathers, to the Creed, and, above all, to Scripture, was by a general Council, professing to be Ecumenical, received as true in the person of its promulgator. If the East could determine a matter of faith independently of the West, certainly the Monophysite heresy was established as Apostolic truth in all its provinces from Macedonia to Egypt. There has been a time in the history of Christianity, when it had been Athanasius against the world, and the world against Athanasius. The need and straitness of the Church had been great, and one man was raised up for her deliverance. In this second necessity, who was the destined champion of her who cannot fail? Whence did he come, and what was his name? He came with an augury of victory upon him, which even Athanasius could not show; it was Leo, Bishop of Rome. Leo's augury of success, which even Athanasius had not, was this, that he was seated in the chair of St. Peter and the heir of his prerogatives ... Such is the external aspect of those proceedings by which the Catholic faith has been established in Christendom against the Monophysites. That the definition passed at Chalcedon is the Apostolic Truth once delivered to the Saints is most firmly to be received, from faith in that overruling Providence which is by special promise extended over the acts of the Church; moreover, that it is in simple accordance with the faith of St. Athanasius, St. Gregory Nazianzen, and all the other Fathers, will be evident to the theological student in proportion as he becomes familiar with their works: but the historical account of the Council is this, that a formula which the Creed did not contain, which the Fathers did not unanimously witness, and which some eminent Saints had almost in set terms opposed, which the whole East refused as a symbol, not once, but twice, patriarch by patriarch, metropolitan by metropolitan, first by the mouth of above a hundred, then by the mouth of above six hundred of its Bishops, and refused upon the grounds of its being an addition to the Creed, was forced upon the Council, not indeed as being such an addition, yet, on the other hand, not for subscription merely, but for acceptance as a definition of faith under the sanction of an anathema, — forced on the Council by the resolution of the Pope of the day, acting through his Legates and supported by the civil power. (*Dev.*, Part II: ch. 6, sec. 3)

If then there is now a form of Christianity such, that it extends throughout the world, though with varying measures of prominence or prosperity in separate places; — that it lies under the power of sovereigns and magistrates, in various ways alien to its faith; — that flourishing nations and great empires, professing or tolerating the Christian name, lie over against it as antagonists; — that schools of philosophy and learning are supporting theories, and following out conclusions, hostile to it, and establishing an exegetical system subversive of its Scriptures; — that it has lost whole Churches by schism, and is now opposed by powerful communions once part of itself; — that it has been altogether or almost driven from some countries; — that in others its line of teachers is overlaid, its flocks oppressed, its Churches occupied, its property held by what may be called a duplicate succession; — that in others its members are degenerate and corrupt, and are surpassed in conscientiousness and in virtue, as in gifts of intellect, by the very heretics whom it condemns; — that heresies are rife and bishops negligent within its own pale; — and that amid its disorders and its fears there is but one Voice for whose decisions the peoples wait with trust, one Name and one See to which they look with hope, and that name Peter, and that see Rome; — such a religion is not unlike the Christianity of the fifth and sixth Centuries. (*Dev.*, Part II: ch. 6, sec. 3)

Cannot I bring as strong passages [in the Fathers] against original sin as you against the Papal Supremacy? ... What are your grounds for holding the necessity of Episcopal Succession, which may not be applied to Papal Supremacy? (*LD* xi, 175; Letter to Henry Wilberforce, 8 June 1846)

I can only lift up my hands in astonishment at your statement that 'the fact is, the Churches did not know or dream of any authority of Rome over them.' Not the Alexandrian Church for instance — of whom Pope

Julius, as St. Athanasius vouches, says, 'Are you ignorant that the custom has been for word to be written first to us, and then for a just sentence to be passed from this place?' While St. Dionysius was actually appealed against to Rome, and responded to the appeal. (*Ward* i, 620 [Appendix to ch. 4]; Letter to Henry Wilberforce, 25 June 1846)

If the Roman Church be the Church, I take it whatever it is—and if I find that Papal Supremacy is a point of faith in it, this point of faith is not to my imagination so strange, to my reason so incredible, to my historical knowledge so utterly without evidence, as to warrant me in saying, 'I *cannot* take it on faith.' ... I believed that our Lord had instituted a Teaching, Sacramental, organised Body called the Church, and that the Roman communion was as an historical fact its present representative and continuation—and therefore, since that communion received the Successor of St Peter as the Vicar of Christ and the Visible Head of the Church, such he was. (*LD* xi, 190-191; Letter to Henry Wilberforce, 4 July 1846)

[I]t is not a greater difficulty to suppose that the patriarchal theory developed into or (if you will) [was] superseded, I should rather say overgrown by, the Papal, than to admit that the Apostles' Creed has been developed into the Athanasian. The Athanasian is at first sight as different from the Apostles,' as the Papal Church from the primitive. If the primitive Church can be proved to be anti-papal, it can as easily (*I* should say as sophistically) be proved to be Arian. (*LD* xi, 238; Letter to Lord Adare, 31 August 1846)

Have I ever said to you that I dislike the 'French school' of theology so called? You will acknowledge there is such a school as Gallicanism, but *that* is dying away. (*LD* xi, 303; Letter to J. D. Dalgairns, 31 December 1846)

The Pope needs all our prayers, we continually think of him, and have no fears that he is divinely guided in all he does. (*LD* xii, 214; Letter to Miss M. R. Giberne, 6 June 1848)

How a Pope bears it, who has the weight of the whole world upon him, I cannot fancy, except that he has so many prayers for him in every country ... it is to me marvelous how a Pope can stand it. (*LD* xii, 361; Letter to Jemima Mozley, 2 December 1848)

[A]gain and again would the civil power, humanly speaking, have taken captive and corrupted each portion of Christendom in turn, but for its union with the rest, and the noble championship of the Supreme Pontiff. Our ears ring with the oft-told tale, how the temporal sovereign persecuted, or attempted, or gained, the local Episcopate, and how the many or the few faithful fell back on Rome. So was it with the Arians in the East and St. Athanasius; so with the Byzantine Empress and St. Chrysostom; so with the Vandal Hunneric and the Africans; so with the 130 Monophysite Bishops at Ephesus and St. Flavian; so was it in the instance of the 500 Bishops, who, by the influence of Basilicus, signed a declaration against the Tome of St. Leo; so in the instance of the Henoticon of Zeno; and so in the controversies both of the Monothelites and of the Iconoclasts. (*Dif.* i, Lecture 6)

[I]t is for the good of every art and science that it should have vigilant guardians. Nor am I comparing such precision (far from it) with that true religious zeal which leads theologians to keep the sacred Ark of the Covenant in every letter of its dogma, as a tremendous deposit for which they are responsible. In this curious sceptical world, such sensitiveness is the only human means by which the treasure of faith can be kept inviolate. There is a woe in Scripture against the unfaithful shepherd. We do not blame the watch-dog because he sometimes flies at the wrong person. I conceive the force, the peremptoriness, the sternness, with which the Holy See comes down upon the vagrant or the robber, trespassing upon the enclosure of revealed truth, is the only sufficient antagonist to the power and subtlety of the world, to imperial comprehensiveness, monarchical selfishness, nationalism, the liberalism of philosophy, the encroachments and usurpations of science. (*Con.*, sec. 1)

[N]o one can have been more loyal to the Holy See than I am. I love the Pope personally into the bargain. (*POL*; Letter to Emily Bowles, 19 May 1863)

I saw that, from the nature of the case, the true Vicar of Christ must ever to the world seem like Antichrist, and be stigmatized as such, because a resemblance must ever exist between an original and a forgery; and thus the fact of such a calumny was almost one of the notes of the Church. (*Apo.*, ch. 3)

Nor is the point which is the direct subject of your question much or at all less an elementary difference of principle between us; viz., the Pope's jurisdiction: — it is a difference of principle even more than of doctrine. That that jurisdiction is universal is involved in the very idea of a Pope at all. I can easily understand that it was only partially apprehended in the early ages of the Church, and that, as Judah in the Old Covenant was not duly recognised and obeyed as the ruling tribe except gradually, so St. Cyprian or St. Augustine in Africa (if so) or St. Basil in Asia Minor (if so) may have fretted under the imperiousness of Rome, and not found a means of resignation in their trouble ready at hand in a clear view (which they had not) that Rome was one of the powers that be, which are ordained of God. It required time for Christians to enter into the full truth, ... there is no use in a Pope at all, except to bind the whole of Christendom into one polity; and that to ask us to give up his universal jurisdiction is to invite us to commit suicide. (*Ward* ii, 222; Letter to Edward B. Pusey, 23 March 1867)

I trust I shall ever give a hearty obedience to Rome, but I never expect in my lifetime any recognition of it. (*Ward* ii, 142; Letter to Fr. Henry Coleridge, 26 April 1867)

Of these heads of accusation, the only one which will be allowed by Catholics is that 'the Pope is the ruler and teacher of the Church;' but this cannot be said to be a mere medieval or modern doctrine; it seems to have been claimed as true and apostolic from the first in the Roman Church itself; *vide* the history of Popes Victor, Stephen, and Dionysius. (*Ess.* ii, sec. X, footnote 2 from 1871)

A Council must not only be 'properly convoked,' according to our doctrine, but its decisions are not binding except so far as they are confirmed

by the Pope. I am not aware he has ever confirmed a decision of the 'superiority of General Councils to him.' (*LD* xxxii, 349; Letter to Henry
Stacke, 12 February 1875)

I say the Pope is the heir of the Ecumenical Hierarchy of the fourth
century, as being, what I may call, heir by default. No one else claims or exercises its rights or its duties. Is it possible to consider the Patriarch of Mos-
cow or of Constantinople, heir to the historical pretensions of St. Ambrose
or St. Martin? Does any Anglican Bishop for the last 300 years recall to our
minds the image of St. Basil? Well, then, has all that ecclesiastical power,
which makes such a show in the Christian Empire, simply vanished, or, if
not, where is it to be found? . . . the course of ages has fulfilled the prophecy
and promise, 'Thou art Peter, and upon this rock I will build My Church;
and whatsoever thou shalt bind on earth, shall be bound in heaven, and
whatsoever thou shalt loose on earth shall be loosed in heaven.' That
which in substance was possessed by the Nicene Hierarchy, that the Pope
claims now . . . I declare it, as my own judgment, that the prerogatives, such
as, and in the way in which, I have described them in substance, which the
Church had under the Roman Power, those she claims now, and never,
never will relinquish; claims them, not as having received them from a
dead Empire, but partly by the direct endowment of her Divine Master,
and partly as being a legitimate outcome of that endowment; claims them,
but not except from Catholic populations, not as if accounting the more
sublime of them to be of every-day use, but holding them as a protection or
remedy in great emergencies or on supreme occasions, when nothing else
will serve, as extraordinary and solemn acts of her religious sovereignty.
And our Lord, seeing what would be brought about by human means, even
had He not willed it, and recognizing, from the laws which He Himself had
imposed upon human society, that no large community could be strong
which had no head, spoke the word in the beginning, as He did to Judah,
'Thou art he whom thy brethren shall praise,' and then left it to the course
of events to fulfil it. (*Dif.* ii, Letter to the Duke of Norfolk, ch. 3, 1875)

Is there then such a duty at all as obedience to ecclesiastical authority now? or is it one of those obsolete ideas, which are swept away, as

unsightly cobwebs, by the New Civilisation? Scripture says, 'Remember them which have the *rule* over you, who have spoken unto you the word of God, whose faith follow.' And, 'Obey them that have the *rule* over you, and *submit yourselves*; for they watch *for your souls*, as they that must give account, that they may do it with joy and not with grief; for that is unprofitable for you.' The margin in the Protestant Version reads, 'those who are your *guides;*' and the word may also be translated 'leaders.' Well, as rulers, or guides and leaders, whichever word be right, they are to be *obeyed* ... Can we be blamed, if, arguing from those texts which say that ecclesiastical authority comes from above, we obey it in that one form in which alone we find it on earth, in that one person who, of all the notabilities of this nineteenth century into which we have been born, alone claims it of us? The Pope has no rival in his claim upon us; nor is it our doing that his claim has been made and allowed for centuries upon centuries, and that it was he who made the Vatican decrees, and not they him. If we give him up, to whom shall we go? (*Dif.* ii, Letter to the Duke of Norfolk, ch. 4, 1875)

I think it was generally received before the Vatican decrees (vid. eg. Perrone), that the confirmation of the pope was necessary for a Council being held as Ecumenical, and therefore infallible in its definitions of faith. (*LD* xxxii, 366; Letter to William Maskell, 15 February 1876)

It seems to me plain from history that the Popes from the first considered themselves to have a universal jurisdiction, and against this positive fact the negative fact that other sees and countries were not clear about it, does not avail. The doctrine doubtless was the subject of a development. There is far less difficulty in a controversial aspect in the proof of the Pope's supremacy than in that of the canon of Scripture. (*VM* i, Lecture 7; footnote 14 from 1877)

Paradox: Christian or Biblical

Religion has (as it were) its very life in what are paradoxes and contradictions in the eye of reason. It is a seeming inconsistency how we can pray for Christ's coming, yet wish time to 'work out our salvation,' and 'make our calling and election sure.' It was a seeming contradiction, how good men were to desire His first coming, yet be unable to abide it; how the Apostles feared, yet rejoiced after His resurrection. And so it is a paradox how the Christian should in all things be sorrowful yet always rejoicing, and dying yet living, and having nothing yet possessing all things. Such seeming contradictions arise from the want of depth in our minds to master the whole truth. We have not eyes keen enough to follow out the lines of God's providence and will, which meet at length, though at first sight they seem parallel. (*PS* v, Sermon 4: 'Shrinking from Christ's Coming,' 4 December 1836)

Penance

Let the case of David suffice. On his repentance Nathan said to him, 'The LORD also *hath put away thy sin; thou shalt not die; howbeit*, because by this deed thou hast given great occasion to the enemies of the LORD to blaspheme, the child also that is born unto thee shall surely die.' 2 Sam. xii. 13, 14. Here is a perspicuous instance of a penitent restored to God's favour at once, yet his sins afterwards visited; and it needs very little experience in life to be aware that such punishments occur continually, though no one takes them to be an evidence that the sufferer himself is under God's displeasure, but rather accounts them punishments even when we have abundant proofs of his faith, love, holiness, and fruitfulness in good works. (*TT #79*, 1836)

When David, for example, said to Nathan, 'I have sinned against the Lord,' this act of repentance was allowed to avail for much. 'Nathan said unto David, the Lord also hath put away thy sin; *thou shalt not die*.' The extreme debt of sin was remitted; yet the Prophet goes on to say, 'Howbeit, because by this deed thou hast given great occasion to the enemies of the Lord to blaspheme, the child also that is born unto thee shall surely die.' [2 Sam. xii. 13, 14.] David then had the prospect of a punishment for his sin after it was remitted, and what did he do in consequence? he sought to deprecate God; he exercised in acts of repentance, that life of

faith and prayer which had been renewed in him, if so be to deprecate
God's wrath. As then he was not allowed to take his restoration as a proof
that God would not punish, neither have we any ground to conclude,
merely because God vouchsafes to work in us what is good, that therefore
what is past will never rise up in judgment against us. It may, or it may not:
we trust, nay may cheerfully confide, that if we go on confessing, repenting, deprecating, and making amends, it will not: but there is no reason
to suppose it will not unless we do. Again: Moses was excluded from the
promised land for speaking unadvisedly with his lips. Was he therefore
'blotted out of God's book?' Was he not in a justified state, though under
punishment? and does not that great Saint show us how to meet the prospect of God's judgments, when he earnestly supplicates God to pardon
him what seemed so small a sin, and to let him go over Jordan? And can
we have a more striking instance of this double condition in which we
stand, after sinning and returning, than when so great a Saint as Moses,
who was faithful in all the house of God, who saw God's face, and was the
mediator for His people, yet beseeches Him, 'O Lord God, … I pray Thee,
let me go over and see the good land that is beyond Jordan, that goodly
mountain, and Lebanon;' and the Almighty remains still unappeased, and
'will not hear' him, and says, 'Let it suffice thee; speak no more unto Me
of this matter?' [Deut. iii. 24-26.] (*PS* iv, Sermon 7: 'Chastisement Amid
Mercy,' 6 August 1837)

Further, it must not be supposed, because sinners have sincerely repented, that therefore they have no punishment for their past sins; and
this puts a vast difference between the state of the innocent and the penitent. In this sense they never can be on a level: the one, if God so wills,
is open to punishment, and the other is not; for God does not so pardon
us, as not also to punish. When His children go wrong they are, in St
Paul's words, 'judged.' He does not abandon them, but He makes their
sin 'find them out.' And, as we well know, it is His merciful pleasure that
this punishment should at the same time act as a chastisement and correction, so that 'when they are judged they are chastened of the Lord,
that they should not be condemned with the world.' [1 Cor. xi. 32.] But
still their visitation is of the nature of a judgment; and no sinner knows

what kind, what number of judgments, he has incurred at the hands of the righteous Judge. I say that repentant sinners are in this respect different from innocent persons; that, it may be, God will bring punishment upon them for their past sins, as He very often does; and it may be God's will to make that punishment the means of their sanctification, as He did in St. Paul's case. Pain, distress, heaviness, may overwhelm them, may be their portion, may be necessary for their attaining that holiness to which they aspire. (SD, Sermon 2: 'Saintliness Not Forfeited by the Penitent,' 16 October 1842)

The promises of forgiveness of sin have as full an application after Baptism as before, but not in the same free instantaneous way. They are regained gradually, with fear and trembling by repentance, prayer, deprecation, penance, patience. (Keb., 207; Letter of 4 March 1843)

[I]t cannot be doubted that the Fathers considered penance as not a mere expression of contrition, but as an act done directly towards God and a means of averting His anger. (Dev., Part II: ch. 9, sec. 3)

Perspicuity (Total Clearness)
of Scripture (Falsity of)

[T]he Bible, though various in its parts, forms a whole, grounded on a few distinct doctrinal principles discernible throughout it; and is in consequence intelligible indeed in its general drift, but obscure in its text; and even tempts the student, if I may so speak, to a lax and disrespectful interpretation of it. (Ari., ch. 1, sec. 3)

No revelation can be complete and systematic, from the weakness of the human intellect; so far as it is not such, it is mysterious. When nothing is revealed, nothing is known, and there is nothing to contemplate or marvel at; but when something is revealed, and only something, for all cannot be, there are forthwith difficulties and perplexities. A Revelation is religious doctrine viewed on its illuminated side; a Mystery is the selfsame doctrine viewed on the side unilluminated. Thus Religious Truth is neither light nor darkness, but both together; it is like the dim view of a country seen in the twilight, with forms half extricated from the darkness, with broken lines, and isolated masses. Revelation, in this way of considering it, is not a revealed *system*, but consists of a number of detached and incomplete truths belonging to a vast system unrevealed, of doctrines and injunctions mysteriously connected together; that is, connected by unknown media, and bearing upon unknown portions of the system. And in this sense we see the propriety of calling St. John's prophecies, though highly mysterious, yet a revelation. (*TT* #73, 1836)

It is one thing to apprehend the Catholic doctrines; quite another to ascertain how and where they are implied in Scripture. Most men of fair education can understand the sacred doctrine debated at Nicaea, as fully as a professed theologian; but few have minds tutored into patient inquiry, attention, and accuracy sufficient to deduce it aright from Scripture. Scripture is not so clear—in God's providential arrangement, to which we submit—as to hinder ordinary persons, who read it for themselves, from being Sabellians, or Independents, or Wesleyans. I do not deny, I earnestly maintain, that orthodoxy in its fullest range is the one and only sense of Scripture; nor do I say that Scripture is not distinct enough to keep the multitude from certain gross forms of heterodoxy, as Socinianism; nor do I presume to limit what God will do in extraordinary cases; much less do I deny that Scripture will place any earnest inquirer in that position of mind which will cause him to embrace the Catholic creed, when offered to him, as the real counterpart and complement of the view which Scripture has given him; but I deny that the mass of Christians, perusing the Scripture merely by themselves, will have that nice and delicate critical power which will secure them from Sabellianism in Germany or America, from Pelagianism in Geneva, or from undervaluing the Sacraments in Scotland. (VM i, ch. 6)

Neither would I deny that individuals, whether from height of holiness, clearness of intellectual vision, or the immediate power of the Holy Ghost, have been and are able to penetrate through the sacred text into some portions of the divine system beyond, without external help from tradition, authority of doctors, and theology ... None, however, it would seem, but a complete and accurately moulded Christian, such as the world has never or scarcely seen, would be able to bring out harmoniously and perspicuously the divine characters in full, which lie hid from mortal eyes within the inspired letter of the revelation. (VM i, ch. 6)

Indeed it certainly does seem presumptuous for a creature, not to say a sinner, to take upon him to say, 'I will believe nothing, unless I am told in the clearest conceivable form.' (VM i, ch. 11)

[T]hough there really is a true creed or system in Scripture, still it is not on the surface of Scripture, but is found latent and implicit within it, and to be maintained only by indirect arguments, by comparison of texts, by inferences from what is said plainly, and by overcoming or resigning oneself to difficulties ... If we will not submit to the notion of the doctrines of the Gospel being hidden under the text of Scripture from the view of the chance reader, we must submit to believe either that there are no doctrines at all in Christianity, or that the doctrines are not in Scripture. (TT #85, Sep. 1838)

If we will have it so, that the doctrines of Scripture should be on the surface of Scripture, though I may have my very definite notion what doctrines *are* on the surface, and you yours, and another his, yet you and he and I, though each of us in appearance competent to judge, though all serious men, earnest, and possessed of due attainments, nevertheless will not agree together *what* those doctrines are; so that, practically, what I have said will come about in the end, — that (if we are candid) we shall be forced to allow, that there is no system, no creed, no doctrine at all lucidly and explicitly set forth in Scripture. (TT #85, Sep. 1838)

As to the nondescript system of religion now in fashion, viz., that nothing is to be believed but what is clearly stated in Scripture, that all its own doctrines are clearly there and none other, and that, as to history, it is no matter what history says and what it does not say, except so far as it must of course be used to prove the canonicity of Scripture, ... it has all the external extravagance of Latitudinarianism without any gain in consistency. (*TT* #85, Sep. 1838)

That He has overruled matters so far as to make the apparently casual writings of the Apostles a complete canon of saving faith, is no reason why He should have given them a systematic structure, or a didactic form, or a completeness in their subject-matter. (*TT* #85, Sep. 1838)

[I]f Scripture contains any religious system at all, it *must* contain it covertly, and teach it obscurely, because it is altogether most immethodical and irregular in its structure; and therefore, that the indirectness of the Scripture proofs of the Catholic system is not an objection to its cogency, except as it is an objection to the Scripture proofs of every other form of Christianity. (*TT* #85, Sep. 1838)

[W]e are nowhere told in Scripture, certainly not in the Old Testament, that the Serpent that tempted Eve was the Devil. The nearest approach to an intimation of it is the last book of the Bible, where the devil is called 'that old serpent.' Can we be surprised that other truths are but obscurely conveyed in Scripture, when this hardly escapes (as I may say) omission? (*TT* #85, Sep. 1838)

The characteristics then, of the narrative portion of Scripture are such as I have described; it is unsystematic and unstudied;—from which I would infer, that as Scripture relates *facts* without aiming at completeness or consistency, so it relates *doctrines* also; ... From which it follows, that we must not be surprised to find in Scripture doctrines of the Gospel, however momentous, nevertheless taught obliquely, and capable only of circuitous proof;—such, for instance, ... the especial Church doctrines, such as the Apostolical Succession, the efficacy of the Holy Eucharist. (*TT* #85, Sep. 1838)

I have been arguing that Scripture is a deep book, and that the peculiar doctrines concerning the Church, contained in the Prayer Book, are in its depths. Now let it be remarked in corroboration, first, that the early

Church always did consider Scripture to be what I have been arguing that it is from its structure, — viz., a book with very recondite meanings; this they considered, not merely with reference to its teaching the particular class of doctrines in question, but as regards its entire teaching. They considered that it was full of mysteries. Therefore, saying that Scripture has deep meanings, is not an hypothesis invented to meet this particular difficulty, that the Church doctrines are not on its surface, but is an acknowledged principle of interpretation independent of it. (*TT* #85, Sep. 1838)

We have reason to believe that God, our Maker and Governor, has spoken to us by Revelation; yet why has He not spoken more distinctly? He has given us doctrines which are but obscurely gathered from Scripture, and a Scripture which is but obscurely gathered from history. (*TT* #85, Sep. 1838)

That Gospel which was to be 'the glory of His people Israel,' [Luke ii. 32.] was a stumblingblock to them, as for other reasons, so especially *because* it was not on the *surface* of the Old Testament. (*TT* #85, Sep. 1838)

All Scripture has its difficulties; but let us not, on account of what is difficult, neglect what is clear. Let us be sure there are many things said in Scripture most clearly, many things which any one, under God's grace, might gain for himself from Scripture, which we do not gain from it; many truths, which all men, if they carefully thought over the sacred text, would one and all agree in finding there. Perchance, if we had learnt from it what we can learn by our own private study, we should be more patient of learning from others those further truths which, though in Scripture, we cannot learn from it by ourselves. (*SD*, Sermon 14: 'The Christian Church a Continuation of the Jewish,' 13 November 1842)

Thus we see how inconsistent is the false philosophy of modern religion. It professes to give the Bible to the poor that they may judge for themselves; yet it will not let them read it in a plain way, lest they read it like the saints of former ages — lest they become too catholic and primitive; but it interposes with its own officious note and comment, to fix upon it a strained figurative meaning. (*SD*, Sermon 15: 'The Principle of Continuity Between the Jewish and Christian Churches,' 20 November 1842)

Scripture, I say, begins a series of developments which it does not finish; that is to say, in other words, it is a mistake to look for every separate proposition of the Catholic doctrine in Scripture. (*US*, Sermon 15: 'The Theory of Developments in Religious Doctrine,' Feb. 1843)

In like manner, Scripture has its unexplained omissions. No religious school finds its own tenets and usages on the surface of it. The remark applies also to the very context of Scripture, as in the obscurity which hangs over Nathanael or the Magdalen. It is a remarkable circumstance that there is no direct intimation all through Scripture that the Serpent mentioned in the temptation of Eve was the evil spirit, till we come to the vision of the Woman and Child, and their adversary, the Dragon, in the twelfth chapter of the Apocalypse. (*Dev.*, Part I: ch. 3, sec. 2)

Surely, then, if the revelations and lessons in Scripture are addressed to us personally and practically, the presence among us of a formal judge and standing expositor of its words, is imperative. It is antecedently unreasonable to suppose that a book so complex, so systematic, in parts so obscure, the outcome of so many minds, times, and places, should be given us from above without the safeguard of some authority; as if it could possibly, from the nature of the case, interpret itself. Its inspiration does but guarantee its truth, not its interpretation. How are private readers satisfactorily to distinguish what is didactic and what is historical, what is fact and what is vision, what is allegorical and what is literal, what is idiomatic and what is grammatical, what is enunciated formally and what occurs *obiter*, what is only of temporary and what is of lasting obligation? Such is our natural anticipation, and it is only too exactly justified in the events of the last three centuries, in the many countries where private judgment on the text of Scripture has prevailed. The gift of inspiration requires as its complement the gift of infallibility ... till the Infallible Authority formally interprets a passage of Scripture, there is nothing heretical in advocating a contrary interpretation, provided of course there is nothing in the act intrinsically inconsistent with the faith, or the *pietas fidei*, nothing of contempt or rebellion, nothing temerarious, nothing offensive or scandalous, in the manner of acting or the circumstances of the case. (*OIS*, sections 15, 17)

Prayer for the Dead

[T]hat the prayers of the living benefit the dead in Christ, is, to say the least, not inconsistent, … with the primitive belief. (*TT* #79, 1836)

Such too is St. Paul's repeated message to the *household* of Onesiphorus, with no mention of Onesiphorus himself, but in one place with the addition of a prayer that 'he might find mercy of the Lord' in the day of judgment, which, taking into account its wording and the known usage of the first centuries, we can hardly deny is a prayer for his soul. (*Dif.* ii, Letter to Pusey, ch. 3, 1865)

Now, was this spiritual bond to cease with life? or had Christians similar duties to their brethren departed? From the witness of the early ages of the Church, it appears that they had; and you, and those who agree with you, would be the last to deny that they were then in the practice of praying, as for the living, so for those also who had passed into the intermediate state between earth and heaven. (*Dif.* ii, Letter to Pusey, ch. 3, 1865)

Prayer (of the Righteous)

'God heareth not sinners;' nature tells us this; but none but God Himself could tell us that He will hear and answer those who are not sinners; for 'when we have done all, we are unprofitable servants, and can claim no reward for our services.' But He has graciously promised us this mercy, in Scripture, as the following texts will show. For instance, St. James says, 'The effectual fervent prayer of a *righteous* man availeth much.' St. John, 'Whatsoever we ask, we receive of Him, *because we keep* His commandments, and do those things that are pleasing in His sight.' [James v. 16.

1 John iii. 22.] Next let us weigh carefully our Lord's solemn announcements uttered shortly before His crucifixion, and, though addressed primarily to His Apostles, yet, surely, in their degree belonging to all who
'believe on Him through their word.' We shall find that consistent obedience, mature, habitual, lifelong holiness, is therein made the condition
of His intimate favour, and of power in Intercession. 'If ye abide in Me,'
he says, 'and My words abide in you, ye shall ask what ye will, and it
shall be done unto you ...' [John xv. 7-15.] From this solemn grant of the
peculiarly Gospel privilege of being the 'friends' of Christ, it is certain,
that as the prayer of repentance gains for us sinners Baptism and justification, so our higher gift of having power with Him and prevailing,
depends on our 'adding to our faith virtue.' Let us turn to the examples
given us of holy men under former dispensations, whose obedience and
privileges were anticipations of the evangelical. St. James, after the passage already cited from his epistle, speaks of Elijah thus: 'Elias was a man
subject to like passions as we are, yet he prayed earnestly that it might
not rain, and it rained not on the earth by the space of three years and six
months.' Righteous Job was appointed by Almighty God to be the effectual intercessor for his erring friends. Moses, who was 'faithful in all the
house' of God, affords us another eminent instance of intercessory power;
as in the Mount, and on other occasions, when he pleaded for his rebellious people, or in the battle with Amalek, when Israel continued conquering as long as his hands remained lifted up in prayer. Here we have
a striking emblem of that continued, earnest, unwearied prayer of men
'lifting up *holy* hands,' which, under the Gospel, prevails with Almighty
God. Again, in the book of Jeremiah, Moses and Samuel are spoken of
as mediators so powerful, that only the sins of the Jews were too great for
the success of their prayers. In like manner it is implied, in the book of
Ezekiel, that three such as Noah, Daniel, and Job, would suffice, in some
cases, to save guilty nations from judgment. Sodom might have been res-
cued by ten. Abraham, though he could not save the abandoned city just
mentioned, yet was able to save Lot from the overthrow; as at another
time he interceded successfully for Abimelech. The very intimation given
him of God's purpose towards Sodom was of course an especial honour,
and marked him as the friend of God. 'Shall I hide from Abraham that

thing which I do, seeing that Abraham shall surely become a great and mighty nation; and all the nations of the world shall be blessed in him?' The reason follows, 'for I know him, that he will command his children and his household after him, and they shall keep the way of the Lord to do justice and judgment, that the Lord may bring upon Abraham that which He hath spoken of him.' [Gen. xviii. 17-19.] (*PS* iii, Sermon 24: 'Intercession,' 22 February 1835)

Intercession thus being a first principle of the Church's life, next it is certain again, that the vital force of that intercession, as an availing power, is, (according to the will of God), sanctity. This seems to be suggested by a passage of St. Paul, in which the Supreme Intercessor is said to be 'the Spirit:'—'the Spirit Himself maketh intercession for us; He maketh intercession for the saints according to God.' And, indeed, the truth thus implied, is expressly brought out for us in other parts of Scripture, in the form both of doctrine and of example. The words of the man born blind speak the common-sense of nature: — 'if any man be a worshipper of God, him He heareth.' And Apostles confirm them: — 'the prayer of a just man availeth much,' and 'whatever we ask, we receive, because we keep his commandments.' Then, as for examples, we read of the Almighty's revealing to Abraham and Moses beforehand, His purposes of wrath, in order that they by their intercessions might avert its execution. To the friends of Job it was said, 'My servant Job shall pray for you; his face I will accept.' Elias by his prayer shut and opened the heavens. Elsewhere we read of 'Jeremias, Moses, and Samuel;' and of 'Noe, Daniel, and Job,' as being great mediators between God and His people. One instance is given us, which testifies the continuance of this high office beyond this life. Lazarus, in the parable, is seen in Abraham's bosom. It is usual to pass over this striking passage with the remark that it is a Jewish mode of speech; whereas, Jewish belief or not, it is recognised and sanctioned by our Lord Himself. What do Catholics teach about the Blessed Virgin more wonderful than this? If Abraham, not yet ascended on high, had charge of Lazarus, what offence is it to affirm the like of her, who was not merely as Abraham, 'the friend,' but was the very 'Mother of God'? (*Dif.* ii, Letter to Pusey, ch. 3, 1865)

There is a power which avails to alter and subdue this visible world, and to suspend and counteract its laws; that is, the world of Angels and Saints, of Holy Church and her children; and the weapon by which they master its laws is the power of prayer. By prayer all this may be done, which naturally is impossible. Noe prayed, and God said that there never again should be a flood to drown the race of man. Moses prayed, and ten grievous plagues fell upon the land of Egypt. Josue prayed, and the sun stood still. Samuel prayed, and thunder and rain came in wheat-harvest. Elias prayed, and brought down fire from heaven. Eliseus prayed, and the dead came to life. Ezechias prayed and the vast army of the Assyrians was smitten and perished. (MD, 'Meditations on the Litany of Loretto, for the Month of May: IV. On the Assumption,' for May 28)

Predestination

In truth, the two doctrines of the sovereign and overruling power of Divine grace, and man's power of resistance, need not at all interfere with each other. They lie in different provinces, and are (as it were) incommensurables. Thus St. Paul evidently accounted them; else he could not have introduced the text in question with the exhortation, 'Work out' or accomplish 'your own salvation with fear and trembling, for it is God which worketh' or acts 'in you.' So far was he from thinking man's distinct working inconsistent with God's continual aiding, that he assigns the knowledge of the latter as an encouragement to the former. Let me challenge then a Predestinarian to paraphrase this text. We, on the contrary, find no insuperable difficulty in it, considering it to enjoin upon us a deep awe and reverence, while we engage in those acts and efforts which are to secure our salvation from the belief that God is in us and with us, inspecting and succouring our every thought and deed ... his argument from it, 'The whole work of salvation is of God, therefore man has no real part in securing it,' in fact runs contrary to the Apostle's own argument from his own words, 'Man must exert himself, because God is present with him.' It is quite certain that a modern Predestinarian never could have written such a sentence. (PS ii, Sermon 26: 'Human Responsibility,' Feb. 1835)

How He separates in His own divine thought, kindness from approbation, time from eternity, what He does from what He foresees, we know not and need not inquire ... He dispenses His favours variously, — gifts, graces, rewards, faculties, circumstances being indefinitely diversified, ... according to His inscrutable purpose, — who chooses whom He will choose, and exalts whom He will exalt, without destroying man's secret responsibilities or His own governance, and the triumph of truth and holiness, and His own strict impartiality in the end. (*PS* iv, Sermon 2: 'Obedience Without Love, as Instanced in the Character of Balaam,' 2 April 1837)

Now, first, it has often happened that, because the elect are few, serious men have considered that this took place in consequence of some fixed decree of God. They have thought that they were few, because it was God's will that they should not be many. Now it is doubtless a great mystery, why this man receives the truth and practices it, and that man does not. We do not know how it comes to pass; but surely we do not tend to solve it, by saying God has so decreed it. If you say that God does absolutely choose the one and reject the other, then *that* becomes the mystery. You do but throw it back a step. It is as difficult to explain this absolute willing or not willing, on the part of Almighty God, as to account for the existence of free will in man. It is as inexplicable why God should act differently towards this man and that, as it is why this man or that should act differently towards God. On the other hand, we are solemnly assured in Scripture that God 'hath no pleasure in the death of the wicked;' that He is 'not willing that any should perish, but that all should come to repentance.' [Ezek. xxxiii. 11. 2 Pet. iii. 9.] (*PS* v, Sermon 18: 'Many Called, Few Chosen,' 10 September 1837)

Precise and absolute as is the teaching of Holy Church concerning the sovereign grace of God, she is as clear and as earnest in teaching also that we are really free and responsible. Every one upon earth might, without any verbal evasion, be saved, as far as God's assistances are concerned. Every man born of Adam's seed, simply and truly, might save himself, if he would, and every man might will to save himself; for grace is given to every one for this end. How it is, however, that in spite of this real freedom of man's will, our salvation still depends so absolutely on God's good pleasure, is unrevealed; divines have devised various modes of reconciling two truths which at first sight seem so contrary to each other; and these explanations have severally been received by some theologians, and not received by others, and do not concern us now. How man is able fully and entirely to do what he will, while God accomplishes His own supreme will also, is hidden from us, as it is hidden from us how God created out of nothing, or how He foresees the future, or how His attribute of justice is compatible with His attribute of love. It is one of those 'hidden things which belong unto the Lord our God;' ... He is the Alpha and Omega, the beginning and the ending, as of all things, so of our salvation. We should have lived and died, every one of us, destitute of all saving knowledge and love of Him, but for a gift which we could not do anything ourselves to secure, had we lived ever so well,—but for His grace; and now that we have known Him, and have been cleansed from our sins by Him, it is quite certain that we cannot do anything, even with the help of grace, to purchase for ourselves perseverance in justice and sanctity, though we live ever so well. His grace begins the work, His grace also finishes it; and now I am going to speak to you of His finishing it; I mean of the necessity under which we lie of His finishing it; else it will never be finished, or rather will be reversed ... It is this gift which our Lord speaks of, when He prays His Father for His disciples, before He departs from them: 'Holy Father, *keep* in Thy name those whom Thou hast given Me; ... I ask not that Thou take them out of the world, but that Thou preserve them from evil.' And St. Paul intends it when he declares to the Philippians that 'He who had begun a good work' in His disciples, 'would perfect it unto the day of Christ Jesus.' St. Peter, too, when he says in like manner, that 'God, who had called His brethren into His eternal glory, would perfect, confirm, and establish them.' And so the Prophet in the Psalms prays that God would 'perfect his walking in His paths, that his steps might not be moved;' and the Prophet Jeremias declares in God's name, 'I will put My fear in their hearts, that they draw not back from Me.' (*Mix.*, Discourse 7: 'Perseverance in Grace')

Another instance of a similar kind is suggested by the general accep-tance in the Latin Church, since the time of St. Augustine, of the doctrine of absolute predestination, as instanced in the teaching of other great saints besides him, such as St. Fulgentius, St. Prosper, St. Gregory, St. Thomas, and St. Buonaventure. Yet in the last centuries a great explanation and modification of this doctrine has been effected by the efforts of the Jesuit School, which have issued in the reception of a distinction between pre-destination to grace and predestination to glory; and a consequent admission of the principle that, though our own works do not avail for bringing us under the action of grace here, that does not hinder their availing, when we are in a state of grace, for our attainment of eternal glory hereafter. Two saints of late centuries, St. Francis de Sales and St. Alfonso, seemed to have professed this less rigid opinion, which is now the more common doctrine of the day. (*Dif.* ii, Letter to the Duke of Norfolk, ch. 9, 1875)

Priesthood; Priests

But again, has not the Gospel Sacraments? and have not Sacraments, as pledges and means of grace, a priestly nature? If so, the question of the existence of a Christian Priesthood is narrowed at once to the simple question whether it is or is not probable that so precious an ordinance as a channel of grace would be committed by Providence to the custody of certain guardians. The tendency of opinions at this day is to believe that nothing more is necessary for acceptance than faith in God's promise of mercy; whereas it is certain from Scripture, that the gift of reconciliation is not conveyed to individuals except through appointed ordinances. Christ has interposed something between Himself and the soul; and if it is not inconsistent with the liberty of the Gospel that a Sacrament should interfere, there is no antecedent inconsistency in a keeper of the Sacrament attending upon it ... Hence, the lamentable spectacle, so commonly seen, of men who deny the Apostolic commission proceeding to degrade the Eucharist from a Sacrament to a bare commemorative rite; or to make Baptism such a mere outward form, and sign of profession, as it would be childish or fanciful to revere. And reasonably; for they who think it superstitious to believe that particular persons are channels of grace, are but consistent in denying virtue to particular ordinances. (*PS* ii, Sermon 25: 'The Christian Ministry,' 14 December 1834)

In Deuteronomy we read that Moses fasted for forty days in the Mount, twice; in Exodus only one fast is mentioned. Now supposing Deuteronomy were not Scripture, but merely part of the Prayer Book, should we not say the latter was in this instance evidently mistaken? This is what men do as regards Episcopacy. Deacons are spoken of by St. Paul in his Epistles to Timothy and Titus, and Bishops; but no third order in direct and express terms. The Church considers that there are two kinds of Bishops, or, as the word signifies, overseers; those who have the oversight of single parishes, or priests, and those who have the oversight of many together, or what are now specially called Bishops. People say, 'Here is a contradiction to Scripture, which speaks of two orders, not of three.' Yes, just as real a contradiction, as the chapter in Deuteronomy is a contradiction of the chapter in Exodus. But this again is to take far lower ground than we need; for we all contend that the doctrine of Episcopacy, even granting it goes beyond the teaching of some passages of Scripture, yet is in exact accordance with others. (*TT* #85, Sep. 1838)

Her priests appeal freely to the consciences of all who encounter them, to say whether they have not a superhuman gift, and that multitude by silence gives consent. They look like other men; they may have the failings of other men; they may have as little worldly advantages as the preachers of dissent; they may lack the popular talents, the oratorical power, the imposing presence, which are found elsewhere; but they inspire confidence, or at least reverence, by their very word. Those who come to jeer and scoff, remain to pray. (*Dif.* i, Preface)

This writer's idea, and the idea of most Protestants is, that we profess that all Priests are angels, but that really they are all devils. No, neither the one nor the other; if these Protestants came to us and asked, they would find that we taught a far different doctrine — viz., that Priests were mortal men, who were intrusted with high gifts for the good of the people, that they might err as other men, that they would fall if they were not watchful, that in various times and places large numbers had fallen, so much so, that the Priesthood of whole countries had before now apostatized, as happened in great measure in England three centuries ago, and that at all times there was a certain remnant scattered about of priests who did not live up to their faith and their profession; still that, on the whole, they had been, as a body, the salt of the earth and the light of the world, through the power of divine grace, and that thus, in spite of the frailty of human nature, they had fulfilled the blessed purposes of their institution. (*PPC*, Lecture 8)

It is true that there is but one Priest and one Sacrifice under the Gospel, but this is because the Priests of the Gospel are *one* with Christ, not because they are only *improperly* called Priests. (*Jfc.*, ch. 8, footnote 9 from 1874)

Private Judgment

[W]hile belief in the document — 'the Bible and the Bible only' — is made the first thing, and belief in the doctrine is only the second, and is considered nothing more than an inference of the private student, it inevitably follows in the case of the multitude, who are not clear-headed or unprejudiced, that the definition of a Christian will be made to turn, not on faith in the doctrine, but on faith in the document. ('Apostolical Tradition,' *British Critic*, Vol. 19, July 1836; in *Ess.* i, sec. III)

[T]here is something so very strange and wild in maintaining that every individual Christian, rich and poor, learned and unlearned, young and old, in order to have an intelligent faith, must have formally examined, deliberated, and passed sentence upon the meaning of Scripture for himself, and that in the highest and most delicate and mysterious matters of faith, that I am unable either to discuss or even to impute such an opinion to another, in spite of the large and startling declarations which men make on the subject. (*VM* i, ch. 6)

[T]he minds of none of us are in such a true state, as to warrant us in judging peremptorily in every case what is from God and what is not. (*TT* #85, Sep. 1838)

Considering the special countenance given in Scripture to quiet, unanimity, and contentedness, and the warnings directed against disorder, insubordination, changeableness, discord, and division; considering the emphatic words of the Apostle, laid down by him as a general principle, and illustrated in detail, 'Let every man abide in the same calling wherein he was called;' considering, in a word, that change is really the characteristic of error, and unalterableness the attribute of truth, of holiness, of Almighty God Himself, we consider that when Private Judgment moves in the direction of innovation, it may well be regarded at first with suspicion and treated with severity ... While, then, the conversions recorded in Scripture are brought about in a very marked way through a teacher, and *not* by means of private judgment, so again, if an appeal *is* made to private judgment, this is done in order to settle who the teacher is, and what are his notes or tokens, rather than to substantiate this or that religious opinion or practice ... We conceive then that on the whole the notion of gaining religious truth for ourselves by our private examination, whether by reading or thinking, whether by studying Scripture or other books, has no broad sanction in Scripture, is neither impressed upon us by its general tone, nor enjoined in any of its commands. The great question which it puts before us for the exercise of private judgment is, — Who is God's prophet, and where? Who is to be considered the voice of the Holy Catholic and Apostolic Church? ('Private Judgment,' *British Critic*, July 1841; in *Ess.* ii, sec. XIV)

[T]hose who maintain that Christian truth must be gained solely by personal efforts are bound to show that methods, ethical and intellectual, are granted to individuals sufficient for gaining it; else the mode of probation they advocate is less, not more, perfect than that which proceeds upon external authority. (*Dev.*, Part I: ch. 2, sec. 2)

Men were told to submit their reason to a living authority. Moreover, whatever an Apostle said, his converts were bound to believe; when they entered the Church, they entered it in order to learn. The Church was their teacher; they did not come to argue, to examine, to pick and choose, but to accept whatever was put before them. No one doubts, no one can doubt this, of those primitive times. A Christian was bound to take without doubting all that the Apostles declared to be revealed; if the Apostles spoke, he had to yield an internal assent of his mind; it would not be enough to keep silence, it would not be enough not to oppose: it was not allowable to credit in a measure; it was not allowable to doubt. No; if a convert had his own private thoughts of what was said, and only kept them to himself, if he made some secret opposition to the teaching, if he waited for further proof before he believed it, this would be a proof that he did not think the Apostles were sent from God to reveal His will; it would be a proof that he did not in any true sense believe at all. Immediate, implicit submission of the mind was, in the lifetime of the Apostles, the only, the necessary token of faith; then there was no room whatever for what is now called private judgment. No one could say: 'I will choose my religion for myself, I will believe this, I will not believe that; I will pledge myself to nothing; I will believe just as long as I please, and no longer; what I believe today I will reject tomorrow, if I choose. I will believe what the Apostles have as yet said, but I will not believe what they shall say in time to come.' No; either the Apostles were from God, or they were not; if they were, everything that they preached was to be believed by their hearers; if they were not, there was nothing for their hearers to believe. To believe a little, to believe more or less, was impossible; it contradicted the very notion of believing: if one part was to be believed, every part was to be believed; it was an absurdity to believe one thing and not another; for the word of the Apostles, which made the one true, made the other true too; they were nothing in themselves, they were all things, they were an infallible authority, as coming from God. The world had either to become Christian, or to let it alone; there was no room for private tastes and fancies, no room for private judgment ... In the Apostles' days the peculiarity of faith was submission to a living authority; this is what made it so distinctive; this is what made it an act of submission at all; this is what destroyed private judgment in matters of religion. If you will not look out for a living authority, and will bargain for private judgment, then say at once that you have not Apostolic faith. (*Mix.*, Discourse 10: 'Faith and Private Judgment')

[W]hen a man has become a Catholic, were he to set about following a doubt which has occurred to him, he has already disbelieved. I have not to warn him against losing his faith, he is not merely in danger of losing it, he has lost it; from the nature of the case he has already lost it; he fell from grace at the moment when he deliberately entertained and pursued his doubt. No one can determine to doubt what he is already sure of; but if he is not sure that the Church is from God, he does not believe it. It is not I who forbid him to doubt; he has taken the matter into his own hands when he determined on asking for leave; he has begun, not ended, in unbelief; his very wish, his purpose, is his sin. I do not make it so, it is such from the very state of the case ... the Church ... speaks to us as a messenger from God,—how can a man who feels this, who comes to her, who falls at her feet as such, make a reserve, that he may be allowed to doubt her at some future day? (*Mix.*, Discourse 11: 'Faith and Doubt')

[I]t is impossible to go into the world without seeing that the idea of taking one's doctrine from an external authority does not enter into their minds. It is always 'I think.' This is what is meant by private judgment—though Scripture, yet they put their own sense on Scripture; they take these books, reject those, etc. This is a most fearful consideration, considering we are saved by faith. (*SN*, 'Faith—III,' 29 May 1859)

To the Fathers the idea of private judgment, and private judgment on Scripture, suggests itself only to be condemned. (*VM* i, Lecture 5; footnote 4 from 1877)

Purgatory

Again, consider what a frightful doctrine purgatory is—not the holiest man who lived but must expect to find himself there on dying, since Christ does not remit all punishment of sin. Now, *if* Christ has promised to wipe away all guilt and all suffering upon death, what a great affront it must be to Him, thus to obscure His mercy, to deprive His people of the full comfort of His work for them! (*POL*; Letter to Mrs. William Wilberforce, 17 November 1834)

Nor would it be surprising if, in God's gracious providence, the very purpose of their remaining thus for a season at a distance from heaven, were, that they may have time for growing in all holy things, and perfecting the inward development of the good seed sown in their hearts. The Psalmist speaks of the righteous as 'trees planted by the rivers of water, that bring forth their fruit in due season;' and when might this silent growth of holiness more suitably and happily take place, than when they are waiting for the Day of the Lord, removed from those trials and temptations which were necessary for its early beginnings? Consider how many men are very dark and feeble in their religious state, when they depart hence, though true servants of God as far as they go. Alas! I know that the multitude of men do not think of religion at all;—they are thoughtless in their youth, and secular as life goes on;—they find their interest lie in adopting a decent profession; they deceive themselves, and think themselves religious, and (to all appearance) die with no deeper religion than such a profession implies. Alas! there are many also, who, after careless lives, amend, yet not truly;—think they repent, but do not in a Christian way. There are a number, too, who leave repentance for their death-bed, and die with no fruits of religion at all, except with so much of subdued and serious feeling as pain forces upon them. All these, as far as we are told, die without hope. But, after all these melancholy cases are allowed for, many there are still, who, beginning well, and persevering for years, yet are even to the end but beginners after all, when death comes upon them;—many who have been in circumstances of especial difficulty, who have had fiercer temptations, more perplexing trials than the rest, and in consequence have been impeded in their course. Nay, in one sense, all Christians die with their work unfinished. Let them have chastened themselves all their lives long, and lived in faith and obedience, yet still there is much in them unsubdued,—much pride, much ignorance, much unrepented, unknown sin, much inconsistency, much irregularity in prayer, much lightness and frivolity of thought. Who can tell then, but, in God's mercy, the time of waiting between death and Christ's coming, may be profitable to those who have been His true servants here, as a time of maturing that fruit of grace, but partly formed in them in this life,—a school-time of contemplation, as this world is a discipline of active service? Such, surely, is the force of the Apostle's words, that 'He that hath begun a good work in us, will perform it *until* the day of Jesus Christ,' *until*, not *at*, not stopping it with death, but carrying it on to the Resurrection. And this, which will be accorded to all Saints, will be profitable to each in proportion to the degree of holiness in which he dies; for, as we are expressly told that in one sense the spirits of the just are *perfected* on their death, it follows that the greater advance each has made here, the higher will be the line of his subsequent growth between death and the Resurrection. (*PS* iii, Sermon 25: 'The Intermediate State,' 1 November 1835)

Tertullian speaks of purification in a subterranean prison; Cyprian of a prison with fire; Origen, Basil, Gregory Nazianzen, Gregory Nyssen, Lactantius, Hilary, Ambrose, Paulinus, Jerome, Augustine, all speak of fire. (*TT* #71, 1836)

[I]f we could consider it as confined to the mere opinion that that good which is begun on earth is perfected in the next world, the tenet would be tolerable. (*TT* #79, 1836)

Some Christians die simply in God's favour with all their sins forgiven; others die out of His favour, as the impenitent, whether Christians or not; but others, and that the great majority, die, according to the Romanists, in God's favour, yet more or less under the bond of their sins. And so far we may unhesitatingly allow to them, or rather we ourselves hold the same, if we hold that after Baptism there is no plenary pardon of sins in this life to the sinner, however penitent, *such* as in Baptism was once vouchsafed to him. If for sins committed after Baptism we have not yet received a simple and unconditional absolution, surely penitents from this time up to the day of judgment may be considered in that double state of which the Romanists speak, their persons accepted, but certain sins uncancelled. Such a state is plainly revealed to us in Scripture as a real one, in various passages, to which we appeal as well as the Romanists. (*TT* #79, 1836)

[I]n the Acts our Lord is declared to have shown Himself to His disciples for forty days. These forty days are a blank in two Gospels. And in like manner, even though Scripture be considered to be altogether silent as to the intermediate state, and to pass from the mention of death to that of the Judgment, there is nothing in this circumstance to disprove the

Church's doctrine, (if there be other grounds for it,) that there *is* an intermediate state, and that it has an important place in the scheme of salvation, that in it the souls of the faithful are purified and grow in grace, that they pray for us, and that our prayers benefit them. (*TT* #85, Sep. 1838)

[S]ome notion of suffering, or disadvantage, or punishment after this life, in the case of the faithful departed, or other vague forms of the doctrine of Purgatory, has in its favour almost a *consensus* of the four first ages of the Church, though some Fathers state it with far greater openness and decision than others. It is, as far as words go, the confession of St. Clement of Alexandria, Tertullian, St. Perpetua, St. Cyprian, Origen, Lactantius, St. Hilary, St. Cyril of Jerusalem, St. Ambrose, St. Basil, St. Gregory of Nazianzus, and of Nyssa, St. Chrysostom, St. Jerome, St. Paulinus, and St. Augustine ... we find, on the one hand, several, such as Tertullian, St. Perpetua, St. Cyril, St. Hilary, St. Jerome, St. Gregory Nyssen, as far as their words go, definitely declaring a doctrine of Purgatory: whereas no one will say that there is a testimony of the Fathers, equally strong, for the doctrine of Original Sin, ... It may be observed, in addition, that, in spite of the forcible teaching of St. Paul on the subject, the doctrine of Original Sin appears neither in the Apostles' nor the Nicene Creed. (*Dev.*, Part I: Introduction)

But I speak of holy souls, souls that will be saved, and I say that to these the sight of themselves will be intolerable, and it will be a torment to them to see what they really are and the sins which lie against them. And hence some writers have said that their horror will be such that of their own will, and from a holy indignation against themselves, they will be ready to plunge into Purgatory in order to satisfy divine justice, and to be clear of what is to their own clear sense and spiritual judgment so abominable. (*FP*, Sermon 2: 'Preparation for the Judgment,' 20 February 1848)

([A]ccording to Bellarmine) they who deny purgatory will never go there. (*LD* xii, 372; Letter to J. M. Capes, 14 December 1848)

[T]hey *do not sin*—no ruffling or impatience; they are the *holy* souls in purgatory. (1) They hate their sin so much that they have greater pleasure in suffering than in not suffering with the feeling of sin. (2) No impatience; they *will* to suffer, for it is God's will. Thus every consolation — full resignation. A holy soul plunging into the place where it sent itself — rather feeling the pains of hell than the least sin ... It is true that its torments are so great that the most extreme pains of this life cannot be compared with it; yet, on the other hand, the internal satisfactions there are such that there is no prosperity or contentment on earth which can equal them. (1) The souls there are in a continual union with God. (2) They are perfectly resigned to His will, or, to speak more exactly, their will is so transformed into His will that they cannot will otherwise than God wills; ... (8) They are there assured of their salvation, with a hope which cannot be confounded in its expectation. (9) Their bitterness, most bitter as it is, is in the midst of peace most profound. (10) Though purgatory be a sort of hell as regards the pain, yet it is a paradise as regards the sweetness which charity spreads abroad in the heart; charity more strong than death, more powerful than hell, the lights of which are all fire and flame. (*SN*, 'Purgatory,' 11 November 1849)

Purgatory is rest compared with this life. (*SN*, 'On Labour and Rest,' 27 January 1850)

The souls in purgatory are without sin, and are visited by angels, yet, though they have higher privileges, they have more pains than we have, and that in spite of their having no bodies to be the seat of the suffering (*Ward* i, 608; Letter to Miss Mary Holmes, 17 October 1861)

This explanation may be given of Bellarmine's proceeding, viz., that a '*consensus* Patrum' is, according to Vincent's Rule, necessary for the validity of the argument from Antiquity; and therefore he had quite a right to adduce in his proof of Purgatory that doctrine in which they all agreed together, while he rejected those points in which they differed from each other. (*VM* i, Lecture 2; footnote 25 from 1877)

[I]t is a great *law*, that punishment follows sin; we differ from Protestants also in considering that, if not undergone by the repentant sinner in this life, he will have the prospect of it *after* this life, that is, before he is admitted into heaven. As we call it 'penance' when undergone by the repentant, reconciled sinner, when undergone in this life, so we call it 'purgatory,' when undergone after this life. Penance and purgatory are names for the 'temporal' punishment of sin, of *forgiven* sin; 'temporal' meaning that punishment which *comes to an end*, and is not eternal. Penance and purgatory are the punishment of *forgiven* sinners, *not* of *unrepentant*. (*LD* xxix, 299; Letter to J. L. Walton, 9 September 1880)

Purgatory as little 'disparages the merits of Christ,' as the 'open penance and punishment of sinners, in this world, that their souls might be saved in the day of the Lord,' spoken of in the Anglican Commination Service. (*TT* #41, footnote 6 of 1883)

There is no doctrine of the Church which so practically and vividly brings home to the mind and engraves upon it the initial element of all true religion, — sense of sin original and actual, as an evil attaching to one and all, — as does Purgatory. As to the thought that friends departed have to endure suffering, our comfort is that we can pray them out of it; but that all, save specially perfect Christians, before they pass to heaven endure, with sensitiveness in proportion to their sins, the pain of fire, is testified by almost a consensus of the Fathers, as is shown in No. 79 of the *Tracts for the Times*. This certainly is the doctrine of Antiquity, whatever want of proof there may be for the exact Roman doctrine. Tertullian speaks of purification in a subterranean prison; Cyprian of a prison with fire; Origen, Basil, Gregory Nazianzen, Gregory Nyssen, Lactantius, Hilary, Ambrose, Paulinus, Jerome, Augustine, all speak of fire. These positive testimonies are not invalidated by other passages which speak generally of rest and peace following upon death to holy souls, which are expressions frequent also in the mouths of Catholics now, in spite of their offering masses for those very dead of whom they thus hopefully speak. (*TT* #71, footnote 7 of 1883)

Here comes in the consolation afforded by the doctrine of Indulgences. Catholics believe that, by their own prayers, works, &c., in their lifetime, as appointed by the Church, and by their friends' prayers for them after their death, their just measure of Purgatory may be shortened or superseded. (*TT* #71, footnote 8 of 1883)

Reform, Catholic

We are sinking into a sort of Novatianism—the heresy which the early Popes so strenuously resisted. Instead of aiming at being a world-wide power, we are shrinking into ourselves, narrowing the lines of communion, trembling at freedom of thought, and using the language of dismay and despair at the prospect before us, instead of, with the high spirit of the warrior, going out conquering and to conquer … I believe the Pope's spirit is simply that of martyrdom, and is utterly different from that implied in these gratuitous shriekings which surround his throne. But the power of God is abroad upon the earth, and He will settle things in spite of what cliques and parties may decide. (*Ward* ii, 127-128; Letter to Emily Bowles, 11 November 1866)

There are those who wish Catholic women, not nuns, to have no higher pursuit than that of dress, and Catholic youths to be shielded from no sin so carefully as from intellectual curiosity. All this is the consequence of Luther, and the separation off of the Teutonic races—and of the imperiousness of the Latin. But the Latin race will not always have a monopoly of the magisterium of Catholicism. We must be patient in our time; but God will take care of His Church—and when the hour strikes, the reform will begin—Perhaps it *has* struck, though we can't yet tell. (*LD* xxv, 326-327; Letter to Emily Bowles, 30 April 1871; cited also in *POL*, 186)

Indeed the outburst of Saints in 1500-1600 after the monstrous corruption seems to me one of the great arguments for Christianity. It is the third marvelous phenomenon in its history; the conversion of the Roman Empire, the reaction under Hildebrand, the resurrection under Ignatius, Teresa, Vincent and a host of others. Think of the contrast between Alexander VI and Pius V, think of the Cardinals of the beginning, and then those of the end of the 16th century. (*LD* xxx, 264; Letter to Richard Holt Hutton, 12 October 1883)

Relics

Elisha's person seems to have been gifted with an extraordinary sanctity and virtue. Even the touch of his relics after his death raised a dead man. Our Saviour had this power, as all others, in its fulness; virtue went out of Him. And His Apostles inherited it in their measure. We are told that 'the people brought forth the sick into the streets, and laid them on beds and couches, that at the least the shadow of Peter passing by might over-shadow some of them.' [Acts v. 15.] And of St. Paul, — that 'God wrought special miracles by the hands of Paul, so that from his body were brought unto the sick handkerchiefs or aprons, and the diseases departed from them, and the evil spirits went out of them.' [Acts xix. 11, 12.] (*SD*, Ser-mon 13: 'Elisha a Type of Christ and His Followers,' 14 August 1836)

'God wrought special miracles by the hands of Paul, so that from his body were brought unto the sick handkerchiefs and aprons, and the dis-eases departed from them, and the evil spirits went out of them.' The grace given him was communicable, diffusive; an influence passing from him to others, and making what it touched spiritual. (*Dev.*, Part II: ch. 8, sec. 2)

As a chief specimen of what I am pointing out, I will direct attention to a characteristic principle of Christianity, whether in the East or in the West, which is at present both a special stumbling-block and a subject of scoffing with Protestants and free-thinkers of every shade and colour: I mean the devotions which both Greeks and Latins show towards bones, blood, the heart, the hair, bits of clothes, scapulars, cords, medals, beads, and the like, and the miraculous powers which they often ascribe to them. Now, the principle from which these beliefs and usages proceed is the doctrine that Matter is susceptible of grace, or capable of a union with a Divine Presence and influence ... it was a fundamental doctrine in the schools, whether Greek or Oriental, that Matter was essentially evil. It had not been created by the Supreme God; it was in eternal enmity with Him; it was the source of all pollution; and it was irreclaimable. Such was the doctrine of Platonist, Gnostic, and Manichee ... the Gnostics, holding the utter malignity of Matter, one and all condemned marriage as sinful, and, whether they observed continence or not, or abstained from eating flesh or not, maintained that all functions of our animal nature were evil and abominable. (*Dev.*, Part II: ch. 10, sec. 1)

Rule of Faith / 'Three-Legged Stool' (Bible-Church-Tradition)

From the very first, that rule has been, as a matter of fact, that the Church should teach the truth, and then should appeal to Scripture in vindication of its own teaching. And from the first, it has been the error of heretics to neglect the information thus provided for them, and to attempt of themselves a work to which they are unequal, the eliciting a systematic doctrine from the scattered notices of the truth which Scripture contains. (*Ari.*, ch. 1, sec. 3)

[I]t must not be supposed, that this appeal to Tradition in the slightest degree disparages the sovereign authority and sufficiency of Holy Scripture, as a record of the truth. In the passage from Irenaeus above cited, Apostolical Tradition is brought forward, not to supersede Scripture, but in conjunction with Scripture, to refute the self-authorized, arbitrary doctrines of the heretics. We must cautiously distinguish, with that Father, between a tradition supplanting or perverting the inspired records, and a corroborating, illustrating, and altogether subordinate tradition. It is of the latter that he speaks, classing the traditionary and the written doctrine together, as substantially one and the same, and as each equally opposed to the profane inventions of Valentinus and Marcion. (*Ari.*, ch. 1, sec. 3)

Doubtless, to forbid in controversy the use of all words but those which actually occur in Scripture, is a superstition, an encroachment on Scripture liberty, and an impediment to freedom of thought; and especially unreasonable, considering that a traditional system of theology, consistent with, but independent of, Scripture, has existed in the Church from the Apostolic age. (*Ari.*, ch. 2, sec. 5)

Such is the judgment that we are obliged to pass on the assumptions on which these friends are content to place their issue. They take it for granted, as beyond all question, that, if we would ascertain the truths which Revelation has brought us, we have nothing else to do but to consult Scripture on the point, with the aid of our own private judgment, and that no doctrine is of importance which the Christian cannot find for himself in large letters there. Not, of course, that, in calling this a mere assumption and a mistake, we would for an instant deny that Scripture has one, and but one, teaching, one direct and definite sense, on the sacred matters of which it treats, and that it is the test of revealed truth; but, as Anglicans, we maintain that it is not its own interpreter, and that, as an historical fact, it has ever been furnished for individuals with an interpreter which is external to its readers and infallible, that is, with an ecclesiastical Tradition, derived in the first instance from the Apostles—a Tradition illuminating Scripture and protecting it; moreover, that this Tradition, and not Scripture itself, is our immediate and practical authority for such high doctrines as these friends discuss. ('Apostolical Tradition,' *British Critic*, Vol. 19, July 1836; in *Ess.* i, sec. III)

Granting that Scripture does not force on us its full dogmatic meaning, that cannot hinder us looking for that meaning elsewhere. Perhaps Tradition is able to supply both interpretation and dogma. ('Apostolical Tradition,' *British Critic*, Vol. 19, July 1836; in *Ess.* i, sec. III)

That authoritative and formal interpretation of the written word, which we have above treated as a probability, is in truth a matter of history in the early Church. The fact of a tradition of revealed truth was an elementary principle of Christianity. ('Apostolical Tradition,' *British Critic*, Vol. 19, July 1836; in *Ess.* i, sec. III)

[T]he phrase 'Rule of Faith,' as applied to Scripture, ... is then used in a novel sense, for the ancient Church made the Apostolic Tradition, as summed up in the Creed, and not the Bible, the 'Regula Fidei' or Rule. (Review of Lectures on the Principal Doctrines and Practices of the Catholic Church, by Nicholas Wiseman, British Critic, vol. 19, Oct. 1836)

Scripture, Antiquity, and Catholicity cannot really contradict one another ... when the sense of Scripture, as interpreted by the Reason of the individual, is contrary to the sense given to it by Catholic Antiquity, we ought to side with the latter. (VM i, ch. 5)

[T]he phrase 'Rule of Faith,' which is now commonly taken to mean the Bible by itself, would seem, in the judgment of the English Church, properly to belong to the Bible and Catholic Tradition taken together. These two together make up a joint rule; Scripture is interpreted by Tradition, Tradition is verified by Scripture; Tradition gives form to the doctrine, Scripture gives life; Tradition teaches, Scripture proves. And hence both the one and the other have, according to the occasion, sometimes the Catholic Creed, sometimes Scripture, been called by our writers the Rule of Faith. (VM i, ch. 11)

The mode pursued by the early Church in deciding points of faith seems to have been as follows. When a novel doctrine was published in any quarter, the first question which the neighbouring Bishops asked each other was, 'Is this part of the Rule of Faith? has this come down to us?' The answer being in the negative, they at once silenced it on the just weight of this presumption. The prevailing opinion of the Church was a sufficient, an overpowering objection against it; nor could truth suffer from proceedings which only subjected it, if it was on the innovating side, to a trial of its intrinsic life and energy. When, however, the matter came before a Council, when it was discussed, when the Fathers reasoned, proved, and decided, they never went in matters of saving faith by Tradition only, but they guided themselves by the notices of the written word, as by landmarks in their course. (VM i, ch. 13)

[W]ho would have conceived that the doctrine of the Resurrection of the Dead lay hid in the words, 'I am the God of Abraham,' etc.? Why may not the doctrines concerning the Church lie hid in repositories which certainly are less recondite? Why may not the Church herself, who is called the pillar and ground of the Truth, be the appointed interpreter of the doctrines about herself? (*TT* #85, Sep. 1838)

[T]he ancient Church made the Apostolic Tradition, as summed up in the Creed, and not the Bible, the *Regula Fidei*, or Rule. (*TT* #90, Jan. 1841)

The 'Rule of Faith' is an ambiguous expression. I cannot answer your question till I know what you mean by it. It has been a received phrase for 'Scripture' only during the last 150 years, as you will see drawn out in Tract 90. Before that time it was sometimes applied to Scripture, sometimes to the creed, sometimes to both, sometimes to Tradition. In antiquity (as by Tertullian) it is the phrase for Tradition. I think that in Tract 90 I have said that it is best to avoid the phrase. (*Keb.*, 207; Letter of 4 March 1843)

The common sense of mankind ... feels that the very idea of revelation implies a present informant and guide, and that an infallible one; not a mere abstract declaration of Truths unknown before to man, or a record of history, or the result of an antiquarian research, but a message and a lesson speaking to this man and that. This is shown by the popular notion which has prevailed among us since the Reformation, that the Bible itself is such a guide; and which succeeded in overthrowing the supremacy of Church and Pope, for the very reason that it was a rival authority, not resisting merely, but supplanting it. In proportion, then, as we find, in matter of fact, that the inspired volume is not adapted or intended to subserve that purpose, are we forced to revert to that living and present Guide, who, at the era of our rejection of her, had been so long recognised as the dispenser of Scripture, according to times and circumstances, and the arbiter of all true doctrine and holy practice to her children. We feel a need, and she alone of all things under heaven supplies it. We are told that God has spoken. Where? In a book? We have tried it and it disappoints; it disappoints us, that most holy and blessed gift, not from fault of its own, but because it is used for a purpose for which it was not given. The Ethiopian's reply, when St. Philip asked him if he understood what he was reading, is the voice of nature: 'How can I, unless some man shall guide me?' The Church undertakes that office; she does what none else can do, and this is the secret of her power ... Nor must it be forgotten in confirmation, that Scripture expressly calls the Church 'the pillar and ground of the Truth,' [1 Tim 3:16] and promises her as by covenant that 'the Spirit of the Lord that is upon her, and His words which He has put in her mouth shall not depart out of her mouth, nor out of the mouth of her seed, nor out of the mouth of her seed's seed, from henceforth and for ever.' [Is. 59:21] (*Dev.*, Part I: ch. 2, sec. 2)

You have made a collection of passages from the Fathers, as witnesses in behalf of your doctrine that the whole Christian faith is contained in Scripture, as if, in your sense of the words, Catholics contradicted you here. And you refer to my Notes on St. Athanasius as contributing passages to your list; but, after all, neither do you, nor do I in my Notes, affirm any doctrine which Rome denies. Those Notes also make frequent reference to a traditional teaching, which (be the faith ever so certainly contained in Scripture), still is necessary as a Regula Fidei, for showing us that it is contained there; ... and this tradition, I know, you uphold as fully as I do in the Notes in question. In consequence, you allow that there is a two-fold rule, Scripture and Tradition; and this is all that Catholics say. How, then, do Anglicans differ from Rome here? I believe the difference is merely one of words; and I shall be doing, so far, the work of an Irenicon, if I make clear what this verbal difference is. Catholics and Anglicans (I do not say Protestants), attach different meanings to the word 'proof,' in the controversy as to whether the whole faith is, or is not, contained in Scripture. We mean that not every article of faith is so contained there, that it may thence be logically proved, *independently* of the teaching and authority of the Tradition; but Anglicans mean that every article of faith is so contained there, that it may thence be proved, *provided* there be added the illustrations and compensations supplied by the Tradition. And it is in this latter sense that the Fathers also speak in the passages which you quote from them. I am sure at least that St. Athanasius frequently adduces passages in proof of points in controversy, which no one would see to be proofs, unless Apostolical Tradition were taken into account, first as suggesting, then as authoritatively ruling their meaning. Thus *you* do not say, that the whole revelation is in Scripture in such sense that pure unaided logic can draw it from the sacred text; nor do *we* say, that it is not in Scripture, in an improper sense, in the sense that the *Tradition* of the Church is able to recognise and determine it there. You do not profess to dispense with Tradition; nor do we forbid the idea of probable, secondary, symbolical, connotative, senses of Scripture, over and above those which properly belong to the wording and context. (*Dif.* ii, Letter to Pusey, ch. 2, 1865)

It seems to us false, and we must ever hold, on the contrary, that the object of faith is *not* simply certain articles, A. B. C. D. contained in dumb documents, but the whole word of God, explicit, and implicit, as dispensed by His living Church. (*Ward* ii, 221-222; Letter to Edward B. Pusey, 23 March 1867)

It is remarkable that he [St. Athanasius] ends, as he began, with a reference to the ecclesiastical scope, or Regula Fidei, which has so often come under our notice, ... as if distinctly to tell us that Scripture did not so force its meaning on the individual as to dispense with an interpreter, and as if his own deductions were not to be viewed merely in their own logical power, great as that power often is, but as under the authority of the Catholic doctrines which those deductions subserve. (VM i, Lecture 13; footnote 3 from 1843; added in 1877)

That the informations of Scripture were of the first importance with the early Church is indisputable, ... when conclusions are in what may be called theological literature, the necessary investigations must lie in books ... mere tradition has not body enough to furnish materials for argument and research; what is needed in controversy is the expression of ideas and of trains of thought in language. The early Christians, when teaching and proving Christianity, had nothing tangible to appeal to but the Scriptures. As time went on, and a theological literature grew up, the appeal exclusively to Scripture ceased. Intermitted it never could be.

Scripture had the prerogative of inspiration, and thereby a sacredness and power, *sui generis*; but, from the nature of the case, it was inferior as an instrument of proof, in directness and breadth, to Councils, to the Schola, and to the Fathers, doctors, theologians, and devotional writers of the Church ... it would appear ... that the differences of Rome and England in the question of Scripture and Tradition are, in the hands of Anglican controversialists, verbal only. Catholic controversialists, while insisting that they need not prove their doctrine from Scripture, always do so prove it; and Anglicans, while insisting that Tradition is unauthoritative, treat it with a deference, which is the correlative of authority. (VM i, Lecture 13; footnote 15 and 27 from 1877)

The recognition of this rule is the basis of St. Athanasius's method of arguing against Arianism ... It is not his aim ordinarily to *prove* doctrine by Scripture, nor does he appeal to the private judgment of the individual Christian in order to determine what Scripture means; but he assumes that there is a tradition, substantive, independent, and authoritative, such as to supply for us the true sense of Scripture in doctrinal matters—a tradition carried on from generation to generation by the practice of catechising, and by the other ministrations of Holy Church. He does not care to contend that no other meaning of certain passages of Scripture besides this traditional Catholic sense is possible or is plausible, whether true or not, but simply that any sense inconsistent with the Catholic is untrue, untrue because the traditional sense is apostolic and decisive. What he was instructed in at school and in church, the voice of the Christian people, the analogy of faith, ... the writings of saints; these are enough for him. He is in no sense an inquirer, nor a mere disputant; he has received, and he transmits. Such is his position, ... He considers the Regula Fidei the principle of interpretation ... he makes the ecclesiastical sense the rule of interpretation, ... This illustrates what he means when he says that certain texts have a 'good,' 'pious,' 'orthodox' sense, i.e. they can be interpreted (in spite, if so be, of appearances) in harmony with the Regula Fidei. It is with a reference to this great principle that he begins and ends his series of Scripture passages, which he defends from the misinterpretation of the Arians. When he begins, he refers to the necessity of interpreting them according to that sense which is not the result of private judgment, but is orthodox. (*Ath.* ii, 'The Rule of Faith')

Athanasius considers Scripture sufficient for the proof of such fundamental doctrines as came into controversy during the Arian troubles; but, while in consequence he ever appeals to Scripture, (and indeed has scarcely any other authoritative document to quote,) he ever speaks against interpreting it by a private rule instead of adhering to ecclesiastical tradition. Tradition is with him of supreme authority, including therein catechetical instruction, the teaching of the *schola*, ecumenical belief, ... the ecclesiastical scope, the analogy of faith, &c ... In interpreting Scripture, Athan. always assumes that the Catholic teaching is true, and the Scripture must be explained by it, vid. art. *Rule of Faith* ... The great and essential difference between Catholics and non-Catholics was that Catholics interpreted Scripture by Tradition, and non-Catholics by their own private judgment. That not only Arians, but heretics generally, professed to be guided by Scripture, we know from many witnesses. (*Ath.* ii, 'Authority of Scripture')

Sacramentals and Sacramentalism

Again, what will the devotion of the country people be, if we strip religion of its external symbols, and bid them seek out and gaze upon the Invisible? Scripture gives the *spirit*, and the Church the *body*, to our worship; and we may as well expect that the spirits of men might be seen by us without the intervention of their bodies, as suppose that the Object of faith can be realized in a world of sense and excitement, without the instrumentality of an outward form to arrest and fix attention, to stimulate the careless, and to encourage the desponding. (*PS* ii, Sermon 7: 'Ceremonies of the Church,' 1 January 1831)

And the case is the same as regards the Sacraments of the Gospel. God does not make for us new and miraculous instruments wherewith to convey His benefits, but He takes, He adopts means already existing. He takes water, which already is the means of natural health and purity, and consecrates it to convey spiritual life. He changes the use of it. Again He selects bread and wine, the chief means and symbols of bodily nourishment, — He takes them, He blesses them; He does not dispense with them, but He uses them. He leaves them in appearance what they were; but He gifts them with a Divine Presence, which before they had not. As He filled the Jewish Temple of wood and stone with glory, on its consecration; as He breathed the breath of life into the dust of the earth, and made it man; so He comes down in power on His chosen symbols, weak though they be in themselves, and makes them what they were not. (*SD*, Sermon 8: 'The Church and the World,' 1 January 1837)

Superstition is the substitution of human for divine means of approaching God. Before He has spoken, it is religious to approach Him in what seems the most acceptable way; but the same principle which leads a pious mind to devise ordinances, when none are given, will lead it, under a Revelation, to adhere to those which are given ... Superstition, then, keeps the mind from Christ, because it originates in a plain act of self-will: a rite is not properly superstitious, unless it is such will-worship. (*Jfc.*, ch. 13)

Again, what should we say, unless we were familarized with it, to the story of Naaman bathing seven times in the Jordan? or rather to the whole system of mystical signs: — the tree which Moses cast into the waters to sweeten them; Elisha's throwing meal into the pot of poisonous herbs; and our Saviour's breathing, making clay, and the like? Indeed, is not the whole of the Bible, Old and New Testament, engaged in a system of outward signs with hidden realities under them, which in the Church's teaching is only continued? Is it not certain, then, that those who stumble at the latter as incredible, will stumble at the former too, as soon as they learn just so much irreverence as to originate objections as well as to be susceptible of them? I cannot doubt that, unless we were used to the Sacraments, we should be objecting, not only to the notion of their conveying virtue, but to their observance altogether, viewed as mere badges and memorials. They would be called Oriental, suited to a people of warm imagination, suited to the religion of other times, but too symbolical, poetical, or (as some might presume to say) theatrical for us; as if there were something far more plain, solid, sensible, practical, and edifying in a sermon, or an open profession, or a prayer. (*TT* #85, Sep. 1838)

Indeed, if persons have already thought it inherently incredible that the hands of Bishop or priest should impart a power, or grace, or privilege, if they have learned to call it profane, and (as they speak) blasphemous to teach this with the early Church, how can it be less so, to consider that God gave virtue to a handkerchief, or apron, or garment, though our Lord's? What was it, after all, but a mere earthly substance, made of vegetable or animal material? (*TT* #85, Sep. 1838)

The doctrine of the Incarnation is the announcement of a divine gift conveyed in a material and visible medium, it being thus that heaven and earth are in the Incarnation united. That is, it establishes in the very idea of Christianity the *sacramental* principle as its characteristic. (*Dev.*, Part II: ch. 7, sec. 1)

Catholics also commonly believe that the benefit arising from the use of holy water accrues, not *ex opere operato*, or by means of the element itself, but, *ex opere operantis*, through the devout mental act of the person using it, and the prayers of the Church. (*Dif.* i, Lecture 3)

Our Lord, by becoming man, has found a way whereby to sanctify that nature, of which His own manhood is the pattern specimen. He inhabits us personally, and this inhabitation is effected by the channel of the Sacraments. (*Ath.* ii, 'The Divine Indwelling')

Sacraments

[T]here is much in Elisha's miracles—nay, and in Elijah's in a degree—typical of the Christian sacraments. Naaman's cleansing in Jordan is a manifest figure of Holy Baptism, in which the leprosy of the soul is washed away by water. Again, the multiplying of the oil is, like the miracle of the loaves, a type of Holy Communion, in which Christ is given to us again and again without failing, all over the world, — to all who believe, — to each of them wholly and entirely, though He is on the right hand of God in heaven. At another time, Elisha multiplied twenty loaves of barley and some corn, so as more than to suffice for one hundred men. (*SD*, Sermon 13: 'Elisha a Type of Christ and His Followers,' 14 August 1836)

[T]he Sacraments may, for what we know, in certain cases, be of benefit to persons unconscious during their administration. (*TT* #82, 3 March 1837)

St. Thomas with the Schola holds generally that the Mosaic Sacraments did not cause grace *ex opere operato* and *physicè*, but only conferred legal sanctity, signifying, not anticipating, Gospel grace. (*TT* #82, 3 March 1837)

Is it not strange that Angels should be represented under brute images? Consider, then, if God has thus made use of brutes in His supernatural acts and in His teaching, as real instruments and as symbols of spiritual things, what is there strange antecedently in supposing He makes use of the inanimate creation also? If Balaam's ass instructed Balaam, what is there fairly to startle us in the Church's doctrine, that the water of Baptism cleanses from sin, that eating the consecrated Bread is eating His Body, or that oil may be blessed for spiritual purposes, as is still done in our Church in the case of a coronation? Of this I feel sure, that those who consider the doctrines of the Church incredible, will soon, if they turn their thoughts steadily that way, feel a difficulty in the serpent that tempted Eve, and the ass that admonished Balaam. (*TT* #85, Sep. 1838)

In these is manifested in greater or less degree, according to the measure of each, that Incarnate Saviour, who is one day to be our Judge, and who is enabling us to bear His presence then, by imparting it to us in measure now. (*PS* v, Sermon 1: 'Worship, a Preparation for Christ's Coming,' 2 December 1838)

If, then, a sacrament be merely *an outward sign of an invisible grace given under it*, the five rites may be sacraments; but if it must be an outward sign *ordained by* God *or* Christ, then only Baptism and the Lord's Supper are sacraments. Our Church acknowledges both definitions. (*TT* #90, Jan. 1841)

Great numbers absolutely confess and believe, that the Christian ordinances are just the same as the Jewish. They own themselves to be in the state in which the Church lay before Christ suffered and rose again. They distinctly assert that Baptism is no more than circumcision. Thus they bear witness against themselves. They do not look for any high mysterious gift in Holy Communion, but they think it the same as the Jewish Passover; each, as they think, figures our Lord's passion; the difference being that, in the one case, it was yet to come, in the other it is past. The Passover prefigured, the Lord's Supper commemorates it; the Jews looked forward, Christians look back. This is what they hold. They *claim* to be in the state of the Jews, in the state of those who had faith without Gospel justification. (*PS* vi, Sermon 13: 'Judaism of the Present Day,' 28 February 1841)

The question sometimes asked is, whether our services, our holy seasons, our rites, our Sacraments, our institutions, really have with them the Presence of Him who thus promised? If so, we are part of the Church; if not, then we are but performers in a sort of scene or pageant, which may be religiously intended, and which God in His mercy may visit, but if He visits, will in visiting go beyond His own promise. (*SD*, Sermon 23: 'Grounds for Steadfastness in Our Religious Profession,' 19 December 1841)

[H]er only idea of what we hold about the Sacraments is that they are 'symbols'! Of course they *are* symbols ... but, if we hold them to be nothing more than symbols, we should be like the Jews or Galatians. We believe our Sacraments to be *means* of grace, as well as symbols. Even our pictures are more than symbols, when blessed by the Priest, but Baptism is an ordinance of Christ Himself. (*LD* xxx, 146; Letter to George T. Edwards, 8 November 1882)

Sacraments and Salvation

[T]he *Sacraments* are evidently in the hands of the Church Visible; and these, we know, are generally necessary to salvation, as the Catechism says. (*TT* #11, 1833)

[T]he Sacraments, not preaching, are the sources of Divine Grace. (*TT*, Advertisement for vol. 1, November 1834)

Catholics hold that there are two justifying Sacraments, in the sense in which the word 'justification' is mainly used in this volume—that is, Sacraments which reconcile the sinner to God, or *sacramenta mortuorum*—viz., Baptism and Penance. The other five are *sacramenta vivorum*, that is, they presuppose the subject of them to be in a state of grace, or justified, and increase his justification. To regard the Holy Eucharist as justifying, in the same light as that in which Baptism justifies, is to confuse the first justification of the sinner with the farther justification of the already just. (*Jfc.*, ch. 6, footnote 9 from 1874)

Saints, Communion of; Veneration of

He is one of a host, and all those blessed Saints he reads of are his brethren in the faith. He finds, in the history of the past, a peculiar kind of consolation, counteracting the influence of the world that is seen. He cannot tell who the Saints are now on earth; those yet unborn are known to God only; but the Saints of former times are sealed for heaven and are in their degree revealed to him. The spirits of the just made perfect encourage him to follow them. This is why it is a Christian's characteristic to look back on former times ... what a world of sympathy and comfort is thus opened to us in the Communion of Saints! ... Blessed be God, He has given us to know them as if we had lived in their day and enjoyed their pattern and instructions. Alas! in spite of the variety of books now circulated among all classes of the community, how little is known about the Saints of past times! How is this? has Christ's Church failed in any age? or have His witnesses betrayed their trust? are they not our bone and our flesh?

Have they not partaken the same spiritual food as ourselves and the same spiritual drink, used the same prayers, and confessed the same creed? If a man merely looks into the Prayer-book, he will meet there with names, about which, perhaps, he knows and cares nothing at all. A prayer we read daily is called the prayer of St. Chrysostom; a creed is called the creed of St. Athanasius; another creed is called the Nicene Creed; in the Articles we read of St. Augustine and St. Jerome; in the Homilies of many other such besides. (*PS* iii, Sermon 17: 'The Visible Church an Encouragement to Faith,' 14 September 1834)

Again the honour paid to the Saints surely is practically a dishonour to the One God. Is it not practically a polytheism? Are not the Saints the Gods of the multitude in Roman Catholic countries? Is there not a natural *tendency* in the human mind to idolatry, and shall the Church, the pillar of the Truth, cherish it instead of repressing it? (*POL*; Letter to Mrs. William Wilberforce, 17 November 1834)

And in some unknown way, that place of rest has a communication with this world, so that disembodied souls know what is going on below. The Martyrs, in the passage before us, cry out, 'How long, O Lord, Holy and True, dost Thou not judge and avenge our blood on them that dwell on the earth?' [Rev 6:9-11] They saw what was going on in the Church, and needed comfort from the sight of the triumph of evil. And they obtained white robes and a message of peace ... Lastly, it is the manner of Scripture to imply that all Saints make up but one body, Christ being the Head, and no real distinction existing between dead and living; as if the Church's territory were a vast field, only with a veil stretched across it, hiding part from us. This at least, I think, will be the impression left on the mind after a careful study of the inspired writers. St. Paul says, 'I bow my knees unto the Father of our Lord Jesus Christ, of whom the *whole* family in heaven and earth is named,' where 'heaven' would seem to include paradise. Presently he declares that there is but 'one body,' not two, as there is but one Spirit ... [Eph. iii. 14, 15; iv. 4] ... What but the vision of all Saints of all ages, whose steps we follow? What but the image of Christ mystical stamped upon our hearts and memories? The early times of purity and truth have not passed away! They are present still! We are not solitary, though we seem so. Few now alive may understand or sanction us; but those multitudes in the primitive time, who believed, and taught, and worshipped, as we do, still live unto God, and, in their past deeds and their present voices, cry from the Altar. They animate us by their example; they cheer us by their company; they are on our right hand and our left, Martyrs, Confessors, and the like, high and low. (*PS* iii, Sermon 25: 'The Intermediate State,' 1 November 1835)

[S]o far is certain, for we have St. Paul's authority for saying it, that in coming to the Church, we approach, not God alone, nor Jesus the Mediator of the New Covenant, nor Angels innumerable, but also, as he says expressly, 'the spirits of the just made perfect.' And in thus speaking, he is evidently speaking neither of saints on earth nor saints after the resurrection, were it only that he designates especially 'the *spirits* of the *just*.' Certainly, then, the Church, in St. Paul's judgment, is made up of the dead as well as of the living ... it may be quite true that in one sense they are at rest, and yet in another active promoters of the Church's welfare, as by prayer; though we know not *how* they are active, or *how* they are at rest, or *how* they can be both at once. (*PS* iv, Sermon 11: 'The Communion of Saints,' 14 May 1837)

O that you would reform your worship, that you would disown the extreme honours paid to St. Mary and the Saints, your traditionary view of Indulgences, and the veneration paid in foreign countries to Images. (*Keb.*, 123; Letter to Rev. Charles Russell, 13 April 1841)

Christianity too has its heroes, and in the supernatural order, and we call them Saints. (*IU*, Part I, Discourse 5: 'Knowledge its Own End,' 1852)

The devotions then to Angels and Saints as little interfered with the incommunicable glory of the Eternal, as the love which we bear our friends and relations, our tender human sympathies, are inconsistent with that supreme homage of the heart to the Unseen, which really does but sanctify and exalt, not jealously destroy, what is of earth. (*Apo.*, ch. 4)

[T]he Saints are ever in our sight, and not as mere ineffectual ghosts or dim memories, but as if present bodily in their past selves. It is said of them, 'Their works do follow them;' what they were here, such are they in heaven and in the Church. As we call them by their earthly names, so we contemplate them in their earthly characters and histories. Their acts, callings, and relations below, are types and anticipations of their present mission above. (*Dif.* ii, Letter to Pusey, ch. 3, 1865)

It would be preposterous to pray for those who are already in glory; but at least they can pray for us, and we can ask their prayers, and in the Apocalypse at least Angels are introduced both sending us their blessing and offering up our prayers before the Divine Presence. We read there of an angel who 'came and stood before the altar, having a golden censer;' and 'there was given to him much incense, that he should offer of the prayers of all saints upon the golden altar which is before the Throne of God.' On this occasion, surely the Angel performed the part of a great Intercessor or Mediator above for the children of the Church Militant below. Again, in the beginning of the same book, the sacred writer goes so far as to speak of 'grace and peace' coming to us, not only from the Almighty, 'but from the seven Spirits that are before His throne,' thus associating the Eternal with the ministers of His mercies; and this carries us on to the remarkable passage of St. Justin, one of the earliest Fathers, who, in his Apology, says, 'To Him (God), and His Son who came from Him and taught us these things, and the host of the other good Angels who follow and resemble Him, and the Prophetic Spirit, we pay veneration and homage.' Further, in the Epistle to the Hebrews, St. Paul introduces, not only Angels, but 'the spirits of the just' into the sacred communion: 'Ye have come to Mount Zion, to the heavenly Jerusalem, to myriads of angels, to God the Judge of all, to the spirits of the just made perfect, and to Jesus the Mediator of the New Testament.' What can be meant by having 'come to the spirits of the just,' unless in some way or other, they do us good, whether by blessing or by aiding us? that is, in a word, to speak correctly, by praying for us, for it is surely by prayer that the creature above is able to bless and aid the creature below. (*Dif.* ii, Letter to Pusey, ch. 3, 1865)

[B]y teaching us also the immortality of man, He sets before us a throng of innumerable souls, once men, who are dead neither to God nor to us, and, who, as having been akin to us, suggest to us, when we think of them, and seem to sanction, acts of mutual intercourse ... First secure in the mind and heart of individuals, in the popular intelligence, a lively faith and trust in Him, and then the *cultus* of Angels and Saints, though ever to be watched with jealousy by theologians, because of human infirmity and perverseness, is a privilege, nay a duty, and has a normal place in revealed Religion ... did they not still pay religious honours to Abraham, up to teaching, as our Lord's language shows, that his bosom was the limbo of holy souls? and did not our Lord sanction them in doing so? and this in spite of the danger of superstition in such beliefs, as shown afterwards in St. Paul's warning against Angel worship in his Epistle to the Colossians. (*VM* i, Preface to the Third Edition, 1877)

As the love of father on earth does not interfere with love of mother, and the love of mother leaves us capable of loving brother and sister so a Catholic loves the Blessed Virgin and the Saints without any harm to the sovereign love and devotion which fills him towards the Holy Trinity in Unity. (*LD* xxxii, 427; Letter to Mrs. Pearson, 1 April 1881)

[Y]ou are fellow citizen with the saints and of the household of God. You are one of that elect body, which has such power with Him, and which is so knit together in one, on earth and in heaven. I recollect how I rejoiced myself on my reception into the Church at being at length under the feet of the Saints and able without introduction or ceremony to address them and make sure of their sympathy. (*LD* xxix, 357; Letter to Mrs. Frederick George Lee, 2 April 1881)

If even while we are in the flesh, soul and body become, by the indwelling of the Word, so elevated above their natural state, so sacred, that to profane them is a sacrilege, is it wonderful that the Saints above should so abound in prerogatives and privileges, and should claim a religious *cultus*, when once in the *pleroma*, and in the sight as in the fruition of the exuberant infinitude of God? (*Ath.* ii, 'The Divine Indwelling')

Saints, Intercession of

As to the doctrine of God's receiving our prayers by the intervention of saints, I am not aware that our Church has given an opinion about it. It speaks against 'the Romish doctrine of invocation.' And it does not in the Prayer Book recognise the doctrine of saints' intercession, but it seems to me to leave it open. (*Moz.* ii; Letter to Miss H., 10 June 1840)

To know too that you are in the Communion of Saints—to know that you have cast your lot among all those Blessed Servants of God who are the choice fruit of His Passion—that you have their intercessions on high—that you may address them—and above all the Glorious Mother of God, what thoughts can be greater than these? (*LD* xii, 224; Letter to Mrs. William Froude, 16 June 1848)

One thing I am sure of, that the more the enemy rages against us, so much the more will the Saints in Heaven plead for us; the more fearful are our trials from the world, the more present to us will be our Mother Mary, and our good Patrons and Angel Guardians; the more malicious are the devices of men against us, the louder cry of supplication will ascend from the bosom of the whole Church to God for us. (*SVO*, Sermon 10: 'The Second Spring,' 13 July 1852)

Our Lord bore the sins of the world: in that work of power and mercy, which is distinct from and above any other, He is the sole mediator, and whatever intercessory power the Saints have is from and in Him. If through gross ignorance this is or has been here or there forgotten, it is not the fault of the Church, which has ever taught it, but of the perversity of human nature. (*TT* #71, footnote 9 of 1883)

Saints, Invocation of

Scripture is as silent about kneeling at the reception of the Elements or crossing in Baptism, as about making mention of the saints, after St. Gregory's manner; on the other hand in our daily service we say, 'O ye spirits and souls of the righteous, O Ananias, Azarias, and Misael, bless ye the Lord,' which would seem to show that there are invocations which are not Romish. (*Keb.*, 65; Letter of 21 May 1840)

[W]e use the Psalms in our daily service, which are frequent in invocations of Angels to praise and bless God ... it is not unnatural, if 'the seven spirits before the Throne' have sent us through St. John the Evangelist, 'grace and peace,' that we, in turn, should send up our thoughts and desires to them. (*TT* #90, Jan. 1841)

[T]he Article opposes, not every sort of calling on beings short of God, (for certain passages in the Psalms do this) but all that *trenches on worship*, (as the Homily puts it) ... in implying that certain modified kinds of Invocation, veneration of Relics, &c., might be Catholic, I did not mean to rule it, that they were so; but considered it an open question, whether they were or not, which I did not wish decided one way or the other, and which I considered the Articles left open. (*VM* ii, IX. 'Letter to Rev. R. W. Jelf in Explanation of Tract 90,' 1841)

I avail myself, however, of the opportunity which this Letter to your Lordship affords me, without any suggestion, as your Lordship knows, from yourself, or from any one else, to state as plainly as I can, lest my brethren should mistake me, my great apprehension concerning the use even of such modified invocations. Every feeling which interferes with God's sovereignty in our hearts, is of an idolatrous nature; and, as men are tempted to idolize their rank and substance, or their talent, or their children, or themselves, so may they easily be led to substitute the thought of Saints and Angels for the one supreme idea of their Creator and Redeemer, which should fill them. It is nothing to the purpose to urge the example of such men as St. Bernard in defence of such invocations. The holier the man, the less likely are they to be injurious to him; but it is another matter entirely when ordinary persons do the same. There is much less of awe and severity in the devotion which rests upon created excellence as its object, and worldly minds will gladly have recourse to it, to be saved the necessity of lifting up their eyes to their Sanctifier and Judge.

And the multitude of men are incapable of many ideas; one is enough for them, and if the image of a Saint is admitted into their heart, he occupies it, and there is no room for Almighty God. (VM ii, X. 'Letter to Richard, Lord Bishop of Oxford, in Explanation of Tract 90,' 1841)

There is nothing in Scripture against invocation of Saints. The practice is right or wrong according as the Church allows it or not but where it is a Church ordinance, still it may be abused. (*Keb.*, 207; Letter of 4 March 1843)

What are the Roman doctrines of the Invocation of Saints etc but vivid realizations of truths which we profess to believe as well as R Catholics? Is it possible to realize that God is 'the God of' St Paul, or St Stephen, without believing that those saints live and are present? (*Ble.*, 331-332; *Diary*, 18 March 1843)

[Y]ou would not think it against the Gospel, I suppose, to ask for yourself the prayers of a good man on earth. Why then should you scruple to ask his prayers, when, having left this world and gone to God, he has become possessed of a far greater power [?]. (*LD* xxxii, 303; Letter to an Unknown Correspondent, 6 November 1869)

Salvation

She teaches that man was originally made in God's image, was God's adopted son, was the heir of eternal glory, and, in foretaste of eternity, was partaker here on earth of great gifts and manifold graces; and she teaches that now he is a fallen being. He is under the curse of original sin; he is deprived of the grace of God; he is a child of wrath; he cannot attain to heaven, and he is in peril of sinking into hell. I do not mean he is fated to perdition by some necessary law; he cannot perish without his own real will and deed; and God gives him, even in his natural state, a multitude of inspirations and helps to lead him on to faith and obedience. There is no one born of Adam but might be saved, as far as divine assistances are concerned; yet, looking at the power of temptation, the force of the

passions, the strength of self-love and self-will, the sovereignty of pride
and sloth, in every one of his children, who will be bold enough to assert
of any particular soul, that it will be able to maintain itself in obedience,
without an abundance, a profusion of grace, not to be expected, as bearing
no proportion, I do not say simply to the claims (for they are none), but
to the bare needs of human nature? We may securely prophesy of every
man born into the world, that, if he comes to years of understanding, he
will, in spite of God's general assistances, fall into mortal sin and lose his
soul. It is no light, no ordinary succour, by which man is taken out of his
own hands and defended against himself. He requires an extraordinary
remedy. (*Mix.*, Discourse 1: 'The Salvation of the Hearer the Motive of
the Preacher,' 2 February 1849)

There is no truth, my brethren, which Holy Church is more earnest
in impressing upon us than that our salvation from first to last is the gift
of God. It is true indeed that we merit eternal life by our works of obedience; but that those works are meritorious of such a reward, this takes
place, not from their intrinsic worth, but from the free appointment and
bountiful promise of God; and that we are able to do them at all, is the
simple result of His grace. That we are justified is of His grace; that we
have the dispositions for justification is of His grace; that we are able
to do good works when justified is of His grace; and that we persevere
in those good works is of His grace. Not only do we actually depend on
His power from first to last, but our destinies depend on His sovereign
pleasure and inscrutable counsel. He holds the arbitration of our future
in His hands; without an act of His will, independent of ours, we should
not have been brought into the grace of the Catholic Church; and without a further act of His will, though we are now members of it, we shall
not be brought on to the glory of the kingdom of Heaven. Though a soul
justified can merit eternal life, yet neither can it merit to be justified, nor
can it merit to remain justified to the end; not only is a state of grace the
condition and the life of all merit, but grace brings us into that state of
grace, and grace continues us in it; and thus, as I began by saying, our
salvation from first to last is the gift of God. (*Mix.*, Discourse 7: 'Perseverance in Grace')

I speak of it, for instance, as teaching the ruined state of man; his utter inability to gain Heaven by any thing he can do himself; the moral certainty of his losing his soul if left to himself; the simple absence of all rights and claims on the part of the creature in the presence of the Creator; the illimitable claims of the Creator on the service of the creature; the imperative and obligatory force of the voice of conscience; and the inconceivable evil of sensuality. I speak of it as teaching, that no one gains Heaven except by the free grace of God, or without a regeneration of nature; that no one can please Him without faith; that the heart is the seat both of sin and of obedience; that charity is the fulfilling of the Law; and that incorporation into the Catholic Church is the ordinary instrument of salvation. (*IU*, Part I, Discourse 8: 'Knowledge Viewed in Relation to Religion,' 1852)

[O]ur Lord's Atonement for sin is not the ordinary instrument of conversion, but the supreme object of devotion … I consider that the faint initial stirrings of religion in the heart, the darkness, the sense of sin, the fear of God's judgment, the contrition, the faith, hope and love, need not be a conscious, clearly defined, experience, but may be, and commonly is, a slow and silent growth, not broken into separate and successive stages, but as regards these spiritual acts composite, and almost simultaneous, strengthening with the soul's strength, advancing with advancing years, till (after whatever relapses and returns, or whatever unswerving fidelity) death comes at length, and seals and crowns with perseverance and salvation what from first to last is a work of grace. Grace is the beginning and end of it. (*LD* xxx, 224-225; Letter to George T. Edwards, 2 June 1883)

Salvation, Absolute Assurance of; Unattainable

And yet though this absolute certainty of our election unto glory be unattainable, and the desire to obtain it an impatience which ill befits sinners, nevertheless a comfortable hope, a sober and subdued belief that God has pardoned and justified us for Christ's sake (blessed be His name!), is attainable, according to St. John's words, 'If our heart condemn us not, then have we confidence towards God.' [1 John iii. 21.] (*PS* i, Sermon 5: 'Self-Denial the Test of Religious Earnestness,' 22 December 1833)

They who make self instead of their Maker the great object of their contemplation will naturally exalt themselves. Without denying that the glory of God is the great end to which all things are to be referred, they will be led to connect indissolubly His glory with their own certainty of salvation; and this partly accounts for its being so common to find rigid predestinarian views, and the exclusive maintenance of justification by Faith in the same persons. And for the same reason, the Scripture doctrines relative to the Church and its offices will be unpalatable to such persons; no one thing being so irreconcileable with another, as the system which makes a man's thoughts centre in himself, with that which directs them to a fountain of grace and truth, on which God has made him dependent. (*PS* ii, Sermon 15: 'Self-Contemplation,' Feb. 1835)

St. Paul speaks as if the Christian course were a race, in which one only out of many could succeed. And what is the conclusion he arrives at? 'I keep under my body, and bring it into subjection, lest that by any means when I have preached to others, I myself should be a castaway.' You see how far the holy Apostle was from security and self-satisfaction, though he, if any one, would have had a right to feel easy about his state. And the exhortation he gives his brethren is, 'So run, that ye may obtain.' Are candidates for a prize confident, because only one can gain it? What is the meaning then of asserting that 'they which run in a race' take it for granted that they are on the winning side? And yet it is quite true that there are men who, in consequence of holding the doctrine that the chosen are few, instead of exerting themselves, become proud and careless. But then, let it be observed, these persons hold another doctrine besides, which is the real cause of their carnal security. They not merely think that Christ's flock is small, but that every man can tell whether or no he belongs to it, and that they do know that they themselves belong to it. Now, if a man thinks he knows for certain that he shall be saved, of course he will be much tempted to indulge in a carnal security, and to look down upon others, and that, whether the true flock of Christ is large or small. It is not the knowledge that the chosen are *few* which occasions these bad feelings, but a man's private assurance that *he* is chosen ... We may know about ourselves, that at present we are sincere and earnest, and so far in

God's favour; we may be able to say that such and such words or deeds are right or wrong in another; but how different is this from having the capacity to decide absolutely about our or his eternal doom! (*PS* v, Sermon 18: 'Many Called, Few Chosen,' 10 September 1837)

He who believes that he can please God of himself, or that obedience can be performed by his own powers, of course has nothing more of awe, reverence, and wonder in his personal religion, than when he moves his limbs and uses his reason, though he might well feel awe then also. And in like manner he also who considers that Christ's passion once undergone on the Cross absolutely secured his own personal salvation, may see mystery indeed in that Cross (as he ought), but he will see no mystery, and feel little solemnity, in prayer, in ordinances, or in his attempts at obedience. He will be free, familiar, and presuming, in God's presence. Neither will 'work out their salvation with fear and trembling;' for neither will realize, though they use the words, that God is in them 'to will and to do.' Both the one and the other will be content with a low standard of duty: the one, because he does not believe that God requires much; the other, because he thinks that Christ in His own person has done all. Neither will honour and make much of God's Law: the one, because he brings down the Law to his own power of obeying it; the other, because he thinks that Christ has taken away the Law by obeying it in his stead. (*PS* v, Sermon 10: 'Righteousness not of us, but in us,' 19 January 1840)

Our Lord speaks of His people as a small flock, as I cited His words when I began: He says, 'Many are called, few are chosen.' St. Paul, speaking in the first instance of the Jews, says that but 'a remnant is saved according to the election of grace.' He speaks even of the possibility of his own reprobation. What a thought in an Apostle! yet it is one with which Saints are familiar; they fear both for themselves and for others. (*Mix.*, Discourse 8: 'Nature and Grace')

Salvation, Moral Assurance of

Now, I suppose, absolute certainty about our state cannot be attained at all in this life; but the nearest approach to such certainty which is possible,

would seem to be afforded by this consciousness of openness and singleness of mind, this good understanding (if I may use such an expression)
between the soul and its conscience, to which St. Paul so often alludes.
'Our rejoicing is this,' he says, 'the testimony of our conscience, that in
simplicity and godly sincerity we have had our conversation in the world.'
He did not rejoice in his faith, but he was justified by faith, because he
could rejoice in his sincerity. Perfectness of heart, simple desire to please
God, 'a spirit without guile,' a true and loyal will, where these are present,
faith is justifying; and whereas those who have this integrity will more or
less be conscious of it, therefore, after all exceptions duly made on the
score of depression of spirits, perplexity of mind, horror at past sins, and
the like, still, on the whole, really religious persons will commonly enjoy
a subdued but comfortable hope and trust that they are in a state of justification. (*PS* v, Sermon 17: 'The Testimony of Conscience,' 9 December
1838)

Sanctification

I suppose a religious man is conscious that God has been with him, and
given him whatever he has of good within him. He knows quite enough
of himself to know how fallen he is from original righteousness, and he
has a conviction, which nothing can shake, that without the aid of his
Lord and Saviour, he can do nothing aright. I do not say he need recollect any definite season when he turned to God and gave up the service
of sin and Satan; but in one sense every season, every year is such a time
of turning. I mean, he ever has experience, just as if he had hitherto been
living to the world, of a continual conversion; ... And this conviction of
a Divine Presence with him is stronger according to the length of time
during which he has served God, and to his advance in holiness. The
multitude of men—nay, a great number of those who think themselves
religious—do not aim at holiness, and do not advance in holiness; but
consider what a great evidence it is that God is with us, so far as we have
it. Religious men, really such, cannot but recollect in the course of years,
that they have become very different from what they were. I say 'in the
course of years:' this it is, among other things, which makes young persons

less settled in their religion. They have not given it a trial; they have not had time to do so; but in the course of years a religious person finds that a mysterious unseen influence has been upon him and has changed him. He is indeed very different from what he was. His tastes, his views, his judgments are different. You will say that time changes a man as a matter of course; advancing age, outward circumstances, trials, experience of life. It is true; and yet I think a religious man would feel it little less than sacrilege, and almost blasphemy, to impute the improvement in his heart and conduct, in his moral being, with which he has been favoured in a certain sufficient period, to outward or merely natural causes. He will be unable to force himself to do so: that is to say, he has a conviction, which it is a point of religion with him not to doubt, which it is a sin to deny, that God has been with him. And this is of course a ground of hope to him that God will be with him still; and if he, at any time, fall into religious perplexity, it may serve to comfort him to think of it. (*SD*, Sermon 23: 'Grounds for Steadfastness in Our Religious Profession,' 19 December 1841)

Satan

Now this delusion arises from Satan's craft, the father of lies, who knows well that if he can get us once to sin, he can easily make us sin twice and thrice, till at length we are taken captive at his will [2 Tim. ii. 26.]. He sees that curiosity is man's great and first snare, as it was in paradise; and he knows that, if he can but force a way into his heart by this chief and exciting temptation, those temptations of other kinds, which follow in life, will easily prevail over us; and, on the other hand, that if we resist the beginnings of sin, there is every prospect through God's grace that we shall continue in a religious way. (*PS* viii, Sermon 5: 'Curiosity a Temptation to Sin,' 26 June 1831)

He has gained a point whenever he can entangle religious persons in some deliberate sin, when he can rouse their pride, inflame their resentment, allure their covetousness, or feed their ambitious hopes. One sin is enough: his work is done, when he can put one single obstacle in their road; and there he leaves it, satisfied. And let it be observed, this applies both to the case of individuals and of the Church itself at a given time. (*PS* iv, Sermon 3: 'Moral Consequences of Single Sins,' 20 March 1836)

Wonderful providence indeed which is so silent, yet so efficacious, so constant, so unerring! This is what baffles the power of Satan. He cannot discern the Hand of God in what goes on; and though he would fain meet it and encounter it, in his mad and blasphemous rebellion against heaven, he cannot find it. Crafty and penetrating as he is, yet his thousand eyes and his many instruments avail him nothing against the majestic serene silence, the holy imperturbable calm which reigns through the providences of God. Crafty and experienced as he is, he appears like a child or a fool, like one made sport of, whose daily bread is but failure and mockery, before the deep and secret wisdom of the Divine Counsels. He makes a guess here, or does a bold act there, but all in the dark. He knew not of Gabriel's coming, and the miraculous conception of the Virgin, or what was meant by that Holy Thing which was to be born, being called the Son of God. He tried to kill him, and he made martyrs of the innocent children; he tempted the Lord of all with hunger and with ambitious prospects; he sifted the Apostles, and got none but one who already bore his own name, and had been already given over as a devil. He rose against his God in his full strength, in the hour and power of darkness, and then he seemed to conquer; but with his utmost effort, and as his greatest achievement, he did no more than 'whatsoever Thy hand and Thy counsel determined before to be done.' [Acts iv. 28.] He brought into the world the very salvation which he feared and hated. He accomplished the Atonement of that world, whose misery he was plotting. Wonderfully silent, yet resistless course of God's providence! (*PS* iv, Sermon 17: 'Christ Manifested in Remembrance,' 7 May 1837)

He has many ways of attack; sometimes he comes openly, sometimes craftily, sometimes he tempts you, sometimes he frightens you, but whether he comes in a pleasing or a frightful form, be sure, if you saw him himself with your eyes, he would always be hateful, monstrous, and abominable. Therefore he keeps himself out of sight. (*PS* viii, Sermon 4: 'The Call of David,' 25 June 1837)

Far be it from any of us to be of those simple ones who are taken in that snare which is circling around us! Far be it from us to be seduced with the fair promises in which Satan is sure to hide his poison! Do you think he is so unskilful in his craft, as to ask you openly and plainly to join him in his warfare against the Truth? No; he offers you baits to tempt you. He promises you civil liberty; he promises you equality; he promises you trade and wealth; he promises you a remission of taxes; he promises you reform … he offers you knowledge, science, philosophy, enlargement of mind. He scoffs at times gone by; he scoffs at every institution which reveres them. He prompts you what to say, and then listens to you, and praises you, and encourages you. He bids you mount aloft. He shows you how to become as gods. Then he laughs and jokes with you, and gets intimate with you; he takes your hand, and gets his fingers between yours, and grasps them, and then you are his. (*TT* #83, 1838)

[H]e is found all over the earth, and within the souls of men, not indeed able to do anything which God does not permit, but still, God not interfering, he possesses immense power, and is able to influence millions upon millions to their ruin. And as the poor epileptic in the gospel was under the mastery of the evil spirit, so that his eyes, his ears, his tongue, his limbs were not his own, so does that same miserable spirit possess the souls of sinners, ruling them, impelling them here and there, doing what he will with them, not indeed doing the same with every one, some he moves one way, some in another, but all in some pitiable, horrible, and ungodly way … as madness was the disorder in which possession by the devil showed itself in Scripture, so this madness of the heart and spirit is the disorder which in all ages the devil produces in the spirit. (*FP*, Sermon 6: 'The World and Sin,' 19 March 1848)

Satan cannot conquer us against ourselves. (*SN*, 'On Christ the Good Samaritan,' 31 August 1851)

Scripture

We read a passage in the Gospels, for instance, a parable perhaps, or the account of a miracle; or we read a chapter in the Prophets, or a Psalm.

Who is not struck with the beauty of what he reads? I do not wish to speak of those who read the Bible only now and then, and who will in consequence generally find its sacred pages dull and uninteresting; but of those who study it. Who of such persons does not see the beauty of it? ... is not Scripture altogether pleasant except in its strictness? (*PS* i, Sermon 3: 'Knowledge of God's Will Without Obedience,' 2 September 1832)

But it may be said that, though the word of God is an infallible rule of faith, yet it requires interpreting, and why, as time goes on, should we not discover in it more than we at present know on the subject of religion and morals? (*PS* vii, Sermon 18: 'Steadfastness in Old Paths,' 1842)

[W]e may be in the practice of reading Scripture carefully, and trying to serve God, and its sense may, as if suddenly, break upon us, in a way it never did before. Some thought may suggest itself to us, which is a key to a great deal in Scripture, or which suggests a great many other thoughts. A new light may be thrown on the precepts of our Lord and His Apostles. We may be able to enter into the manner of life of the early Christians, as recorded in Scripture, which before was hidden from us, and into the simple maxims on which Scripture bases it. We may be led to understand that it is very different from the life which men live now. Now knowledge is a call to action: an insight into the way of perfection is a call to perfection. (*PS* viii, Sermon 2: 'Divine Calls,' 1843)

The actual course of the *events* which Scripture relates is one thing, and the course of the *narrative* is another; for the sacred writers do not state events with that relative prominence in which they severally occurred in fact. Inspiration has interfered to select and bring into the foreground the most cogent instances of Divine interposition, and has identified them by a number of distinct details; on the other hand, it has covered up from us the 'many other signs' which 'Jesus did in the presence of His disciples,' 'the which, if they should be written every one, even the world itself,' as St. John speaks, 'could not contain the books that should be written.' And doubtless there are doctrinal reasons also for this circumstance, if we had means of ascertaining them. (*Mir.*, Essay Two: 'The Miracles of Early Ecclesiastical History,' 1843)

Scripture is a refuge in any trouble; only let us be on our guard against seeming to use it further than is fitting, or doing more than sheltering ourselves under its shadow. Let us use it according to our measure. It is far higher and wider than our need; and its language veils our feelings while it gives expression to them. It is sacred and heavenly; and it restrains and purifies, while it sanctions them. (*SD*, Sermon 26: 'The Parting of Friends,' 25 September 1843)

This moreover should be considered, — that great questions exist in the subject-matter of which Scripture treats, which Scripture does not solve; questions too so real, so practical, that they must be answered, and, unless we suppose a new revelation, answered by means of the revelation which we have, that is, by development. Such is the question of the Canon of Scripture and its inspiration: that is, whether Christianity depends upon a written document as Judaism; — if so, on what writings and how many; — whether that document is self-interpreting, or requires a comment, and whether any authoritative comment or commentator is provided; — whether the revelation and the document are commensurate, or the one outruns the other; — all these questions surely find no solution on the surface of Scripture, nor indeed under the surface in the case of most men, however long and diligent might be their study of it. Nor were these difficulties settled by authority, as far as we know, at the commencement of the religion; yet surely it is quite conceivable that an Apostle might have dissipated them all in a few words, had Divine Wisdom thought fit. But in matter of fact the decision has been left to time, to the slow process of thought, to the influence of mind upon mind, the issues of controversy, and the growth of opinion. (*Dev.*, Part I: ch. 2)

But the whole Bible, not its prophetical portions only, is written on the principle of development. As the Revelation proceeds, it is ever new, yet ever old. St. John, who completes it, declares that he writes no 'new commandment unto his brethren,' but an old commandment which they 'had from the beginning.' And then he adds, 'A new commandment I write unto you.' The same test of development is suggested in our Lord's words on the Mount, as has already been noticed, 'Think not that I am come to destroy the Law and the Prophets; I am not come to destroy, but to fulfil.' He does not reverse, but perfect, what has gone before. Thus with respect to the evangelical view of the rite of sacrifice, first the rite is enjoined by Moses; next Samuel says, 'to obey is better than sacrifice;' then Hosea, 'I will have mercy and not sacrifice;' Isaiah, 'Incense is an abomination unto me;' then Malachi, describing the times of the Gospel, speaks of the 'pure offering' of wheatflour; and our Lord completes the development, when He speaks of worshipping 'in spirit and in truth.' (*Dev.*, Part I: ch. 2)

Christianity developed, as we have incidentally seen, into the form, first, of a Catholic, then of a Papal Church. Now it was Scripture that was made the rule on which this development proceeded in each case, and Scripture moreover interpreted in a mystical sense ... The divines of the Church are in every age engaged in regulating themselves by Scripture, appealing to Scripture in proof of their conclusions, and exhorting and teaching in the thoughts and language of Scripture. Scripture may be said to be the medium in which the mind of the Church has energized and developed ... And this has been the doctrine of all ages of the Church, as is shown by the disinclination of her teachers to confine themselves to the mere literal interpretation of Scripture. Her most subtle and powerful method of proof, whether in ancient or modern times, is the mystical sense, which is so frequently used in doctrinal controversy as on many occasions to supersede any other ... we find this method of interpretation to be the very basis of the proof of the Catholic doctrine of the Holy Trinity. Whether we betake ourselves to the Ante-nicene writers or the Nicene, certain texts will meet us, which do not obviously refer to that doctrine, yet are put forward as palmary proofs of it ... On the other hand, the School of Antioch, which adopted the literal interpretation, was, as I have noticed above, the very metropolis of heresy ... the Jews clung to the literal sense of the Scriptures and hence rejected the Gospel; the Christian Apologists proved its divinity by means of the allegorical. The formal connexion of this mode of interpretation with Christian theology is noticed by Porphyry, who speaks of Origen and others as borrowing it from heathen philosophy, both in explanation of the Old Testament and in defence of their own doctrine. It may be almost laid down as an historical fact, that the mystical interpretation and orthodoxy will stand or fall together ... The use of Scripture then, especially its spiritual or second sense, as a medium of thought and deduction, is a characteristic principle of doctrinal teaching in the Church. (*Dev.*, Part II: ch. 7, sec. 4)

It has ever seemed to me that the Scripture text has often various meanings, over and above that first and direct sense which may be dogmatic, ethical or historical; and that the Hebrew or Greek words may have in certain passages a depth (mystical, philosophical, or theological) which is supernatural, which one language may admit and another may not, and which therefore a translation cannot preserve. This defect incident to a translation need not interfere with its authenticity in matters of faith and morals ... it would suggest a sacredness in the original which no mere version can claim. (*LD* xxx, 260; Letter to Bishop William Clifford of Clifton, 3 October 1883)

Scripture, ... Apostolic, unerring Truth. (*OIS*, sec. 4)

Many truths may be predicated about Scripture and its contents which are not obligatory on our faith, viz., such as are private conclusions from premises, or are the *dicta* of theologians. Such as about the author of the Book of Job, or the dates of St. Paul's Epistles. These are not obligatory upon us, because they are not the subjects of *ex cathedrâ* utterances of the Church. Opinions of this sort may be true or not true, and lie open for acceptance or rejection, since no divine utterance has ever been granted to us about them, or is likely to be granted. We are not bound to believe what St. Jerome said or inferred about Scripture; nor what St. Augustine, or St. Thomas, or Cardinal Caietan or Fr. Perrone has said; but what the Church has enunciated, what the Councils, what the Pope, has determined. We are not bound to accept with an absolute faith what is not a dogma, or the equivalent of dogma. (*OIS*, sec. 5)

As to the authority of Scripture, we hold it to be, in all matters of faith and morals, divinely inspired throughout; as to its interpretation, we hold

that the Church is, in faith and morals, the one infallible expounder of
that inspired text ... The Vatican Council speaks more distinctly, saying
that the entire books with all their parts, are divinely inspired, and adding
an anathema upon impugners of this definition. (*OIS*, sections 8-9)

But while the Councils, as has been shown, lay down so emphatically
the inspiration of Scripture in respect to 'faith and morals,' it is remarkable that they do not say a word directly as to inspiration in matters of
fact. Yet are we therefore to conclude that the record of facts in Scripture
does not come under the guarantee of its inspiration? We are not so to
conclude ... Scripture is inspired, not only in faith and morals, but in all
its parts which bear on faith, including matters of fact. (*OIS*, sec. 13)

Nor is it *de fide* ... that inspired men, at the time when they speak from
inspiration, should always know that the Divine Spirit is visiting them.
The Psalms are inspired; but, when David, in the outpouring of his deep
contrition, disburdened himself before his God in the words of the *Miserere*, could he, possibly, while uttering them, have been directly conscious
that every word he uttered was not simply his, but another's? Did he not
think that he was personally asking forgiveness and spiritual help? (*OIS*,
sec. 21)

Moses may have incorporated in his manuscript as much from foreign
documents as is commonly maintained by the critical school; yet the existing Pentateuch, with the miracles which it contains, may still (from
that personal inspiration which belongs to a prophet) have flowed from
his mind and hand on to his composition. He new-made and authenti-
cated what till then was no matter of faith. This being considered, it follows that a book may be, and may be accepted as, inspired, though not a
word of it is an original document. (*OIS*, sec. 23)

Nor does it matter whether one or two Isaiahs wrote the book which
bears that Prophet's name; the Church, without settling this point, pronounces it inspired in respect of faith and morals, both Isaiahs being
inspired; and, if this be assured to us, all other questions are irrelevant

and unnecessary. Nor do the Councils forbid our holding that there are interpolations or additions in the sacred text, say, the last chapter of the Pentateuch, provided they are held to come from an inspired penman, such as Esdras, and are thereby authoritative in faith and morals. (*OIS*, sec. 24)

These two Councils [Trent, Vatican I] decide that the Scriptures are inspired, and inspired throughout, but they do not add to their decision that they are inspired by an immediately divine act, but they say that they are inspired through the instrumentality of inspired men; that they are inspired in all matters of faith and morals, meaning thereby, not only theological doctrine, but also the historical and prophetical narratives which they contain, from Genesis to the Acts of the Apostles; and lastly, that, being inspired because written by inspired men, they have a human side, which manifests itself in language, style, tone of thought, character, intellectual peculiarities, and such infirmities, not sinful, as belong to our nature, and which in unimportant matters may issue in what in doctrinal definitions is called an *obiter dictum*. (*SE*, Essay II, sec. 30, May 1884)

I do not, then, feel it any difficulty when I am told by the infallible voice of more than one Ecumenical Council, that the writers of Scripture, whether under the New Covenant or the Old, ethical and religious writers as they were, have had assigned to them a gift and promise in teaching which is in keeping with this antecedent idea which we form of the work of Evangelists and Prophets. If they are to teach us our duty to God and man, it is natural that inspiration should be promised them in matters of faith and morals; and if such is the actual promise, it is natural that Councils should insist upon its being such; — but how otherwise are we to account for the remarkable stress laid on the inspiration of Scripture in matters of faith and morals, both in the Vatican and at Trent, if after all faith and morals, in view of inspiration, are only parts of a larger gift? Why was it not simply said once for all that in all matters of faith or fact, not only in all its parts, but on every subject whatever, Scripture was inspired? If nothing short of the highest and exact truth on all subjects must be contemplated as the gift conveyed to the inspired writers, what is gained by singling out faith and morals as the legitimate province of Inspiration, and thereby throwing the wider and more complete view of Scripture truth into the shade? (*SE*, Essay II, sec. 32, May 1884)

When I say that the writers of Scripture were divinely inspired in all matters of faith and morals, what matters are included in the range of such inspiration? Are historical statements of fact included? It makes me smile to think that any one could fancy me so absurd as to exclude them, especially since in a long passage in my Essay I have expressly included them. (*SE*, Essay II, sec. 33, May 1884)

The subject which naturally comes next to be considered is that of the possible presence of *obiter dicta* in inspired Scripture: by *obiter dicta* being meant phrases, clauses, or sentences in Scripture about matters of mere fact, which, as not relating to faith and morals, may without violence be referred to the human element in its composition ... And next, why does he always associate an *obiter dictum* with the notion of error or moral infirmity, or, even as he sometimes expresses himself, with 'falsehood'? At least what right has he to attribute such an association to me? I have implied no such thing. I very much doubt whether I have even once used the word 'error' in connexion with the phrase 'obiter dictum,' though (as I shall show directly) no harm follows if I have ... *Obiter dictum* means, as I understand it, a phrase or sentence which, whether a statement of literal fact or not, is not from the circumstances binding on our faith. The force of the 'obiter' is negative, not positive. To say, 'I do not accept a statement as a literal fact,' is not all one with saying that it is *not* a fact; I can *not hold* without *holding not*. The very comfort of an *obiter dictum* to the Catholic, whether in its relation to infallibility or to inspiration, whether in dogma or in Scripture, is, that it enables him in controversy to pass by a difficulty, which else may be pressed on him without his having the learning perhaps, or the knowledge, or the talent, to answer it; that it enables him to profess neither Yes nor No in questions which are beyond him, and on which nothing depends. In difficult questions it leaves the Catholic student in peace ... let us consider his [St. Thomas Aquinas'] words: ... 'In all matters which Scripture delivers after the manner of historical narrative, we must hold, as a fundamental fact, the truth of the history.' ... when St. Thomas says that the test of historical truth is the inspired penman's writing in the historical style, he certainly implies that there are, or might be, statements of fact, which in their literal sense come short of the historic style and of historic truth, or are what I should call *obiter dicta*. I repeat, *obiter dicta* are but 'unhistoric statements.' ... I ... see little difficulty, supposing (which of course he does not grant) that the literal sense was not historic, or was doubtful, in interpreting the whole account spiritually or even figuratively. Therefore, if the case occurred of small inaccuracies of fact in Scripture history, instead of countenancing me in saying that, in matters which did not infringe upon faith and morals, such apparent error was of no serious consequence, I grant that he would have preferred, (and with St. Augustine,) to interpret a passage, so characterised, in a spiritual sense, or according to some other secondary sense, which he thinks it possible to give to Scripture. Here it is, I grant, that I should not have his countenance; he would not indeed forbid me to say that a statement was *literally* inaccurate, but he would rather wish me to find some interpretation for it which would give it an edifying sense. (*SE*, Essay II, sec. 34, May 1884)

[I]f the whole of Scripture in all its parts is inspired, how can inspiration be restricted to the matters of faith and morals? Yet I conceive this difficulty admits of an easy reply ... still we may ask the question, In what respect, and for what purpose? ... though Scripture be plenarily inspired, it is a question still, for what purposes, and in what way. (*SE*, Essay II, sec. 36, May 1884)

He says that error cannot co-exist with inspiration, more than sin with grace; but grace *can* co-exist with sin. His parallel just turns against him. Good Christians are each 'the Temple of God,' 'partakers of the Divine Nature,' nay 'gods,' and they are said '*portare Deum in corpore suo;*' and priests, I consider, have not less holiness than others; yet every priest in his daily Mass asks pardon '*pro innumerabilibus peccatis et offensionibus et negligentiis meis.*' Grace brings a soul nearer to God than inspiration, for Balaam and Caiphas were inspired; yet the Professor tells us that, though sin is possible in spite of grace, error is impossible because of inspiration. (*SE*, Essay II, sec. 37, May 1884)

Scripture, Canon of

[W]e receive through Tradition both the Bible itself, and the doctrine that it is divinely inspired ... To deride Tradition therefore as something irrational or untrustworthy in itself, is to weaken the foundation of our own faith in Scripture. (VM i, ch. 1)

[T]he first Father who expressly mentions Commemorations for the Dead in Christ ... is Tertullian, about a hundred years after St. John's death. This, it is said, is not authority early enough to prove that that Ordinance is Apostolical, though succeeding Fathers, Origen, St. Cyprian, Eusebius, St. Cyril of Jerusalem, etc., bear witness to it ever so strongly ... yet Tertullian is also the first who refers to St. Paul's Epistle to Philemon, and even he without quoting or naming it ... Now, I ask, why do we receive the Epistle to Philemon as St. Paul's, and not the Commemorations for the faithful departed as Apostolical also? ... If it be said that from historical records we have good reasons for thinking that the Epistle of St. Paul to Philemon, with his other Epistles, was read from time immemorial in Church, ... quite as much evidence can be given for the solemn Commemorations of the Dead in the Holy Eucharist which I speak of. They too were in use in the Church from time immemorial. (*TT* #85, Sep. 1838)

Again: the early Church with one voice testifies in favour of Episcopacy, as an ordinance especially pleasing to God. Ignatius, the very disciple of the Apostles, speaks in the clearest and strongest terms; and those who follow fully corroborate his statements for three or four hundred years. And besides this, we know the fact, that a succession of Bishops from the Apostles did exist in all the Churches all that time. At the end of that time, one Father, St. Jerome, in writing controversially, had some strong expressions against the divine origin of the ordinance. And this is all that can be said in favour of any other regimen. Now, on the other hand, what is the case as regards the Epistle to the Hebrews? Though received in the

East, it was not received in the Latin Churches, till that same St. Jerome's time. St. Irenaeus either does not affirm or actually denies that it is St. Paul's. Tertullian ascribes it to St. Barnabas. Caius excluded it from his list. St. Hippolytus does not receive it. St. Cyprian is silent about it. It is doubtful whether St. Optatus received it. Now, that this important Epistle is part of the inspired word of God, there is no doubt. But why? Because the testimony of the fourth and fifth centuries, when Christians were at leisure to examine the question thoroughly, is altogether in its favour. I know of no other reason, and I consider this to be quite sufficient: but with what consistency do persons receive this Epistle as inspired, yet deny that Episcopacy is a divinely ordained means of grace? (*TT* #85, Sep. 1838)

Again: the Epistles to the Thessalonians are quoted by six writers in the first two hundred years from St. John's death; first, at the end of the first hundred, by three Fathers, Irenaeus, Clement, and Tertullian; and are by implication acknowledged in the lost work of Caius, at the same time, and are in Origen's list some years after. On the other hand, the Lord's table is always called an Altar, and is called a Table only in one single passage of a single Father, during the first three centuries. It is called Altar in four out of the seven Epistles of St. Ignatius. It is called Altar by St. Clement of Rome, by St. Irenaeus, Tertullian, St. Cyprian, Origen, Eusebius, St. Athanasius, St. Ambrose, St. Gregory Nazianzen, St. Optatus, St. Jerome, St. Chrysostom, and St. Austin. It is once called Table by St. Dionysius of Alexandria ... I do not know on what ground we admit the Epistles to the Thessalonians to be the writing of St. Paul, yet deny that the use of Altars is Apostolic. (*TT* #85, Sep. 1838)

Again: much stress, as I have said, is laid by objectors on the fact that there is so little evidence concerning Catholic doctrine in the very first years of Christianity. Now, how does this objection stand, as regards the Canon of the New Testament? The New Testament consists of twenty-seven books in all, though of varying importance. Of these, fourteen are not mentioned at all till from eighty to one hundred years after St. John's death, in which number are the Acts, the Second to the Corinthians, the Galatians, the Colossians, the Two to the Thessalonians, and St. James.

Of the other thirteen, five, viz., St. John's Gospel, the Philippians, the First of Timothy, the Hebrews, and the First of John, are quoted but by one writer during the same period. Lastly, St. Irenaeus, at the close of the second century, quotes all the books of the New Testament but five, and deservedly stands very high as a witness. Now, why may not so learned and holy a man, and so close on the Apostles, stand also as a witness of some doctrines which he takes for granted, as the invisible but real Presence in the Holy Eucharist, the use of Catholic tradition in ascertaining revealed truth, and the powers committed to the Church? If men then will indulge that eclectic spirit which chooses part and rejects part of the primitive Church system, I do not see what is to keep them from choosing part and rejecting part of the Canon of Scripture. (*TT* #85, Sep. 1838)

It seems, then, that the objections which can be made to the evidence for the Church doctrines are such as also lie against the Canon of Scripture; so that if they avail against the one, they avail against both. (*TT* #85, Sep. 1838)

[T]he Church doctrines may also be proved from Scripture, but no one can say that the Canon of Scripture itself can be proved from Scripture to be a Canon; no one can say, that Scripture anywhere enumerates all the books of which it is composed, and puts its seal upon them ever so indirectly, even if it might allowably bear witness to itself. (*TT* #85, Sep. 1838)

I must explain myself, when I say that we depend for the Canon and Creed upon the fourth and fifth centuries. We depend upon them thus: As to Scripture, former centuries certainly do not speak distinctly, frequently, or unanimously, except of some chief books, as the Gospels: but still we see in them, as we believe, an ever-growing tendency and approximation to that full agreement which we find in the fifth. (*TT* #85, Sep. 1838)

Lower, as you will, the evidence for the Creed; you do nothing thereby towards raising the evidence for the Canon. The first Fathers, in the midst of the persecutions, had not, as I have said, time and opportunity to ascertain always what was inspired and what was not; and, since nothing but an agreement of many, of different countries, will prove to us what the Canon is, we must betake ourselves of necessity to the fourth and fifth centuries, to those centuries which did hold those very doctrines, which, it seems, are to be rejected as superstitions and corruptions. But if the Church then was in that miserable state of superstition, which belief in those doctrines is supposed to imply, then I must contend, that blind bigotry and ignorance were not fit judges of what was inspired and what was not. I will not trust the judgment of a worldly-minded partizan, or a crafty hypocrite, or a credulous fanatic in this matter. Unless then you allow those centuries to be tolerably free from doctrinal corruptions, I conceive, you cannot use them as witnesses of the canonicity of the Old and New Testament, as we now have them; but, if you do consider the fourth and fifth centuries enlightened enough to decide on the Canon, then I want to know why you call them not enlightened in point of doctrine. (*TT* #85, Sep. 1838)

The degrees of evidence are very various for one book and another ... For instance, as to the Epistle of St. James. It is true, it is contained in the old Syriac version in the second century; but Origen, in the third century, is the first writer who distinctly mentions it among the Greeks; and it is not quoted by name by any Latin till the fourth. St. Jerome speaks of its gaining credit 'by degrees, in process of time.' Eusebius says no more than that it had been, up to his time, acknowledged by the majority; and he classes it with the Shepherd of St. Hermas and the Epistle of St. Barnabas ... Again, St. Jerome tells us, that in his day, towards A.D. 400, the Greek Church rejected the Apocalypse, but the Latin received it ... On what ground, then, do we receive the Canon as it comes to us, but on the authority of the Church of the fourth and fifth centuries? The Church at that era decided,—not merely bore testimony, but passed a judgment on former testimony,—decided, that certain books were of authority. (*Dev.*, Part I: ch. 4, sec. 1)

Scripture, Material Sufficiency of

Now that the doctrine of the Atonement is so essential a doctrine that none other is more so, (true as it is,) does not at all hinder other doctrines in their own place being so essential that they may not be moved one inch from it, or made to converge towards that doctrine ever so little, beyond the sanction of Scripture. (*TT* #73, 1836)

We do not for an instant suppose that the Catholic doctrine is not in Scripture, and that clear and unprejudiced readers will not find it there. ('Apostolical Tradition,' *British Critic,* Vol. 19, July 1836; in *Ess.* i, sec. III)

We do not deny that many things may be true which are not in Scripture; but we deny such are points of what is emphatically called the *faith,* i.e. points necessary to be believed in order to salvation ... we do not think that she may declare points to be necessary to be believed in order to salvation, and may act accordingly, unless she professes to derive them from Scripture. (Review of *Lectures on the Principal Doctrines and Practices of the Catholic Church,* by Nicholas Wiseman, *British Critic,* vol. 19, Oct. 1836)

The sixth Article speaks as follows: 'Holy Scripture containeth all things necessary to salvation, so that whatsoever is not read therein, nor may be proved thereby, is not to be required of any man, that it should be believed as an article of the faith, or be thought requisite or necessary to salvation.' Now, this statement is very plain and clear except in one point, viz., who is to be the *judge* what is and what is not contained in Scripture. Our Church is silent on this point, — very emphatically so. This is worth observing; in truth, she does not admit, strictly speaking, of any judge at all. (*VM* i, ch. 11)

Holy Scripture contains all things necessary to salvation, that is, either as being read therein or deducible therefrom; not that Scripture is the only ground of the faith, or ordinarily the guide into it and teacher of it, or the source of all religious truth whatever, or the systematizer of it, or the instrument of unfolding, illustrating, enforcing, and applying it; but that it is the document of ultimate appeal in controversy, and the touchstone of all doctrine. (*VM* i, ch. 13)

[A]t least as regards matters of faith, it *does* (as we in common with all Protestants hold) contain all that is necessary for salvation; it has been overruled to do so by Him who inspired it. By parallel acts of power, He both secretly inspired the books, and secretly formed them into a perfect rule or canon ... It is enough that Scripture has been overruled to contain the whole Christian faith, and that the early Church so taught. (*TT* #85, Sep. 1838)

Doubtless, Scripture *contains* all things necessary to be *believed*; but there may be things *contained* in it, which are not *on the surface*, and things which belong to the *ritual* and not to *belief*. Points of faith may lie *under* the surface, points of observance need not be in Scripture *at all*. (*TT* #85, Sep. 1838)

The Tracts nowhere say that anything need be believed in order to salvation which is not contained in, or [cannot] be proved from Scripture. (*Keb.*, 207; Letter of 4 March 1843)

Of no doctrine whatever, which does not actually contradict what has been delivered, can it be peremptorily asserted that it is not in Scripture ... It may be added that, in matter of fact, all the definitions or received judgments of the early and medieval Church rest upon definite, even though sometimes obscure sentences of Scripture. Thus Purgatory may appeal to the 'saving by fire,' and 'entering through much tribulation into the kingdom of God;' the communication of the merits of the Saints to our 'receiving a prophet's reward' for 'receiving a prophet in the name of a prophet,' and 'a righteous man's reward' for 'receiving a righteous man in the name of a righteous man;' the Real Presence to 'This is My Body;' Absolution to 'Whosesoever sins ye remit, they are remitted;' Extreme Unction to 'Anointing him with oil in the Name of the Lord;' Voluntary poverty to 'Sell all that thou hast;' obedience to 'He was in subjection to His parents.' (*Dev.*, Part I: ch. 2)

Nor am I aware that later Post-tridentine writers deny that the whole Catholic faith may be proved from Scripture, though they would certainly maintain that it is not to be found on the surface of it, nor in such sense that it may be gained from Scripture without the aid of Tradition. (*Dev.*, Part II: ch. 7, sec. 4)

Again, there is another principle of Scripture interpretation which we should hold as well as you, viz., when we speak of a doctrine being contained in Scripture, we do not necessarily mean that it is contained there in direct categorical terms, but that there is no satisfactory way of accounting for the language and expressions of the sacred writers, concerning the subject-matter in question, except to suppose that they held concerning it the opinion which we hold, — that they would not have spoken as they have spoken, *unless* they held it. For myself I have ever felt the truth of this principle, as regards the Scripture proof of the Holy Trinity; I should not have found out that doctrine in the sacred text without previous traditional teaching; but, when once it is suggested from without, it commends itself as the one true interpretation, from its appositeness, — because no other view of doctrine, which can be ascribed to the inspired writers, so happily solves the obscurities and seeming inconsistencies of their teaching. (*Dif.* ii, Letter to Pusey, ch. 3, 1865)

Sheol / Hades / Limbo of the Fathers

There is another word used in Scripture to express the abode of just men made perfect, which gives us the same meaning. Our Lord is said in the Creed to have 'descended into *hell*,' which word has a very different sense there from that which it commonly bears. Our Saviour, as we suppose, did not go to the abyss assigned to the fallen Angels, but to those mysterious mansions where the souls of all men await the judgment. That He went to the abode of blessed spirits is evident, from His words addressed to the robber on the cross, when He also called it paradise; that He went to some other place besides paradise, may be conjectured from St. Peter's saying, He 'went and preached to the spirits in prison, who had once been disobedient.' [1 Pet. iii. 19, 20.] The circumstance then that these two abodes of disembodied good and bad, are called by one name, Hades, or (as we happen to express it) hell, seems clearly to show that paradise is not the same as Heaven, but a resting-place at the foot of it. Let it be further remarked, that Samuel, when brought from the dead, in the witch's cavern, said, 'Why hast thou disquieted me, to bring me *up*?' [1 Sam. xxviii. 15.] words which would seem quite inconsistent with his being then already in Heaven. (*PS* iii, Sermon 25: 'The Intermediate State,' 1 November 1835)

Sin, Mortal

If we do so sin, we *cease* to be in that state of salvation; we fall back into a state resembling our original state of wrath, and must pass back again from wrath to grace (if it be so), as we best may, in such ways as God has appointed: … some men of name in the world have, before now, laid it down as a great and high principle, that there is no mortal sin but one, and that is want of faith; and have hereby meant, not that he who commits mortal sin cannot be said to have faith, but that he who has faith cannot be said to commit mortal sin; or, to speak more clearly, they have, in fact, defined a state of salvation to be nothing more or less than a state *in which* our sins are forgiven; a state of mere acceptance, not of substantial holiness. Persons who hold these opinions, consider that the great difference between a state of nature and a state of salvation is, that, in a state of nature when we sin, we are not forgiven (which is true); but that, in a state of salvation, when we sin, our sins are forgiven us, because we *are* in that state … they who do sin are *not* in a state of grace. For instance, 'If we say that we have fellowship with Him, and walk in darkness, we lie, and do not the truth.' 'He that saith he is in the light, and hateth his brother, is in darkness even until now.' Again, 'Whosoever committeth sin, transgresseth also the law, for sin is the transgression of the law … Whosoever sinneth, hath not seen Him, neither known Him.' 'He that committeth sin is of the devil.' 'Whosoever transgresseth, and abideth not in the doctrine of Christ, hath not God.' [1 John i. 6; ii. 9; iii. 4, 6, 8. 2 John 9.] … If we do commit greater sins, we have not faith. Faith we cannot use to blot out the greater sins, for faith we have not at all, if we commit such. That faith which has not power over our hearts to keep us from transgressing, has not power with God to keep Him from punishing. (*PS* v, Sermon 13: 'The State of Salvation,' 18 March 1838)

This distinction in the character of sins, viz., that some argue absence of faith and involve the loss of God's favour, and that others do not, is a very important one to insist upon, even though we cannot in all cases draw the line and say what sins imply the want of faith, and what do not; because, if we know that there *are* sins which do throw us out of grace, though we do not know *which* they are, this knowledge, limited as it is, will, through God's mercy, put us on our guard against acts of sin of any kind; both from the dread we shall feel lest these in particular, whatever they are, may be of that fearful nature, and next, from knowing that at least they tend that way ... I would force upon men's notice that there are sins which do forfeit grace; and then if, as is objected, that we cannot draw the line between one kind of sin and another, this very circumstance will make us shrink not only from transgressions, but also from infirmities. From hatred and abhorrence of large sins, we shall, please God, go on to hate and abhor the small. (*PS* v, Sermon 14: 'Transgressions and Infirmities,' 25 March 1838)

The poor infant passes through his two, or three, or five years of innocence, blessed in that he cannot yet sin; but at length (oh woeful day!) he begins to realise the distinction between right and wrong. Alas! sooner or later, for the age varies, but sooner or later the awful day has come; he has the power, the great, the dreadful, the awful power of discerning and pronouncing a thing to be wrong, and yet doing it. He has a distinct view that he shall grievously offend his Maker and his Judge by doing this or that; and while he is really able to keep from it, he is at liberty to choose it, and to commit it. He has the dreadful power of committing a mortal sin. Young as he is, he has as true an apprehension of that sin, and can give as real a consent, as did the evil spirit, when he fell. (*Mix.*, Discourse 1: 'The Salvation of the Hearer the Motive of the Preacher,' 2 February 1849)

Sola Scriptura / Bible Alone (Falsity of)

[T]he doctrines in question have never been learned merely from Scripture. Surely the Sacred Volume was never intended, and is not adapted, to teach us our creed; however certain it is that we can prove our creed from it, when it has once been taught us, and in spite of individual producible exceptions to the general rule. (*Ari.*, ch. 1, sec. 3)

Such men act, in the solemn concerns of religion, the part of the self-sufficient natural philosopher, who should obstinately reject Newton's theory of gravitation, and endeavour, with talents inadequate to the task, to strike out some theory of motion by himself. The insufficiency of the mere private study of Holy Scripture for arriving at the exact and entire truth which Scripture really contains, is shown by the fact, that creeds and teachers have ever been divinely provided, and by the discordance of opinions which exists wherever those aids are thrown aside; as it is also shown by the very structure of the Bible itself. (*Ari.*, ch. 1, sec. 3)

Their first principle really is inconsistent with there being any certainties in Revelation whatever; for, if nothing is to be held as revealed but what every one perceives to be in Scripture, there is nothing that can be so held, considering that in matter of fact there is no universal agreement as to what Scripture teaches and what it does not teach: and why are one man's opinions to be ruled by the readings of another? The right which each man has of judging for himself *ipso facto* deprives him of the right of judging for other inquirers. He is bound to tolerate all other creeds by virtue of the very principle on which he claims to choose his own. Thus ultra-Protestantism infallibly leads to Latitudinarianism. ('Apostolical Tradition,' *British Critic*, Vol. 19, July 1836; in *Ess.* i, sec. III)

But when the Ultra-Protestant comes upon them, and catches up and perverts their words, and says, 'You admit the Bible is a rule of faith; therefore it is our sole *guide*,' we answer, as our Church has ever answered, 'No; it is our sole document, basis of proof, record, standard of appeal, touchstone of the faith, not the sole guide, for the Church is a guide, having 'authority in matters of faith." (Review of *Lectures on the Principal Doctrines and Practices of the Catholic Church*, by Nicholas Wiseman, *British Critic*, vol. 19, Oct. 1836)

A widely extended shape of Protestantism in this country, and that which professes to be the most religious of all, maintains ... that Scripture is the only divine instrument given us; that everything else is human; that the Church is human; that rites and sacraments are human; that teachers are human; that the Fathers are but fallible men; that creeds and confessions, primitive faith, Apostolical Traditions, are human systems, and doctrines of men; that there is no need of proving this in particular instances, because it is an elementary principle, which holds good of them all; and that till we acknowledge and accept this principle we are still in the flesh. It follows that to inquire about the early Church, the consent of Fathers, uninterrupted testimonies, or the decisions of Councils, to inquire when the Church first became corrupt, or to make the early writers a comment upon the inspired text, are but melancholy and pernicious follies ... divine influence, but not in Baptism, is supposed, according to this popular form of Protestantism, to assure the soul without proof that the Bible is the only instrument of divine knowledge. (VM i, ch. 6)

[W]ere the whole new creation against him, Bishops, Doctors, Martyrs, Saints, the Holy Church Universal, the very companions of the Apostles, the unanimous suffrage of the most distinct times and places, and the most gifted and holiest men, yet according to the popular doctrine, though he was aware of this, he ought ultimately to rest in his own interpretations of Scripture, and to follow his private Judgment, however sorry he might be to differ from such authorities. (VM i, ch. 11)

[T]hey desire more adequate and explicit *Scripture proof* of its truth. They find that the proof is *rested* by us on Scripture, and therefore they require more explicit *Scripture proof*. They say, 'All this that you say about the Church is very specious, and very attractive; but where is it to be found in the inspired Volume?' And that it is *not* found there (that is, I mean not found as fully as it might be), seems to them proved at once by the simple fact, that all persons (I may say all, for the exceptions are very few),—all those who try to form their Creed by Scripture only, fall away from the Church and her doctrines, and join one or other sect or party, as if showing that, whatever is or is not scriptural, at least the Church, by consent of all men, is not so. (*TT* #85, Sep. 1838)

There is not a single text in the Bible enjoining infant baptism: the Scripture warrant on which we baptize infants consists of inferences carefully made from various texts ... Again, there is not a single text telling us to keep holy the first day of the week, and that *instead* of the seventh ... There is nothing on the surface of Scripture to prove that the sacredness conferred in the beginning on the seventh day now by transference attaches to the first. Again, there is scarcely a text enjoining our going to Church for joint worship ... our Lord did not use social prayer: even when with His disciples He prayed by Himself; and His directions in Matt. vi. about *private* prayer, with the silence which He observes about *public*, might be as plausibly adduced as an argument against public, as the same kind of silence in Scripture concerning turning to the east, or making the sign of the Cross, or concerning commemorations for the dead in Christ, accompanied with its warnings against formality and ceremonial abuses, is now commonly urged as an argument against these latter usages ... Once more: —On how many texts does the prohibition of polygamy depend, if we set about counting them? (*TT* #85, Sep. 1838)

The inquirer who rejects a doctrine which has but one text in its favour, on the ground that if it were important it would have more, may, even in a case when a doctrine is mentioned often, always find occasion to wonder that still it is not mentioned in this or that particular place, where it might be expected. (*TT* #85, Sep. 1838)

If the Eucharist is never distinctly called a Sacrifice, or Christian Ministers never called Priests, still, let me ask (as I have already done), is the Holy Ghost ever expressly called God in Scripture? Nowhere; we infer it from what is said then; we compare parallel passages. If the words Altar, Absolution, or Succession, are not in Scripture (supposing it), neither is the word Trinity. Again: how do we know that the New Testament is inspired? does it anywhere declare this of itself? nowhere; *how*, then, do we know it? we infer it from the circumstance that the very office of the

Apostles who wrote it was to publish the Christian Revelation, and from the Old Testament being said by St. Paul to be inspired.

Again: whence do Protestants derive their common notion, that every one may gain his knowledge of revealed truth from Scripture for himself? ... Again: on how many texts does the doctrine of Original Sin rest, that is, the doctrine that we are individually born under God's displeasure, in consequence of the sin of Adam? on one or two. (*TT* #85, Sep. 1838)

[T]here must be some fault somewhere in this specious argument; that it does not follow that a doctrine or rite is not divine, because it is not directly stated in Scripture; that there are some wise and unknown reasons for doctrines being, as we find them, not clearly stated there. To be sure, I might take the other alternative, and run the full length of scepticism, and openly deny that any doctrine or duty, whatever it is, is divine, which is not stated in Scripture beyond all contradiction and objection. But for many reasons I cannot get myself to do this. (*TT* #85, Sep. 1838)

Why, for instance, should a certain number of letters, more or less private, written by St. Paul and others to particular persons or bodies, contain the whole of what the Holy Spirit taught them? ... You will say that its writers wrote in order to communicate religious truth; true, but not all religious truth: that is the point. They did not sit down with a design to commit to paper all they had to say on the whole subject. (*TT* #85, Sep. 1838)

The argument which has been last engaging us is this: Objection is made to the indirectness of the evidence from Scripture on which the peculiar Church doctrines are proved; — I have answered, that sacred *history* is for the most part marked by as much apparent inconsistency, as recorded in one part of Scripture and another, as there is inconsistency as regards *doctrine* in the respective informations of Scripture and the Church; one event being told us here, another there; so that we have to compare, compile, reconcile, adjust. As then we do not complain of the history being conveyed in distinct, and at times conflicting, documents, so too we have no fair reason for complaining of the obscurities and intricacies under which doctrine is revealed through its two channels. (*TT* #85, Sep. 1838)

The only reason commonly given is, that their Christianity contains many notions and many usages and rites not *in* Scripture, and which, because not *in* Scripture, are to be considered, it seems, as if *against* Scripture. But this surely is no sound argument, unless it is true also that the canonicity itself of the Old and New Testament, not being declared in Scripture, is therefore unscriptural. (*TT* #85, Sep. 1838)

[T]he common complaint of Protestants against the Church of Rome is, not simply that she has added to the primitive or the Scriptural doctrine, (for this they do themselves,) but that she contradicts it, and moreover imposes her additions as fundamental truths under sanction of an anathema. For themselves they deduce by quite as subtle a method, and act upon doctrines as implicit and on reasons as little analyzed in time past, as Catholic schoolmen. What prominence has the Royal Supremacy in the New Testament, or the lawfulness of bearing arms, or the duty of public worship, or the substitution of the first day of the week for the seventh, or infant baptism, to say nothing of the fundamental principle that the Bible and the Bible only is the religion of Protestants? These doctrines and usages, true or not, which is not the question here, are surely not gained by the direct use and immediate application of Scripture, nor by a mere exercise of argument upon words and sentences placed before the eyes, but by the unconscious growth of ideas suggested by the letter and habitual to the mind. And, indeed, when we turn to the consideration of particular doctrines on which Scripture lays the greatest stress, we shall see that it is absolutely impossible for them to remain in the mere letter of Scripture, if they are to be more than mere words, and to convey a definite idea to the recipient. When it is declared that 'the Word became flesh,' three wide questions open upon us on the very announcement. What is meant by 'the Word,' what by 'flesh,' what by 'became'? The answers to these involve a process of investigation, and are developments. Moreover, when they have been made, they will suggest a series of secondary questions; and thus at length a multitude of propositions is the result, which

gather round the inspired sentence of which they come, giving it externally the form of a doctrine, and creating or deepening the idea of it in the
mind. (*Dev.*, Part I: ch. 2)

[I]t soon turned out that it was a new idea to the gentleman in question, that I was not bound to prove the point in debate simply by Scripture; he considered that Scripture was to be the sole basis of the discussion. This was quite another thing ... had I accepted this gratuitous and
officious proposition, you see I should have been simply recognising a
Protestant principle, which I disown. He would not controvert with me
at all, unless I subscribed to a doctrine which I believe to be, not only a
dangerous, but an absurd error; and, because I would not allow him to
assume what it was his business to prove, before he brought it forward,
and because I challenged him to prove that Scripture was, as he assumed,
the Rule of Faith, he turned away as happy and self-satisfied as if he had
gained a victory. That all truth is contained in Scripture was his first principle; he thought none but an idiot could doubt it; none but a Jesuit could
deny it; he thought it axiomatic; he thought that to offer proof was even
a profanation of so self-evident a point, and that to demand it was a *re-
ductio ad absurdum* of the person demanding; — but this, I repeat, was no
extraordinary instance of Protestant argumentation; it occurs every other
day ... Let it be observed, that the fallacy involved in the Protestant Rule
of Faith is this, — that its upholders fancy, most unnaturally, that the accidental and occasional writings of an Apostle convey to them of necessity
his whole mind. It does not occur to them to ask themselves, whether, as
he has in part committed his teaching to writing so possibly he may not
have expressed it in part through other channels also. (*PPC*, Lecture 8)

Consider what is called Scriptural Religion, or the Religion of the
Bible. The fault which the theologian, over and above the question of
private judgment, will find with a religion logically drawn from Scripture
only, is, not that it is not true, as far as it goes, but that it is not the whole
truth; that it consists of only some out of the whole circle of theological
doctrines, and that, even in the case of those which it includes, it does not
always invest them with certainty, but only with probability. If, indeed,

the Religion of the Bible is made subservient to Theology, it is but a specimen of useful induction; but if it is set up, as something complete in itself against Theology, it is turned into a mischievous paralogism. (*IU*, Part II, ch. 7: 'Christianity and Physical Science,' November 1855)

There is another great conflict of first principles, and that among Christians, which has occupied a large space in our domestic history, during the last thirty or forty years, and that is the controversy about the Rule of Faith. I notice it as affording an instance of an assumption so deeply sunk into the popular mind, that it is a work of great difficulty to obtain from its maintainers an acknowledgment that it is an assumption. That Scripture is the Rule of Faith is in fact an assumption so congenial to the state of mind and course of thought usual among Protestants, that it seems to them rather a truism than a truth. If they are in controversy with Catholics on any point of faith, they at once ask, 'Where do you find it in Scripture?' and if Catholics reply, as they must do, that it is not necessarily in Scripture in order to be true, nothing can persuade them that such an answer is not an evasion, and a triumph to themselves. Yet it is by no means self-evident that all religious truth is to be found in a number of works, however sacred, which were written at different times, and did not always form one book; and in fact it is a doctrine very hard to prove. (GA, Part II, ch. 9, sec. 3)

At Ephesus, for example, the General Council did not refer to a single passage of Scripture before condemning Nestorius, but principally to the Creed of Nicaea, and to ten or twelve passages from the Fathers. And in the fourth General Council at Chalcedon the language of its members was from first to last, 'to keep to the faith of Nicaea, of Constantinople, of Athanasius, Cyril, Hilary, Basil,' &c., Scripture being hardly once mentioned. (VM i, Lecture 13; footnote 2 from 1877)

Total Depravity

[H]ere again some men go wrong; and while they go so far as to acknowledge that there is a new state, or kingdom, into which souls must be brought, in order to salvation, yet they consider it as a state, not of holiness and righteousness, but merely or mainly of acceptance with God. It has been maintained by some persons, that human nature, even when regenerate, is not, and cannot be, really holy; nay, that it is idle to suppose that, even with the aid of the Holy Spirit, it can do any thing really good in any degree; that our best actions are sins; and that we are always sinning, not only in slighter matters, but so as to need pardon in all we do, in the same sense in which we needed it when we were as yet unregenerate; and, consequently, that it is vain to try to be holy and righteous, or, rather, that it is presumptuous. (*PS* v, Sermon 13: 'The State of Salvation,' 18 March 1838)

As to the difference of 'sinful tendencies' and 'tendencies towards sin,' the two phrases seem to mark the difference between the Catholic and Protestant views of original sin respectively. We do not hold human nature to be sinful—Protestants on the contrary speak of an innate radical corruption and wickedness. We consider human nature so debilitated, wounded, sick, that it is seen to fall into sin without divine grace—but not such that, as in the virtuous heathen, it may not do works morally good, though not such works as (according to the promises of God) has [sic] the reward of eternal life. (*LD* xxxii, 330; Letter to J. J. Murphy, 1 June 1873)

Tractarianism; Oxford Movement; *Via Media*

It is clear, then, that the English Church holds all that the primitive Church held, even in ceremonies, *except* there be some particular reasons assignable for not doing so in this or that instance; ... Thus the Church stands in a *Via Media*; the first five Articles being directed against extreme Protestantism, the remaining ones against Rome ... our Apostolical communion inherits, as the promises, so the faith, enjoyed by the Saints in every age; the faith which Ignatius, Cyprian, and Gregory received from the Apostles. (*TT* #82, 3 March 1837)

Protestantism and Popery are real religions; no one can doubt about them; they have furnished the mould in which nations have been cast: but

the *Via Media,* viewed as an integral system, has never had existence except on paper; it is known, not positively but negatively, in its differences
from the rival creeds, not in its own properties; and can only be described
as a third system, neither the one nor the other, but with something of
each, cutting between them, and, as if with a critical fastidiousness, trifling
with them both, and boasting to be nearer Antiquity than either. What is
this but to fancy a road over mountains and rivers, which has never been
cut? When we profess our *Via Media,* as the very truth of the Apostles, we
seem to bystanders to be mere antiquarians or pedants, amusing ourselves
with illusions or learned subtleties, and unable to grapple with things as
they are. They accuse us of tendering no proof to show that our view is not
self-contradictory, and if set in motion, would not fall to pieces, or start
off in different directions at once ... To take for instance the subject of
Private Judgment; our theory here is neither Protestant nor Roman; and
has never been duly realized. Our opponents ask, What is it? Is it more
than a set of words and phrases, of exceptions and limitations made for
each successive emergency, of principles which contradict each other? It
cannot be denied there is force in these representations, though I would
not adopt them to their full extent; it still remains to be tried whether
what is called Anglo-Catholicism, the religion of Andrewes, Laud, Hammond, Butler, and Wilson, is capable of being professed, acted on, and
maintained on a large sphere of action and through a sufficient period, or
whether it be a mere modification or transition-state either of Romanism
or of popular Protestantism, according as we view it. It may be plausibly
argued that whether the primitive Church agreed more with Rome or
with Protestants, and though it agreed with neither of them exactly, yet
that one or the other, whichever it be, is the nearest approximation to
the ancient model which our changed circumstances admit; that either
this or that is the modern representative of primitive principles; that any
professed third theory, however plausible, must necessarily be composed
of discordant elements, and, when attempted, must necessarily run into
one or the other, according to the nearness of the attracting bodies, and
the varying sympathies of the body attracted, and its independence of
those portions of itself which interfere with the stronger attraction. It may
be argued that the Church of England, as established by law, and existing

in fact, has never represented a doctrine at all or been the development of a principle, has never had an intellectual basis; that it has been but a name, or a department of the state, or a political party, in which religious opinion was an accident, and therefore has been various. In consequence, it has been but the theatre of contending religionists, that is, of Papists and Latitudinarians, softened externally, or modified into inconsistency by their birth and education, or restrained by their interests and their religious engagements. Now all this is very plausible, and is here in place, as far as this, that there certainly is a call upon us to exhibit our principles in action. (VM i, Introduction)

The Protestant sectary alleges that we differ from the Romanist only in minute and unintelligible points; the Romanist retorts, on the other hand, that in heart we are Protestants, but in controversy are obliged by our theory to profess a devotion while we evade an obedience to the teaching of Antiquity. Such is the position of the *Via Media*. (VM i, ch. 8)

We are accused, it seems, of drawing fine, and over-subtle distinctions; as if, like the Semi-arians of old, we were neither on the one side nor the other. (VM i, ch. 8)

You speak as if the opinions held by the writers you censure were novel in our Church, and you connect them with the 'revival of Popery.' Does any one doubt that on all points of *doctrine* on which a question can occur, there is a large school in our Church, consisting of her far most learned men, mainly agreeing with those writers? Does any one doubt that their statements are borne out in the main by Hooker, Andrewes, Laud, Montague, Hammond, Bramhall, Taylor, Thorndike, Bull, Beveridge, Ken, and Wilson, not to mention others? ... I will but ask by which of the Articles, by what part of the Prayer Book, is a member of our Church bound to acknowledge the Reformers, or to profess himself a Protestant? Nowhere ... we are not Cranmerites, nor Jewelists, but Catholics, members not of a sect or party, but of the Catholic and Apostolic Church. (VM ii, VI. 'On Froude's Statements Concerning the Holy Eucharist,' 1838)

[A]s *a whole,* he [Pusey] is not *reviving* any thing that *ever* was *any*
where for 1800 years. There is a tradition of High Church and of Low
Church—but none of what *now* is *justly* called *Puseyism.* (*LD* xii, 157;
Letter to Henry Wilberforce, 19 January 1848)

Dr. Pusey ... cannot name the individual for 1800 years who has ever
held his circle of doctrines; he cannot first put down his own creed, and
then refer it to doctor, or school before him ... I want to know what single
individual that ever belonged to the Anglican Church does he follow.
Not Laud, for Laud on the scaffold avowed himself an honest Protestant;
not Hooker, for *he* gives up the Real Presence; not Taylor for *he* blames
both the Athanasian and Nicene Creeds; not Bull for *he* considers that
Transubstantiation 'bids defiance to all the reason and sense of mankind;'
not Ussher, for he was a Calvinist; not Jewell, for he gave up the Priesthood; nor the Articles, for Dr. P. *puts* an *interpretation* on them; nor the
Prayer book, for he believes about twice as much as the Prayer Book contains. Who before him ever joined the circle of Roman doctrine to the
Anglican ritual and polity? ... converts smile at confession in the Anglican Church;—they smile, not at those who religiously take part in the
ordinance, but at those who out of their own heads invent rites or ceremonies, or again, who borrow the rites, while they disown the authority
of the Catholic Church. (*LD* xii, 273-274; Letter to Catherine Ward, 25
September 1848)

Now, if we are advocates of doctrines, however true, with no *authority*
to back us, it is the story of the Oxford Tracts over again—we shall be in a
false position. (*LD* xii, 278; Letter to Frederick W. Faber, 4 October 1848)

[N]or do I think he nor any other anglo-catholic would submit to put
down his entire creed on paper, and lay it before the world. (*LD* xii, 290;
Letter to Catherine Ward, 12 October 1848)

Free thinkers and broad thinkers, Laudians and Prayer-Book Christians, high-and-dry and Establishment-men, all these he would understand; but what he would feel so prodigious is this,—that such as you, my

brethren, should consider Christianity given from heaven once for all, should protest against private judgment, should profess to transmit what you have received, and yet from diligent study of the Fathers, from your thorough knowledge of St. Basil and St. Chrysostom, from living, as you say, in the atmosphere of Antiquity, that you should come forth into open day with your new edition of the Catholic faith, different from that held in any existing body of Christians anywhere, which not half-a-dozen men all over the world would honour with their *imprimatur*; and then, withal, should be as positive about its truth in every part, as if the voice of man-kind were with you instead of being against you ... [Y]ou are purer than Rome; you know more than St. Bernard; you judge how far St. Thomas was right, and where he is to be read with caution, or held up to blame. You can bring to light juster views of grace, or of penance, or of invocation of saints, than St. Gregory or St. Augustine ... You have in all respects an eclectic or an original religion of our own. You dare not stand or fall by Andrewes, or by Laud, or by Hammond, or by Bull, or by Thorndike, or by all of them together. There is a *consensus* of divines, stronger than there is for Baptismal Regeneration or the Apostolical Succession, that Rome is, strictly and literally, an anti-Christian power:—Liberals and High Churchmen in your Communion in this agree with Evangelicals; you put it aside. There is a *consensus* against Transubstantiation, besides the declaration of the Article; yet many of you hold it notwithstanding. Nearly all your divines, if not all, call themselves Protestants, and you anathematize the name. Who makes the concessions to Catholics which you do, yet remains separate from them? Who, among Anglican authori-ties, would speak of Penance as a Sacrament, as you do? Who of them encourages, much less insists upon, auricular confession, as you? or makes fasting an obligation? or uses the crucifix and the rosary? or reserves the consecrated bread? or believes in miracles as existing in your communion? or administers, as I believe you do, Extreme Unction? In some points you prefer Rome, in others Greece, in others England, in others Scotland; and of that preference your own private judgment is the ultimate sanc-tion ... do not come to me with the latest fashion of opinion which the world has seen, and protest to me that it is the oldest. Do not come to me at this time of day with views palpably new, isolated, original, *sui generis*, warranted old neither by Christian nor unbeliever, and challenge me to answer what I really have not the patience to read. Life is not long enough for such trifles. Go elsewhere, not to me, if you wish to make a proselyte. Your inconsistency, my dear brethren, is on your very front. Nor pretend that you are but executing the sacred duty of defending your own Communion: your Church does not thank you for a defence, which she has no dream of appropriating. (*Dif.* i, Lecture 5)

Such, then, is the Anglican Church and its *Via Media,* and such the practical application of it; it is an interposition or arbitration between the extreme doctrines of Protestantism on the one hand, and the faith of Rome which Protestantism contradicts on the other. At the same time, though it may be unwilling to allow it, it is, from the nature of the case, but a particular form of Protestantism. I do not say that in secondary principles it may not agree with the Catholic Church; but, its essential idea being that she has gone into error, whereas the essential idea of Catholicism is the Church's infallibility, the *Via Media* is really nothing else than Protestant. Not to submit to the Church is to oppose her, and to side with the heretical party; for medium there is none. The *Via Media* assumes that Protestantism is right in its protest against Catholic doctrine, only that that protest needs correcting, limiting, perfecting. This surely is but a matter of fact; for the *Via Media* has adopted all the great Protestant doctrines, as its most strenuous upholder and the highest of Anglo-Catholics will be obliged to allow; the mutilated canon, the defective Rule of Faith, justification by faith only, putative righteousness, the infection of nature in the regenerate, the denial of the five Sacraments, the relation of faith to the Sacramental Presence, and the like; its aim being nothing else than to moderate, with Melancthon, the extreme statements of Luther, to keep them from shocking the feelings of human nature, to protect them from the criticism of common sense, and from the pressure and urgency of controversial attack. Thus we have three parties on the historical stage; the See and Communion of Rome; the original pure Protestant, violent, daring, offensive, fanatical in his doctrines; and a cautious middle party, quite as heretical in principle and in doctrinal elements as Protestantism itself, but having an eye to the necessities of controversy, sensible in its ideas, sober in its tastes, safe in its statements, conservative in its aims, and practical in its measures. Such a *Via Media* has been represented by the line of Archbishops of Canterbury from Tillotson downwards, as by Cranmer before them. Such in their theology, though not in their persons or their histories, were Laud and Bull, Taylor and Hammond, and I may say nearly all the great authorities of the Established Church ... Now this sketch of the relative positions of the See of Rome, Protestantism, the *Via Media*, and the State, which we see in the history of the last three centuries, is, I repeat, no novelty in history; it is almost its rule, certainly its rule during the long period when relations existed between the Byzantine Court and the Holy See; and it is impossible to resist the conclusion, which the actual inspection of the history in detail forces upon us, that what the See of Rome was then such is it now; that what Arius, Nestorius, or Eutyches were then, such are Luther and Calvin now; what the Eusebians or Monophysites then, such the Anglican hierarchy now; what the Byzantine Court then, such is now the Government of England, and such would have been many a Catholic Court, had it had its way. That ancient history is not dead, it lives; it prophesies of what passes before our eyes; it is founded in the nature of things; we see ourselves in it, as in a glass, and if the *Via Media* was heretical then, it is heretical now. (*Dif.* i, Lecture 12)

Even if the *Via Media* were ever so positive a religious system, it was not as yet objective and real; it had no original anywhere of which it was the representative. It was at present a paper religion ... I trusted that some day it would prove to be a substantive religion ... hardly any two persons, who took part in the Movement, agreed in their view of the limit to which our general principles might religiously be carried. (*Apo.*, ch. 2)

I had a scorn of the imputations which were heaped upon me. It was true that I held a large bold system of religion, very unlike the Protestantism of the day, but it was the concentration and adjustment of the statements of great Anglican authorities, and I had as much right to hold it, as the Evangelical, and more right than the Liberal party could show, for asserting their own respective doctrines. As I declared on occasion of Tract 90, I claimed, in behalf of who would in the Anglican Church, the right

of holding with Bramhall a comprecation with the Saints, and the Mass
all but Transubstantiation with Andrewes, or with Hooker that Transubstantiation itself is not a point for Churches to part communion upon, or
with Hammond that a General Council, truly such, never did, never shall
err in a matter of faith, or with Bull that man had in paradise, and lost on
the fall, a supernatural habit of grace, or with Thorndike that penance is
a propitiation for post-baptismal sin, or with Pearson that the all-powerful name of Jesus is no otherwise given than in the Catholic Church ...
though the object of the Movement was to withstand the Liberalism of
the day, I found and felt this could not be done by mere negatives. It was
necessary for us to have a positive Church theory erected on a definite
basis. This took me to the great Anglican divines; and then of course
I found at once that it was impossible to form any such theory, without
cutting across the teaching of the Church of Rome ... In its formal creed
Anglicanism was not at a great distance from Rome: far otherwise, when
viewed in its insular space, the traditions of its establishment, its historical characteristics, its controversial rancour, and its private judgment. I
disavowed and condemned those excesses, and called them 'Protestantism' or 'Ultra-Protestantism.' (*Apo.*, ch. 3)

These then were the *parties* in the controversy: — the Anglican *Via
Media* and the popular religion of Rome. And next, as to the *issue*, to
which the controversy between them was to be brought, it was this: — the
Anglican disputant took his stand upon Antiquity or Apostolicity, the
Roman upon Catholicity. The Anglican said to the Roman: 'There is but
One Faith, the Ancient, and you have not kept to it;' the Roman retorted: 'There is but One Church, the Catholic, and you are out of it.'
The Anglican urged: 'Your special beliefs, practices, modes of action, are
nowhere in Antiquity;' the Roman objected: 'You do not communicate
with any one Church besides your own and its offshoots, and you have
discarded principles, doctrines, sacraments, and usages, which are and
ever have been received in the East and the West.' The true Church, as
defined in the Creeds, was both Catholic and Apostolic; now, as I viewed
the controversy in which I was engaged, England and Rome had divided
these notes or prerogatives between them: the cause lay thus, Apostolicity

versus Catholicity ... I considered that the special point or plea of Rome in the controversy was Catholicity, as the Anglican plea was Antiquity. Of course I contended that the Roman idea of Catholicity was not an-cient and apostolic ... he triumphantly referred to the Treatise of Vincen-tius of Lerins upon the 'Quod semper, quod ubique, quod ab omnibus,' in proof that the controversialists of Rome, in spite of their possession of the Catholic name, were separated in their creed from the Apostolical and primitive faith. (*Apo.*, ch. 3)

[W]hereas the Creeds tell us that the Church is One, Holy, Catholic, and Apostolic, I could not prove that the Anglican communion was an integral part of the One Church, on the ground of its teaching being Ap-ostolic or Catholic, without reasoning in favour of what are commonly called the Roman corruptions; and I could not defend our separation from Rome and her faith without using arguments prejudicial to those great doctrines concerning our Lord, which are the very foundation of the Christian religion. The *Via Media* was an impossible idea. (*Apo.*, ch. 4)

I have said that these Lectures are 'more or less' directed against points in Catholic teaching, and that I should consider 'how far,' because it must be borne in mind that the formal purpose of the Volume was, not an at-tack upon that teaching, but the establishment of a doctrine of its own, the Anglican *Via Media*. It only indirectly comes into collision with the theology of Rome. That theology lay in the very threshold of the author's experiment; he came across it, whether he would or no, and, while he attacked it at considerable length in its details, he adopted its main prin-ciples and many of its conclusions; and, as obliterating thereby or ignoring the very rudiments of Protestantism, he acted far more as an assailant of the religion of the Reformation than of what he called 'Popery.' ... large portions of these Lectures are expositions, nay, recommendations of prin-ciples and doctrines, recognised in the Catholic Church ... the *Via Media*, ... a doctrine, wanting in simplicity, hard to master, indeterminate in its provisions, and without a substantive existence in any age or country ... I readily grant in particular that there is much truth in Anglican teach-ing, and that, so far, it does and will, while it lasts, powerfully affect the multitude of men, to whom it comes; but I cannot allow to the Church of England itself what is true of much of its teaching and many of its teachers, for that teaching and those teachers, who are so effective, know nothing of the *Via Media*. (VM i, Preface to the Third Edition, 1877)

[H]e found in early history a veritable *Via Media* in both the Semi-Arian and the Monophysite parties, and they, as being heretical, broke his attachment to middle paths. (VM i, Introduction; footnote 3 from 1877)

Tradition, Apostolic

And, indeed, without formal proofs of the existence and the authority in primitive times of an Apostolical Tradition, it is plain that there must have been such tradition, granting that the Apostles conversed, and their friends had memories, like other men. (*Ari.*, ch. 1, sec. 3)

They agree in ignoring the existence, in fact—nay, the probability, or the very possibility—of an Apostolical Tradition, supplementary to and interpretative of Scripture. The idea of such an aid to Christian teaching does not seem even to enter into their comprehension. They take for granted that the accumulated knowledge about our Lord and His religion which must have flowed from the lips of the Apostles upon their converts, in their familiar conversations, catechizings, preachings, ecclesiastical determinations, prayers, was clean swept away and perished with the closing of the canon and the death of St. John. All the information of the great forty days came to nought, except so far as it accidentally strayed into one or other passage of the Apostolic Epistles. No one had ever any curiosity to ask the Apostles, during the remnant of their lives, any point of faith; no one had felt interest enough to ascertain from them who their Master was, why He died, and with what results. No one retained any memory of their teaching concerning God, or the human soul, or the unseen state, or the world of saints and angels, or the Church on earth; no one had sought for explanation of any verse in St. Matthew or St. Luke, of the doctrine contained in the first or in the sixth chapters of St. John, or of the symbol of 'the Lamb,' or of the nature of 'the Spirit;' or, anyhow, nothing had been asked, nothing answered, but what already was recorded by a singular chance in the books of the New Testament, or at least nothing that was of the slightest importance and worth preserving. The great Churches of the day, at Corinth, Rome, Antioch, and Ephesus, the learned school of Alexandria, knew in the year A.D. 100 and onwards as much of all these matters as we do now, and no more. Their interpretations of the sacred writings were just on a par with the private judgments of clever commentators, orthodox or heterodox, now—one as good as another, conjectural, personal, inferential, unauthoritative. ('Apostolical Tradition,' *British Critic*, Vol. 19, July 1836; in *Ess.* i, sec. III)

[T]raditions, 'devised by men's imagination,' are not Divine traditions, ... it as little follows that Catholic Traditions are to be rejected because Jewish and Roman are, as that the Christian Sabbath is abolished because the Jewish is abolished. (*TT* #82, 3 March 1837)

[I]t is not true that a traditionary doctrine cannot be 'plainly revealed;' for the transference of the sabbatical rest from the seventh day to the Lord's day, comes to us upon Tradition. (*VM* i, ch. 11)

They evidently did not in Scripture say out all they had to say; this is evident on the face of Scripture, evident from what they do say. St. Paul says, '*The rest* will I set in order when I come.' St. John, 'I had *many things* to write, but I will not with ink and pen write unto thee; but I trust I shall shortly see thee, and we shall *speak* face to face.' This he says in two Epistles. (*TT* #85, Sep. 1838)

[A]fter St. Paul has declared some plain truths to the Corinthians, he says, 'Be ye followers of me: *for this cause* have I sent unto you Timotheus, who is my beloved son, and faithful in the Lord, *who shall bring you into remembrance of my ways*, which be in Christ, as I *teach* everywhere in every Church.' [1 Cor. iv. 17.] He refers them to an authority beyond and beside his epistle,—to Timothy, nay to his doctrine *as* he had taught in every Church. (*TT* #85, Sep. 1838)

It is remarkable how frequent are the allusions in the Epistles to *other* Apostolic teaching beyond themselves, that is, besides the written authority. For instance; in the same chapter [1 Cor. 11], 'I *praise* you, brethren, that ye *remember* me in all things, and *keep the traditions*, as I delivered them to you.' Again, 'I have also received,' or had by tradition, 'of the Lord that which also I delivered unto you,' that is, which I gave by tradition unto you. This giving and receiving was not in writing. Again, 'If any man seem to be contentious, we have no such custom, neither the churches of God:' he appeals to the received custom of the Church. Again, 'I declare unto you the Gospel which I preached unto you, which also ye have received, and wherein ye stand, ... for I delivered unto you (gave by tradition) first of all that which I also received' (by tradition). Again, 'Stand fast, and hold the traditions which ye have been taught, whether by word or our epistle.' [1 Cor. xi. 2, 16, 23; xv. 1-3; 1 Thess. ii. 15.] Such passages prove, as all will grant, that at the time there were means of gaining knowledge distinct from Scripture, and sources of information in addition to it ... the mere circumstance that it is in addition, is no proof against its being Apostolic; that it is extra-scriptural is no proof that it is unscriptural, for St. Paul himself tells us in Scripture, that there are truths not in Scripture. (*TT* #85, Sep. 1838)

[T]he Book of Ecclesiastes contains no prophecy, is referred to in no part of the New Testament, and contains passages which at first sight are startling. Again: that most sacred Book, called the Song of Songs, or Canticles, is a continued type from beginning to end. Nowhere in Scripture, as I have already observed, are we told that it is a type; nowhere is it hinted that it is not to be understood literally. Yet it is only as having a deeper and hidden sense, that we are accustomed to see a religious purpose in it. (*TT* #85, Sep. 1838)

'In vain do they worship Me, teaching doctrines and commandments of *men*.' As is the origin, so is the tradition; when the origin is true, the tradition will be true; when the origin is false, the tradition will be false. There can most surely be true traditions, that is, traditions from true sources; but such traditions, though they really be true, do not profess to prove themselves; they come accompanied by other arguments; the true traditions of Divine Revelation are proved to be true by miracle, by prophecy, by the test of cumulative and collateral evidences, which directly warrant and verify them. Such were not the traditions of the Pharisee—they professed to speak for themselves, they bore witness to themselves, they were their own evidence; and, as might have been expected, they were not trustworthy—they were mere frauds. (*PPC*, Lecture 2)

All the world knows that Catholics hold that the Apostles made over the Divine Revelation to the generation after them, not only in writing, but by word of mouth, and in the ritual of the Church. We consider that the New Testament is not the whole of what they left us; that they left us a number of doctrines, not in writing at all, but living in the minds and mouths of the faithful; Protestants deny this. They have a right to deny it; but they have no right to assume their denial to be true without proof, and to use it as self-evident, and to triumph over us as beaten, merely because we will not admit it. Yet this they actually do; can anything be more preposterous? (*PPC*, Lecture 8)

[I]n a question of doctrine, we must have recourse to the great source of doctrine, Apostolical Tradition, and a Father must represent his own people, and that people must be the witnesses of an uninterrupted Tradition from the Apostles, if anything decisive is to come of any theological statement which is found in his writings ... a doctrine reported by the Fathers, in order to have dogmatic force, must be a Tradition in its *source* or *form*, next, what is a Tradition, considered in its *matter*? It is a belief, which, be it *affirmative* or *negative*, is *positive*. The mere absence of a tradition in a country, is not a tradition the other way ... The proposition 'Christ is God,' serves as an example of what I mean by an affirmative tradition; and 'no one born of woman is born in God's favour,' is an example of a negative tradition. I observe then, in the third place, that a tradition does not carry its own full explanation with it; it does but land (so to say) a proposition at the feet of the Apostles, and its interpretation has still to be determined,—as the Apostles' words in Scripture, however much theirs, need an interpretation ... Further, there are *explicit* traditions and *implicit*. By an explicit tradition I mean a doctrine which is conveyed in the letter of the proposition which has been handed down; and by implicit, one which lies in the force and virtue, not in the letter of the proposition. Thus it might be an Apostolical tradition that our Lord was the very Son of God, of one nature with the Father, and in all things equal to Him; and again a tradition that there was but one God: these would be explicit, but in them would necessarily be conveyed, moreover, the implicit tradition, that the Father and the Son were numerically one. Implicit traditions are positive traditions, as being strictly conveyed in positive. Lastly, there are at least two ways of determining an Apostolical tradition: — (1.) When credible witnesses declare that it *is* Apostolical; as when three hundred Fathers at Nicaea stopped their ears at Arius's blasphemies: (2.) When, in various places, independent witnesses enunciate one and the same doctrine, as St. Irenaeus, St. Cyprian, and Eusebius assert, that the Apostles founded a Church, Catholic and One. (*Dif.* ii, Letter to Pusey, Note III, 1865)

How can history, that is, words and deeds which are dead and gone, act as an effectual living decider of quarrels between living men? To apply past principles, doctrines, laws, precedents to present cases requires an applier, that is, a living and present mind; and if neither the body is to decide nor the individual member of it, who is there to decide when questions arise, as they will to the end of time? (*VM* i, Lecture 11; footnote 3 from 1877)

What can be the instrument, what the guarantee, of trustworthy tradition, but a promise from above of infallibility? (*LD* xxx, 391; Letter to W. S. Lilly, 17 August 1884)

Transubstantiation

Such seems to be the connexion between the feast with which our Lord began, and that with which He ended His ministry. Nay, may we not add without violence, that in the former feast He had in mind and intended to foreshadow the latter? for what was that first miracle by which He manifested His glory in the former, but the strange and awful change of the element of water into wine? and what did He in the latter, but change the Paschal Supper and the typical lamb into the sacrament of His aton- ing sacrifice, and the creatures of bread and wine into the verities of His most precious Body and Blood? He began His ministry with a miracle; He ended it with a greater. (*SD*, Sermon 3: 'Our Lord's Last Supper and His First,' 26 February 1843)

People say that the doctrine of Transubstantiation is difficult to be- lieve; I did not believe the doctrine till I was a Catholic. I had no dif- ficulty in believing it, as soon as I believed that the Catholic Roman Church was the oracle of God, and that she had declared this doctrine to be part of the original revelation. It is difficult, impossible, to imagine, I grant; — but how is it difficult to believe? ... I cannot indeed prove it, I cannot tell *how* it is; but I say, 'Why should it not be? What's to hinder it? What do I know of substance or matter? just as much as the greatest philosophers, and that is nothing at all;' — so much is this the case, that there is a rising school of philosophy now, which considers phenomena to constitute the whole of our knowledge in physics. The Catholic doc- trine leaves phenomena alone. It does not say that the phenomena go; on the contrary, it says that they remain; nor does it say that the same phenomena are in several places at once. It deals with what no one on earth knows any thing about, the material substances themselves. (*Apo.*, ch. 5)

The Catholic doctrine is as follows; ... Our Lord is *in loco* in heaven, not (in the same sense) in the Sacrament. He is present in the Sacra- ment only in substance, *substantive*, and substance does not require or imply the occupation of place. But if place is excluded from the idea of the Sacramental Presence, therefore division or distance from heaven is excluded also, for distance implies a measurable interval, and such there cannot be except between places. Moreover, if the idea of distance is ex- cluded, therefore is the idea of motion. Our Lord then neither descends from heaven upon our altars, nor moves when carried in procession. The visible species change their position, but He does not move. He is in the

Holy Eucharist after the manner of a spirit. We do not know how; we have
no parallel to the 'how' in our experience. We can only say that He is
present, not according to the natural manner of bodies, but *sacramentally*.
His Presence is substantial, spirit-wise, sacramental; an absolute mystery,
not against reason, however, but against imagination, and must be received by faith ... St. Thomas says ... that our Lord is *not* under the species *localiter*. (VM ii, VI. 'On Froude's Statements Concerning the Holy
Eucharist,' originally 1838; footnote from 1883)

Trent, Council of

I do not think that there is anything very erroneous or very blameable
in such a belief; and it seems to be a very satisfactory omen in its favour,
that at the Council of Trent, such protests, as are quoted in the Tract,
were entered against so many of the very errors and corruptions which our
Articles and Homilies also condemn. I do not think it is any great excess
of charity towards the largest portion of Christendom, to rejoice to detect
such a point of agreement between them and us, as a joint protest against
some of their greatest corruptions, though they in practice cherish them,
and though there are still other points in which they differ from us ... I
should not be honest if I did not add, that I consider our own Church,
on the other hand, to have in it a traditionary system, as well as the
Roman, beyond and beside the letter of its formularies, and to be ruled
by a spirit far inferior to its own nature. And this traditionary system, not
only inculcates what I cannot receive, but would exclude any difference
of belief from itself. To this exclusive modern system, I desire to oppose
myself. (VM ii, IX. 'Letter to Rev. R. W. Jelf in Explanation of Tract 90,'
1841)

When Trent was the last Council, we enjoyed the stability and edifica-
tion of three hundred years. A series of the ablest divines had examined,
interpreted, adjusted, located, illustrated every sentence of the definitions.
We were all of us on sure ground, and could speak with confidence, after
Suarez, Lambertini, and a host of others. (*POL*; Letter to Lord Howard of
Glossop, 27 April 1872)

Trinitarianism; Holy Trinity

[A]s regards the doctrine of the Trinity, the mere text of Scripture is not calculated either to satisfy the intellect or to ascertain the temper of those who profess to accept it as a rule of faith … the text of Scripture being addressed principally to the affections, and of a religious, not a philosophical character. (*Ari.*, ch. 2, sec. 1)

There are persons who think the Catholic doctrine of the Holy Trinity 'scholastic;' and so it is, but it is something more, it is Apostolic also. It is no proof that the distinction in question is not Scriptural, that it is, if it is, scholastic. (*TT* #82, 3 March 1837)

It must be asked, moreover, how much direct and literal testimony the Ante-nicene Fathers give, one by one, to the divinity of the Holy Spirit? This alone shall be observed, that St. Basil, in the fourth century, finding that, if he distinctly called the Third Person in the Blessed Trinity by the Name of God, he should be put out of the Church by the Arians, pointedly refrained from doing so on an occasion on which his enemies were on the watch; and that, when some Catholics found fault with him, St. Athanasius took his part. Could this possibly have been the conduct of any true Christian, not to say Saint, of a later age? that is, whatever be the true account of it, does it not suggest to us that the testimony of those early times lies very unfavourably for the application of the rule of Vincentius? Let it not be for a moment supposed that I impugn the orthodoxy of the early divines, or the cogency of their testimony among *fair* inquirers; but I am trying them by that *unfair* interpretation of Vincentius, which is necessary in order to make him available against the Church of Rome. And now, as to the positive evidence which those Fathers offer in behalf of the Catholic doctrine of the Trinity, it has been drawn out by Dr. Burton and seems to fall under two heads. One is the general *ascription of glory* to the Three Persons together, both by fathers and churches, and that on continuous tradition and from the earliest times. Under the second fall certain *distinct statements* of *particular* fathers; thus we find the word 'Trinity' used by St. Theophilus, St. Clement, St. Hippolytus, Tertullian, St. Cyprian,

Origen, St. Methodius; and the Divine *Circumincessio*, the most distinctive portion of the Catholic doctrine, and the unity of power, or again, of substance, are declared with more or less distinctness by Athenagoras, St. Irenaeus, St. Clement, Tertullian, St. Hippolytus, Origen, and the two SS. Dionysii. This is pretty much the whole of the evidence. (*Dev.*, Part I: Introduction)

[I]n like manner, of that majestic Article of the Anglican as well as of the Catholic Creed, — the doctrine of the Trinity in Unity. What do I know of the Essence of the Divine Being? I know that my abstract idea of three is simply incompatible with my idea of one; but when I come to the question of concrete fact, I have no means of proving that there is not a sense in which one and three can equally be predicated of the Incommunicable God. (*Apo.*, ch. 5)

[T]o apply arithmetical notions to Him may be as unphilosophical as it is profane. Though He is at once Father, Son, and Holy Ghost, the word 'Trinity' belongs to those notions of Him which are forced on us by the necessity of our finite conceptions, the real and immutable distinction which exists between Person and Person implying in itself no infringement of His real and numerical Unity. (GA, Part I, ch. 4, sec. 1)

Bibliography and Abbreviations

(listed alphabetically by source abbreviations)

[multiple dates = first date of publication/date of uniform edition (preceding publisher); date of volume used for quotations (following publisher)]

Apo.   *Apologia pro Vita Sua* (1865; London: Longmans, Green, and Co., 1908).

Apo. ii   *Apologia pro Vita Sua* (1864-1865 combined edition, edited by Wilfrid Ward; London: Oxford University Press, 1913).

Ari.   *Arians of the Fourth Century* (1833/1871; London: Longmans, Green, and Co., 3rd edition, 1908).

Ath. ii   *Select Treatises of St. Athanasius*, Vol. II: *Being an Appendix of Illustrations* (1881; London: Longmans, Green, and Co., 1903).

Ble.   [Vincent Ferrer Blehl] *Pilgrim Journey: John Henry Newman: 1801-1845* (New York: Paulist Press, 2001).

Con.   *On Consulting the Faithful in Matters of Doctrine* (*Rambler*: July 1859; portion of *Conscience, Consensus, and the Development of Doctrine*, New York: Doubleday Image Books, 1992).

Dev.   *An Essay on the Development of Christian Doctrine* (1845/2nd edition, 1878; London: Longmans, Green, and Co., 1909).

Dif. i *Certain Difficulties Felt by Anglicans in Catholic Teaching Considered*, vol. 1 (1850; London: Longmans, Green, and Co., 1901).

Dif. ii *Certain Difficulties Felt by Anglicans in Catholic Teaching Considered*, vol. 2 (contains *Letter to Pusey*, 1865 and *Letter to the Duke of Norfolk*, 1875/1875; London: Longmans, Green, and Co., 1900).

Ess. i *Essays Critical and Historical*, vol. 1 (1829, 1836-1840/1871; London: Longmans, Green, and Co., 1907).

Ess. ii *Essays Critical and Historical*, vol. 2 (1840-1842, 1846/1871; London: Longmans, Green, and Co., 1907).

FP *Faith and Prejudice and Other Unpublished Sermons* (1848, 1870, 1873; New York: Sheed & Ward, 1956).

GA *An Essay in Aid of a Grammar of Assent* (1870; London: Longmans, Green, and Co., 1903).

IU *The Idea of a University* (1852, 1858/1873; London: Longmans, Green, and Co., 1907).

Jfc. *Lectures on the Doctrine of Justification* (1838/1874; London: Longmans, Green, and Co., 3rd edition, 1908).

Keb. *Correspondence of John Henry Newman with John Keble and Others, 1839-45* (edited at the Birmingham Oratory, London: Longmans, Green, and Co., 1917).

Ker [Ian Ker]: *John Henry Newman: A Biography* (Oxford: Oxford University Press, 1988).

LD viii *The Letters and Diaries of John Henry Newman*, vol. VIII: *Tract 90 and the Jerusalem Bishopric: January 1841 — April 1842* (edited by Gerard Tracey, Oxford University Press, USA, 2000).

LD xi *The Letters and Diaries of John Henry Newman*, vol. XI: *Littlemore to Rome: October 1845 to December 1846* (edited by Charles Stephen Dessain, London: Thomas Nelson and Sons, 1961).

LD xii *The Letters and Diaries of John Henry Newman*, vol. XII: *Rome to Birmingham: January 1847 to December 1848* (edited by Charles Stephen Dessain, London: Thomas Nelson and Sons, 1962)

LD xxv *The Letters and Diaries of John Henry Newman*, vol. XXV: *The Vatican Council, January 1870 to December 1871* (edited by Charles Stephen Dessain, Oxford University Press, USA, 1974)

LD xxvi *The Letters and Diaries of John Henry Newman*, vol. XXVI: *Aftermaths, January 1872 to December 1873* (edited by Charles Stephen Dessain, Oxford University Press, USA, 1974)

LD xxix *The Letters and Diaries of John Henry Newman*, vol. XXIX: *The Cardinalate: January 1879 to September 1881* (edited by Charles Stephen Dessain and Thomas Gornall, S.J., London: Oxford University Press, 1976)

LD xxx *The Letters and Diaries of John Henry Newman*, vol. XXX: *A Cardinal's Apostolate: October 1881 to December 1884* (edited by Charles Stephen Dessain and Thomas Gornall, S.J., London: Oxford University Press, 1976)

LD xxxii *The Letters and Diaries of John Henry Newman*, vol. XXXII: *Supplement* (edited by Francis J. McGrath, Oxford University Press, USA, 2008)

MD *Meditations and Devotions of the Late Cardinal Newman* (edited by William P. Neville; London: Longmans, Green, and Co., 1907)

Mir. *Two Essays on Biblical and Ecclesiastical Miracles* (1826, 1843/1870; London: Longmans, Green, and Co., 1907)

Mix. *Discourses Addressed to Mixed Congregations* (1849; London: Longmans, Green, and Co., 1906)

Moz. ii *Letters and Correspondence of John Henry Newman During His Life in the English Church*, vol. 2 [starting from December 1833] (edited by Anne Mozley; 1891; London: Longmans, Green, and Co., 1903)

OIS *On the Inspiration of Scripture* (*The Nineteenth Century*, vol. 15, no. 84, February 1884; reprinted in *On the Inspiration of Scripture*, edited by J. Derek Holmes and Robert Murray, Washington, D.C.: Corpus Books, 1967)

POL *A Packet of Letters: A Selection from the Correspondence of John Henry Newman*, edited by Joyce Sugg (Oxford: Clarendon Press, 1983)

PPC *Lectures on the Present Position of Catholics in England* (1851; London: Longmans, Green, and Co., 1908)

PS i-viii *Parochial and Plain Sermons* (8 volumes: i 1834, ii 1835, iii 1836, iv 1839, v 1840, vi 1842, vii 1842, viii 1843/1869; London: Longmans, Green, and Co., 1907 [i, iii, v-vii], 1908 [ii, viii], 1909 [iv])

Say. *Sayings of Cardinal Newman* (London: Burns & Oates, 1890)

SD *Sermons Bearing on Subjects of the Day* (1831-1843/1869; London: Longmans, Green, and Co., 1902)

SE *Stray Essays on Controversial Points Variously Illustrated* (privately printed, 1890)

SN *Sermon Notes of John Henry Cardinal Newman: 1849-1878* (edited by the Fathers of the Birmingham Oratory; London: Longmans, Green, and Co., 1913)

SVO   *Sermons Preached on Various Occasions* (1850-1859, 1866, 1873 / 1874; London: Longmans, Green, and Co., 1908)

Trev. ii   [Meriol Trevor] *Newman: Light in Winter* (Garden City, New York: Doubleday & Co., Inc., 1963)

TT   *Tracts for the Times* (#1-3, 6-8, 10-11, 15, 19-21, 31, 33-34, 38, 41, 45, 47, 71, 73-76, 79, 82-83, 85, 88, 90; 1833-1840; London: J.G.F. & J. Rivington, 1840; #38, 41, 71, 82, and 90 also appeared in *Via Media*, vol. 2; #73 in *Essays Critical and Historical*, vol. 1 (1871; London: Longmans, Green, and Co., 1907); #83, 85 in *Discussions and Arguments on Various Subjects* (1872; London: Longmans, Green, and Co., 1907); these later versions are used here, with Newman's corrections and comments)

US   *Oxford University Sermons* (1826-1843/1871; London: Longmans, Green, and Co., 1909)

VM i   *The Via Media of the Anglican Church: Illustrated in Lectures, Letters and Tracts Written Between 1830 and 1841*, vol. 1; aka *Lectures on the Prophetical Office of the Church* (1837/1877; London: Longmans, Green, and Co., 3rd edition, 1901)

VM ii   *The Via Media of the Anglican Church: Illustrated in Lectures, Letters and Tracts Written Between 1830 and 1841*, vol. 2 (1830-1845/1883; London: Longmans, Green, and Co., 1908)

Ward i, ii   [Wilfrid Ward] *The Life of John Henry Cardinal Newman* (two volumes: London: Longmans, Green, and Co., 1912)

About the Author

Dave Armstrong is a Catholic writer, apologist, and evangelist who has been actively proclaiming and defending Christianity for more than twenty years. Formerly a campus missionary, as a Protestant, Armstrong was received into the Catholic Church in 1991 by the late, well-known catechist and theologian Fr. John A. Hardon, S.J. Armstrong's conversion story appeared in the best-selling book *Surprised by Truth*, and his articles have been published in a number of Catholic periodicals, including *The Catholic Answer*, *This Rock*, *Envoy*, *Hands On Apologetics*, *The Coming Home Journal*, and *The Latin Mass*. His apologetic and writing apostolate was the subject of a feature article in the May 2002 issue of *Envoy*. Armstrong is the author of the books *A Biblical Defense of Catholicism* and *More Biblical Evidence for Catholicism* and of forty-four apologetics articles in *The Catholic Answer Bible*. His website, Biblical Evidence for Catholicism (www.biblicalcatholic.com), online since March 1997, received the 1998 Catholic Website of the Year award from *Envoy*, which also nominated Armstrong himself for Best New Evangelist. Armstrong and his wife, Judy, and their four children live near Detroit, Michigan.

An Invitation

Reader, the book that you hold in your hands was published by Sophia Institute Press.

Sophia Institute seeks to restore man's knowledge of eternal truth, including man's knowledge of his own nature, his relation to other persons, and his relation to God.

Our press fulfills this mission by offering translations, reprints, and new publications. We offer scholarly as well as popular publications; there are works of fiction along with books that draw from all the arts and sciences of our civilization. These books afford readers a rich source of the enduring wisdom of mankind.

Sophia Institute Press is the publishing arm of the Thomas More College of Liberal Arts and Holy Spirit College. Both colleges are dedicated to providing university-level education in the Western tradition under the guiding light of Catholic teaching.

If you know a young person who might be interested in the ideas found in this book, share it. If you know a young person seeking a college that takes seriously the adventure of learning and the quest for truth, bring our institutions to his attention.

www.SophiaInstitute.com
www.ThomasMoreCollege.edu
www.HolySpiritCollege.org

SOPHIA INSTITUTE PRESS

THE PUBLISHING DIVISION OF